Contents at a Glance

44 Manage Your IM Contacts
45 Carry On an IM Conversation
46 About Instant Messaging Services

CHAPTER 8: Browsing the Wireless Web PAGE 183

47 About BlackBerry Web Browsing
48 Navigate to a Web Page
49 Create and Manage Bookmarks
50 Install a New Application Over-the-Air
51 Download New Wallpaper
52 Download New Ring Tones
53 Tweak Browser Options

CHAPTER 9: BlackBerry As the Ultimate Mobile Phone PAGE 211

54 About the BlackBerry Phone
55 Make and Receive Phone Calls
56 Make a Conference Call
57 Forward Calls
58 Manage the Speed Dial List
59 Take Advantage of Smart Dialing
60 Work with Call Logs
61 Tweak Phone Options
62 Access a 411 Phone Directory

CHAPTER 10: Using Bluetooth for Short-range Wireless Networking PAGE 247

63 About Bluetooth
64 Turn Bluetooth On and Off
65 Pair Up with a Bluetooth Headset or Car Kit
66 Tweak Bluetooth Options
67 About Bluetooth Security

PART III: GETTING PRODUCTIVE WITH YOUR BLACKBERRY 7100

CHAPTER 11: Using the Address Book to Never Lose a Contact PAGE 269

68 Create and Manage Contacts
69 Create and Manage Mailing Lists
70 Apply Categories to Contacts
71 Tweak Address Book Options
72 Access the SIM Phone Book

CHAPTER 12: Managing Your Time with the Calendar PAGE 285

73 About the Calendar
74 Navigate in the Calendar
75 Create and Manage Appointments
76 Tweak Calendar Options

CHAPTER 13: Organizing Your To-Do List with Tasks PAGE 303

77 Create and Manage Tasks
78 Apply Categories to Tasks
79 Tweak Task Options

CHAPTER 14: Getting the Most Out of Helper Applications PAGE 315

80 Stay on Schedule with an Alarm
81 Make Notes with the MemoPad
82 Crunch Numbers with the Calculator
83 Manage Pictures with the Photo Album
84 Monitor Traffic and Surveillance Remotely
85 Use Your Device As a Flashlight and Mirror
86 Use Your Device As a High-tech Golf Scorecard

CHAPTER 15: Securing Your BlackBerry Device PAGE 339

87 About BlackBerry Security
88 Secure the SIM Card
89 Turn On the Firewall
90 Protect Your Content
91 Safely Store IDs and Passwords on Your Device
92 Register Your Device with StuffBak

BlackBerry®

Michael Morrison

Sams Publishing, 800 East 96th Street, Indianapolis, Indiana 46240 USA

BlackBerry® in a Snap

Copyright © 2006 by Sams Publishing

All rights reserved. No part of this book shall be reproduced, stored in a retrieval system, or transmitted by any means, electronic, mechanical, photocopying, recording, or otherwise, without written permission from the publisher. No patent liability is assumed with respect to the use of the information contained herein. Although every precaution has been taken in the preparation of this book, the publisher and author assume no responsibility for errors or omissions. Nor is any liability assumed for damages resulting from the use of the information contained herein.

International Standard Book Number: 0672-32-670-1

Library of Congress Catalog Card Number: 2003099242

Printed in the United States of America

First Printing: July 2005

09 08 07 06   4 3 2 1

Trademarks

All terms mentioned in this book that are known to be trademarks or service marks have been appropriately capitalized. Sams Publishing cannot attest to the accuracy of this information. Use of a term in this book should not be regarded as affecting the validity of any trademark or service mark.

BlackBerry is registered trademark of Research In Motion Limited.

Warning and Disclaimer

Every effort has been made to make this book as complete and as accurate as possible, but no warranty or fitness is implied. The information provided is on an "as is" basis. The author and the publisher shall have neither liability nor responsibility to any person or entity with respect to any loss or damages arising from the information contained in this book.

Bulk Sales

Sams Publishing offers excellent discounts on this book when ordered in quantity for bulk purchases or special sales. For more information, please contact

    U.S. Corporate and Government Sales
    1-800-382-3419
    corpsales@pearsontechgroup.com

For sales outside of the United States, please contact

    International Sales
    1-317-428-3341
    international@pearsontechgroup.com

Acquisitions Editor
Betsy Brown

Development Editors
Jon Steever
Alice Martina Smith

Managing Editor
Charlotte Clapp

Senior Project Editor
Matthew Purcell

Indexer
Erika Millen

Proofreader
Katie Robinson

Technical Editor
James Barnett

Team Coordinator
Vanessa Evans

Designer
Gary Adair

Page Layout
Bronkella Publishing

About the Author

Michael Morrison is a writer, developer, toy inventor, and author of a variety of computer technology books and interactive web-based courses. In addition to his primary profession as a writer and freelance nerd-for-hire, Michael is the creative lead at Stalefish Labs, an entertainment company he cofounded with his wife, Masheed. The commercial debut for Stalefish Labs is a traditional social/trivia game called *Tall Tales: The Game of Legends and Creative One-Upmanship* (http://www.talltalesgame.com/). When not glued to his computer, playing hockey, skateboarding, or watching movies with his wife, Michael enjoys hanging out by his koi pond while he checks email on his BlackBerry. You can visit Michael on the Web and discuss this book at http://www.michaelmorrison.com/.

Dedication

To my parents, who always indulged my desire to have the latest and greatest electronic gadgets.

Acknowledgments

Thanks to Betsy Brown, Alice Martina Smith, and Gary Adair for guiding this project along smoothly despite my best attempts to derail it! Also thanks to my skateboarding buddy Jeff Hottle for helping out with screenshots and sharing BlackBerry thoughts during some of our skate sessions. I owe an enormous thanks to my wife, Masheed, for being my best friend and biggest supporter. And finally, thanks to the legions of loyal BlackBerry users who suffer chronic "BlackBerry thumb" all in the name of more efficient digital communication!

Tell Us What You Think!

As the reader of this book, *you* are our most important critic and commentator. We value your opinion and want to know what we're doing right, what we could do better, what areas you'd like to see us publish in, and any other words of wisdom you're willing to pass our way.

As a publisher for Sams, I welcome your comments. You can fax, email, or write me directly to let me know what you did or didn't like about this book— as well as what we can do to make our books stronger.

Please note that I cannot help you with technical problems related to the topic of this book, and that due to the high volume of mail I receive, I might not be able to reply to every message.

When you write, please be sure to include this book's title and author as well as your name and phone or fax number. I will carefully review your comments and share them with the author and editors who worked on the book.

Fax: 317-428-3310

Email: consumer@samspublishing.com

Mail: Mark Taber
        Sams Publishing
        800 East 96th Street
        Indianapolis, IN 46240 USA

Reader Services

For more information about this book or others from Sams Publishing, visit our website at www.samspublishing.com. Type the ISBN of the book (excluding hyphens) or the title of the book you're looking for in the Search box.

PART I

Getting Started with Your BlackBerry 7100

IN THIS PART:

CHAPTER 1	Start Here	3
CHAPTER 2	Hit the Ground Running with Your BlackBerry	17
CHAPTER 3	Managing Your BlackBerry from a Desktop PC	41
CHAPTER 4	Fine-tuning Your BlackBerry	71

1

✔ Start Here

For the past several years there has been talk of a "wireless revolution" that is going to hit at any moment. And year after year, that moment has come and gone with plenty of wires and no revolution. That is, until now. It was a few years late in coming, but the wireless revolution has begun in terms of traditional desktop computers, household appliances and—more importantly to this book—mobile handheld devices. Sure, wireless mobile phones have been around for a while now, but it wasn't until recently that technologies converged to give us multipurpose handheld devices.

Before I get too carried away with this talk of a revolution, allow me to point out that we're still in the very early stages of the wireless revolution. Wireless short-range networks have made it possible for us to roam around the house with a constant Internet connection, as well as drift into and out of spheres of connectivity in public spaces. The next level of wireless Internet access is now visible on the horizon, where high-speed wireless connections can be made across miles of separation. But this applies to broadband wireless connectivity, which doesn't entirely correlate to handheld devices. More specifically, mobile phones use a different type of network connection for shuttling voice and data, as compared to a notebook PC that is concerned with only a high-speed data connection.

> **NOTE**
> For the record, Voiceover Internet Protocol (VoIP) stands to turn this discussion on its ear by allowing you to use a wireless broadband connection to carry out phone conversations. VoIP is still relatively new and won't have a sweeping impact on mobile phones until long-range wireless broadband becomes more commonplace. Even so, services such as Vonage are quickly bringing VoIP into the mainstream, and popular wireless routers are making it possible to forego traditional analog phone lines in lieu of VoIP communication.

The wireless revolution as it applies to mobile handheld devices involves several evolving technologies, including advances in wireless networks and dramatic improvements in mobile device hardware. The wireless networks used by mobile handheld devices for voice and data communication have evolved rapidly, now giving mobile devices access to a fast enough data transfer rate to browse the Web at tolerable speeds. I use the word *tolerable* a bit loosely here because the transfer rate of most current wireless voice/data networks is still quite slow by any true networking standard. However, it's just fast enough to allow device manufacturers to combine Internet applications (email, web browsing, instant messaging, and so on) with a mobile phone to create truly revolutionary wireless communication devices. The BlackBerry 7100 series devices represent one of these kinds of devices.

The combination of Internet applications with a mobile phone is not new to the BlackBerry 7100. In fact, device manufacturers have been trying to marry the two for years now, but they've typically leaned heavily on one end of the spectrum or the other. For example, Research In Motion (RIM), the maker of the BlackBerry 7100, released several BlackBerry devices with mobile phone capabilities before the 7100 series. However, each of the devices was essentially a text-messaging device with a mobile phone tacked onto it. Mobile phone users, already accustomed to a certain shape and size for their phones, were reluctant to adopt a clunky phone even if its messaging capabilities were stellar.

On the other end of the spectrum, practically every mobile phone manufacturer has attempted to cram Internet features into their phones. But with tiny screens and extremely limited keyboards, it's very difficult to browse meaningful websites on such phones. Don't even get me started on the difficulty in typing text messages on such phones—it's no fun at all. So, the point is that, until recently, no one had hit just the right blend of handheld computer and mobile phone when developing a device that mixes both.

The BlackBerry 7100 device represents one of the first devices to nimbly walk the tightrope and balance the form factor of a mobile phone with the functionality of a handheld computer. This explains why the device has instantly become so popular.

If you've missed out on the BlackBerry craze, you might want to buckle your seatbelt because the BlackBerry 7100 series of mobile handheld devices takes the popular BlackBerry text messaging platform to a whole new level. Often referred to as "CrackBerry" because of the addictive nature of its text messaging feature, the BlackBerry platform has been the mobile text communication darling of corporate North America for several years now. Similar to the pervasiveness of Short Message Service (SMS) in Europe and parts of Asia, BlackBerry has played a similar role in business text messaging in the United States and Canada. However, before the 7100 series, most BlackBerry devices were positioned purely as text messaging devices with secondary mobile phone capabilities, or none at all.

▶ **NOTE**
BlackBerry devices are so heavily used that some doctors are now concerned about "BlackBerry thumb," which is basically tendonitis of the thumb caused by repetitive typing on a BlackBerry or similar mobile device. Although BlackBerry thumb appears to be blown a bit out of proportion, it isn't unrealistic to think that hardcore users could develop repetitive stress-related problems from all the thumb typing.

The 7100 dramatically changes the BlackBerry platform's pure text messaging perception by adding a mobile phone to the equation, along with a more compact, mobile phone form factor. Because of its slim-line form factor, the 7100 series devices aren't quite as rugged as their traditional text messaging ancestors, but the trade-off is hardly a negative when you consider that you're able to combine two devices into one.

BlackBerry 7100 series devices use the familiar BlackBerry operating system, which is intuitive and relatively easy to use. Even so, there are numerous tricks and tips you can employ to optimize the BlackBerry experience and streamline your mobile communications. Throughout this book, you'll find a healthy dose of practical BlackBerry usage tips and tricks, as well as techniques for tweaking the device settings to suit your needs and using third-party applications to pick up where the standard applications leave off. Before getting into all that, however, it's worth getting acquainted with the BlackBerry 7100 and how it fits into the wireless landscape in general, and the BlackBerry product line in particular.

Taking a Look at Mobile Wireless Networks

All BlackBerry devices, mobile phones, and many handheld computers are generally referred to as *wireless devices*, which simply means they can transmit and receive information over invisible radio waves without the aid of wires. Wireless devices have been around for a while, as evidenced by garage door openers, television remote controls, two-way radios, and cordless phones. What primarily distinguishes these devices from BlackBerry devices is the range of the wireless communication being carried out. More specifically, BlackBerry devices communicate over a wide area network (WAN) that spans many miles, whereas the other devices mentioned are limited to a range more easily measured in tens or hundreds of feet.

▶ **NOTE**
Such shorter range wireless networks typically fall under the category of personal area networks (PANs) or local area networks (LANs), depending on their specific wireless range.

In many ways, you can compare the networking capabilities of a BlackBerry device with those of a Wi-Fi device such as a laptop or high-end handheld computer. Like BlackBerry devices, these devices can transmit and receive complex data over a wireless network connection. However, they currently suffer from the same range problem as more primitive wireless devices such as garage door openers, even though the technology is dramatically different. Granted, Wi-Fi hubs are popping up everywhere, which is making it increasingly easier to find an access point, but the fact remains that there is no unified wide area Wi-Fi network to tap into, as there is for BlackBerry devices and mobile phones. On the other hand, the BlackBerry 7100 series devices use a relatively slow data connection as compared to Wi-Fi. It seems as if we're still a few years away from having our cake and eating it too (widespread wireless access at high speeds).

Getting back to WANs, which is the type of network used by BlackBerry devices, it's important to understand where wireless WANs came from in evolving to their current form. The first generation of wireless WANs (also known as *1g* for *first generation*) was designed exclusively for carrying analog voice data. This network was used to considerable success in early cell phones and formed the basis for creating a market for mobile communication devices. However, the network is analog, which eliminates any decent chance of carrying out meaningful data communications beyond voice conversations.

The second generation of mobile phone networks (also known as *2g* for *second generation*) was created as a digital network that can support both voice and data communications. 2g networks have served their purpose of putting mobile phones into the digital domain, but their communication speeds are considerably lacking. More specifically, 2g networks typically offer data speeds capped at 9.6Kbps, which is quite slow by modern computing standards. To put this in practical terms, it takes anywhere from 30 to 40 minutes to download a 3-minute MP3 song over a 2g network connection. Popular 2g networks include Code Division Multiple Access (CDMA), Global System for Mobile Communications (GSMC), Time Division Multiple Access (TDMA), and Integrated Digital Enhanced Network (iDEN), which are still used by many mobile phones worldwide.

▶ **NOTE**

In addition to offering digital data communications, 2g networks were a necessary replacement for 1g networks to accommodate a wider spectrum of frequencies for the rapidly growing number of mobile phone users.

Confusingly, the generation of WANs after 2g isn't called 3g, as you might expect. This is because the network succeeding 2g was designed more as an incremental improvement over 2g as opposed to a full-blown next-generation network. I'm referring to the network type known as *2.5g*, which improves upon the 2g data transfer limitations by offering a theoretical maximum speed of 115Kbps. Unfortunately, few if any 2.5g wireless networks offer speeds anywhere near this theoretical maximum speed. A more realistic speed range for 2.5g networks is 40Kbps–60Kbps, which still represents a significant improvement over 2g networks. Going back to the MP3 download example, it takes anywhere from 6 to 9 minutes to download a 3-minute MP3 song over a 2.5g network connection.

All BlackBerry 7100 series devices currently operate on the 2.5g network and have varying network speeds unique to each specific wireless service provider. The only 2.5g network is General Packet Radio Service (GPRS), which is used by many wireless providers to support most of the current mobile handheld devices that combine both voice and data communications.

▶ **NOTE**

To make the whole 2g/2.5g/3g discussion even more confusing, there is a network standard considered to be 2.75g. I'm referring to Enhanced Data GSM Environment (EDGE), which is considered an improvement over 2g and 2.5g that offers data transfer speeds up to 384Kbps. EDGE represents an option for some wireless service providers who aren't ready or able to make the significant move up to a 3g network.

The true third-generation wireless mobile network (also known as *3g*) has been around for a couple of years but is still somewhat limited in terms of provider and device support, especially in North America. 3g networks provide data transfer speeds in the range of 144Kbps–2Mbps, which is a significant improvement over earlier networks. Using the MP3 download example one more time, it takes anywhere from 11 to 90 seconds to download a 3-minute MP3 song over a 3g network connection. Major 3g networks include W-CDMA (Wideband CDMA) and CDMA2000.

▶ **NOTE**

BlackBerry currently offers two devices designed for 3g networks—the 6750 and 7750—which have a much larger form factor than the 7100. Although currently no 7100 devices support 3g networks, it is likely only a matter of time before RIM expands the 7100 product line for 3g.

✔ **Start Here**

The BlackBerry Device Family Past and Present

To fully appreciate the BlackBerry 7100, it's helpful to understand how it fits into the BlackBerry device family. This is important because the 7100 has, in many ways, evolved from the BlackBerry devices that came before it. Although the BlackBerry operating system has evolved considerably over the years, many of the devices have remained relatively unchanged in terms of their appearances. This is a testament to the fact that the devices were well-designed to begin with. The 7100 is by far the most dramatic departure from the familiar, rugged, rectangular BlackBerry device profile.

The earliest BlackBerry device, the BlackBerry 950, was released by RIM in 1998 as a pure text-messaging device that supports two-way text messaging on the Mobitex pager network developed by Ericsson. The BlackBerry 950 built on RIM's original Interactive Pager, released in 1996 as the first two-way messaging pager. The BlackBerry 950 put RIM on the map and allowed it to jump from the Toronto Stock Exchange to the NASDAQ under the ticker symbol RIMM in 1999. Also in 1999, RIM expanded the BlackBerry product line with the BlackBerry 850, as well as the BlackBerry Enterprise Server (BES) software for wireless corporate email integration.

Throughout 2000 and 2001, the BlackBerry family of text-messaging devices built steam and developed a loyal corporate user base while picking up numerous technological awards along the way. In 2002, a new generation of BlackBerry devices was introduced to support mobile phone features. Models included the 5810, 6710, 6720, 6510, and 6750. The 6510 was unique in that it supports Nextel's walkie-talkie feature, while the 6750 supports the speedy CDMA2000 3g network standard. The only drawback to this generation of devices is their use of a monochrome screen, which severely inhibits serious mobile web browsing. However, the devices were on par with other mobile devices of the day, so the monochrome screen wasn't perceived as a weakness.

In 2003, RIM's status as a technology player increased when it was promoted to the NASDAQ-100 Index, putting it in the top 100 companies listed on the NASDAQ. That year, RIM also introduced the 6200 series of devices, which were to be the last new BlackBerry devices with monochrome screens. Quickly on the heels of the 6200 series arrived the first color BlackBerry devices in the 7200 and 7700 series.

The year 2004 represented a significant milestone in the history of RIM: It celebrated its 20th anniversary by crossing the one million subscriber mark. And less than 10 months later, still in 2004, the BlackBerry subscriber count doubled to more than two million users—an impressive level of growth by any standard. Perhaps more importantly to this discussion, in 2004 RIM released the 7100 and 7500 series of devices, with the former being the first device to adopt a look and feel more closely approximating a mobile phone.

▶ **NOTE**
The 7100 series of BlackBerry devices were code-named "Charm" devices when they were under development, and you occasionally still see them referred to by that name on the Web.

As of this writing, the latest development in the BlackBerry saga is the long-awaited release of version 4.0 of the BlackBerry operating system, which hit the street in early 2005. Unfortunately, version 4.0 was released between the releases of some of the 7100 models, so users of the first 7100 series devices (7100t and 7100r, for example) will have to manually upgrade their devices to the 4.0 operating system. This turns out to be a fairly simple task—see the section later in this chapter titled "Upgrading Your Device to the Latest BlackBerry OS."

Now that we've arrived at the 7100 series of devices in the storied history of the BlackBerry platform, it's worth clarifying exactly why I have to refer to the devices as a *series* as opposed to a single device. There are actually a few different devices with the 7100 name, and some of them look surprisingly different from each other. For example, the 7100t (T-Mobile in the United States) and 7100v (Vodafone in Europe and Asia-Pacific) aren't even shaped the same, although they do hold to roughly the same dimensions.

To understand how the 7100 series of devices represents such a departure for RIM in terms of form factor, take a look at the 7780, which follows the more traditional square shape of BlackBerry text-messaging devices.

Getting back to the 7100 series, as of this writing there are five 7100 devices, each of which is tailored to the specific wireless service providers that offer it:

Model	Service Provider (Location)
7100t	T-Mobile (United States and Europe)
7100r	Rogers Wireless (Canada)
7100g	Cingular and Cellular One (United States), Optus and Telstra (Australia), SingTel and Starhub (Singapore), 3 and CSL (Hong Kong)
7100v	Vodafone (Europe, Australia, and New Zealand)
7100x	O2 (Europe)

✔ **Start Here**

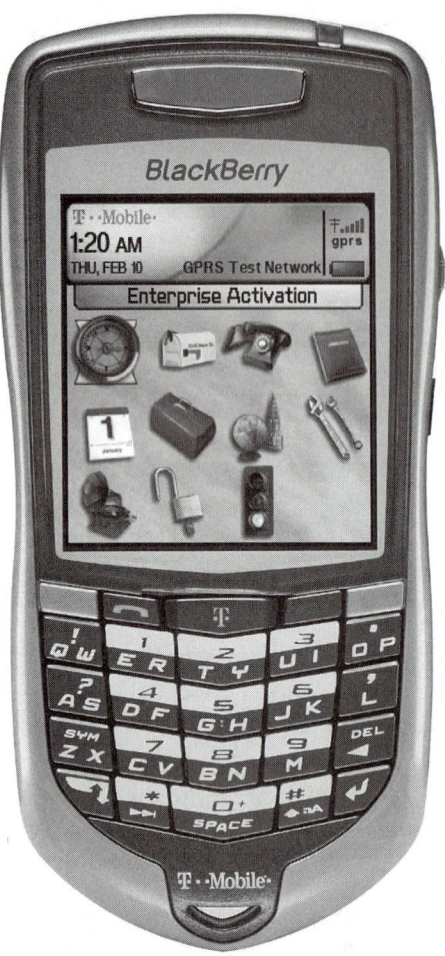

The BlackBerry 7100t, which is available from T-Mobile in the United States, packs the functionality of a larger BlackBerry device into the slim form factor of a mobile phone.

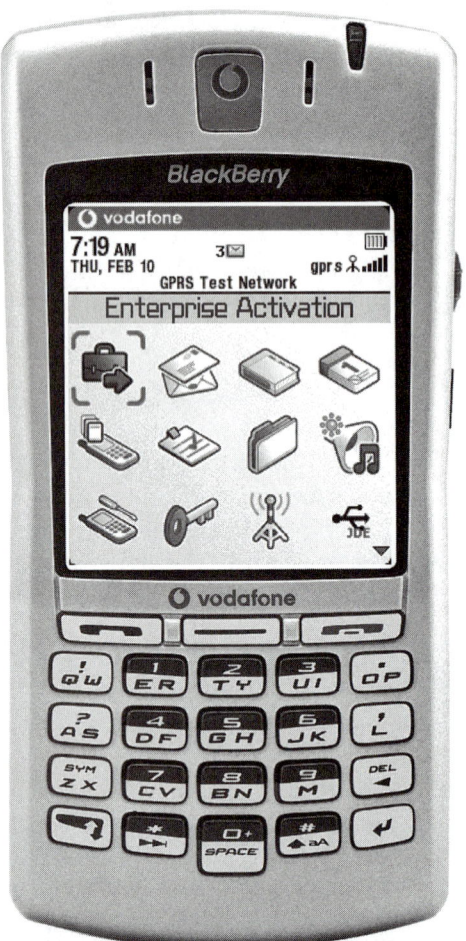

The BlackBerry 7100v, which is available from Vodafone in Europe, Australia, and New Zealand, is similar in size to the 7100t but with much straighter lines.

Undoubtedly, even more BlackBerry 7100 devices will roll out, especially in the United States, as wireless providers scramble to keep up with each other and meet user demand for the first "BlackBerry phone."

✔ **Start Here** 11

The BlackBerry 7780 offers features similar to the 7100 series of devices, but its shape and size make it considerably less appealing as a mobile phone replacement.

Assessing the BlackBerry Platform

Okay, so you get the idea that the BlackBerry 7100 series of devices represents a unique merger of wireless text messaging and mobile phone functionality, but I haven't really said a lot about what makes the BlackBerry platform as a whole so appealing.

Until recently, the BlackBerry platform was widely regarded as a business-only platform for mobile devices tailored to the corporate set. Although corporate users still represent a significant portion of the BlackBerry user base, a major part of the goal in the 7100 series is to bring BlackBerry to the masses. POP/IMAP email support, web browsing, and instant messaging are features in the BlackBerry operating system that appeal to a broad range of users. But that doesn't explain why the BlackBerry platform etched its name so deeply in the corporate world.

The secret to the success of the BlackBerry can be summed up in two words: push email. *Push* refers to a type of email in which messages are pushed from the email server to the remote device immediately, as opposed to the device polling the server for new messages on regular intervals. The practical significance of push email is that it is immediate. Push email is the text equivalent of the walkie-talkie feature popular on Nextel mobile phones. Business users responded in huge numbers to the benefits of push email by adopting BlackBerry as the platform of choice for robust, rapid-fire text messaging. The push email phenomenon has been limited primarily to business users because a dedicated mail server has been required for it to work; checking a POP email account with Outlook Express is not push email.

▶ **NOTE**
Other companies have offered devices with push email, and still do, but RIM established in the BlackBerry platform the most reliable and affordable system for push email that integrated well with corporate email servers.

The corporate side of BlackBerry email support is made possible thanks to the BES, a software package that integrates wireless push email with popular groupware servers such as Microsoft Exchange and Lotus Domino. A BES is by no means required to use BlackBerry email, but it does provide advanced synchronization features that benefit business users. For example, with the BES, you can send and receive wireless meeting invitation requests and synchronize your calendar accordingly. The other thing the BES does is provide an infrastructure for allowing universal connectivity between different wireless network providers. In other words, you can have people using devices on different wireless providers that seamlessly communicate through a BES server.

Although push email and the BES are central in the success of BlackBerry devices, they don't represent the end of the story. Following are some other significant hallmarks of the BlackBerry name that also contributed to its success:

- **Long battery life**—BlackBerry devices have traditionally offered considerably longer battery life than other mobile handheld devices.

- **Rough and rugged**—BlackBerry devices are known as very rugged devices thanks to their thick, rigid outer shells. Unfortunately, the 7100 represents a departure from this design for the sake of making it slimmer and lighter.

✔ **Start Here**

- **Data protection**—Because data is stored in Flash ROM, your data can survive without the main device battery; some handheld devices suffer from data loss if you lose battery power.

- **Security**—Encryption is a standard part of the BlackBerry OS, and all applications must be digitally signed to verify the publisher.

- **Stability**—Generally speaking, BlackBerry devices have been proven to require far fewer system restarts than competing devices and can operate over longer continuous periods of time without any glitches.

- **Always-on connection**—The wireless connection for BlackBerry devices is always on, which means you never have to manually establish a connection unless you've deliberately disabled the wireless radio.

So, I've done a decent sales job for BlackBerry devices. Now allow me to point out some of the deficiencies in the BlackBerry platform that are still standing in the way of the 7100 becoming a true consumer device. Following are some major mobile handheld features you won't currently find on any BlackBerry devices:

- MP3 music support
- An FM tuner
- A digital camera (still or video)
- Bluetooth synchronization with a desktop computer
- A wide selection of entertainment software

The lack of inclusion of these features into the 7100 series can be attributed to two things: security and the business past of the BlackBerry platform. RIM has been extremely guarded about including anything in its devices that isn't ultra-secure, which is an important issue for its corporate clientele. This same clientele isn't so turned on by downloading Top 40 songs to their devices or taking pictures to send to friends. However, if RIM hopes to truly bridge the gap from its business user base to a consumer user base, it will eventually have to address some of these missing ingredients. The reality is that it isn't just teenagers who appreciate the convenience of snapping a quick picture with their phone or listening to music on a commute.

▶ **NOTE**
I have to admit that I really like being able to listen to the FM radio on my phone when I'm exercising, and I sorely missed this feature when I switched to the BlackBerry 7100 as my all-in-one device.

So, what's on the horizon for the BlackBerry platform? In addition to expecting some new 7100 devices, an explosion in BlackBerry software development is underway. This is a much-needed area of improvement for BlackBerry devices, and it is thankfully underway. Expect to see many more options in the near future for all kinds of new applications, including some open-source applications. Rumors even abound regarding a possible Linux synchronization application, which would be quite interesting.

Upgrading Your Device to the Latest BlackBerry OS

If you purchased a 7100 device that shipped with a version of the BlackBerry operating system (OS) older than 4.0, it's important for you to upgrade the OS to 4.0 because that is the major release of the OS currently supported by RIM. If you aren't sure which version OS your device has, follow these steps to find out:

1 Open the Tools Screen

Scroll to the **Tools** icon on the **Home** screen and click the trackwheel. The **Tools** screen appears, offering a list of tool options.

2 Open the Settings Screen

Scroll to the **Settings** icon and click the trackwheel. A list of options for which you can change the settings appears.

3 Open the About Screen

Scroll to the **About** option in the list of settings and click the trackwheel. The **About** screen opens, which shows a great deal of information about the system software installed on your device.

4 Check the Version Number of the OS

Near the top of the **About** screen you'll see a line that shows the version of the BlackBerry OS. Check whether the first number in the version is 4, which indicates that you have version 4.0 of the OS. If the number is 3, it means you probably need to upgrade to get the latest and greatest BlackBerry OS.

✔ **Start Here** 15

If your device indeed needs to be upgraded to a newer version of the BlackBerry OS, you'll have to visit the website of your wireless service provider to download the upgrade software for your specific device. But first you should download the latest version of the BlackBerry desktop software, the BlackBerry Desktop Manager. The latest version of the BlackBerry Desktop Manager is available for

✔ **Start Here**

downloading directly from RIM at http://www.blackberry.com/support/downloads/. After downloading the new desktop software, see **8** **Install the BlackBerry Desktop Software** for details on how to install it.

With the Desktop Manager software updated and ready to roll on your desktop computer, you can then move on to downloading and installing the latest BlackBerry OS. It's important to note that the latest BlackBerry OS is not in any way required to get the most out of this book—it's just a good idea in terms of improving your device's stability and smoothing over minor issues in performance and reliability. But feel free to dive in and start learning how to maximize your BlackBerry 7100—you can always upgrade later!

2

Hit the Ground Running with Your BlackBerry

IN THIS CHAPTER:

1. About the BlackBerry User Interface
2. Select a Display Language
3. Set the Date and Time
4. Make Yourself the Owner
5. Lock and Unlock Your Device
6. Password-Protect Your Device
7. Choose a Theme

CHAPTER 2: Hit the Ground Running with Your BlackBerry

Unlike a traditional mobile phone, your BlackBerry 7100 is a very personal mobile device. Not only do you use it to communicate in a variety of ways, but you also use it to house a great deal of personal information. Knowing this, it only makes sense to get started with your BlackBerry by personalizing it. A few personal tweaks here and there can make the difference in giving your BlackBerry a familiar feel.

As you get started customizing your BlackBerry for your own personal tastes, you'll also begin to get acquainted with the BlackBerry user interface. Whether you're moving to the 7100 series from an earlier BlackBerry device or from a more traditional mobile phone, you'll find that the user interface in the 7100 series devices has a great deal to offer. There is a small learning curve, but you'll likely start feeling at home relatively quickly.

1 About the BlackBerry User Interface

BlackBerry 7100 series devices are built on the popular BlackBerry operating system, which has evolved quite a bit from its earlier days in simple text messaging devices. The user interface is just as much about hardware as it is about software—the keys on the 7100 series devices are carefully designed to mesh with the software visuals you see on the screen. The first thing you might notice about the 7100 that sets it apart from other BlackBerry devices—and virtually all handheld devices, for that matter—is the unusual keyboard.

There are significantly fewer keys on the 7100 keyboard than on a traditional computer keyboard, certainly not enough for every letter in the alphabet. In fact, many of the keys on the 7100 keyboard include two letters instead of one. The magic at work in this compact keyboard is a technology called *SureType*, which allows you to peck away at each letter of a word without worrying too much about what shows up onscreen until you get near the end. The vast majority of the time, you'll find that SureType does an excellent job of figuring out what you wanted to type even though you probably used only a handful of keys.

▶ KEY TERM

SureType—Research In Motion's (RIM) key-entry technology that intelligently analyzes what you type and figures out which letter you intend from the context of what you're typing. SureType keyboards are unique in that they include multiple letters on a single key.

About the BlackBerry User Interface

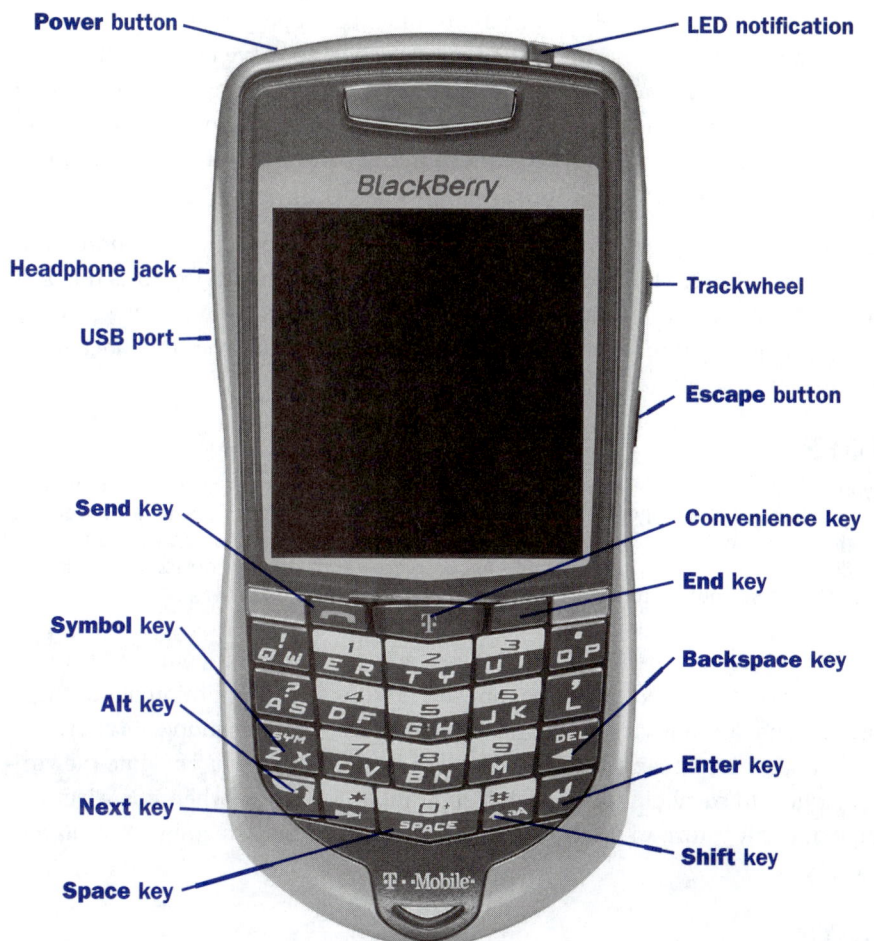

The BlackBerry 7100 series device consists of a vertically oriented screen and a compact keyboard.

You'll notice some familiar keys on the keyboard that are carry-overs from traditional computer keyboards. The **Alt** key is used in a variety of ways to execute alternate commands. The **Shift**, **Enter**, **Backspace**, and **Space** keys also play roles similar to a traditional keyboard. The **Send** and **End** keys are associated with the underlying mobile phone within the 7100 series devices. The **Next** key is used to cycle through items in lists, among other things. And finally, the **Symbol** key provides access to important symbols such as hyphens (-) and the at symbol (@).

Aside from the keyboard, the trackwheel and **Escape** button are the two most important aspects of the 7100 user interface. You can scroll the trackwheel to navigate menus and generally move around within the BlackBerry user interface. Most of the time the trackwheel defaults to up/down scrolling, but in some cases it also allows you to move left/right if the context is appropriate. For example, when setting the time you can rotate the trackwheel to move horizontally between the hours, minutes, and AM/PM setting. The trackwheel is also useful for making and confirming selections. To use it in this manner, you simply push in on it, which is also known as *clicking* it; in many cases you'll find that clicking the trackwheel is equivalent to pressing the **Enter** key.

The **Escape** button just below the trackwheel is used to cancel actions and back out of applications. The **Power** button along the top of the device turns the device on and off. The action of the **Convenience** key can be unique to each wireless service provider, but most of them set the key so that it launches the BlackBerry web browser.

▶ **NOTE**

If you quickly press the **Power** button to turn off your device, the device doesn't actually turn off. Instead, it simply turns off the screen to conserve battery power. If the radio is on, you'll still receive phone calls, email, and text messages; the screen will automatically kick on in the event of a phone call. To completely turn off your device, you must hold down the **Power** button for a few seconds.

The **Home** screen is the first screen you see when you turn on your device, and it consists of a status area along the top with a variety of information about the current state of the device as well as a list of icons for the available services. The main area of the screen (where all the icons live) is where you navigate the various services to carry out tasks. Each icon highlights to show when it is selected. You can easily return to the **Home** screen from any other screen by pressing the **End** key.

▶ **NOTE**

If, for some reason, you've already tinkered with the theme on your device, the **Home** screen might not appear as I'm showing it in the figure. Your **Home** screen also might be different depending on your wireless service provider. Most of the figures for this book are based on the default T-Mobile theme. However, all themes are somewhat similar, so you shouldn't have too much trouble following along even if your device's theme is different.

▶ **NOTE**

The services on your particular device might vary slightly from those in the figure. For example, your device might be missing the Enterprise Activation service but might have additional services unique to your particular wireless carrier, such as instant messaging.

2 Select a Display Language

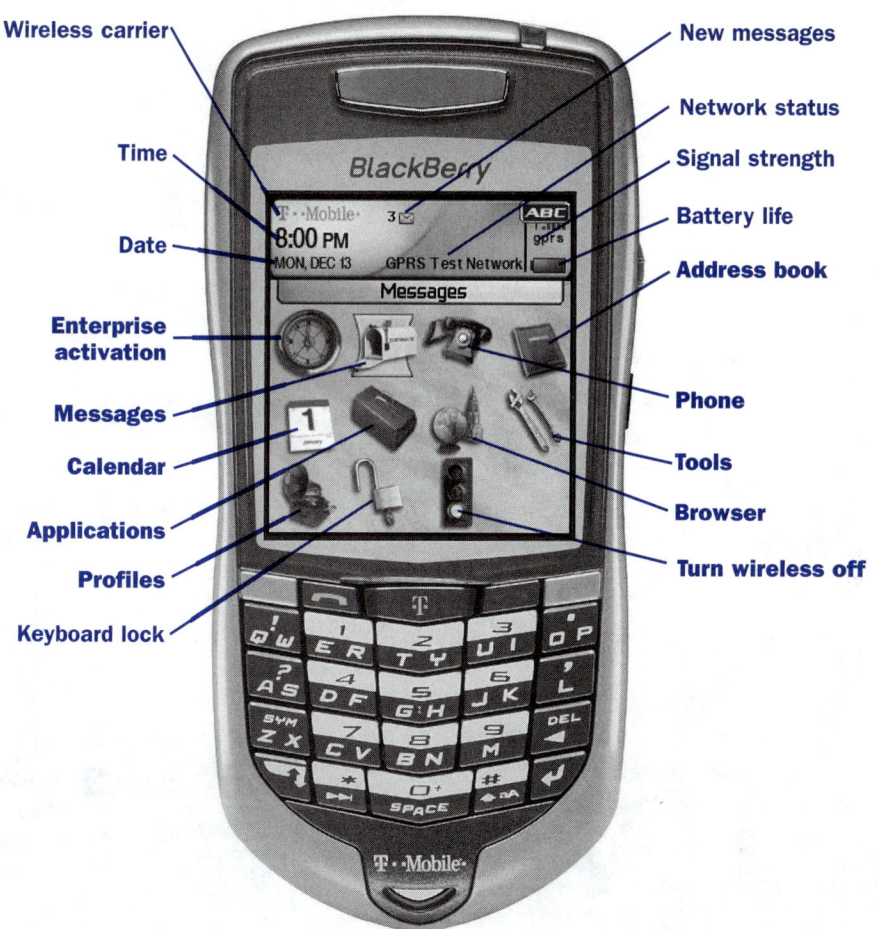

The **Home** screen includes a status area along the top and a main area with icons for available services.

2 Select a Display Language

✔ **BEFORE YOU BEGIN**

1 About the BlackBerry User Interface

CHAPTER 2: Hit the Ground Running with Your BlackBerry

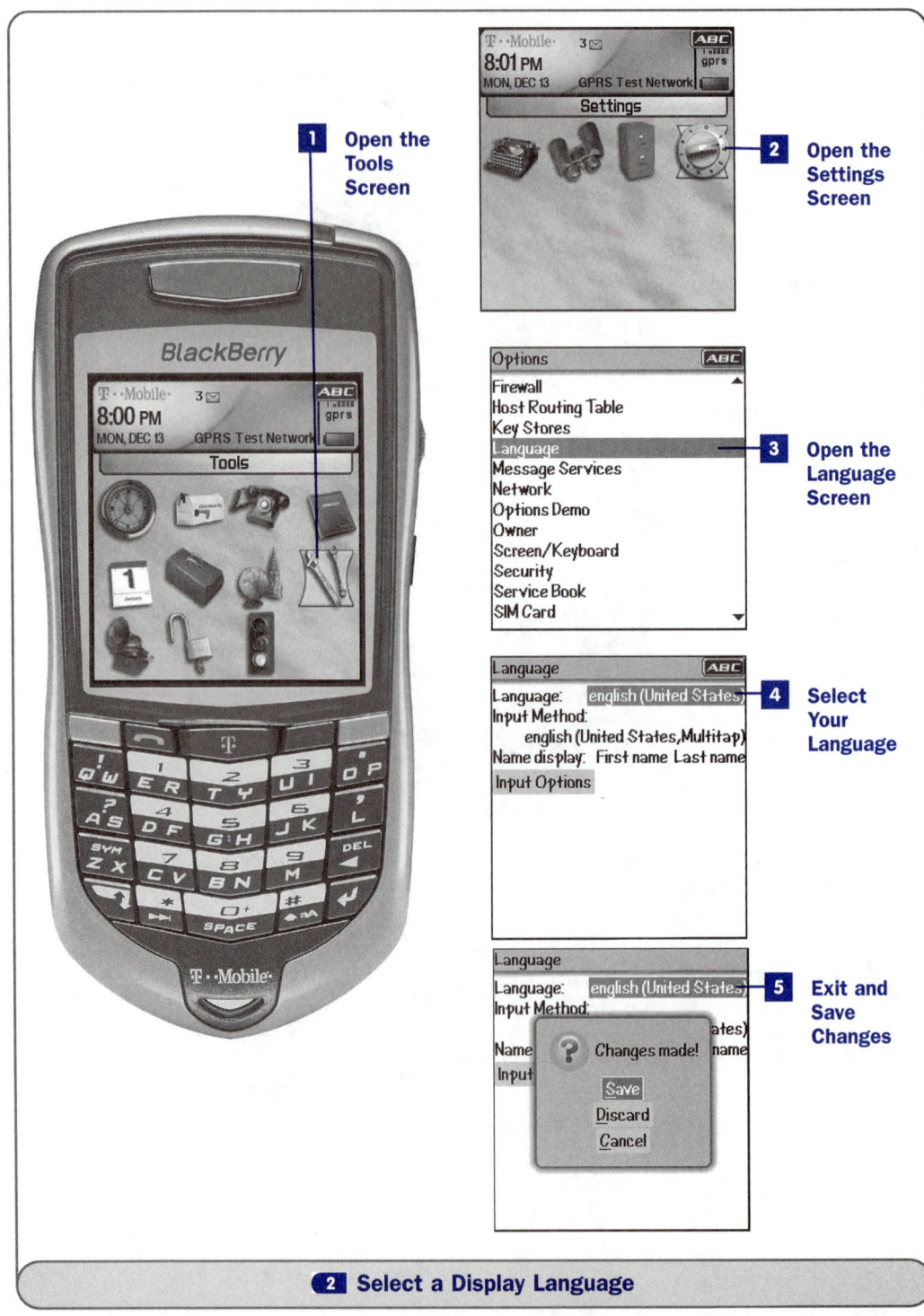

2 Select a Display Language

Your BlackBerry device is essentially a personal communicator, and as such it is important for it to speak the same language you speak. Although BlackBerry devices can be configured to operate using a variety of languages, your device likely came configured to support only those languages common to where you live. Regardless of that, you'll want to ensure that your device is set to use the proper language. In all likelihood, this is a setting you probably won't need to change, but it's worth taking a quick peek just to be safe.

1 Open the Tools Screen

Scroll to the **Tools** icon on the **Home** screen and click the trackwheel. The **Tools** screen appears, offering a list of tool options.

2 Open the Settings Screen

Scroll to the **Settings** icon and click the trackwheel. A list of options for which you can change the settings appears.

3 Open the Language Screen

Scroll to the **Language** option in the list of settings and click the trackwheel. The **Language** screen opens.

▶ TIP

You can quickly navigate to the **Language** option on the **Settings** screen by pressing the **L** key on the keyboard.

4 Select Your Language

If the language you want your BlackBerry unit to use differs from the language that appears on the **Language** screen, use the trackwheel to highlight the text in the **Language** field and click the trackwheel; then click **Change Option** in the menu that appears. A list of alternative language options appears.

Scroll the trackwheel through the list of alternative languages, and click to accept the choice you've made.

▶ TIP

To quickly change an option without having to go through the two trackwheel clicks required to open a menu and select **Change Option**, highlight the option and press the **Alt** key to view a list of choices. Then scroll to the desired choice and click the trackwheel to select it. An even faster shortcut involves cycling to the next available choice by pressing the **Space** key; pressing **Shift+Space** cycles to the previous choice.

CHAPTER 2: Hit the Ground Running with Your BlackBerry

▶ **NOTE**

The BlackBerry 7100 series supports language dialects for different locales. For example, there are variations of English for the United States and Great Britain. Because wireless providers usually target a specific locale, your device might already be configured with the correct language setting.

5 Exit and Save Changes

Press the **Escape** button to exit the **Language** screen. If you changed the language, you're prompted to save or discard the changes. When prompted, scroll the trackwheel to the **Save** option and click to save the changes. You're returned to the **Settings** screen. Press the **Escape** button twice to navigate back to the **Home** screen, or just press the **End** key once.

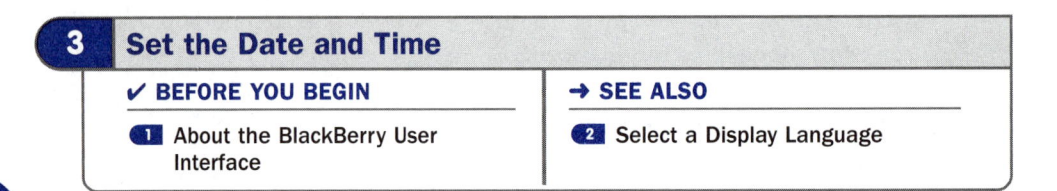

3 Set the Date and Time

✔ BEFORE YOU BEGIN	→ SEE ALSO
1 About the BlackBerry User Interface	2 Select a Display Language

Just about everything you do with your BlackBerry is dependent on the date and time. Phone calls, emails, and text messages all carry a time stamp that is important in establishing the context of a communication. The BlackBerry 7100 series devices allow you to directly set the date, time, time zone, and time format. You can also elect to allow the device to automatically retrieve the date and time from the wireless network or from your desktop computer when it's synchronizing data.

When getting started with your device, you'll probably want to directly set the date and time. From then on, you might choose to let it automatically update from the network or from your desktop computer.

1 Open the Tools Screen

Scroll to the **Tools** icon on the **Home** screen and click the trackwheel. The **Tools** screen opens.

▶ **TIP**

To immediately jump to the **Home** screen from any other screen, press the **End** key. Optionally, you can press the **Escape** button repeatedly to navigate backward through the user interface to return to the **Home** screen.

3 Set the Date and Time

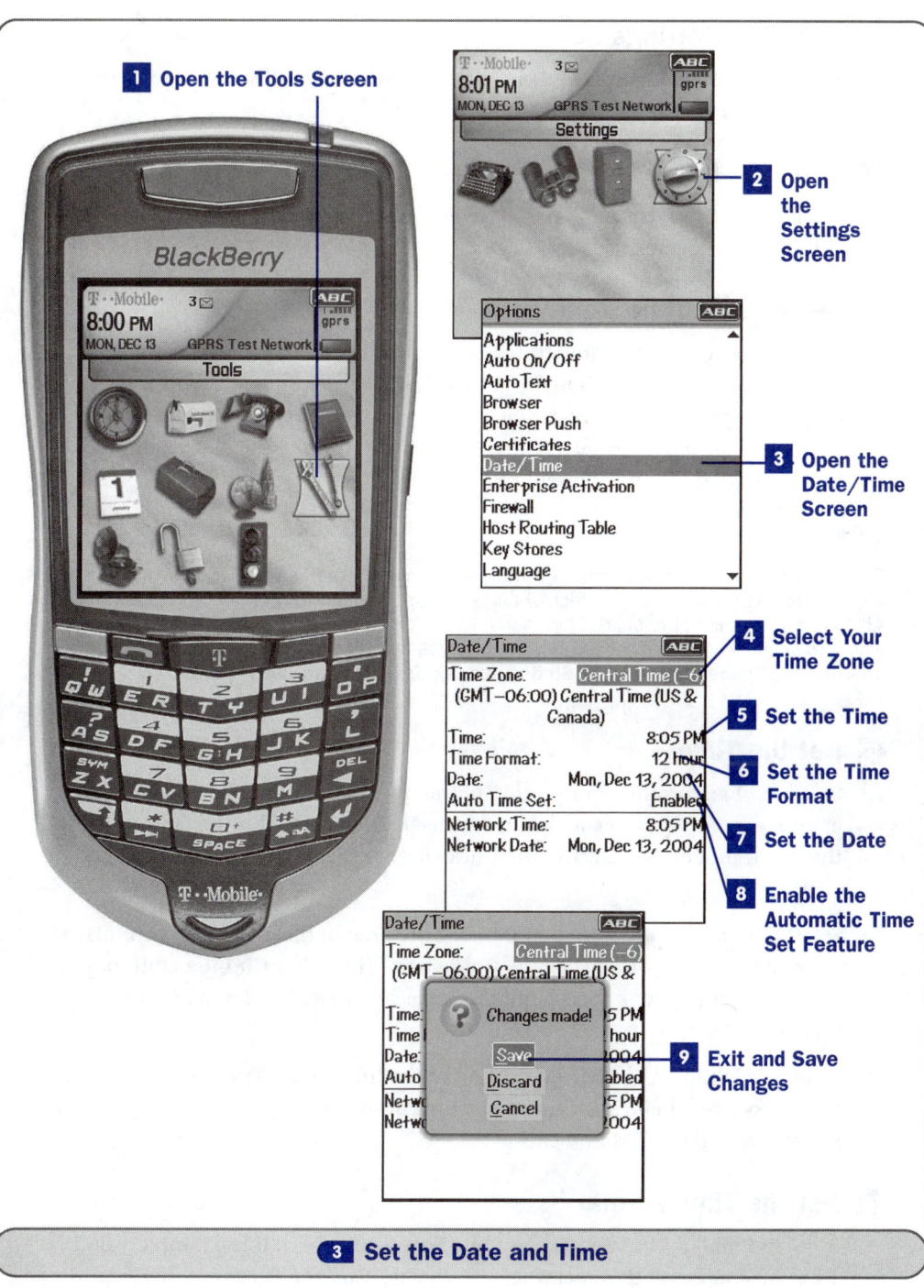

1. Open the Tools Screen
2. Open the Settings Screen
3. Open the Date/Time Screen
4. Select Your Time Zone
5. Set the Time
6. Set the Time Format
7. Set the Date
8. Enable the Automatic Time Set Feature
9. Exit and Save Changes

3 Set the Date and Time

2 Open the Settings Screen

Scroll to the **Settings** icon and click the trackwheel. A list of options for which you can change the settings appears.

3 Open the Date/Time Screen

Scroll to the **Date/Time** option in the list, and click the trackwheel. The **Date/Time** screen opens.

4 Select Your Time Zone

Use the trackwheel to highlight the text in the **Time Zone** field—in this example, select the text **Central Time (–6)**—and click the trackwheel. Then click **Change Option** in the menu that appears. A list of alternative time zones appears. Scroll through the list of options to select the desired time zone and click the trackwheel to select that option.

▶ **TIP**

To quickly change an option without having to go through the two trackwheel clicks required to open a menu and select **Change Option**, highlight the option and press the **Alt** key to view a list of choices. Then scroll to the desired choice and click the trackwheel to select it. An even faster shortcut involves cycling to the next available choice by pressing the **Space** key; pressing **Shift+Space** cycles to the previous choice.

5 Set the Time

Scroll to highlight the hour portion of the time in the **Time** field—in this example, select **8**—and click the trackwheel. Then click **Change Option** in the menu that appears. Scroll the trackwheel to select the desired hour and click.

Scroll to highlight the minute portion of the time in the **Time** field—in this example, select **05**—and click the trackwheel. Then click **Change Option** in the menu that appears. Scroll the trackwheel to select the desired minutes and click.

Scroll to highlight the **AM/PM** portion of the time in the **Time** field and click the trackwheel; then click **Change Option** in the menu that appears. Scroll to select either **AM** or **PM** and click.

6 Set the Time Format

Scroll to highlight the text in the **Time Format** field—in this example, select **12 hour**—and click the trackwheel. Then click **Change Option** in the menu that appears. From the next menu, select either **12 hour** (to see time displayed as **1:00 AM** and **1:00 PM**) or **24 hour** (to see time displayed as **01:00** and **13:00**) and click.

▶ **NOTE**

The **24 hour** time format is handy if you're accustomed to military time, which is officially known as Universal Military Time (UMT). According to UMT, the hours of the day are listed from 0 to 24 with no notion of a.m. or p.m.; actually, 0 and 24 are equivalent (midnight) in UMT.

7 Set the Date

Scroll to highlight the month portion of the date in the **Date** field—in this example, select **Dec**—and click the trackwheel. Then click **Change Option** in the menu that appears. Scroll to select the month and click.

Repeat this step to select and set the day and year portions of the date.

▶ **NOTE**

You don't have the option to set the day of the week—it is automatically selected based on the date you set.

8 Enable the Automatic Time Set Feature

If the automatic time set feature isn't already enabled, scroll to select the **Auto Time Set** field and click the trackwheel. Then click **Change Option**. From the menu that appears, select **Enabled** to allow your BlackBerry unit to retrieve the current local time and date from your service provider or the wireless network to which you are connected; select **Disabled** to force the device to use only the time and date you have specified on this screen.

9 Exit and Save Changes

Press the **Escape** button to exit the **Date/Time** screen. When prompted to save or discard your changes, scroll the trackwheel to **Save** and click to save the changes.

---

4 Make Yourself the Owner

✔ **BEFORE YOU BEGIN**

1 About the BlackBerry User Interface

→ **SEE ALSO**

5 Lock and Unlock Your Device
6 Password-Protect Your Device

28 CHAPTER 2: Hit the Ground Running with Your BlackBerry

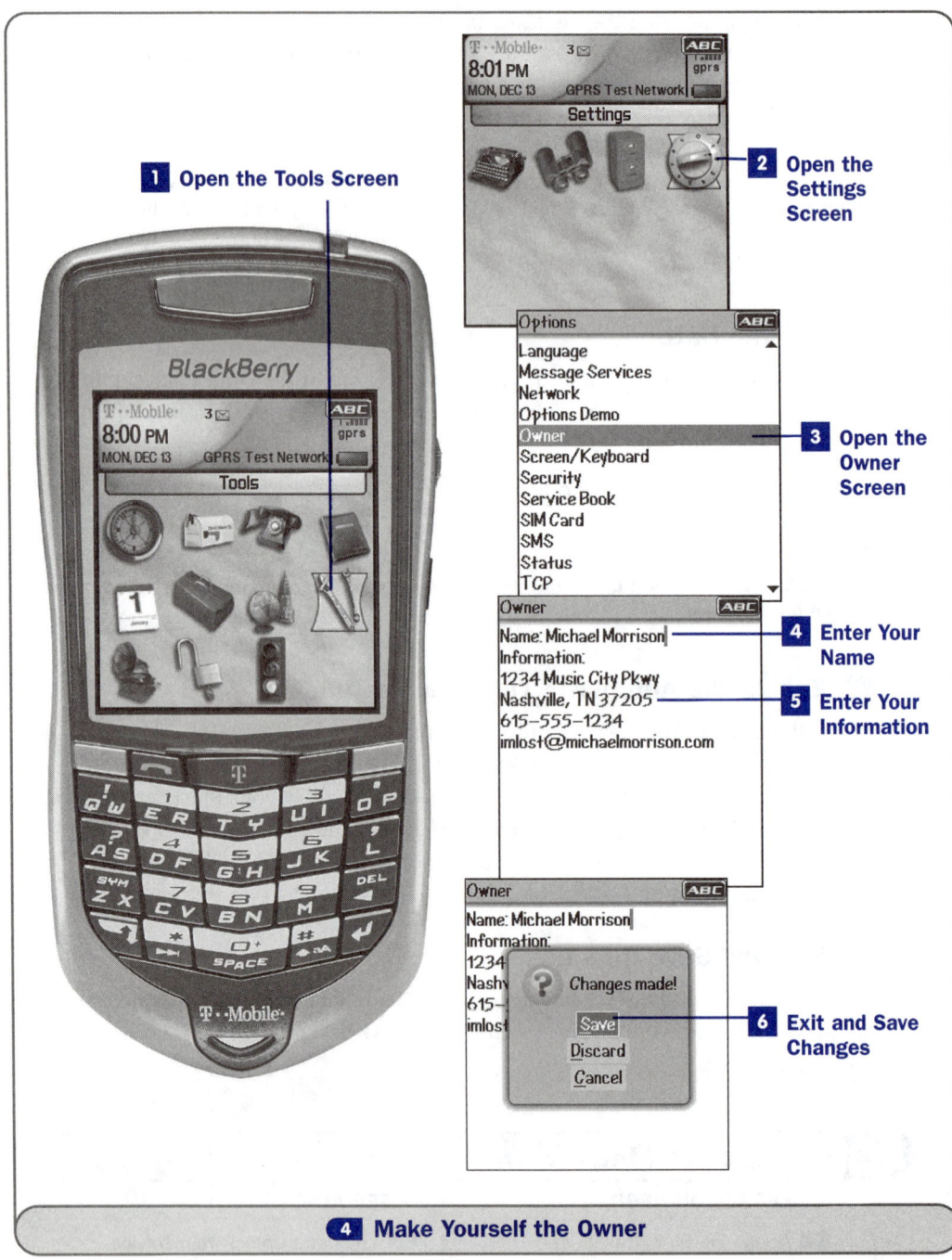

4 Make Yourself the Owner

4 Make Yourself the Owner

As the proud owner of a BlackBerry 7100 series device, it's important that you take ownership of your device. More specifically, I'm referring to you entering your name and any relevant personal information so that your device is associated with *you*. This information is important because it is displayed on the **Home** screen when you lock the device. You will typically lock your device to prevent accidental key presses from having any effect, to protect the device from others, or both. See **5** **Lock and Unlock Your Device**.

1 Open the Tools Screen

Scroll to the **Tools** icon on the **Home** screen and click the trackwheel. The **Tools** screen opens.

▶ **TIP**

To immediately jump to the **Home** screen from any other screen, press the **End** key.

2 Open the Settings Screen

Scroll to the **Settings** icon and click the trackwheel. A list of options for which you can change the settings appears.

3 Open the Owner Screen

Scroll to the **Owner** option in the list and click the trackwheel. The **Owner** screen opens.

4 Enter Your Name

Using the keyboard, enter your name as you'd like it to appear on the device when the device is locked. With SureType, all you have to do is press the key corresponding to each letter of your name and the device will figure out the rest. If you want, you can switch to *multitap* input mode instead by holding down the **Next** key for a second or so. Press the **Enter** key when you're finished entering your name.

▶ **TIP**

If you have trouble entering your name with SureType, hold down the **Next** key (the key with the asterisk on it) for about a second to switch to multitap input mode. With multitap input mode enabled, press each key multiple times to access the different letters. Hold down the **Next** key again for a second or so to switch back to SureType input mode.

▶ KEY TERM

Multitap—A popular handheld input mode in which keys are pressed multiple times to access the additional letters, numbers, and symbols printed on the face of the key. You switch from SureType mode to multitap mode by holding down the **Next** key for about a second. As an example, to access the letter *r*, hold down the **Next** key for a second to switch to multitap mode, and then tap the **E R** key twice: The first tap displays the letter *e*, and the second tap displays the letter *r*. You may briefly hold down the key to convert the letter to uppercase. To access the number *1*, you must press the **Shift** key before pressing the **E R** key.

5 Enter Your Information

Using the keyboard, enter any additional information you'd like to be visible below your name when your device is locked.

▶ TIP

The **Information** field is a great place to include your home or office phone number, your mailing address, or some other information about how to get in touch with you should someone find your device if it gets lost. If you prefer to be a bit more private with personal information, just list a home or work email address. To learn more about BlackBerry loss prevention, see **94 Register Your Device with StuffBak**.

6 Exit and Save Changes

Press the **Escape** button to exit the **Owner** screen. When prompted to save or discard changes, scroll the trackwheel to **Save** and click to save the changes.

---

5 Lock and Unlock Your Device

✔ BEFORE YOU BEGIN	→ SEE ALSO
1 About the BlackBerry User Interface	**4** Make Yourself the Owner **6** Password-Protect Your Device

---

BlackBerry 7100 series devices don't have protected keyboards that are hidden away when not in use (as is the case with flip phones), so you will likely need to lock your device to prevent accidental key presses when you aren't using the device. You might also opt to password-protect your device; if you then lock your device, you will have to enter the password before you can use the BlackBerry unit. Although entering a password every time you want to use your device can be cumbersome, it's a handy way to kill two birds with one stone (keyboard lock and password protection). See **6 Password-Protect Your Device**.

5 Lock and Unlock Your Device

1 Lock the Device

2 Unlock the Device

5 Lock and Unlock Your Device

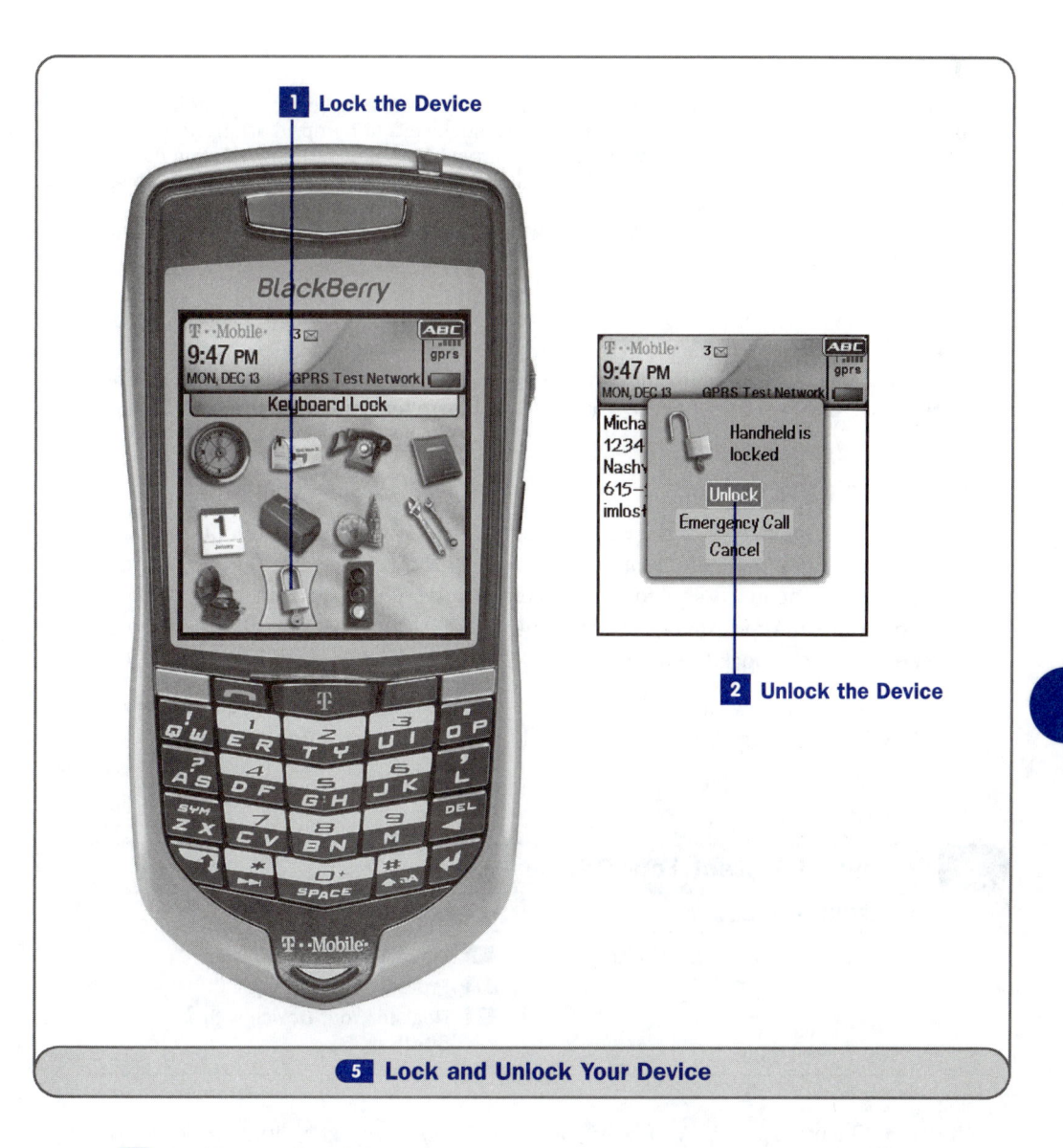

1 Lock the Device

Scroll to the **Keyboard Lock** icon on the **Home** screen and click the trackwheel. Optionally, in many circumstances you can simply hold down the **Next** key (the key with the asterisk on it) to lock the device. The **Owner** screen appears to indicate that the device is locked.

▶ **TIP**

Lock your device whenever you don't plan to use it for a while or before you put it in an outside coat pocket or a purse where it might be subjected to bumps. Locking your BlackBerry unit prevents the keyboard and trackwheel from inadvertently sending commands to the device so that it accidentally dials someone from your address book while you discuss business strategy at lunch. I have a friend who inadvertently overheard harsh criticism of himself from a customer who didn't lock her mobile phone and dialed my friend by accident. Ouch!

▶ **TIP**

You can configure your device so that it automatically locks itself when you place it in its holster. See **6 Password-Protect Your Device** to learn how to enable this option.

2 Unlock the Device

Click the trackwheel and a pop-up menu appears with a default option of **Unlock**. Click the **Unlock** option; because **Unlock** is the default option on the menu, this action is equivalent to double-clicking the trackwheel to unlock your device. Alternatively, you can simply press the **Next** key followed by the **Send** key to unlock the device.

If you have password-protected your device (see **6 Password-Protect Your Device**), you must type your password before you can resume using your device.

---

6 Password-Protect Your Device

✔ BEFORE YOU BEGIN	→ SEE ALSO
5 Lock and Unlock Your Device	**4** Make Yourself the Owner **91** Protect Your Content **94** Register Your Device with StuffBak

---

If you're like most people, you keep your BlackBerry device close to your person at almost all times. Although this goes a long way toward keeping your device secure, there is always the possibility of someone else picking up your device and looking through your data or, in the worst case, of your device getting lost or stolen and falling into unknown hands. For this reason, you might want to consider password-protecting your device, which simply means that a password is required to unlock the device. You still lock your device as normal, but you need to enter a password to unlock it. Although entering a password to unlock your device can be cumbersome, it can offset the inherent risks associated with an unsecured device.

6 Password-Protect Your Device

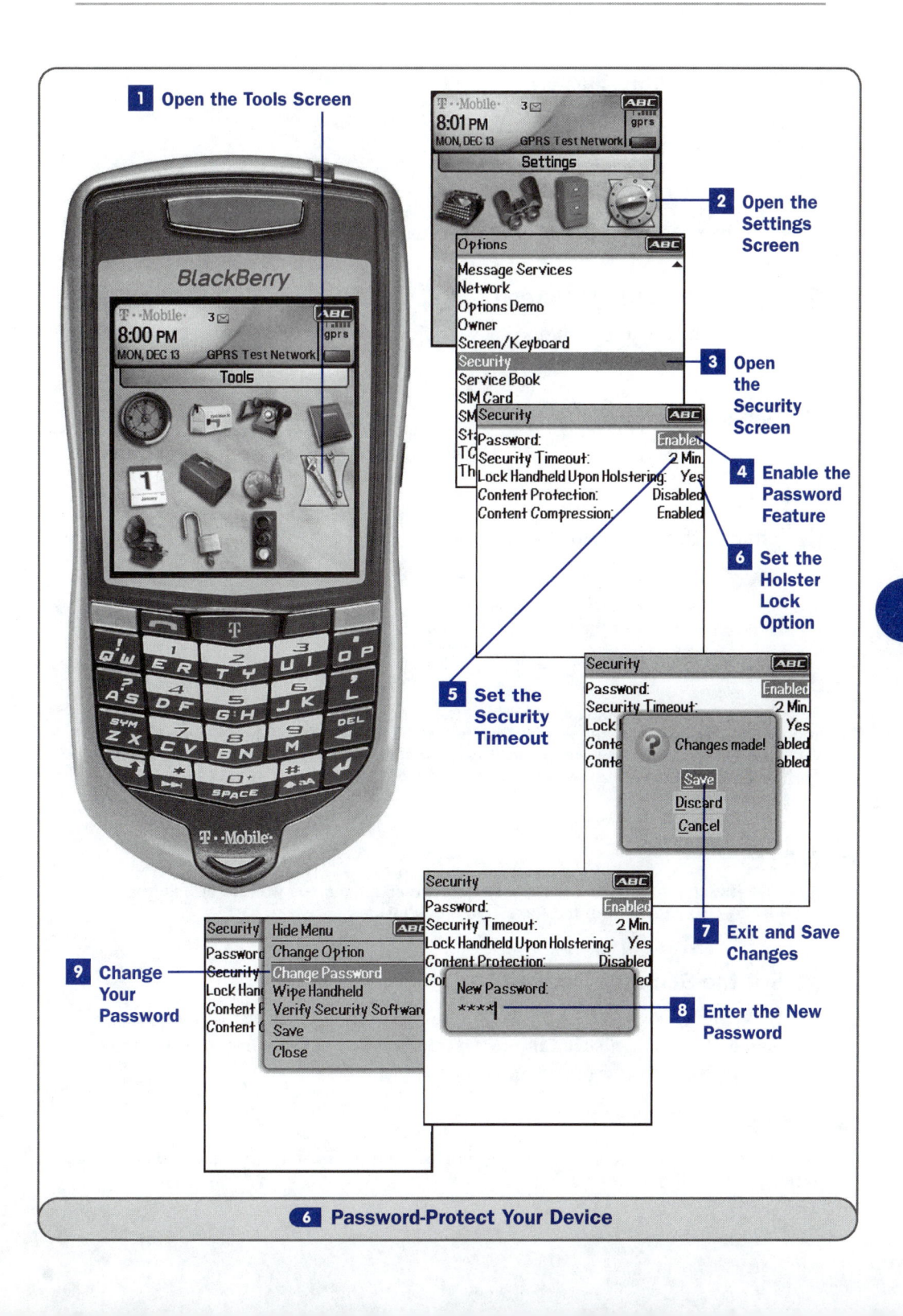

1 Open the Tools Screen

2 Open the Settings Screen

3 Open the Security Screen

4 Enable the Password Feature

6 Set the Holster Lock Option

5 Set the Security Timeout

7 Exit and Save Changes

8 Enter the New Password

9 Change Your Password

6 Password-Protect Your Device

CHAPTER 2: Hit the Ground Running with Your BlackBerry

1. Open the Tools Screen

Scroll to the **Tools** icon on the **Home** screen and click the trackwheel. The **Tools** screen opens.

▶ **TIP**

To immediately jump to the **Home** screen from any other screen, press the **End** key.

2. Open the Settings Screen

Scroll to the **Settings** icon and click the trackwheel. A list of options for which you can change the settings appears.

3. Open the Security Screen

Scroll to the **Security** option in the list and click the trackwheel. The **Security** screen opens.

4. Enable the Password Feature

Click the trackwheel on the text at the right end of the **Password** field (either the word **Enabled** or **Disabled**) and then click **Change Option**. In the menu that appears, scroll the trackwheel to select **Enabled** and click to accept it.

▶ **TIP**

To quickly change an option without having to go through the two trackwheel clicks required to open a menu and select **Change Option**, press the **Alt** key to view a list of options. Then scroll to the desired choice and click the trackwheel to select it. An even faster shortcut involves cycling to the next available choice by pressing the **Space** key.

▶ **NOTE**

If your BlackBerry device is currently password-protected and you want to disable the feature, select **Disabled** from the **Password** menu instead.

5. Set the Security Timeout

Scroll the trackwheel to the value at the right end of the **Security Timeout** field and click; then click **Change Option**. Scroll the trackwheel to select the security timeout in minutes, and click to accept it.

▶ **NOTE**

The security timeout specifies how long your device must sit idle before automatically locking itself.

6 Password-Protect Your Device   35

6 Set the Holster Lock Option

Scroll the trackwheel to the **Yes** or **No** at the right end of the **Lock Handheld Upon Holstering** field and click; then click **Change Option**. From the menu that appears, scroll to select **Yes** or **No** and click to accept this setting.

▶ **NOTE**

When enabled, the **Lock Handheld Upon Holstering** option causes your device to be automatically locked anytime it is placed in the holster. This is a handy setting if you are the kind of person who constantly locks and unlocks your device to prevent accidental key presses.

▶ **TIP**

You can use the **Lock Handheld Upon Holstering** option even if you choose not to password-protect your device.

▶ **NOTE**

If you're curious about how your BlackBerry device knows when it is placed in its holster, I'll let you in on a secret: A small round magnet inside the front of the holster is sensed by your device when it is seated in the holster. You can verify this by holding your device against the outside front of the holster—it will lock itself as if you had slid it in the holster…magic!

7 Exit and Save Changes

Press the **Escape** button to exit the **Security** screen. When prompted to save or discard your changes, scroll the trackwheel to **Save** and click to save the changes.

8 Enter the New Password

A dialog box appears prompting you for the new password. Using the keyboard, enter the password, making sure that it is at least four characters long. When you enter a password, each character is shown briefly as you type it before it is turned into an asterisk. This is helpful because your password will likely require different keystrokes depending on whether you use alphabetic or numeric input mode. Password entry is always carried out in multitap mode, but you can switch between alphabetic and numeric characters by briefly holding down the **Next** key (asterisk). Alphabetic multitap mode is always selected by default when you enter a password, so I recommend sticking with an alphabetic password as opposed to a numeric one. In numeric mode, the familiar **ABC** icon in the upper-right corner of the screen changes to **123**.

▶ **TIP**

Keep in mind that you will be entering the password every time you unlock your device, which will likely be frequently, especially if you have the security timeout set to a low value or you're using the **Lock Handheld Upon Holstering** option. For this reason, you should specify a password you can enter quickly. I prefer thinking of it as more of a PIN code, which means sticking with the minimum of four characters.

▶ **TIP**

Alphabetic multitap mode is the default mode for entering passwords, which means you'll have to constantly switch to numeric mode to enter a numeric password or press the **Shift** key for each number. So, I recommend using an alphabetic PIN code instead of a numeric one so you don't have to change to numeric mode every time you enter the password.

Press the **Enter** key when you're finished entering the password. Another screen appears, prompting you to verify the new password. Enter it again and press the **Enter** key.

Your BlackBerry unit is now password-protected. This password protection goes into effect whenever the timeout value expires, you place the device in its holster with the **Lock Handheld Upon Holstering** option set, or you manually lock it. You will now have to enter your password to unlock your device so you can use it again.

▶ **TIP**

Even with a device locked, you are able to make emergency calls. Just use the trackwheel to select and click **Emergency Call** on the **Unlock** screen that appears when you attempt to unlock the device.

You might have noticed additional options on the **Security** screen for **Content Protection** and **Content Compression**. The **Content Protection** option allows you to take your BlackBerry security to another level by protecting the content on your device. To learn how, **see 91 Protect Your Content**. The **Content Compression** option, which is enabled by default, compresses all the content on your device to conserve space. Because there is no noticeable performance loss when using content compression, you should leave it on.

9 Change Your Password

At some point, you might need to change your password. In fact, some experts recommend changing your password regularly for an added level of security. You change the password from the **Security** screen by clicking **Enabled** on the **Password** field with the trackwheel and then clicking **Change Password** from the menu that appears. Enter the old password, click the trackwheel, and then enter the new password.

7 Choose a Theme 37

▶ **TIP**

If your device is locked, you don't have to press a key or click the trackwheel to view the password entry screen and enter your password. Just start typing your password on the locked device—even if the device's screen is off—and the password entry screen automatically appears. This saves you an extra key press.

7 Choose a Theme

→ **SEE ALSO**

21 Change the Wallpaper
22 Install a New Theme

1 Open the Tools Screen
2 Open the Settings Screen
3 Open the Theme Screen
4 Select and Activate a Theme
5 View the New Theme

7 Choose a Theme

You might be familiar with *themes* from your desktop computer, where they impact the background wallpaper, icons, font family, font size, and color scheme of your daily work. Themes play a similar role on the BlackBerry 7100 series devices. In fact, in some ways, themes are even more important on BlackBerry devices than on desktop computers because the user interface is compacted into such a small space. For example, icons largely define the **Home** screen, which means a theme change dramatically affects the appearance of all the major services. Although the default theme on your device will certainly suffice, it's worth experimenting with a few themes to find one you really like. Everyone has his own tastes, and there's a good chance you'll find a theme that suits your style better than the default.

▶ **KEY TERM**

Theme—A set of images, icons, fonts, and colors that determines the visual look and feel of the BlackBerry user interface. A BlackBerry theme is similar to a theme on a desktop computer.

▶ **NOTE**

For consistency, this book uses the standard **T-Mobile** theme throughout, which features a retro look for icons. Other wireless carriers typically provide their own themes, which can vary considerably from the **T-Mobile** theme.

1 Open the Tools Screen

Scroll to the **Tools** icon on the **Home** screen and click the trackwheel. The **Tools** screen opens.

2 Open the Options Screen

Scroll to the **Options** icon and click the trackwheel. A list of options for which you can change the settings appears.

▶ **NOTE**

Depending on your specific 7100 device, the **Options** screen might be named **Settings** instead.

3 Open the Theme Screen

Scroll to the **Theme** option in the list and click the trackwheel. The **Theme** screen opens.

4 Select and Activate a Theme

Scroll the trackwheel to select a theme and then click. From the menu that appears, click **Activate** to activate the selected theme.

5 View the New Theme

The theme is now activated and visible, but to really see its true effect, you must press the **End** key to return to the **Home** screen.

▶ **NOTE**

There is no guarantee that your device comes configured with more than one theme. However, you can download and install additional themes. See **22 Install a New Theme**.

In the example shown here, you can see the difference a theme change makes to the appearance of the **Home** screen. Step 1 shows the **T-Mobile** theme that is initially set on devices offered by T-Mobile, while this step shows the **Home** screen again but this time with the **Default** theme that is also available on most devices.

3

Managing Your BlackBerry from a Desktop PC

IN THIS CHAPTER:

- **8** Install the BlackBerry Desktop Software
- **9** Connect Your Device to Your PC
- **10** Synchronize PIM Data with Your PC
- **11** Install a New Application to Your Device
- **12** Remove an Application from Your Device
- **13** Back Up Your Device
- **14** Restore Your Device
- **15** Clear Personal Data from Your Device

CHAPTER 3: Managing Your BlackBerry from a Desktop PC

Your BlackBerry 7100 series device is by many accounts a powerful computer that can be used entirely on its own to carry out a lot of interesting and useful tasks. However, to truly get the most out of your device you must occasionally connect the device to your desktop PC. This is important because your desktop PC is probably already your center for storing and retrieving contacts and email messages and carrying out other personal information management. Not only that, your desktop PC is your device's window into a much larger world of BlackBerry applications. In other words, you can use your desktop PC to install new applications to your device. Your desktop PC can also serve as an excellent backup system for your BlackBerry device. Speaking of desktop PCs, the standard BlackBerry desktop software supports only Windows computers, but third-party applications are available that allow you to interface with your BlackBerry device using a Macintosh computer.

Your BlackBerry shipped with a CD-ROM containing the BlackBerry Desktop Software, which includes the BlackBerry Desktop Manager. This application runs on your desktop PC and provides several features for communicating between your device and your PC. Through this software you can synchronize PIM data, install and remove applications, and back up and restore device data.

8 Install the BlackBerry Desktop Software

→ **SEE ALSO**

- **9** Connect Your Device to Your PC
- **10** Synchronize PIM Data with Your PC

The BlackBerry Desktop Software is included on the CD-ROM that shipped with your BlackBerry device and is also available online directly from Research In Motion (RIM) on the Web at https://www.blackberry.com/Downloads/—be sure you enter the URL exactly as shown with the *s* in https. You can either install the software straight from the CD-ROM or check for a newer version online. Either way, the purpose of installing the software is to gain access to the BlackBerry Desktop Manager, which is the PC application that allows you to communicate with your device. After the BlackBerry Desktop Manager is installed, you can begin interacting with your device from your desktop PC, including synchronizing PIM data, installing new applications, and performing backups.

1 Insert the BlackBerry Desktop Software CD-ROM

Insert the **BlackBerry Desktop Software** CD-ROM into your desktop PC. The first step of the installation wizard appears, which prompts you to click **Next** with the mouse to continue with the installation. After you click **Next** to get started with the installation, the **Country or Region Selection** window appears.

8 Install the BlackBerry Desktop Software

1 Insert the BlackBerry Desktop Software CD-ROM

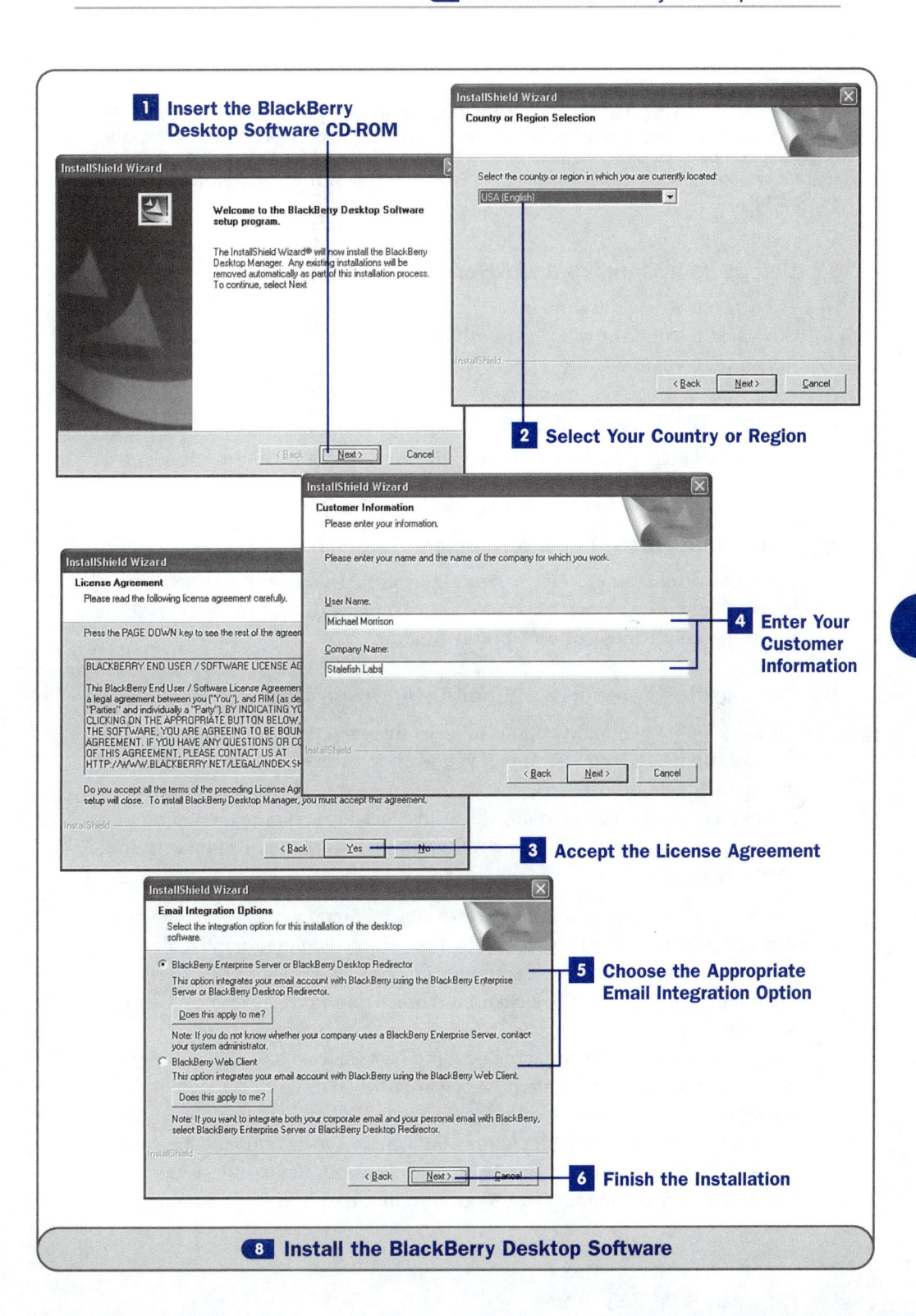

2 Select Your Country or Region

3 Accept the License Agreement

4 Enter Your Customer Information

5 Choose the Appropriate Email Integration Option

6 Finish the Installation

8 Install the BlackBerry Desktop Software

▶ NOTE

The BlackBerry Desktop Manager is currently supported only on Windows-based PCs. To synchronize your device with an Apple Macintosh computer, you should consider a third-party application such as PocketMac by Information Appliance Associates. You can learn more about PocketMac by visiting the PocketMac website at http://www.pocketmac.net/.

2. Select Your Country or Region

Click the drop-down list and select your country or region by clicking it. Then click **Next** to continue with the installation, which shows the **License Agreement** window.

3. Accept the License Agreement

Click **Yes** to accept the license agreement. The **Customer Information** window appears.

4. Enter Your Customer Information

Enter your **User Name**, which is typically your first and last name, followed by your **Company Name**. Click **Next** to continue with the installation, which shows the **Email Integration Options** window.

5. Choose the Appropriate Email Integration Option

Click one of the two radio buttons to select the email integration option for the BlackBerry Desktop Software. If you want to access a corporate email account with your BlackBerry, choose the first option. If you only want to access a personal email account with your BlackBerry, choose the second option. If you plan on accessing both corporate and personal email accounts, choose the first option.

The remainder of the installation varies depending on which email integration option you select. If you select the first option, you're prompted to select the email system used in your corporate environment, such as **Microsoft Exchange** (Microsoft Outlook client) or **Lotus Domino** (Lotus Notes client). Select the email system and click **Next**. You're then prompted to select whether you'd like your corporate email to be redirected to your BlackBerry device via the BlackBerry Enterprise Server or the BlackBerry Desktop Redirector. If your company uses the BlackBerry Enterprise Server, select the **Redirect email using the BlackBerry Enterprise Server** option. Otherwise, select **Redirect email using the BlackBerry Desktop Redirector** as the **Email Redirection** option. Click **Next** to continue with the installation.

9 Connect Your Device to Your PC 45

▶ **NOTE**
If you don't know whether your company uses the BlackBerry Enterprise Server, you might want to ask a network administrator. If available, the BlackBerry Enterprise Server is the preferable approach for redirecting email to your device. However, the BlackBerry Desktop Redirector is sufficient if your company doesn't use the BlackBerry Enterprise Server.

6 Finish the Installation

The remainder of the installation for the BlackBerry Desktop Software follows the familiar flow of installing any Windows application. Just continue to click **Next** to accept the default installation settings, and the software will be successfully installed. To begin using the software with your BlackBerry device, see **9** Connect Your Device to Your PC and **10** Synchronize PIM Data with Your PC.

9 Connect Your Device to Your PC

✔ **BEFORE YOU BEGIN**
8 Install the BlackBerry Desktop Software

→ **SEE ALSO**
10 Synchronize PIM Data with Your PC

Connecting your device to your PC probably doesn't seem like it should require a task all its own, but the first time you do it there are a few hoops you must jump through. The main issue is detecting the proper type of connection and then generating a unique encryption key. These are one-time issues that you won't have to worry about again after you've successfully connected your device the first time. After the initial setup, connecting your device to your desktop PC involves nothing more than plugging the device in to the computer, usually via a USB cable.

1 Run the BlackBerry Desktop Manager on Your Desktop PC

From your desktop PC, click the **Start** button on the Windows taskbar to open the main Windows system menu. Then select **All Programs**, **BlackBerry**, **Desktop Manager**. The Desktop Manager application appears. If the Desktop Manager application prompts you for a user ID, domain, and password for a Microsoft Exchange account, enter them and click **OK**. Depending on your settings, it might also prompt you to select an Outlook user profile; select the user profile you normally use with Outlook and click **OK**.

CHAPTER 3: Managing Your BlackBerry from a Desktop PC

1 Run the BlackBerry Desktop Manager on Your Desktop PC

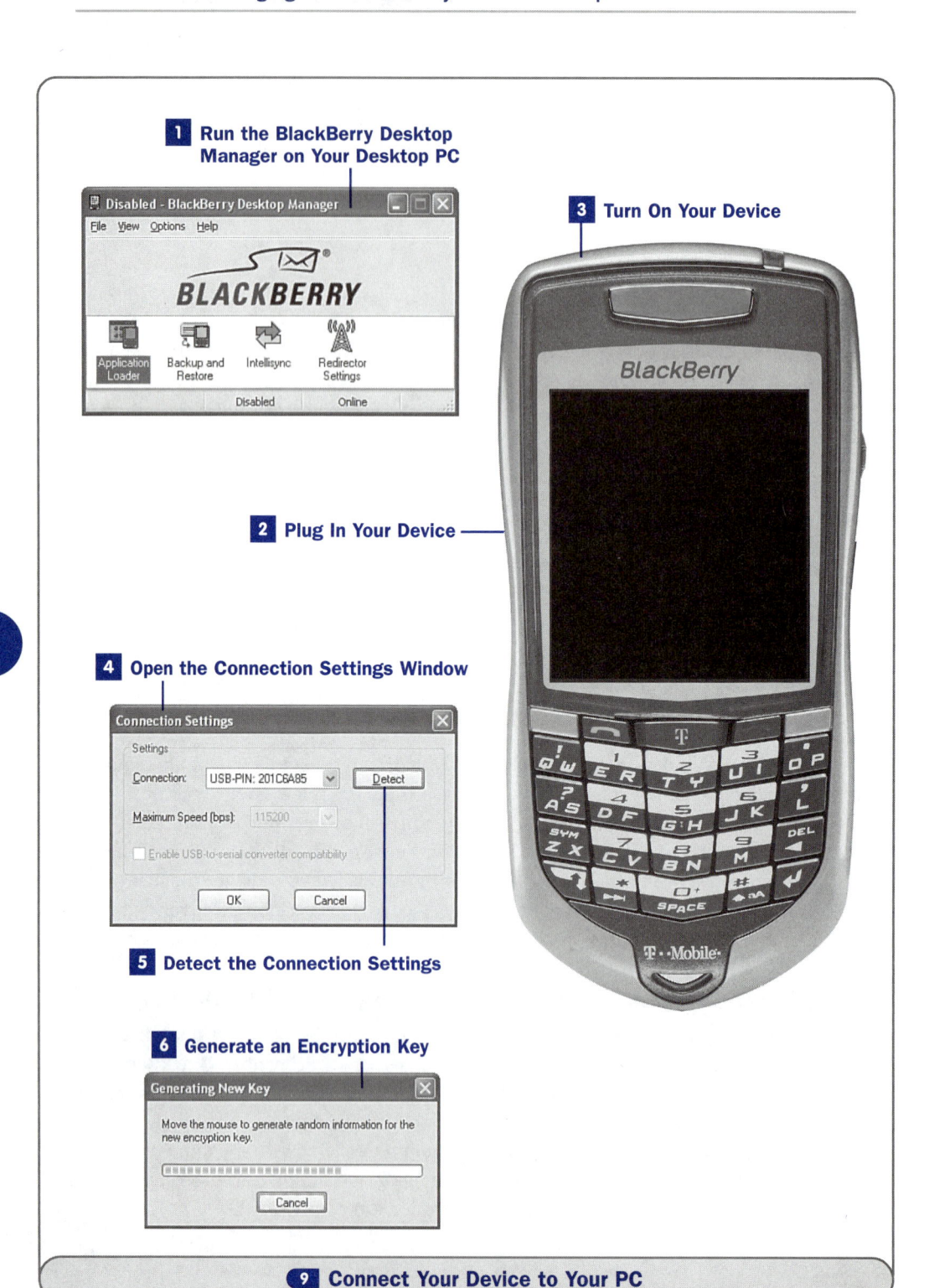

3 Turn On Your Device

2 Plug In Your Device

4 Open the Connection Settings Window

5 Detect the Connection Settings

6 Generate an Encryption Key

9 Connect Your Device to Your PC

▶ **NOTE**

Some Windows systems might be configured differently, in which case their menus might not appear exactly as I've described them here. For example, some Windows configurations have the **All Programs** menu named **Programs** instead. You should still be able to follow along, even if your Windows configuration is a little different from what I describe.

2 **Plug In Your Device**

Connect your device to the PC using the USB cable that came with the device; some devices ship with multiple cables, in which case you can use either one. The smaller end of the cable plugs in to a port on the device, while the larger end can plug in to any available USB port on your desktop PC.

▶ **NOTE**

BlackBerry 7100 series devices use the USB connection to a desktop computer as a means of charging the device battery. As long as you have the BlackBerry Desktop Manager installed, your device will automatically begin charging when you plug it in to your desktop PC as long as your computer is on. You can tell it is charging by looking for a small lightning bolt icon near or on top of the battery level indicator on the **Home** screen.

3 **Turn On Your Device**

Press the **Power** button to turn on your device. The **Add/Remove Hardware** window might pop up on your desktop PC, but you can ignore it.

4 **Open the Connection Settings Window**

For the BlackBerry Desktop Manager to connect to your device for the first time, you must allow it to detect the connection settings. On the **BlackBerry Desktop Manager** menu, click **Options**, followed by **Connection Settings**. The **Connection Settings** window appears.

5 **Detect the Connection Settings**

Click the **Detect** button on the **Connection Settings** window. The **Connection Settings** window should report that a USB device has been found, along with a *PIN* for the device. Click **OK** to accept the connection settings.

▶ **NOTE**

If you have password protection turned on for your device, you're prompted to enter the password on your desktop PC when you first turn on your device after connecting it to your PC. This is important because your device shouldn't be open to desktop synchronization without providing the password. If you haven't already secured your device with a password, **see** **6** **Password-Protect Your Device**.

CHAPTER 3: Managing Your BlackBerry from a Desktop PC

▶ **KEY TERM**

PIN—Stands for personal identification number, which is a "number" up to eight alphanumeric characters long that uniquely identifies your BlackBerry device. Not only is your device's PIN used for configuration purposes, but it can also be used as a means of communication; you can send text messages directly to another BlackBerry device if you know its PIN. See **36** **Send a PIN Message**.

You are next prompted to assist in generating a new encryption key for the device. After clicking **OK**, the **Generating New Key** window appears.

6 Generate an Encryption Key

All you have to do to generate an encryption key is wiggle the mouse around for a few seconds—the fuel gauge in the **Generating New Key** window will increase as you continue to move the mouse. This random mouse motion is used as the basis for generating a unique encryption key. When the encryption key is finished generating, your device is successfully connected to your desktop PC.

10 Synchronize PIM Data with Your PC

✔ **BEFORE YOU BEGIN**

8 Install the BlackBerry Desktop Software
9 Connect Your Device to Your PC

→ **SEE ALSO**

68 Create and Manage Contacts
75 Create and Manage Appointments
77 Create and Manage Tasks
81 Make Notes with the MemoPad

One of the most important reasons to connect your BlackBerry device to your desktop PC is to synchronize PIM data such as contacts, calendar events, tasks, and notes. You synchronize PIM data with your PC by enabling each type of data that you'd like to synchronize and then specifying a translator application for each. For example, in the case of Microsoft Outlook, it serves as the translator application for all PIM data types because it has support for the various data types (contacts, events, tasks, and notes).

For the purposes of synchronization, email is handled differently from the other PIM data types. Your ability to synchronize, or reconcile, email depends largely on what type of email account you have and whether your company uses the BlackBerry Enterprise Server. If you don't have access to the BlackBerry Enterprise Server, you'll probably want to use the BlackBerry Web Client. See **23** **About Email and the BlackBerry Web Client** to get started.

10 Synchronize PIM Data with Your PC

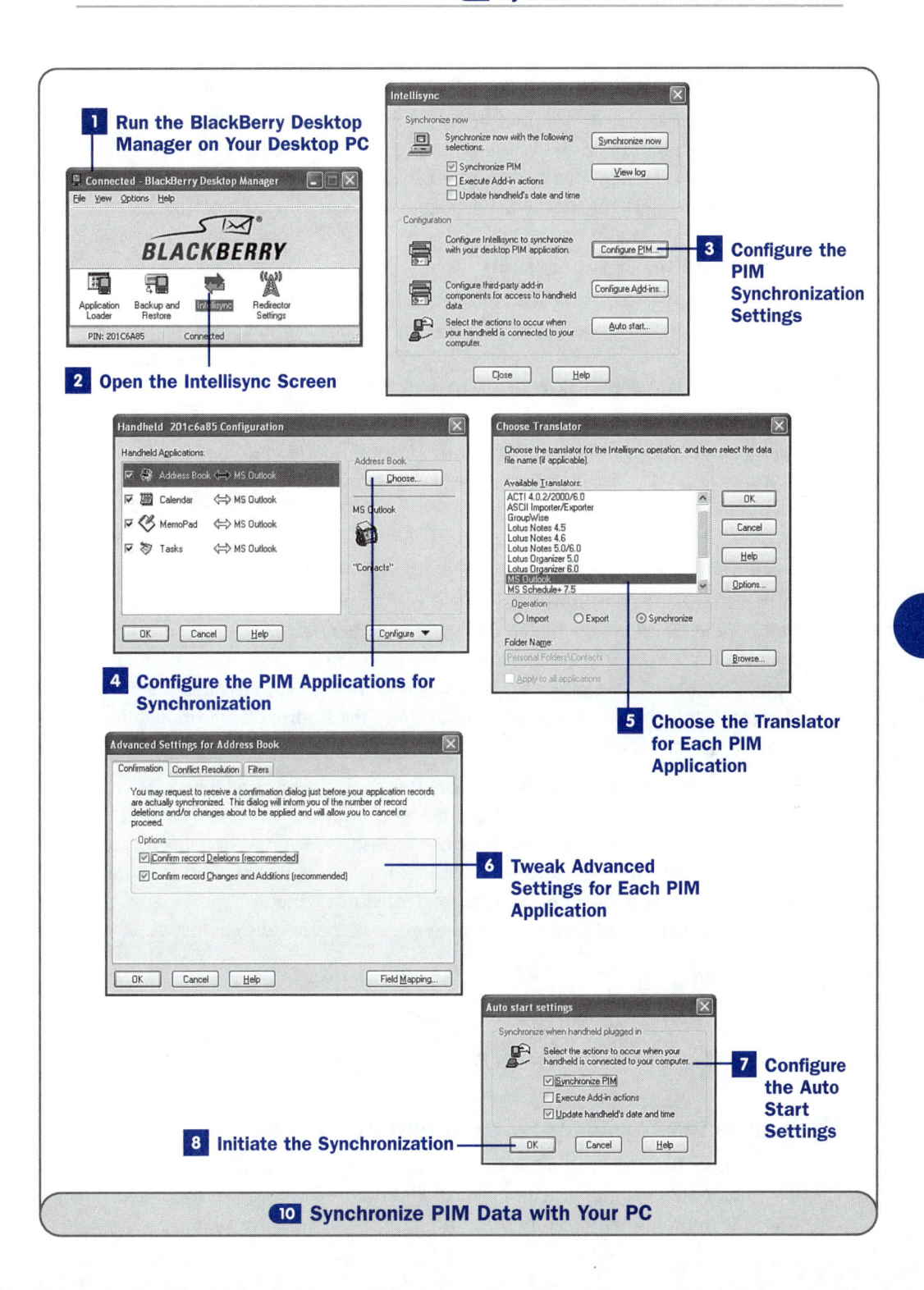

1 Run the BlackBerry Desktop Manager on Your Desktop PC

2 Open the Intellisync Screen

3 Configure the PIM Synchronization Settings

4 Configure the PIM Applications for Synchronization

5 Choose the Translator for Each PIM Application

6 Tweak Advanced Settings for Each PIM Application

7 Configure the Auto Start Settings

8 Initiate the Synchronization

10 Synchronize PIM Data with Your PC

1 **Run the BlackBerry Desktop Manager on Your Desktop PC**

With your BlackBerry device plugged in to your desktop PC and turned on, click the **Start** button on the Windows taskbar of your desktop PC to open the main Windows system menu. Then select **All Programs**, **BlackBerry**, **Desktop Manager**. The BlackBerry Desktop Manager application appears.

2 **Open the Intellisync Screen**

Double-click the **Intellisync** icon in the BlackBerry Desktop Manager. The **Intellisync** window appears, offering several synchronization options.

3 **Configure the PIM Synchronization Settings**

Before you synchronize for the first time, you should configure the PIM synchronization settings. Click the **Configure PIM** button to view the **Handheld Configuration** window, where you tweak PIM synchronization settings for each PIM application.

4 **Configure the PIM Applications for Synchronization**

In the **Handheld Configuration** window is a list of handheld applications that handle PIM data. To the left of each application is a check box you can click to turn synchronization on and off for that particular application/data type. For example, you might want to synchronize only contacts and no other PIM data, in which case you would check the **Address Book** application and uncheck the others.

To change the desktop *translator application* that synchronizes with a particular handheld application, click the handheld application in the list and then click the **Choose** button. The **Choose Translator** window appears for the handheld application you selected. As an example, if you click **Address Book** as the handheld application, the **Choose Translator** window appears with the available desktop translator applications that can handle contact data.

▶ **KEY TERM**

Translator application—An application that handles the translation of PIM data between your device and your desktop PC. This application is typically just the client application that you already use to view and manage PIM data on your desktop PC.

5 **Choose the Translator for Each PIM Application**

The **Choose Translator** window displays a list of desktop translator applications associated with a particular type of PIM data, such as contacts or tasks. Click the appropriate translator application in the list. The translator application you choose will likely be the same application you already use on your desktop PC to manage PIM data. For example, I use Microsoft Outlook for my contacts, calendar, memo notes, and tasks, not to mention email.

If you want to carry out a one-way exchange of PIM information, select **Import** or **Export** as the **Operation** instead of **Synchronize** just below the list of translator applications. The **Import** operation imports PIM data from your desktop PC to your BlackBerry with no information exchange in the other direction. Conversely, the **Export** operation exports data from your device to your PC only.

To exert maximum control over the synchronization of PIM data, you must dig deeper into the advanced settings for each type of data. Click **OK** to return to the **Handheld Configuration** window; then click the **Configure** button. Click **Advanced Settings** in the menu that appears, and the **Advanced Settings for Address Book** window appears.

6 Tweak Advanced Settings for Each PIM Application

The **Advanced Settings for Address Book** window displays a series of tabbed panes with advanced options associated with address book (contacts) data. The **Confirmation** tab allows you to specify whether contact record changes, additions, and deletions must be confirmed during synchronization. I'd recommend leaving the default setting for both of these options, which is to leave them both turned on.

Other tabbed panes allow you to specify **Conflict Resolution** options and **Filter** options for contact data. Other PIM data types can also include additional panes that provide options specific to that type of data. For example, the **Advanced Settings for Calendar** window includes a **Date Range** tab that allows you to get very specific about which appointments and events are synchronized. You can limit the synchronization to appointments and events that take place only within a certain date range.

▶ **TIP**

Unless you have some specific synchronization needs in mind, I suggest you start with the default settings for all the advanced PIM synchronization options.

Click **OK** to accept your changes and close the **Advanced Settings for Address Book** window, or click **Cancel** to exit the window without making any changes. Then click **OK** in the **Handheld Configuration** window to return to the main **Intellisync** window. Here you can set the BlackBerry

Desktop Manager so that it automatically synchronizes PIM data when you connect your device to your desktop PC. Click the **Auto start** button to open the **Auto start settings** window.

7 Configure the Auto Start Settings

The auto start settings consist of three options that allow you to automatically synchronize PIM data, execute *add-in* actions, and update the device's date and time from your desktop PC. The first option, **Synchronize PIM**, is the only option that directly relates to synchronization, although you might want to enable the last option—**Update handheld's date and time**—if you want to ensure that your desktop and device time are always in sync. Click **OK** to accept the auto start settings and return to the **Intellisync** window.

▶ **KEY TERM**

Add-in—A special helper application that is installed on your device to carry out a specific task, such as allowing you to view a file of an unsupported type. As an example, you might install an add-in that enables you to view Microsoft Excel spreadsheets on your device.

8 Initiate the Synchronization

Click the **Synchronize now** button to initiate the synchronization of your BlackBerry with your PC. A window appears that provides you with a status report on the synchronization process. You might be required to okay changes to information based on the advanced **Confirmation** settings you saw in step 6. When your device finishes synchronizing, click the **Close** button in the **Intellisync** window to return to the main BlackBerry Desktop Manager window.

You can either leave your device connected to your PC to charge the battery or disconnect it. You'll probably want to minimize the BlackBerry Desktop Manager application instead of closing it so it remains available for synchronization later; otherwise, you'll need to launch it again the next time you need to synchronize. BlackBerry Desktop Manager is a reasonably lean application, so it shouldn't tax your system too much to leave it running.

▶ **TIP**

An option in the BlackBerry Desktop Manager application hides the application from the Windows taskbar when the application is minimized. This provides the visual effect of the application being closed, although it is still ready and available for synchronizing the next time you connect your device. To enable this option, click **Options** on the main BlackBerry Desktop Manager menu, and then click **Hide When Minimized**.

11 Install a New Application to Your Device

✔ BEFORE YOU BEGIN
- 8 Install the BlackBerry Desktop Software
- 9 Connect Your Device to Your PC

→ SEE ALSO
- 12 Remove an Application from Your Device
- 50 Install a New Application Over-the-Air

If you simply plugged in your desktop PC the day you got it and have since been happily using it without ever installing any additional applications, you might not see the significance of this task. More realistically, you've probably installed numerous applications on your desktop PC ranging from productivity applications to games. Your BlackBerry device is no different from your desktop PC in regard to expanding its software capabilities through third-party applications. There is a surprisingly wide range of available applications, most of them priced reasonably—and some are even available for free download.

It's worth noting that BlackBerry devices have been around for several years, and not all of them are as full-featured as the 7100 series. For this reason, you should pay close attention to any applications you consider installing to ensure that they specifically take advantage of the newer features in the 7100. Otherwise, you might end up with an application that is designed to run on a much smaller black-and-white screen. An application designed specifically for the 7100 will take advantage of the larger color screen and phone features that are built in to the device.

▶ TIP
Speaking of installing applications, the following are a few websites you might want to visit to find useful BlackBerry applications: http://www.handango.com/, http://www.rimroad.com/software.html, and http://www.magmic.com/.

▶ NOTE
You can download and install an application directly to your BlackBerry device from the Web. See 50 **Install a New Application Over-the-Air** to find out how.

1 Download the Application to Your Desktop PC

Whether you have purchased a commercial application or found an application that is freely available for download, you must first download the application to your desktop PC before you can install it to your BlackBerry device. The website from which you are obtaining the application should provide a link for downloading the application. When prompted to open or save the downloaded application file, click **Save** to save the file; you will then get an opportunity to open the file and execute it on your desktop PC after it finishes downloading.

CHAPTER 3: Managing Your BlackBerry from a Desktop PC

1 Download the Application to Your Desktop PC

2 Install the Application Files to Your Desktop PC

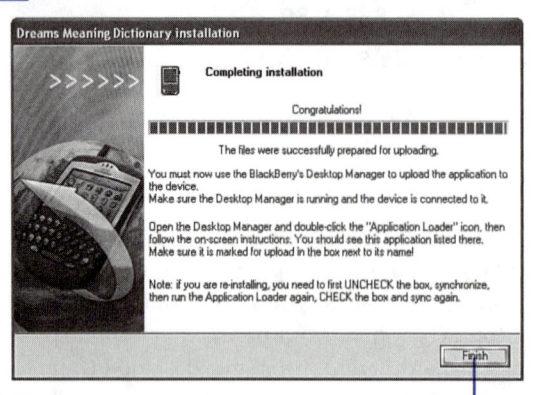

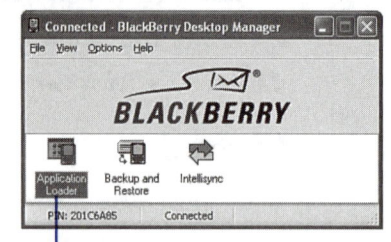

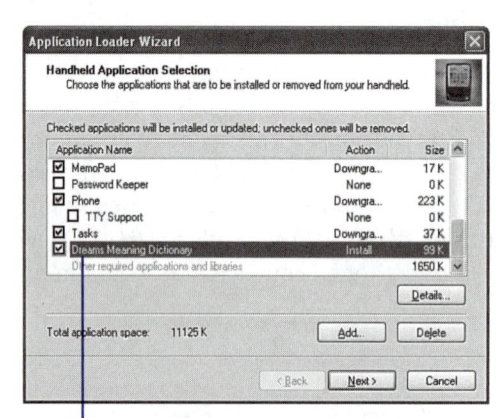

3 Launch the Application Loader Wizard

4 Select the New Application for Installation

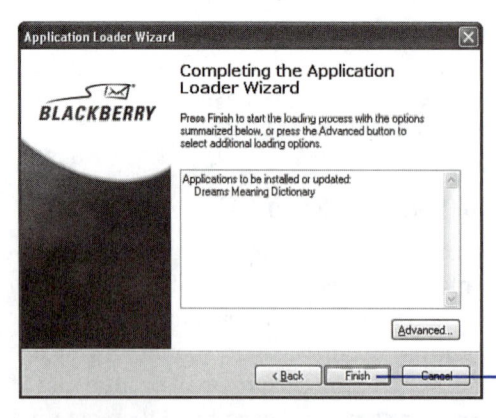

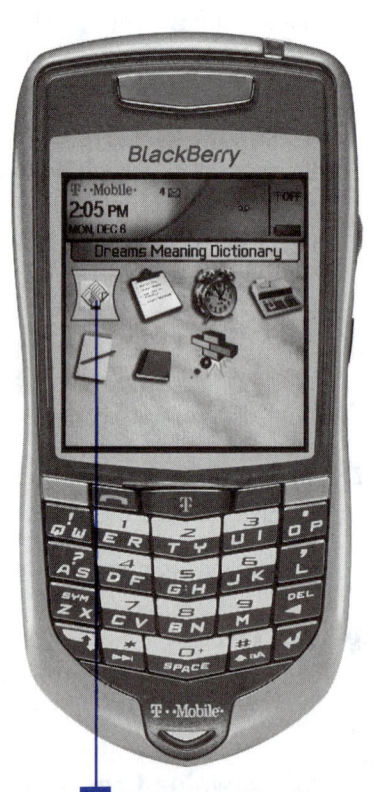

5 Install the Application to Your Device

6 Run the Application on Your Device

11 Install a New Application to Your Device

2 Install the Application Files to Your Desktop PC

Most BlackBerry applications include an installation program that simply places a special file on your desktop PC that is used by the BlackBerry Desktop Manager to install the application on your device. Follow the instructions for the specific application to install this file on your desktop PC, being sure to remember the location on your desktop hard drive.

▶ **TIP**

If you download a BlackBerry application that is stored in a Zip file instead of an executable installation program (EXE), you'll need to unzip the application yourself. Just use Windows Explorer to extract the application files from the Zip file to a new folder. The primary file you're looking for is a file with an extension of **.alx**, which is the file used by the BlackBerry Desktop Manager to install the application.

3 Launch the Application Loader Wizard

With your BlackBerry device plugged in to your desktop PC and turned on, click the **Start** button on the Windows taskbar of your desktop PC to open the Windows **Start** menu. Then select **All Programs**, **BlackBerry**, **Desktop Manager**. The BlackBerry Desktop Manager application appears.

Double-click the **Application Loader** icon in the BlackBerry Desktop Manager. The **Application Loader Wizard** window appears.

4 Select the New Application for Installation

Click the **Next** button to get started with the Application Loader Wizard. The wizard will take a few moments to analyze your device and then display the **Handheld Application Selection** window. This window includes all the applications installed on your device, including core operating system components. The new application you are installing is not listed yet because you haven't added it to the list.

▶ **TIP**

You must be careful when using the Application Loader Wizard because it allows you to make sweeping changes to the applications installed on your device, including critical core applications such as the phone and security features. Unless you really want to remove an application from your device, you should never uncheck an application in the **Application Loader Wizard** because it will be uninstalled. Generally speaking, it's not a good idea to uncheck standard applications unless you fully understand the implications.

Click the **Add** button to add the new application to the list of available applications. Navigate to the folder on your desktop PC where you installed the application files. Click the file with the **.alx** extension, and then click the **Open** button. After returning to the **Handheld Application Selection** window, you now see the new application at the bottom of the application list.

If it isn't already checked, click the check box next to the application name to select it for installation to your device. Click the **Next** button to continue in the wizard. The completion window of the Application Loader Wizard appears.

5 Install the Application to Your Device

The **Advanced** button enables you to tweak the installation settings associated with application data and currently installed applications. More specifically, you can specify that all application data be erased from your device prior to installation. You can also specify that all applications be erased from your device before installation. These are both fairly aggressive measures intended to serve as somewhat of a cleanup of your device's state. They are recommended only if you are having problems, and even then you should perform a backup of your device prior to proceeding with any erasure.

▶ **TIP**

If you click the **Advanced** button to tweak advanced installation settings, you might have to progress through several screens to return to the familiar **Finish** button that allows you to finish the installation process. Just accept the default settings along the way if you aren't sure how to answer.

Click the **Finish** button to install the application to your device. After installing the application to your device, the BlackBerry Desktop Manager automatically synchronizes the device with your desktop PC. The new application is now ready to run on your device.

6 Run the Application on Your Device

On the **Home** screen of your device, scroll to the **Applications** icon and click the trackwheel. The **Applications** screen appears, offering a sequence of applications, including the new application you installed. In this example, I installed the Dreams Meaning Dictionary by Beiks LLC, which enables me to type a word and find out what it means if I dream about it. Scroll to the application icon with the trackwheel and click to launch the application.

12 Remove an Application from Your Device

✔ BEFORE YOU BEGIN	→ SEE ALSO
11 Install a New Application to Your Device	50 Install a New Application Over-the-Air

12 Remove an Application from Your Device

1 Launch the Application Loader Wizard

2 Select the Application for Removal

3 Remove the Application from Your Device

12 Remove an Application from Your Device

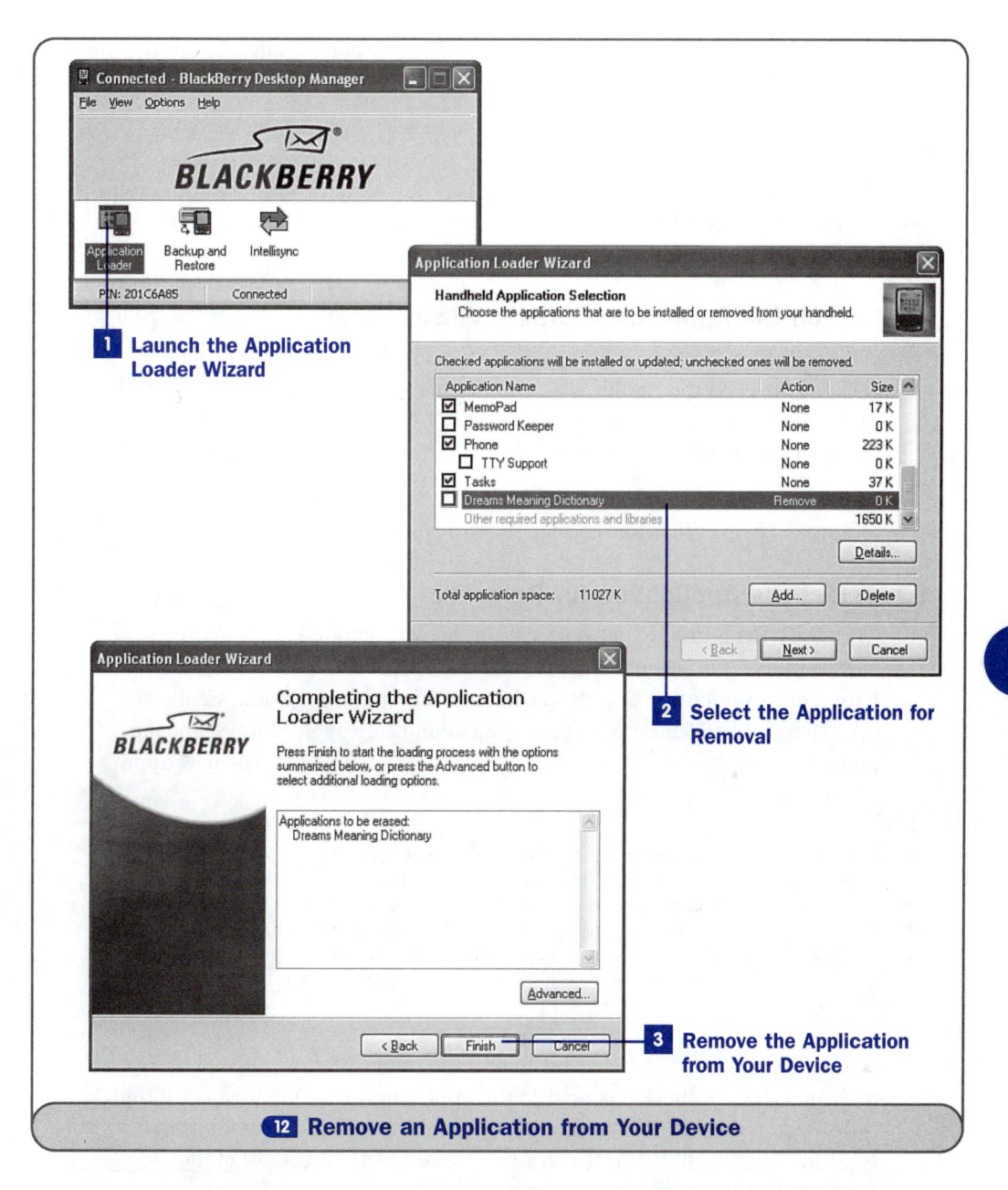

Once you realize how easy it is to expand your BlackBerry device by installing new applications, it's easy to get carried away and install everything you run across. There is a downside to this strategy, however, in that your device has a limited amount of memory that can get eaten up if you go wild installing unnecessary applications. The general rule of thumb is to keep only applications you use on a regular basis, which to me means weekly. Anything less than that, and

I'd recommend removing the application and only installing it later on an as-needed basis.

Before you remove any applications, you should know that the BlackBerry Desktop Manager enables you to remove any application from your device, including many of the built-in applications. For this reason, you should be careful when removing applications so you don't accidentally remove an application you really do need.

1 Launch the Application Loader Wizard

With your BlackBerry device plugged in to your desktop PC and turned on, click the **Start** button on the Windows taskbar of your desktop PC to open the main Windows system menu. Then select **All Programs**, **BlackBerry**, **Desktop Manager**. The BlackBerry Desktop Manager application appears.

Double-click the **Application Loader** icon in the BlackBerry Desktop Manager. The **Application Loader Wizard** window appears.

2 Select the Application for Removal

Click the **Next** button to get started with the Application Loader Wizard. The wizard will take a few moments to analyze your device and then display the **Handheld Application Selection** window. This window includes all the applications installed on your device, including core operating system components.

▶ **TIP**

You must be careful when using the **Application Loader Wizard** because it allows you to make sweeping changes to the applications installed on your device, including critical core applications such as the phone and security features. Unless you really want to remove an application from your device, you should never uncheck an application in the **Application Loader Wizard** because it will be uninstalled. Generally speaking, it's not a good idea to uncheck standard applications unless you fully understand the implications of doing so.

Scroll down in the application list to find the application you would like to remove. Click the check box next to the application name to uncheck it and indicate that the application is to be removed from your device. Click the **Next** button to continue in the wizard. The completion window of the Application Loader Wizard appears.

3 Remove the Application from Your Device

The **Advanced** button enables you to tweak the installation settings associated with application data and currently installed applications. More specifically, you can specify that all application data be erased from your device prior to removal. You can also specify that all applications be erased from your device before removal. These are both fairly aggressive measures intended to serve as somewhat of a cleanup of your device's state. They are recommended only if you are having problems, and even then you should perform a backup of your device prior to proceeding with any erasure.

▶ **TIP**

If you click the **Advanced** button to tweak advanced installation settings, you might have to progress through several screens to return to the familiar **Finish** button that allows you to finish the installation process. Just accept the default settings along the way if you aren't sure how to answer.

Click the **Finish** button to remove the application from your device. After removing the application from your device, the BlackBerry Desktop Manager automatically synchronizes the device with your desktop PC.

13 Back Up Your Device

✔ **BEFORE YOU BEGIN**

- 8 Install the BlackBerry Desktop Software
- 9 Connect Your Device to Your PC

→ **SEE ALSO**

- 14 Restore Your Device
- 15 Clear Personal Data from Your Device

If this is your first foray into using a handheld device that handles a variety of electronic communications, you might not immediately see the importance of backing up your device's data. There just isn't that big of a need for backing up data on a traditional mobile phone. But the BlackBerry 7100 isn't a traditional mobile phone, and you will eventually store enough data on your device to make a backup a good idea—if not a necessity.

Depending on the sensitivity of your mobile data and how much it changes, backing up your device might or might not be a priority to you. Just keep in mind that we usually only appreciate a backup when it's too late. So, think in terms of prevention when it comes to preserving your data, and try to back up your device a little more frequently than you think might be necessary. Typical backup scheduling scenarios range from daily to monthly, although the latter option is really pushing it in terms of putting your data at risk.

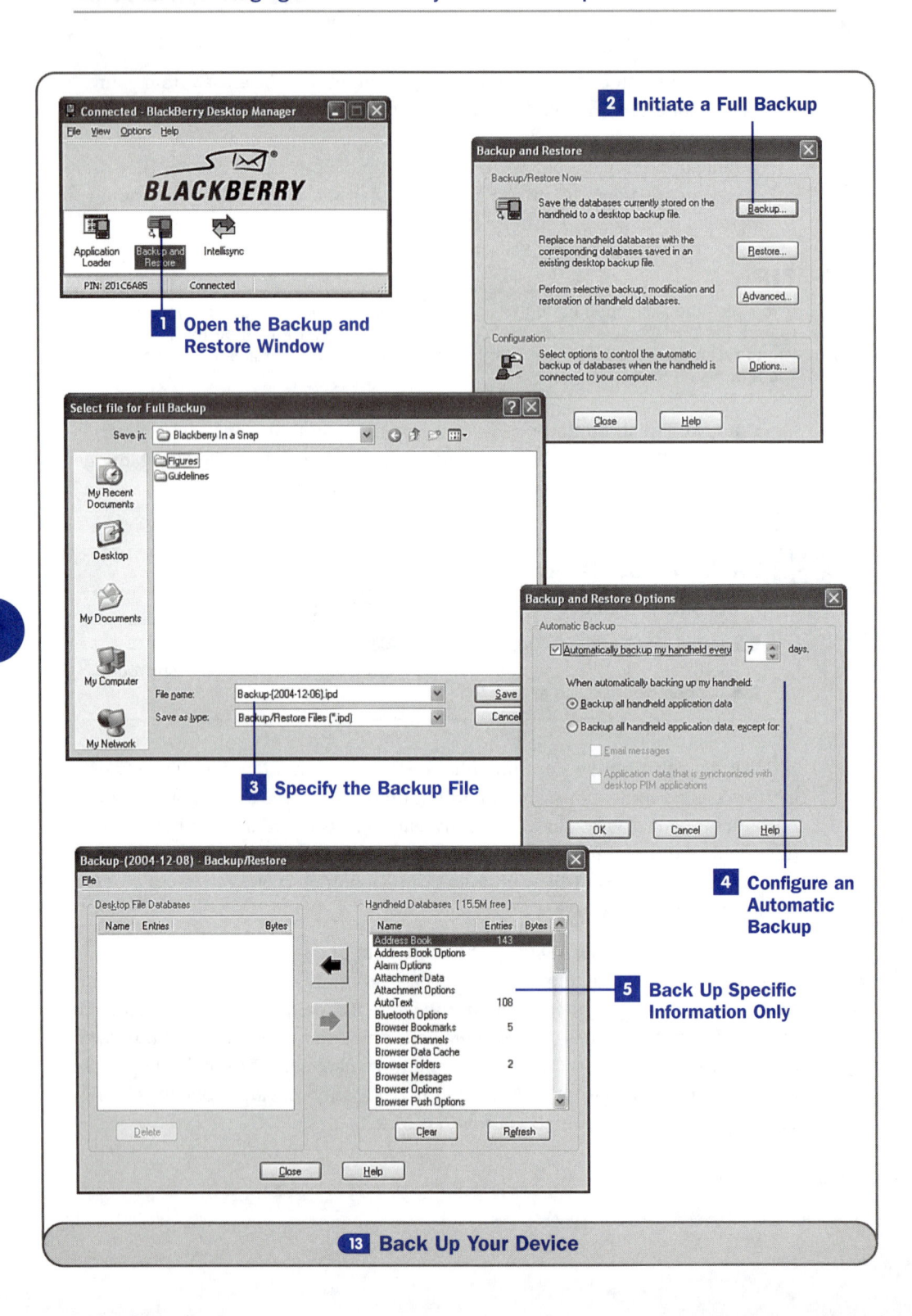

CHAPTER 3: Managing Your BlackBerry from a Desktop PC

1 Open the Backup and Restore Window

2 Initiate a Full Backup

3 Specify the Backup File

4 Configure an Automatic Backup

5 Back Up Specific Information Only

13 Back Up Your Device

1 Open the Backup and Restore Window

With your BlackBerry device plugged in to your desktop PC and turned on, click the **Start** button on the Windows taskbar of your desktop PC to open the main Windows system menu. Then select **All Programs**, **BlackBerry**, **Desktop Manager**. The BlackBerry Desktop Manager application appears.

Double-click the **Backup and Restore** icon in the BlackBerry Desktop Manager. The **Backup and Restore** window appears.

2 Initiate a Full Backup

Click the **Backup** button to get started fully backing up your BlackBerry device. The **Select file for Full Backup** window appears and prompts you for the name of the file to which the backup is stored.

3 Specify the Backup File

Navigate to a suitable folder on your desktop PC, and then click the **Save** button to accept the default backup filename. Feel free to change the filename to some other name if you choose, but keep in mind that you should include the backup date in the filename as is done in the default name.

▶ **TIP**

You might want to create a special folder on your desktop PC to store your BlackBerry backup files. That way, you'll have them all in one place should you ever need to restore the device from a specific date.

After you accept the backup filename, the backup proceeds and stores a full backup of your device in the specified file on your desktop PC. This file can then be used at any time in the future to restore your device to the current state; see **14 Restore Your Device**.

The **Options** button in the **Backup and Restore** window enables you to configure automatic backup options, which are useful because they make backups a regularly occurring event without you having to remember. When you click the **Options** button, the **Backup and Restore Options** window appears.

4 Configure an Automatic Backup

To set up the BlackBerry Desktop Manager for automatic backup, check the **Automatically backup my handheld every** option. The default backup time frame is seven days, which simply means your device will be backed up once a week. You can tweak this setting to suit your own specific needs, but seven days is probably a reasonable backup time frame for most users. One scenario in which you might want to use a shorter time frame is if the data on your device changes a great deal from day to day. In this case, you might shorten the backup time frame to every two days, or maybe even daily.

▶ **NOTE**
Don't forget that every time you back up your device, a unique backup file is created on your desktop PC. This isn't a problem, but it can mean that a lot of files pile up if you back up very frequently. For this reason, consider cleaning up your backup folder every so often to eliminate older backup files you no longer need.

When performing an automatic backup, you have the option of excluding email messages and synchronized PIM data. The idea behind excluding this information from a backup is that you likely already have a copy of it on your desktop PC due to synchronization. Even so, unless you find that your backup files are taking up too much space on your desktop PC, it's safer to select the first option, **Backup all handheld application data**, so all the data on your device is included in automatic backups.

Click the **OK** button to accept the automatic backup settings. In the future, the BlackBerry Desktop Manager will automatically back up your device according to the specified backup schedule.

In addition to performing a full backup, in some instances you might need to take greater control over your backup files. Click the **Advanced** button to open the **Backup/Restore** window.

5 Back Up Specific Information Only

Although a full backup of your device is recommended in most instances to safely save device data, there might be special circumstances where you want to back up only a specific piece of information. For example, maybe you want to clear out your device and start over with nothing more than your address book data. In this case, you want to back up only the contacts from the address book. Or maybe you've added a new web browser bookmark you want to back up, so you need to quickly update the latest backup file with the bookmark data. Both of these scenarios are possible in the **Backup/Restore** window.

The **Backup/Restore** window appears to be a list of general options for fine-tuning how a backup is carried out. While this is true to some extent, what you're really looking at is the current PIM data on your device next to the data stored in the backup file for today. The right pane in the **Backup/Restore** window shows the data on your device that is available for backup, whereas the left pane shows the data that has been backed up to today's backup file. If you haven't performed a backup today, the left pane of the

14 Restore Your Device

window is empty to indicate that no data has been backed up yet. If you've just performed a full backup today, the left pane matches the right pane.

▶ **NOTE**

As you might suspect, the **Backup/Restore** window also enables you to restore data to your device from a backup file. To find out exactly how this is done, see **14 Restore Your Device**. Similarly, you can use the **Backup/Restore** window to clear data from your device. See **15 Clear Personal Data from Your Device** to find out how.

To perform a selective backup of a certain piece of information, click the entry in the right pane and then click the **Backup** button (the large left arrow) between the panes. You can use this technique to selectively back up a subset of the device data to a limited backup file. Or, if you've already performed a full backup, you can use the same technique to update a particular piece of information. Using the address book example from earlier, if you want to create a backup file containing only your contacts, just click **Address Book** in the right pane and then click the **Backup** button. This assumes that you haven't already performed a full backup; if you have, the address book information will simply be updated in the backup file.

▶ **TIP**

To select more than one piece of information for backup, hold down the **Ctrl** key on your desktop keyboard while clicking the entries in the right pane of the **Backup/Restore** window.

▶ **TIP**

If information on your device changes while you have the **Backup/Restore** window open, click the **Refresh** button to update the right pane so the changes are reflected.

Click the **Close** button to exit the **Backup/Restore** window and return to the main **Backup and Restore** window. If you're prompted to save changes before exiting this window, click **Yes** to accept the changes. To return to the main **BlackBerry Desktop Manager** window, click the **Close** button once more.

14 Restore Your Device

✔ **BEFORE YOU BEGIN**
- **8** Install the BlackBerry Desktop Software
- **9** Connect Your Device to Your PC
- **13** Back Up Your Device

→ **SEE ALSO**
- **15** Clear Personal Data from Your Device

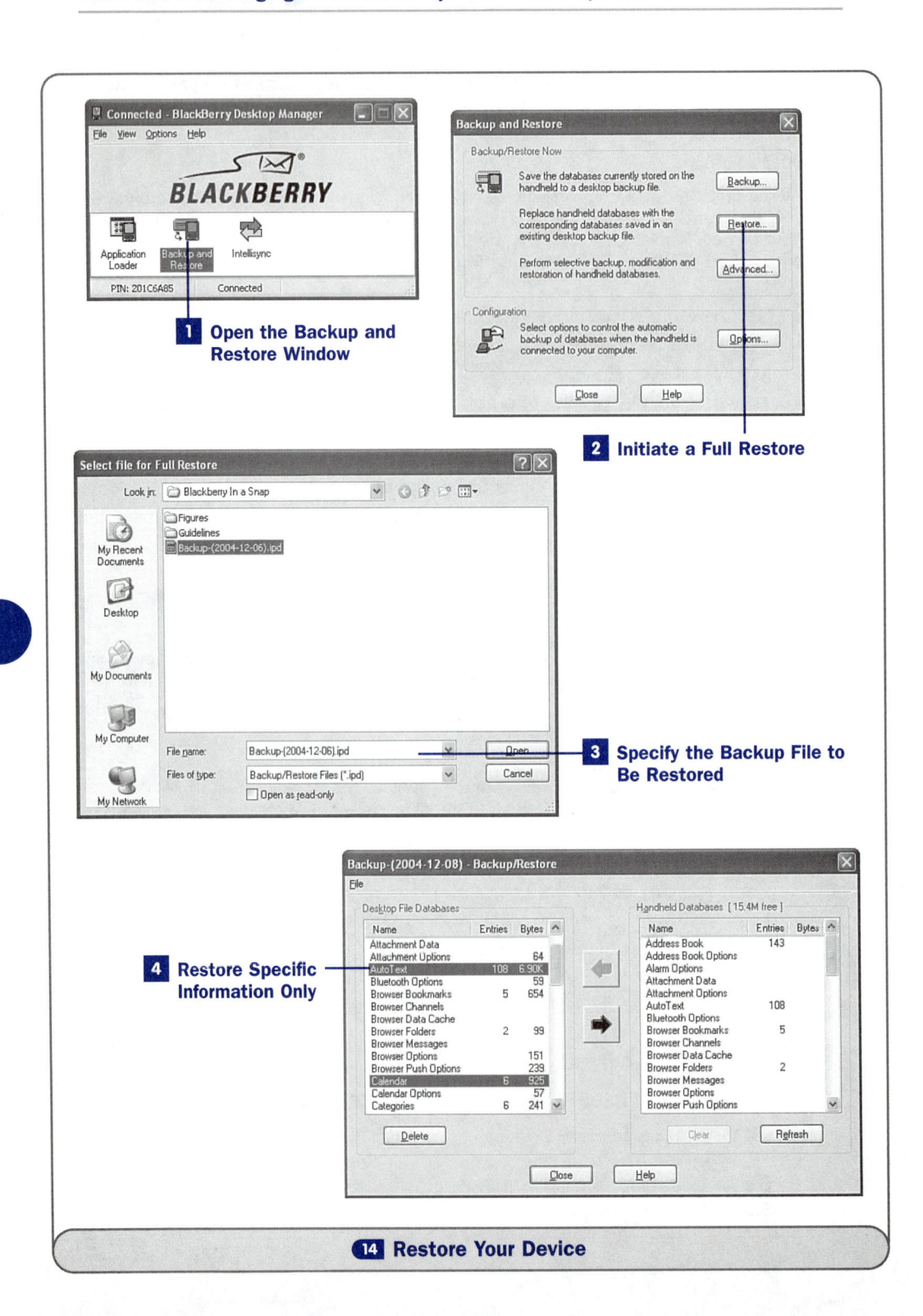

CHAPTER 3: Managing Your BlackBerry from a Desktop PC

1 Open the Backup and Restore Window

2 Initiate a Full Restore

3 Specify the Backup File to Be Restored

4 Restore Specific Information Only

14 Restore Your Device

14 Restore Your Device

Hopefully, you'll never need to actually use this task, and you're just reading it now to be thorough. Or maybe you've been conscientious about making regular backups and your commitment to preserving your data has paid off when you needed it most. Either way, restoring backed-up data to your device is an important and often necessary part of being a BlackBerry user. Just keep in mind that your ability to restore data is limited only by your willingness to back it up on a regular basis. I apologize if I sound a bit preachy in regard to backing up regularly, but I've been burned before. And I can tell you it is a terrible feeling to know that you lost some valuable information only because you didn't take the time to back it up.

1 Open the Backup and Restore Window

With your BlackBerry device plugged in to your desktop PC and turned on, click the **Start** button on the Windows taskbar of your desktop PC to open the main Windows system menu. Then select **All Programs**, **BlackBerry**, **Desktop Manager**. The BlackBerry Desktop Manager application appears.

Double-click the **Backup and Restore** icon in the BlackBerry Desktop Manager. The **Backup and Restore** window appears.

2 Initiate a Full Restore

Click the **Restore** button to get started fully restoring your BlackBerry device. The **Select file for Full Restore** window appears and prompts you for the name of the backup file from which you'd like to restore.

3 Specify the Backup File to Be Restored

Navigate to the folder on your desktop PC where you store your device's backup files, and then click to select the backup file from which you'd like to restore. Click the **Open** button to accept the backup filename. The restoration proceeds and copies all the data from the specified backup file to your device.

In addition to performing a full restore, in some instances you might need to take greater control over the restoration of device data from backup files. From the **Backup and Restore** window, click the **Advanced** button to open the **Backup/Restore** window.

4 Restore Specific Information Only

A full restore is a quick and easy way to restore all the data on your device, but in some circumstances it can be overkill. For example, you might want to restore only calendar events so that you don't change other data on your device. Or maybe you've made some AutoText changes you want to roll back to their previous settings (**see 17 Customize the AutoText Feature**). The **Backup/Restore** window enables you to specify individual pieces of information for a selective restore.

In the **Backup/Restore** window you'll find the current PIM data on your device next to the data available in the backup you selected for restoration. The right pane in the **Backup/Restore** window shows the current data on your device, whereas the left pane shows the data in the specified backup file. Depending on how old the backup file is and whether you performed a full backup to the file, the left pane will more or less match the right pane.

▶ **NOTE**

The **Backup/Restore** window also lets you back up data from your device to a backup file. For more information, see ⑬ **Back Up Your Device**. Similarly, you can use the **Backup/Restore** window to clear data from your device. See ⑮ **Clear Personal Data from Your Device** to find out how.

To perform a selective restoration of a certain piece of information, click the entry in the left pane and then click the **Restore** button (the large right arrow) between the panes. You can use this technique to selectively restore a subset of the backup file to your device. Using the calendar events and AutoText examples from earlier, if you want to restore only calendar and AutoText information from a backup file, just hold down the **Ctrl** key and click **AutoText** and **Calendar** in the right pane; then click the **Restore** button.

▶ **TIP**

To select more than one piece of information for restoration, hold down the **Ctrl** key on your desktop keyboard while clicking the entries in the left pane of the **Backup/Restore** window.

▶ **TIP**

If information on your device changes while you have the **Backup/Restore** window open, click the **Refresh** button to update the right pane so the changes are reflected.

Click the **Close** button to exit the **Backup/Restore** window and return to the main **Backup and Restore** window. To return to the main **BlackBerry Desktop Manager** window, click the **Close** button once more.

15 Clear Personal Data from Your Device

✔ BEFORE YOU BEGIN	→ SEE ALSO
⑧ Install the BlackBerry Desktop Software ⑨ Connect Your Device to Your PC ⑬ Back Up Your Device	⑭ Restore Your Device

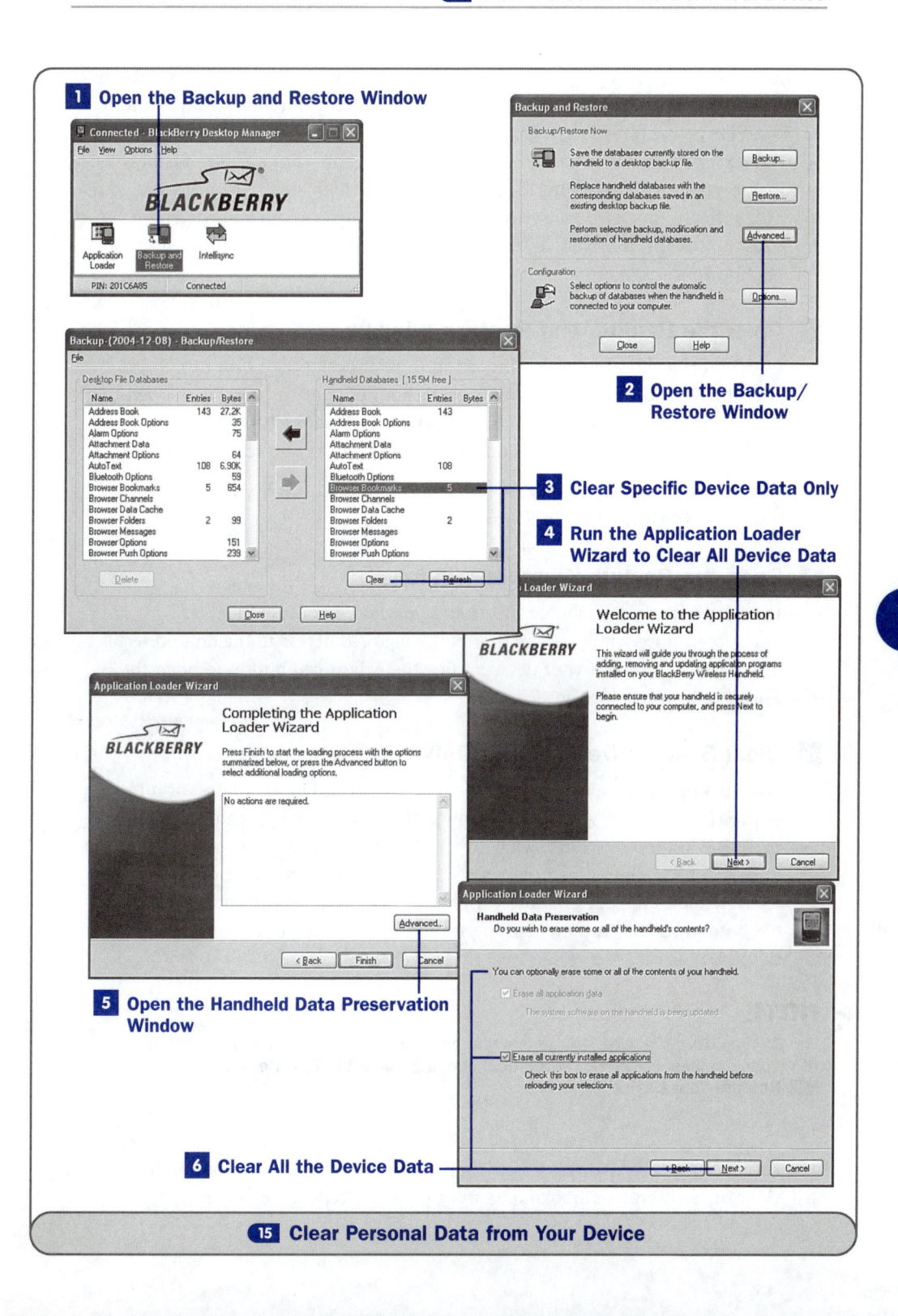

15 Clear Personal Data from Your Device

1 Open the Backup and Restore Window

2 Open the Backup/Restore Window

3 Clear Specific Device Data Only

4 Run the Application Loader Wizard to Clear All Device Data

5 Open the Handheld Data Preservation Window

6 Clear All the Device Data

15 Clear Personal Data from Your Device

So, the time has come to sell your cherished BlackBerry device on eBay. What am I thinking, you can't get rid of your BlackBerry 7100! But maybe you have another reason for needing to clear the device of all your personal data. Maybe you've been using it personally and now you need to shift gears with a clean business install. Or maybe you just want to start over with a clean slate. Regardless of your motive, there is a quick and easy way to blitz your device of all your personal data. Just be careful and back up the data before you clear the device, just in case you change your mind later.

1 Open the Backup and Restore Window

With your BlackBerry device plugged in to your desktop PC and turned on, click the **Start** button on the Windows taskbar of your desktop PC to open the main Windows system menu. Then select **All Programs**, **BlackBerry**, **Desktop Manager**. The BlackBerry Desktop Manager application appears.

Double-click the **Backup and Restore** icon in the BlackBerry Desktop Manager. The **Backup and Restore** window appears.

2 Open the Backup/Restore Window

To selectively clear personal data from your device you use the **Backup/Restore** window, which provides detailed access to the databases of information stored on your device. Click the **Advanced** button to open the **Backup/Restore** window.

3 Clear Specific Device Data Only

The **Backup/Restore** window allows you to clear individual pieces of information from your device. The window consists of two panes that show the current PIM data on your device next to the data available for restoration from today's backup file, if one exists. The right pane in the **Backup/Restore** window shows the current data on your device, whereas the left pane shows the data in the backup file. The right pane is the only pane of interest for clearing data.

▶ **NOTE**

The **Backup/Restore** window also lets you back up and restore data on your device using backup files. For more information, see **13** **Back Up Your Device** and **14** **Restore Your Device**.

To perform a selective clearing of a certain piece of information, click the entry in the right pane and then click the **Clear** button. As an example, to clear the web browser bookmarks from your device, click **Browser**

Bookmarks in the right pane and then click the **Clear** button. The browser bookmark data will be removed from the device.

▶ **TIP**

To select more than one piece of information for clearing, hold down the **Ctrl** key on your desktop keyboard while clicking the entries in the right pane of the **Backup/Restore** window.

▶ **TIP**

If information on your device changes while you have the **Backup/Restore** window open, click the **Refresh** button to update the right pane so that the changes are reflected.

Click the **Close** button to exit the **Backup/Restore** window and return to the main **Backup and Restore** window. To return to the main **BlackBerry Desktop Manager** window, click the **Close** button once more.

4 Run the Application Loader Wizard to Clear All Device Data

You might decide that clearing selective data from your device isn't enough and you need to take more sweeping measures. In this case you might want to consider clearing all the personal data from your device. Double-click the **Application Loader** icon in the BlackBerry Desktop Manager to get started. The **Application Loader Wizard** window appears.

Click the **Next** button to get started with the Application Loader Wizard. The wizard will take a few moments to analyze your device and then display the **Handheld Application Selection** window. This window includes all the applications installed on your device, which aren't important for simply clearing the device's data.

▶ **TIP**

You must be careful when using the **Application Loader Wizard** because it allows you to make sweeping changes to the applications installed on your device, including critical core applications such as the phone and security features. Unless you really want to remove an application from your device, you should never uncheck an application in the **Application Loader Wizard** because it will be uninstalled. Generally speaking, it's not a good idea to uncheck standard applications unless you fully understand the implications of doing so.

Click **Next** to continue along in the wizard. The completion window of the Application Loader Wizard appears.

5 Open the Handheld Data Preservation Window

The **Advanced** button is what provides access to the wholesale clearing of device data. Click the **Advanced** button to view the **Handheld Data Preservation** window.

6 Clear All the Device Data

The **Handheld Data Preservation** window provides a couple of options for clearing information from your device. The first option, **Erase all application data**, clears all the data associated with applications—this is data you've created while using the applications and is what you're interested in clearing. The second option, **Erase all currently installed applications**, clears the applications themselves from your device. Even though the latter option might sound harsh, what it means is that the applications are erased prior to being reinstalled. In other words, the BlackBerry Desktop Manager performs a clean install of the applications onto your device. The bottom line is that, to successfully clear your device of all data, you must check both options and click the **Next** button. The end result is a device with a clean install of the applications and no application data.

After clicking the **Next** button, you might be prompted to automatically back up your device before carrying out the data clearing. This is a good idea just in case you change your mind later about clearing your device of all data. Just accept the default option to back up your device, and then click **Next** to continue.

Click the **Finish** button in the Application Loader Wizard to proceed with clearing all the data from your device.

4

Fine-tuning Your BlackBerry

IN THIS CHAPTER:

- **16** Automatically Turn Your Device On and Off
- **17** Customize the AutoText Feature
- **18** Tweak the Profiles
- **19** Adjust the Screen and Keyboard
- **20** Organize Application Icons
- **21** Change the Wallpaper
- **22** Install a New Theme

CHAPTER 4: Fine-tuning Your BlackBerry

If you haven't already realized it, your BlackBerry 7100 series device is a very personal piece of electronic equipment. No two people use BlackBerry devices in exactly the same way, so it is expected that you'll want to customize the device to suit your exact needs. In some ways, this entire book is focused on customizing your device to how you work and play and help solve problems unique to you. This chapter takes a direct approach to the customization issue by showing several key ways to fine-tune your BlackBerry device to maximize its usefulness.

16 Automatically Turn Your Device On and Off

→ **SEE ALSO**

- **5** Lock and Unlock Your Device
- **6** Password-Protect Your Device

It might seem like a strange proposition to have your device automatically turn itself on and off, but it is actually a very useful feature. One of the biggest challenges in all of mobile computing is preserving battery life. Even though BlackBerry devices require far less battery power than full-size notebook computers, they still have fairly limited battery resources. For this reason, you should do all you can to help your device conserve power. One of the best ways to conserve power is to configure your device so it automatically powers itself off at the end of the day when you're finished using it.

1 Open the Tools Screen

Scroll to the **Tools** icon on the **Home** screen and click the trackwheel. The **Tools** screen appears, offering a list of tools options.

2 Open the Settings Screen

Scroll to the **Settings** icon and click the trackwheel. A list of options for which you can change the settings appears.

3 Open the Auto On/Off Screen

Scroll to the **Auto On/Off** option in the list of settings and click the trackwheel. The **Auto On/Off** screen opens.

4 Enable the Auto On/Off Feature for Weekdays

If the auto on/off feature isn't already enabled, scroll to select the **Weekday** field and click the trackwheel. Then click **Change Option**. From the menu that appears, select **Enabled** to specify that your BlackBerry unit should automatically turn on and off at the specified times each weekday.

16 Automatically Turn Your Device On and Off

1 Open the Tools Screen

2 Open the Settings Screen

3 Open the Auto On/Off Screen

4 Enable the Auto On/Off Feature for Weekdays

5 Enable the Auto On/Off Feature for Weekends

6 Exit and Save Changes

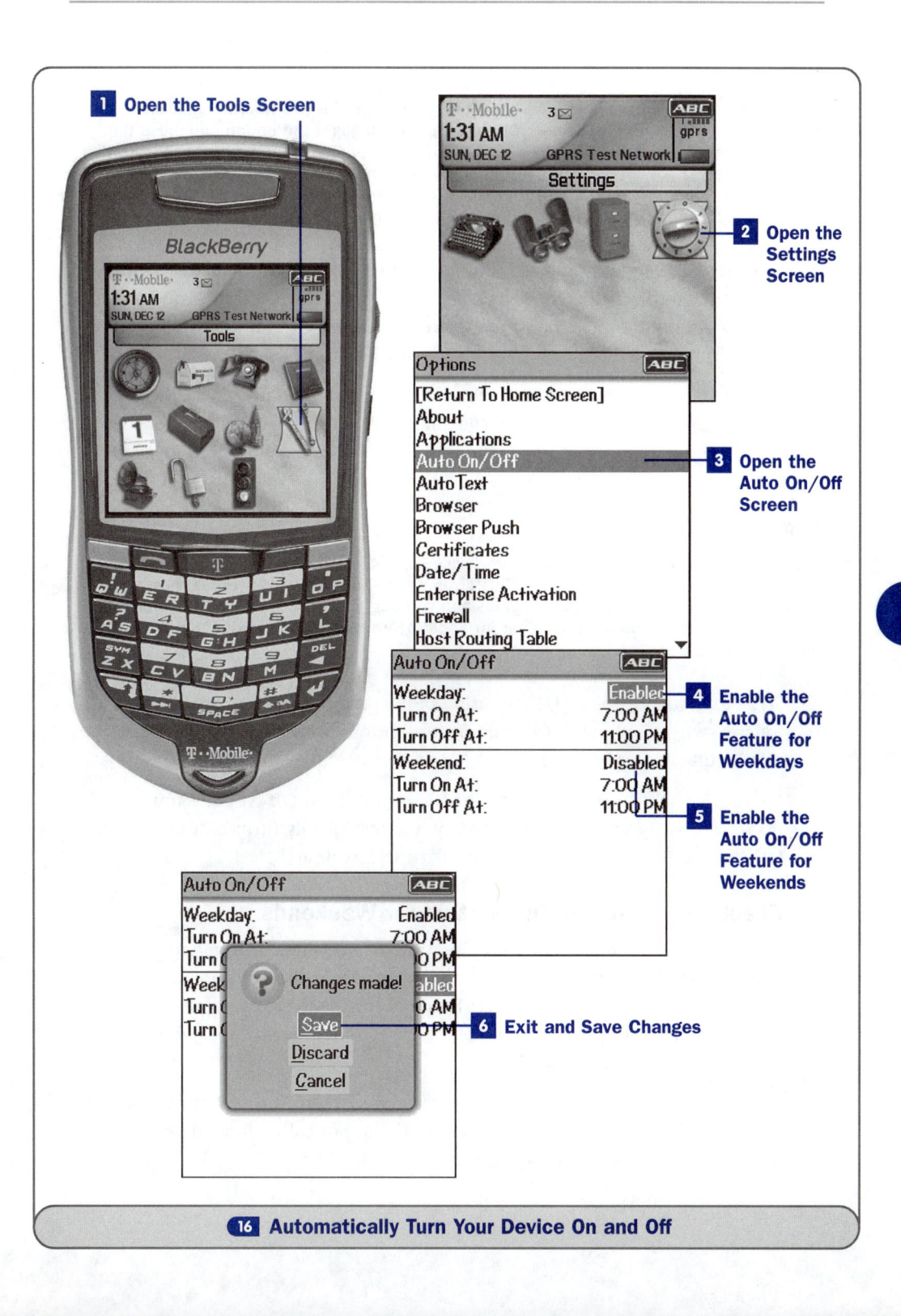

16 Automatically Turn Your Device On and Off

▶ TIP

To quickly change an option without having to go through the two trackwheel clicks required to open a menu and select **Change Option**, highlight the option and press the **Alt** key to view a list of choices. Then scroll to the desired choice and click the trackwheel to select it. An even faster shortcut involves cycling to the next available choice by pressing the **Space** key; pressing **Shift+Space** cycles to the previous choice. You can also jump immediately to a choice by typing the first character in the choice's name.

To change the default auto on/off times, scroll to highlight the hour portion of the time in the **Turn On At** field—in this example, select the 7—and click the trackwheel; then click **Change Option** in the menu that appears. Scroll through the list of options to select the desired hour and click.

Scroll to highlight the minute portion of the time in the **Turn On At** field—in this example, select the **00**—and click the trackwheel. Then click **Change Option** in the menu that appears. Scroll through the list of options to select the desired minutes and click.

▶ TIP

You should set the auto on time for your device so that it comes on a few minutes before you plan on using it each day. This gives it time to retrieve your email messages so they will be ready and waiting for you when you begin using the device. Generally speaking, I like to set the auto on time for about 15 minutes prior to when I start using the device each day.

Scroll to highlight the **AM/PM** portion of the time in the **Time** field and click the trackwheel; then click **Change Option** in the menu that appears. Scroll to select either **AM** or **PM** and click.

Repeat this procedure to change the time for the **Turn Off At** field. Your device is now set so that every weekday it automatically turns on at the **Turn On At** time and then turns off at the **Turn Off At** time.

5. Enable the Auto On/Off Feature for Weekends

You can also enable the auto on/off feature for weekends by scrolling to select the **Weekend** field and clicking the trackwheel. Then click **Change Option**. From the menu that appears, select **Enabled** to specify that your device should automatically turn on and off at the specified times during the weekend.

Repeat the procedure for setting the weekend **Turn On At** and **Turn Off At** time fields. Your device is now set so that it automatically turns on and off on the weekends as well as on weekdays.

6 Exit and Save Changes

Press the **Escape** button to exit the **Auto On/Off** screen. You're prompted to save or discard your changes. When prompted, scroll the trackwheel to the **Save** option and click to save the changes. You're then returned to the **Settings** screen. Press the **Escape** button twice to navigate back to the **Home** screen, or just press the **End** key once.

17 Customize the AutoText Feature

→ **SEE ALSO**

4 About the BlackBerry User Interface

If you have any experience using an "intelligent" word processor such as Microsoft Word, you understand how handy it can be to have spelling mistakes and typos automatically fixed as you type. The BlackBerry operating system includes a feature called AutoText that serves as somewhat of a simplified spell checker. AutoText isn't a true spell checker because it focuses more on commonly mistyped words, as opposed to including an entire dictionary of correct spellings. However, AutoText goes beyond the call of duty for a spell checker by carrying out a more general text replacement.

In addition to correcting misspelled words, AutoText allows you to specify any word and corresponding replacement text for that word. Any time you type the specified word, the replacement text is plugged in to replace it. If you pay close attention to the words and phrases you use regularly, you'll find that creating AutoText entries for them will save you a lot of time. As an example, by default, the word *sig* is set so that it is replaced by your owner information (**see** 4 **Make Yourself the Owner**). This enables you to quickly use your owner information as an email signature by simply typing the word *sig*.

1 Open the Tools Screen

Scroll to the **Tools** icon on the **Home** screen and click the trackwheel. The **Tools** screen appears, offering a list of tools options.

2 Open the Settings Screen

Scroll to the **Settings** icon and click the trackwheel. A list of options for which you can change the settings appears.

3 Open the AutoText Screen

Scroll to the **AutoText** option in the list of settings and click the trackwheel. The **AutoText** screen opens.

CHAPTER 4: Fine-tuning Your BlackBerry

1 Open the Tools Screen

2 Open the Settings Screen

3 Open the AutoText Screen

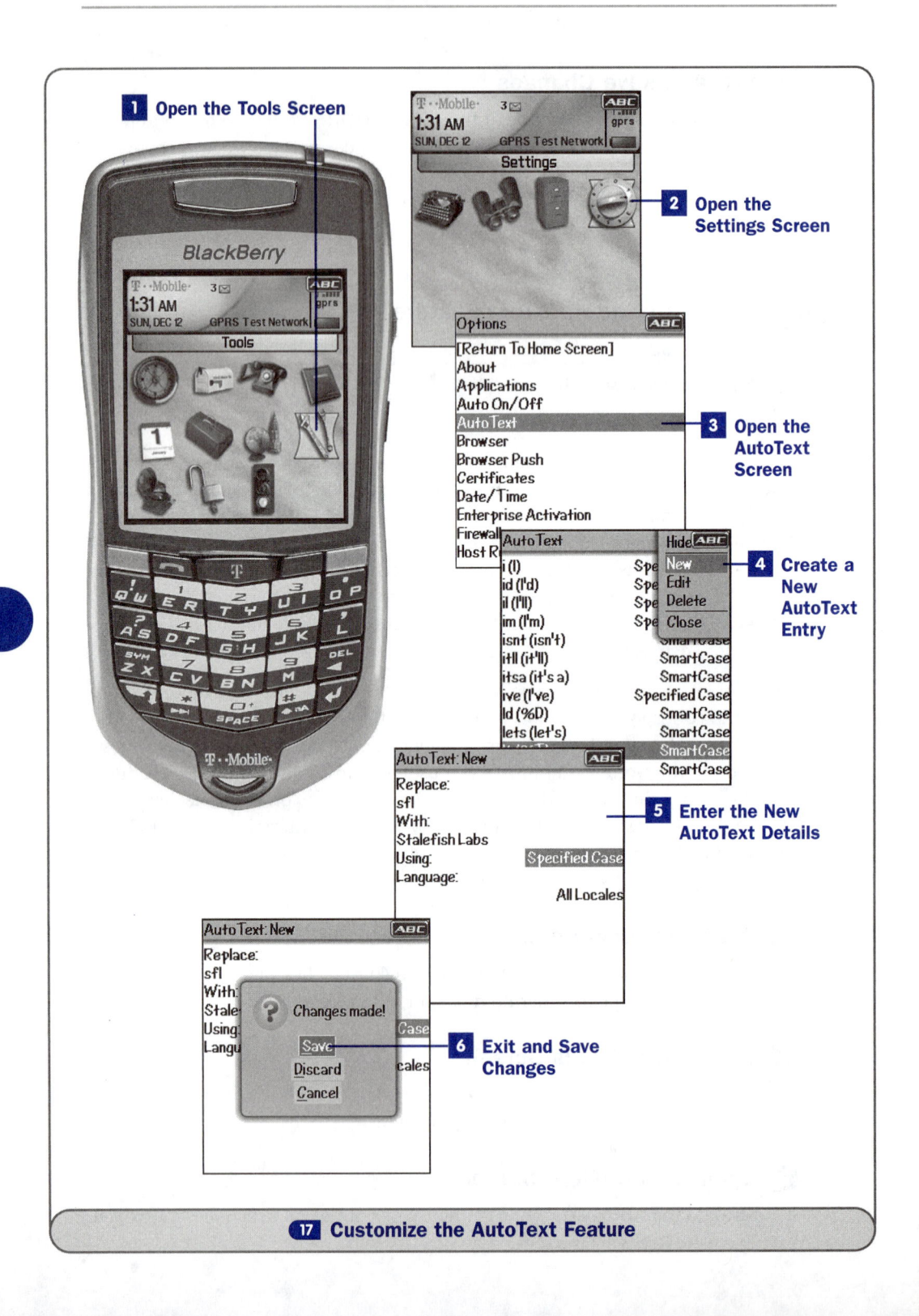

4 Create a New AutoText Entry

5 Enter the New AutoText Details

6 Exit and Save Changes

17 Customize the AutoText Feature

4 Create a New AutoText Entry

The AutoText screen consists of a fairly large list of words and their respective replacement text. The idea behind AutoText is to recognize a word when you type it and then replace it with another word, phrase, or *macro*. Many commonly misspelled words are already listed, as well as a few handy replacement shortcuts such as **lt**, which gets replaced by the current time (in long format, which includes **AM** or **PM**).

▶ **TIP**

To quickly filter the AutoText list so you can view a specific set of entries, type the first few characters in the entry. For example, if you type **the**, you will see the AutoText entries that add apostrophes to words such as *they'd*, *they'll*, *there's*, and so on.

▶ **KEY TERM**

Macro—A special symbol that references a piece of information stored on your device such as the date, time, owner name, or phone number. Using AutoText, macros enable you to insert such information by simply typing a short word. For example, the AutoText word *sig* is replaced by the owner information so you can quickly enter it as your signature at the bottom of a message. See 4 **Make Yourself the Owner.**

To create a new AutoText entry, click the trackwheel and then click **New** on the menu that appears. The **AutoText: New** screen appears.

▶ **TIP**

Just as you can create new AutoText entries, you can also edit existing entries. Just click the entry with the trackwheel, and then click **Edit** from the menu that appears. The **AutoText: Edit** screen appears and is very similar to the **AutoText: New** screen that is used to create a new entry.

5 Enter the New AutoText Details

The **AutoText: New** screen includes several fields for filling in the details of a new AutoText entry. The **Replace** field shows the word to be replaced, and the **With** field contains the word, phrase, or macro that replaces it. In the example, the word **sfl** is replaced by the phrase **Stalefish Labs**, which is the name of my company. Because I use the name fairly often in email correspondence, it can get tedious having to type it over and over. This AutoText entry provides an extremely efficient way to enter the name.

If you choose to use a macro in the replacement text for an AutoText entry, you must take advantage of special codes that identify the macros. All these codes begin with a percent symbol (%), as shown in the table. To enter a macro in the **Replace** field, just type the code corresponding to the macro in the table.

Macro Codes Available for Use in AutoText Entries

Macro	Code	AutoText Word
Owner Name	%o	usrid
Owner Info	%O	sig
Phone Number	%p	mynumber
Handheld PIN	%P	mypin
OS Version	%V	myver
Short Date	%d	
Long Date	%D	ld
Short Time	%t	st
Long Time	%T	lt
Backspace	%b	rb
Delete	%B	br
% Symbol	%%	

You might notice a couple of other fields in the **AutoText: New** screen. The **Using:** field specifies how the case of the replacement text is determined. The default setting of **SmartCase** means that the case of the text is determined based on the context in which it is used. For example, if the text appears at the beginning of a sentence, it is automatically capitalized. In the case of my company name, I always want it to be capitalized, so the other option is more appropriate, **Specified Case**. If you select **Specified Case**, the replacement text is capitalized exactly as you've entered it.

The last field in the **AutoText: New** screen allows you to apply the AutoText entry to all locales or a specific *locale*. Unless you switch locales frequently and are creating language-specific AutoText entries, the default setting of **All Locales** makes the most sense for this setting.

▶ KEY TERM

Locale—A combination of a country/region and a language. Locales are used in BlackBerry devices to reflect language and cultural differences throughout the user interface and applications.

6 Exit and Save Changes

Press the **Escape** button to exit the **AutoText: New** screen. You're prompted to save or discard your changes. When prompted, scroll the trackwheel to the **Save** option and click to save the changes. You're then returned to the **AutoText** screen. Press the **Escape** button three times to navigate back to the **Home** screen, or just press the **End** key once.

18 Tweak the Profiles

> **→ SEE ALSO**
>
> **5** Lock and Unlock Your Device
> **7** Choose a Theme
>
> **19** Adjust the Screen and Keyboard

Every BlackBerry device includes several built-in profiles that determine how the device responds to notifications such as an incoming phone call or email message. Each profile is tailored to a certain usage scenario. For example, the **Default** profile is a general-purpose profile that will work most of the time when you aren't overly concerned about the sound of the ringer, whereas the **Vibrate** profile is intended for meetings, movies, and places where you don't want the device to be heard.

In addition to tweaking the standard profiles, you can also create custom profiles of your own. I encourage you to create a custom profile so you can experiment with different settings and still have the default profiles to fall back on should you change your mind. You should experiment with different ring tones, as well as different options for how your device handles notifications when in its holster as opposed to when you have it out of the holster.

1 Open the Profiles Screen

Scroll to the **Profiles** icon on the **Home** screen and click the trackwheel. The **Profiles** screen appears, offering a list of profiles from which to choose.

2 Select a Different Profile

Not surprisingly, the default profile is named **Default**. The **Default** profile is intended for general device usage and results in a ring/vibrate combination for phone calls and only a vibration for new messages. The profile also describes device behavior for other notifications such as calendar events and due tasks. The device behavior can vary based on whether the device is in the holster. Changing the profile can be handy in situations where you need your device to behave differently when communicating notifications to you. For example, the **Vibrate** profile is useful in meetings, movies, or other places where you don't want your device to make noise. In contrast to the **Vibrate** profile, the **Loud** profile is useful at outdoor events and places where you might not hear the device notifications at their normal sound levels.

▶ **TIP**

To quickly switch between the **Default** and **Vibrate** profiles from the **Home** screen, hold down the **Shift** key (#) for a second or so.

CHAPTER 4: Fine-tuning Your BlackBerry

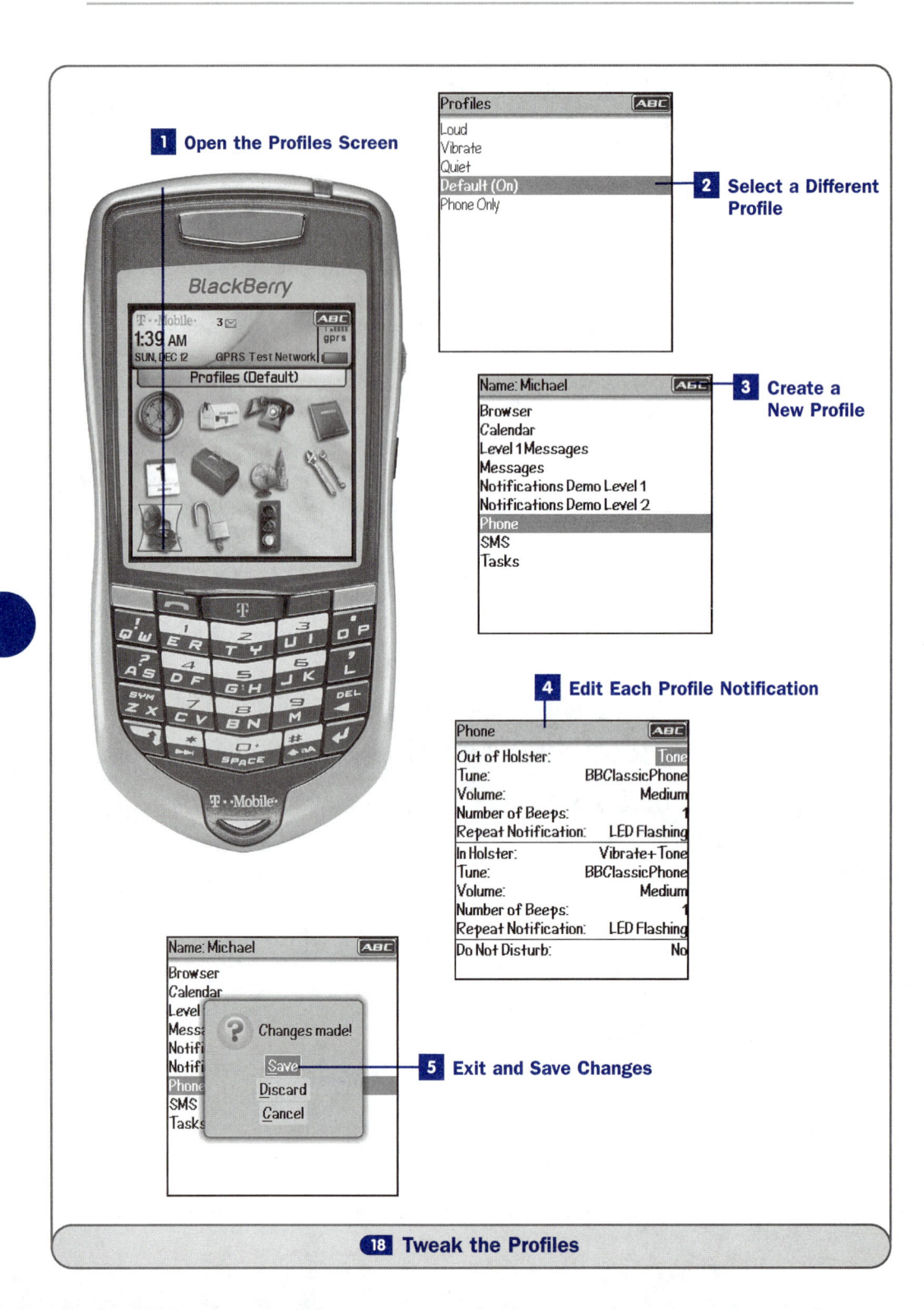

1. **Open the Profiles Screen**
2. **Select a Different Profile**
3. **Create a New Profile**
4. **Edit Each Profile Notification**
5. **Exit and Save Changes**

18 Tweak the Profiles

18 Tweak the Profiles

▶ **NOTE**
You might be tempted to use the **Quiet** profile in meetings and quiet places, but you should know that it effectively eliminates all notifications. In other words, your device won't make noise or vibrate when it is in **Quiet** mode. This might be desirable at times, but if your goal is simply to mute the device, use the **Vibrate** profile so that you'll get vibration notifications.

To select a different profile, scroll to the profile in the list with the trackwheel and click. Then click **Enable** in the menu that appears to select the profile. You are automatically returned to the **Home** screen after changing the profile.

▶ **TIP**
To quickly select a profile, scroll the trackwheel to select the profile and then press the **Space** key.

You gain a much better appreciation of the differences between profiles when you create one of your own. To create a new profile, click any of the profiles in the list with the trackwheel and then click **New** in the menu that appears. A new profile screen appears.

3 Create a New Profile

The first step in creating a new profile on the new profile screen is to name the profile. Type and enter the name of the profile in the edit field at the top of the screen. Click the trackwheel or press the **Enter** key to accept the profile name.

Each of the notifications in the list shown on the new profile screen corresponds to something that can take place on your device that is worthy of being notified about. For example, the **Phone** notification informs you of a phone call. Similarly, the **Messages** notification lets you know when you've received an email message. All the notifications are initially set to default values that are equivalent to the **Default** profile.

▶ **NOTE**
In case you're wondering, a "level 1" message is a PIN message. So, the **Level1Message** notification applies only to PIN messages you receive. Similarly, the SMS notification applies only to SMS messages. See **36** Send a PIN Message and **37** Send an SMS Message.

To change a notification in the profile, scroll the trackwheel to select one of the notifications—**Phone** for example—and click. Then click **Edit** in the menu that appears. The **Phone** notification screen appears.

▶ **NOTE**

Although you can delete profiles you create by selecting **Delete** from the profile menu, you are not allowed to delete any of the built-in profiles.

4 Edit Each Profile Notification

The **Phone** notification screen is similar to the edit screen for all the notifications. The screen is divided into two main sections, each of which corresponds to a different holster state: device in holster or device out of holster. The idea is that the notification is different based on whether the device is in the holster. The **Out of Holster** and **In Holster** fields can be set to one of four possible values: **None**, **Tone**, **Vibrate**, or **Vibrate+Tone**.

The **Tune** field determines what the tone sounds like if you've selected **Tone** or **Vibrate+Tone** in the respective holster field. When you change the **Tune** value, you can scroll through the available tones and listen to each of them. The **Volume** field determines the volume of the tune and can be set to **Mute**, **Low**, **Medium**, **High**, or **Escalating**. The **Mute** value results in no sound, whereas the **Escalating** value results in a volume level that increases as the tune is played. The **Number of Beeps** field specifies how many times the tune is played for each notification. However, in the case of the **Phone** notification, the tune plays until the phone is answered or the call is dumped to voice mail.

▶ **TIP**

You can access the tunes directly from the **Profiles** screen by clicking any of the profiles with the trackwheel and then clicking **Show Tunes** in the menu that appears. The **Tunes** screen appears and allows you to scroll through the tunes and play them by clicking and selecting **Play** from the menu.

The **Repeat Notification** field applies to messages (voice mail messages in the case of the **Phone** notification) and determines whether the LED on the device should flash to indicate that new messages are available. The last field on the **Phone** notification screen, **Do Not Disturb**, is unique to the **Phone** notification and specifies whether your device notifies you of incoming calls. If you don't want any notification to take place at all for phone calls, set this field to **Yes**.

Press the **Escape** button to return to the new profile screen. If you made any changes, you are prompted to save them before returning to the new profile screen. You can edit and customize each of the other notifications just as you did the **Phone** notification.

▶ TIP

It's probably a good idea to change the **In Holster** field to **None** for the **Messages** notification. The default setting causes your device to vibrate every time you receive an email message, which can be annoying if you receive a lot of email.

5 Exit and Save Changes

Press the **Escape** button to exit the new profile screen. You're prompted to save or discard your changes; scroll the trackwheel to the **Save** option and click to save the changes. You're then returned to the **Home** screen.

---

19 Adjust the Screen and Keyboard

✔ **BEFORE YOU BEGIN**

1 About the BlackBerry User Interface

➜ **SEE ALSO**

7 Choose a Theme
21 Change the Wallpaper
22 Install a New Theme

Alongside the trackwheel, the screen and keyboard represent the primary hardware components in the BlackBerry user interface. We all have different eyesight and hand/eye coordination abilities, so it only makes sense that you'll want to customize the screen and keyboard settings to suit your specific needs. The screen font is one of the key customizations you can make. If your vision can stand it, I recommend sizing the font a bit smaller so you can fit more information on the screen. Speaking of the screen, you can alter the brightness to accommodate varying amounts of ambient lighting. Because the screen brightness directly impacts battery life, you should lower the brightness when you're in a dimly lit area that doesn't require as much backlighting.

The keyboard settings consist of adding a tone to every key press—which can honestly get a bit annoying—and adjusting the key rate. The key rate impacts the speed of cursor moves when you hold down the **Backspace**, **Enter**, or **Space** key, as well as the speed at which a letter is converted to uppercase when you hold down a letter key while typing.

1 Open the Tools Screen

Scroll to the **Tools** icon on the **Home** screen and click the trackwheel. The **Tools** screen appears, offering a list of tools options.

2 Open the Settings Screen

Scroll to the **Settings** icon and click the trackwheel. A list of options for which you can change the settings appears.

CHAPTER 4: Fine-tuning Your BlackBerry

1. Open the Tools Screen
2. Open the Settings Screen
3. Open the Screen/Keyboard Screen
4. Customize the Font Settings
5. Tweak the Screen Settings
6. Fine-tune the Key Settings
7. Exit and Save Changes

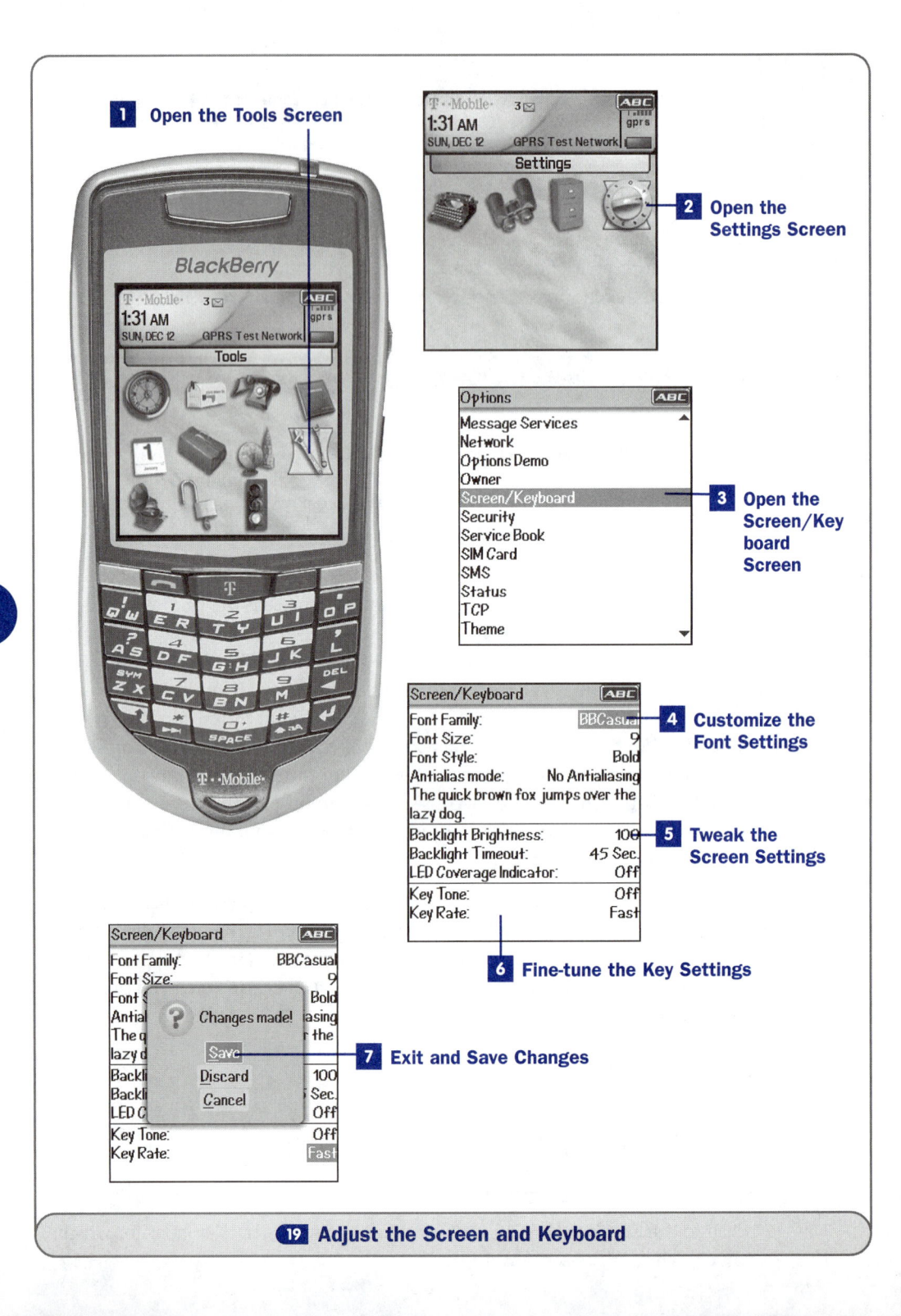

19 Adjust the Screen and Keyboard

3 Open the Screen/Keyboard Screen

Scroll to the **Screen/Keyboard** option in the list of settings and click the trackwheel. The **Screen/Keyboard** screen opens.

4 Customize the Font Settings

The first block of settings on the **Screen/Keyboard** screen involves the font used throughout the BlackBerry operating system. The default font settings depend on the theme you have selected. To change the font family, scroll the trackwheel to select the **Font Family** field and click the trackwheel; then click **Change Option** in the menu that appears. A list of alternative font family options appears.

▶ **TIP**

To quickly change an option without having to go through the two trackwheel clicks required to open a menu and select **Change Option**, highlight the option and press the **Alt** key to view a list of choices. Then scroll to the desired choice and click the trackwheel to select it. An even faster shortcut involves cycling to the next available choice by pressing the **Space** key; pressing **Shift+Space** cycles to the previous choice. You can also jump immediately to a choice by typing the first character in the choice's name.

Scroll the trackwheel through the list of alternative font families, and click to accept the choice you've made. You might notice that the sample text below the font fields changes as you scroll through the list of font families.

The **Font Size** and **Font Style** fields are used to further customize the font by changing its size and appearance. Use the trackwheel to select and modify these settings as desired, being sure to pay attention to the sample text as you make changes. Some font selections might eliminate the **Antialias mode** option, which simply means you won't be able to turn antialiasing on and off for the font—the font either uses antialiasing automatically or doesn't use it at all.

▶ **TIP**

If you don't have a problem reading small text, you might find that a smaller font is useful because it allows your device to present more information on the screen. Similarly, you might opt for a larger font if you tend to be more farsighted.

5 Tweak the Screen Settings

The screen settings on the **Screen/Keyboard** screen consist of **Backlight Brightness**, **Backlight Timeout**, and **LED Coverage Indicator**. The **Backlight Brightness** option determines the brightness of the screen's backlight as a value in the range from **0** (dark) to **100** (bright); **100** is the default setting. If you're working in a poorly lit area, you might require less brightness and be able to lower this value, which helps save battery life. Just click the trackwheel on the option and scroll to change the value.

The **Backlight Timeout** option is used to help preserve battery life by automatically turning off the backlight when your device sits idle. You specify the amount of time (in seconds) that the device must sit idle before the backlight is turned off; the default setting is **30** seconds. If you find that your screen is turning off too quickly, you can increase this value a bit. Just keep in mind that the backlight is a big battery drain, so you should avoid having it on when you aren't actually using your device.

The **LED Coverage Indicator** option determines whether the device's LED flashes to indicate wireless network coverage. More specifically, the LED flashes green when you have a wireless network connection. This flash isn't always a desirable thing. As an example, it tends to act more as a strobe night light if you keep your device near your bed while traveling.

6 Fine-tune the Key Settings

The key settings are the last block of options in the **Screen/Keyboard** window. The **Key Tone** option allows your device to play a short tone in response to every key press. Most people find this option annoying when enabled, so you can stick with the default setting of **Off**. Try it by turning it **On** if you aren't sure.

The **Key Rate** option is a little more useful in that it allows you to alter the speed of cursor moves when you hold down the **Backspace**, **Enter**, or **Space** key. The **Key Rate** option also impacts the speed at which a letter is converted to uppercase when you hold down a letter key while typing. The default setting is **Fast**, which is probably acceptable unless you have trouble typing.

7 Exit and Save Changes

Press the **Escape** button to exit the **Screen/Keyboard** screen. If you made any changes, you're prompted to save or discard the changes. When prompted, scroll the trackwheel to the **Save** option and click to save the changes. You're then returned to the **Settings** screen. Press the **Escape** button twice to navigate back to the **Home** screen, or just press the **End** key once.

20 Organize Application Icons

✔ BEFORE YOU BEGIN	→ SEE ALSO
1 About the BlackBerry User Interface	11 Install a New Application to Your Device
	12 Remove an Application from Your Device

20 Organize Application Icons

1 Activate the Application Menu

2 Move an Application Icon

3 Hide an Application Icon

4 Show an Application Icon

20 Organize Application Icons

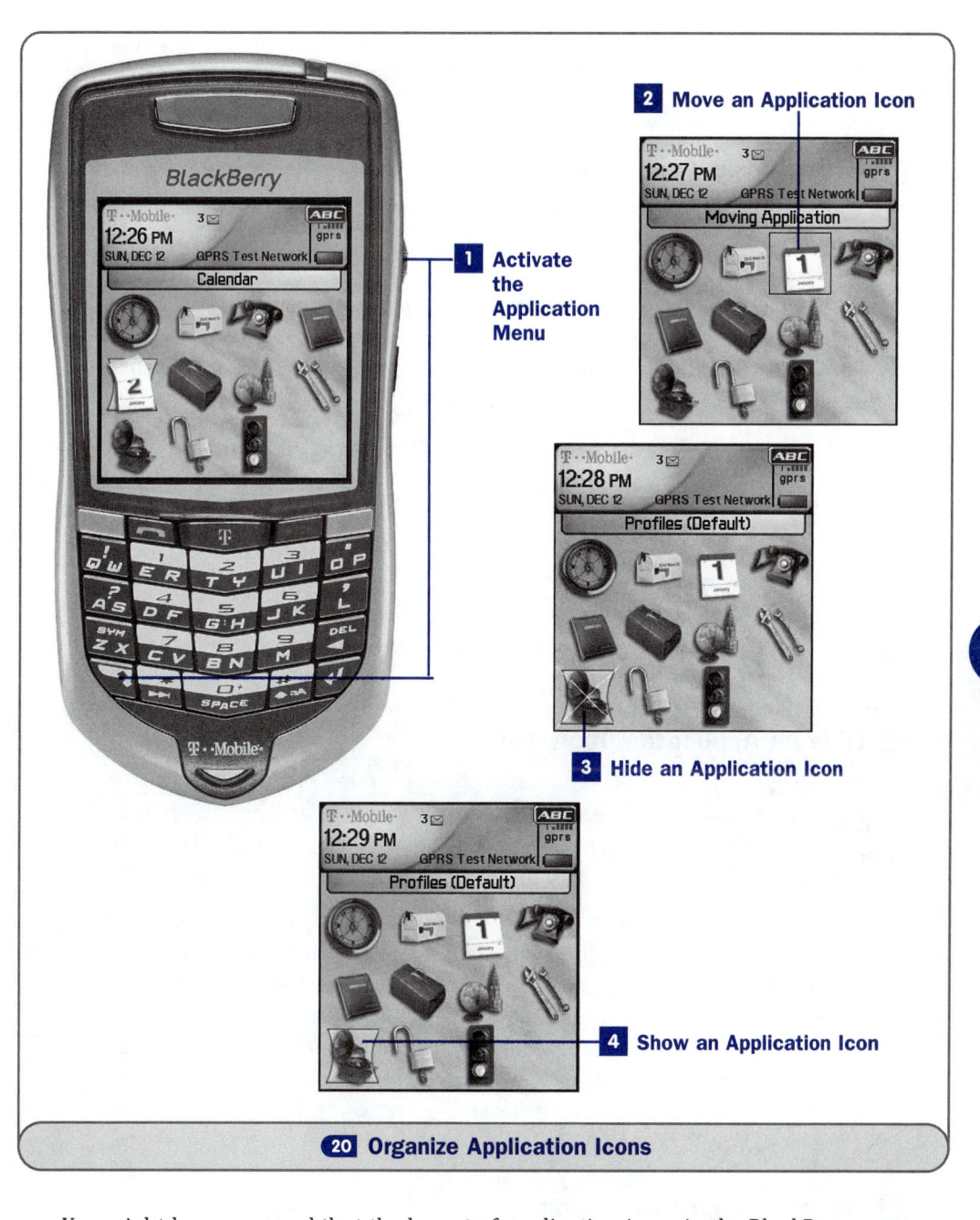

You might have assumed that the layout of application icons in the BlackBerry user interface is set in stone. But like much of the BlackBerry 7100 experience, application icons can be altered to achieve a customized look and feel. More specifically, you can rearrange and even hide icons as you see fit, which is a good idea because there might be applications you never use. I encourage you to move the icons of the most frequently used applications to the top of the screen so they are more accessible and then hide any icons of applications you don't use. You can always go back and rearrange or unhide icons later if you change your mind.

1 Activate the Application Menu

Scroll the trackwheel to select an icon from a screen that displays application icons, such as the **Home** screen. Open the application menu by pressing the **Alt** key and then clicking the trackwheel. The application menu appears and provides commands for moving and hiding applications.

2 Move an Application Icon

Scroll the trackwheel to select **Move Application** from the application menu, and click. The selected application is now highlighted. Scroll the trackwheel to move the application icon around among the other icons on the screen. When you're satisfied with the application's new position, click the trackwheel.

Although moving application icons is handy, a more aggressive, and often more useful, technique involves hiding application icons. To hide an icon, press the **Alt** key and click the trackwheel to display the application menu again.

3 Hide an Application Icon

Scroll to select **Hide Application** from the application menu, and click. The selected application icon disappears from view. Hiding an application icon in this manner is useful if there is an application you never use. It's never a bad idea to remove clutter and streamline the BlackBerry user interface to suit your exact needs.

But what happens if you change your mind and need to show an application icon you've hidden? No problem. Just open the application menu by pressing the **Alt** key and then clicking the trackwheel. The application menu appears and now includes a command for showing all application icons, both visible and hidden. Scroll to select **Show All** from the application menu, and click. The hidden application icon appears with an **X** over it to indicate that it is actually hidden.

4 Show an Application Icon

With the hidden application icon selected, open the application menu again by pressing the **Alt** key and then clicking the trackwheel. You'll notice that the **Hide Application** option is checked to indicate that the application is hidden. Scroll to select **Hide Application** from the menu, and click. The **X** is removed from the selected application to indicate that it is no longer hidden from view.

Now all you have left to do is turn off the **Show All** option to return to the normal application view. Open the application menu once more by pressing the **Alt** key and then clicking the trackwheel. Scroll to select **Show All** from the menu, and click.

21 Change the Wallpaper

✔ BEFORE YOU BEGIN

- **1** About the BlackBerry User Interface

→ SEE ALSO

- **19** Adjust the Screen and Keyboard
- **22** Install a New Theme
- **51** Download New Wallpaper

The background image on BlackBerry screens that show application icons is known as *wallpaper*. And like wallpaper on your desktop or notebook PC, your BlackBerry's wallpaper can be set to any image you choose. Even though the wallpaper appears on more than one screen on your device, it is also sometimes referred to as the *home screen image*. Several images, or pictures, are included by default in every BlackBerry device, and all these images are available for use as wallpaper. You can also download custom images to your device and use them as wallpaper.

1 Open the Applications Screen

Scroll to the **Applications** icon on the **Home** screen and click the trackwheel. The **Applications** screen appears, offering a list of applications you can launch.

2 Launch the Photo Album Application

Scroll to the **Photo Album** application icon and click the trackwheel. The **Photo Album** appears with a list of pictures and their thumbnails.

3 Select a Picture to Use As Wallpaper

You can use any of the pictures in the **Photo Album** as wallpaper that is displayed behind application icons throughout the BlackBerry user interface. Scroll the trackwheel through the list of pictures, and click to select a picture. In the menu that appears, scroll to **Open** and click to open and view the full picture. Press the **Escape** button to return to the list of pictures. You can continue viewing the pictures in this manner until you find the one you want to use as the wallpaper.

CHAPTER 4: Fine-tuning Your BlackBerry

1 Open the Applications Screen

2 Launch the Photo Album Application

3 Select a Picture to Use As Wallpaper

4 View the New Wallpaper

21 Change the Wallpaper

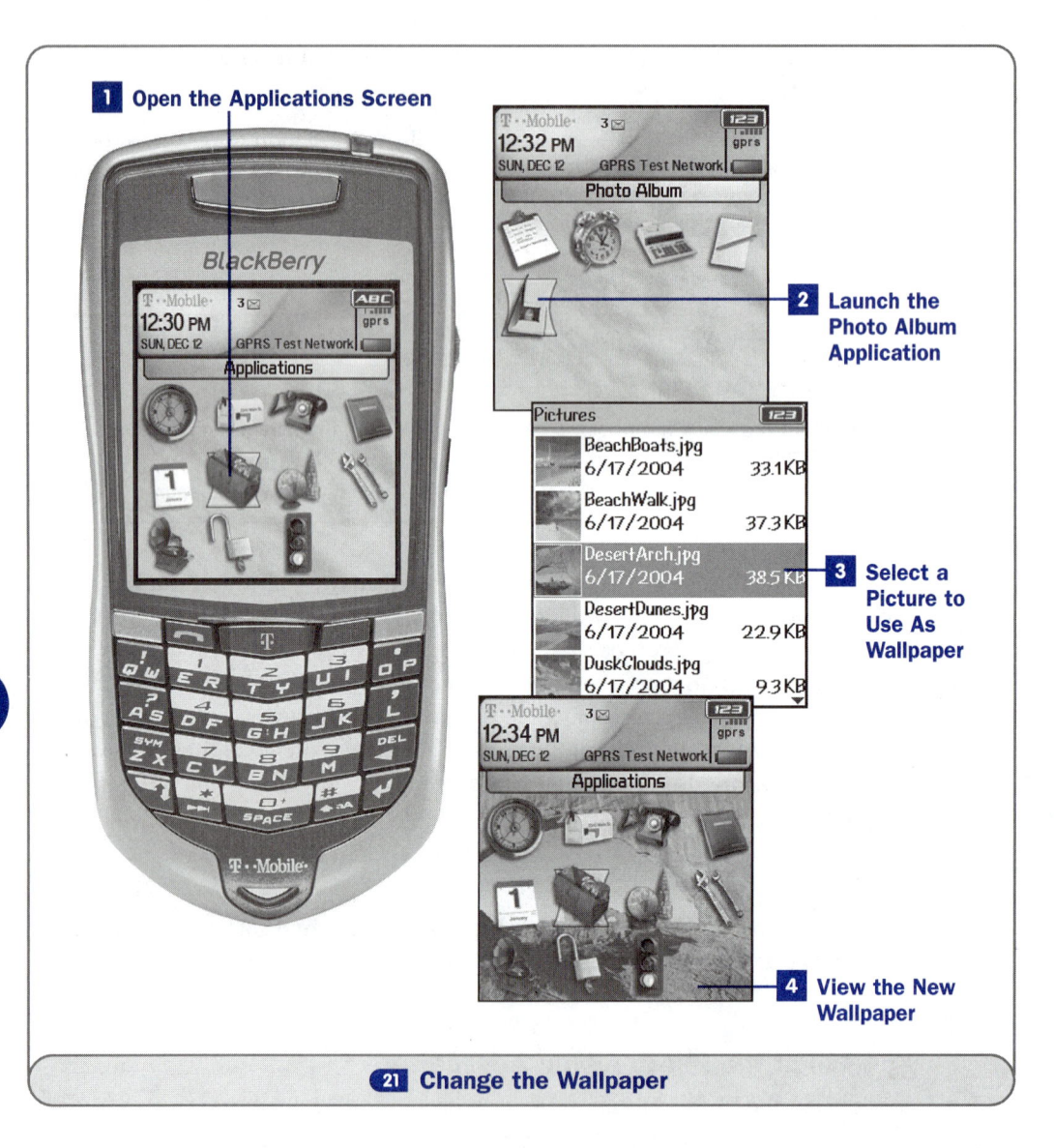

When you decide on a picture to use as wallpaper, scroll the trackwheel to select the picture in the list and click. In the menu that appears, scroll to **Set as Home Screen Image** and click to set the picture as the wallpaper.

▶ **TIP**

You can use your own custom pictures as wallpaper provided that you make them available for download on the Web. You then browse to the picture file using the BlackBerry browser and download it to your device. The picture is stored to the **Photo Album**, where you can set it as wallpaper. See **51** Download New Wallpaper for more details.

▶ **TIP**

To restore the wallpaper to the default picture for the currently selected theme, click any picture in the **Photo Album** with the trackwheel and then click **Reset Home Screen Image** in the menu that appears. See **7** Choose a Theme for more information about changing themes.

4 View the New Wallpaper

Press the **Escape** button to exit the **Photo Album** application. You're then returned to the **Applications** screen, where you can see the new wallpaper behind the application icons. Press the **Escape** button again to navigate back to the **Home** screen, or just press the **End** key.

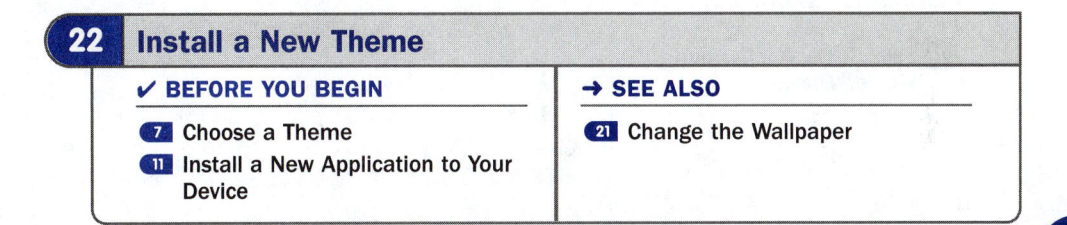

22 Install a New Theme

✔ BEFORE YOU BEGIN	→ SEE ALSO
7 Choose a Theme	**21** Change the Wallpaper
11 Install a New Application to Your Device	

Nothing has a more dramatic impact on the look and feel of your BlackBerry device than the theme. Every device ships with at least one default theme, and usually an extra theme you can use if you so desire. Themes determine the layout, color scheme, font size, and various other user interface components within the BlackBerry operating system. Even if you're happy with the default theme on your device, I encourage you to experiment with some other themes just to see how they work. You might be surprised that a different theme might actually make your device more usable.

1 Download the Theme to Your Desktop PC

After you've located a theme for your device, the first step is to download it to your PC so you can install it to your device. The website from which you are obtaining the theme should provide a link for downloading the theme. When prompted to open or save the downloaded theme file, click **Save** to save the file; you will then get an opportunity to open the file and execute it on your desktop PC after it finishes downloading.

▶ **TIP**

Although a web search for BlackBerry 7100 themes is probably your best bet for finding new themes, you can download the standard Vodafone and T-Mobile themes in a single Zip file from the following URL: http://www.kalkounis.com/files/Themes.zip. You might also want to check a website such as BlackBerry Forums for additional themes. Just visit http://www.blackberryforums.com/ and search for "themes".

CHAPTER 4: Fine-tuning Your BlackBerry

1 Download the Theme to Your Desktop PC

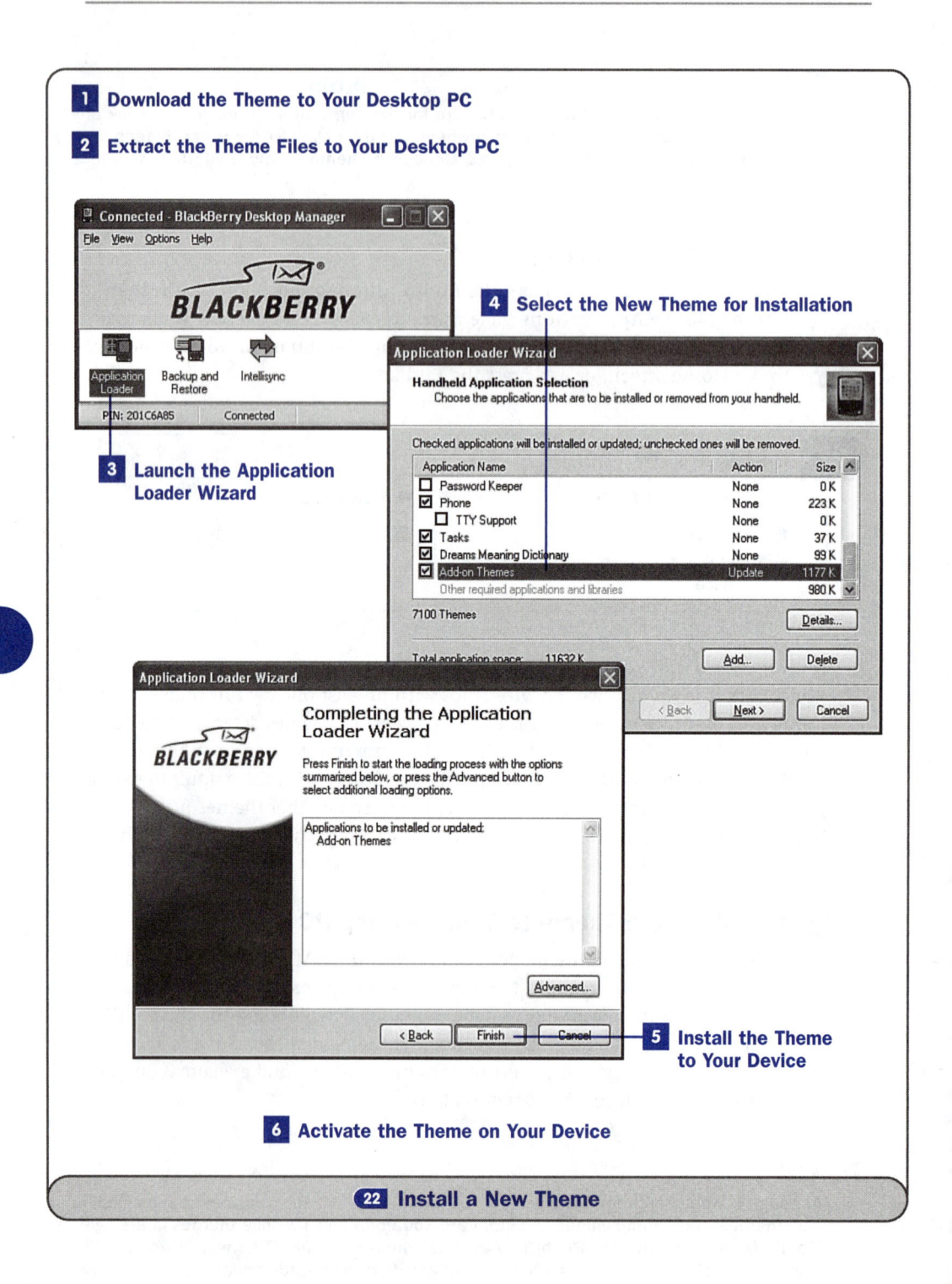

2 Extract the Theme Files to Your Desktop PC

3 Launch the Application Loader Wizard

4 Select the New Theme for Installation

5 Install the Theme to Your Device

6 Activate the Theme on Your Device

22 Install a New Theme

2 Extract the Theme Files to Your Desktop PC

Most themes are stored in compressed Zip files so they take up less space and can be downloaded more quickly. You'll need to unzip the theme by using Windows Explorer to extract the theme files from the Zip file to a new folder. The theme files should include a file that ends in **.alx**, which is the file used by the BlackBerry Desktop Manager to install the theme. There will also be at least one file with an extension of **.cod**, which is the theme itself. After these files are successfully extracted, you're ready to launch the BlackBerry Desktop Manager and install the theme.

▶ **NOTE**

You can download and install several themes at once. In this case, there is still a single **.alx** file but there are multiple **.cod** files—one for each theme.

3 Launch the Application Loader Wizard

With your BlackBerry device plugged in to your desktop PC and turned on, click the **Start** button on the Windows taskbar of your desktop PC to open the Windows **Start** menu. Then select **All Programs**, **BlackBerry**, **Desktop Manager**. The BlackBerry Desktop Manager application appears.

Double-click the **Application Loader** icon in the BlackBerry Desktop Manager. The **Application Loader Wizard** window appears.

4 Select the New Theme for Installation

Click the **Next** button to get started with the Application Loader Wizard. The wizard will take a few moments to analyze your device and then display the **Handheld Application Selection** window. This window includes all the applications installed on your device, including core operating system components. The new theme you are installing is not listed yet because you haven't added it to the list.

▶ **TIP**

You must be careful when using the Application Loader Wizard because it allows you to make sweeping changes to the applications installed on your device, including critical core applications such as the phone and security features. Generally speaking, it's not a good idea to check or uncheck standard applications unless you fully understand the implications.

Click the **Add** button to add the new theme to the list of available applications. Navigate to the folder on your desktop PC where you extracted the theme files. Click the file with the **.alx** extension, and then click the **Open** button. After returning to the **Handheld Application Selection** window, you now see the new theme at the bottom of the application list.

If it isn't already checked, click the check box next to the theme name to select it for installation to your device. Click the **Next** button to continue in the wizard. The completion window of the Application Loader Wizard appears.

5 Install the Theme to Your Device

Click the **Finish** button to install the theme to your device, after which the BlackBerry Desktop Manager automatically synchronizes the device with your desktop PC. The new theme is now installed and ready for activation on your device.

6 Activate the Theme on Your Device

See **7 Choose a Theme** to select the new theme and activate it.

▶ **NOTE**

It's important to note that, when you change themes, any modifications you've made to the screen settings—such as the font family and size—are lost. Each theme defines its own specific font settings that override any customizations you might have made.

PART II

Staying in Touch with Your BlackBerry 7100

IN THIS PART:

CHAPTER 5	Taking Control of Email with the BlackBerry Web Client	97
CHAPTER 6	Digging Deeper into Email and Text Messages	129
CHAPTER 7	Instant Messaging with Your BlackBerry	167
CHAPTER 8	Browsing the Wireless Web	183
CHAPTER 9	BlackBerry As the Ultimate Mobile Phone	211
CHAPTER 10	Using Bluetooth for Short-range Wireless Networking	247

5

Taking Control of Email with the BlackBerry Web Client

IN THIS CHAPTER:

- **23** About Email and the BlackBerry Web Client
- **24** Create a BlackBerry Web Client Account
- **25** Configure Web Client Options
- **26** Import Your Address Book
- **27** Compose an Email Message Using the Web Client
- **28** Create an Auto Reply Message
- **29** Change the Sent from Email Address
- **30** Copy Your Email Messages to Another Account
- **31** Add Another Email Account to the Web Client
- **32** Create an Email Filter

CHAPTER 5:   Taking Control of Email with the BlackBerry Web Client

The BlackBerry Web Client is a web-based email tool that enables you to control your device's wireless email functionality through a web interface. Although this might sound a bit odd at first, the idea makes a lot of sense when you consider that the Web provides a ubiquitous access point for tweaking wireless email options and generally managing your mobile email. You aren't tied to a particular email client application, and you can log on to your account from any computer. Although the BlackBerry Web Client isn't for everyone, especially hardcore corporate email users who have access to the BlackBerry Enterprise Server, it is a godsend for the rest of us who desperately need a simple yet effective means of integrating existing email accounts with our BlackBerry 7100 devices and otherwise keeping our handheld email running smoothly.

23 About Email and the BlackBerry Web Client

→ **SEE ALSO**

24 Create a BlackBerry Web Client Account

There is often confusion among users new to BlackBerry devices regarding email. It seems as if there are a dozen options for how to access and integrate email with your device, and it's hard to tell which options overlap and which ones are really necessary. So let me cut to the chase and attempt to explain the whole email scenario. I'll also point out where the BlackBerry Web Client fits into the email picture because it is an important component of BlackBerry email access.

There are four fundamental approaches to accessing email from your BlackBerry device. Let's take a quick look at each of them:

- **The BlackBerry Web Client**—A web-based email solution for individuals that includes a handheld email account, it also allows you to integrate other existing email accounts into your BlackBerry email. The Web Client is useful for the handheld email account, as well as for anyone with a POP or IMAP email account with an Internet service provider, such as Earthlink, Comcast, Yahoo!, AOL, MSN, or Hotmail. The handheld email account included with the BlackBerry Web Client is a true *push email* account.

▶ **KEY TERM**

Push email—A type of email delivery in which email is sent immediately to the email client without the client having to periodically check for available messages. Push email feels more instantaneous because, when someone sends you an email, as soon as the server receives it, it's sent to your BlackBerry; it doesn't sit on the server and wait until you retrieve it. Sent messages are handled just as efficiently—as soon as you send a message, it is transmitted to the server and pushed to the recipient.

▶ **NOTE**
The BlackBerry Web Client can retrieve and integrate email from up to 10 email accounts.

- **Email forwarding**—An email solution for individuals in which you set a rule in your existing email client to forward messages to your handheld email address. This solution requires a BlackBerry Web Client account but doesn't require you to integrate your existing email accounts with the BlackBerry Web Client.

- **BlackBerry Redirector**—An email solution similar to email forwarding; however, instead of relying on your email client, a special application called the BlackBerry Redirector is installed and used to forward messages from your desktop PC to your BlackBerry device. This solution is primarily geared toward corporate email users who don't have access to the BlackBerry Enterprise Server. The only hitch to this solution is that your computer must be up and running for the BlackBerry Redirector to redirect messages.

- **BlackBerry Enterprise Server**—A server-based email solution for multiple users that involves using the BlackBerry Server software with an email server such as Microsoft Exchange or Lotus Domino. This email solution is powerful and offers complete email synchronization—when you delete a message on your device, it is deleted from your desktop email client. BlackBerry Enterprise Server email is also true push email, which makes it efficient.

▶ **NOTE**
Another email option I neglected to mention involves third-party mobile email applications. You can download and install these email clients on your device in lieu of the default Messages application, which is covered in Chapter 6, "Digging Deeper into Email and Text Messages." These applications are typically designed to tie into an existing POP or IMAP email account. For overall usability, I've found the built-in Messages application to be as good as most third-party options, except in the case of dealing with email attachments; see **35 View an Email Attachment**.

To sum up the various email approaches, the BlackBerry Enterprise Server is by far the best option if you work at a company that offers it or you don't mind shelling out the money to buy and run your own email server. If the BlackBerry Enterprise Server is not an option but you use a corporate email account that isn't easily accessed using POP or IMAP, you will probably need to use the BlackBerry Redirector application to redirect messages to your device. And finally, the BlackBerry Web Client is for everyone else, whether you choose to use only the Web Client account, integrate your email accounts into the Web Client, or forward other email to your Web Client account. Just because I mention it last in this discussion doesn't mean it doesn't do a good job—you'll likely find that the BlackBerry Web Client solves most of your mobile email needs.

▶ **TIP**

If you have multiple email accounts and want to use more than one of them with your BlackBerry device, it's worth pointing out that you can use any combination of the email solutions mentioned here. This flexibility is ultimately what makes BlackBerry such a powerful platform for mobile email.

24 Create a BlackBerry Web Client Account

✔ **BEFORE YOU BEGIN**

23 About Email and the BlackBerry Web Client

→ **SEE ALSO**

25 Configure Web Client Options
26 Import Your Address Book
27 Compose an Email Message Using the Web Client
41 Redirect Messages with the BlackBerry Redirector

Unless you are using corporate email only through the BlackBerry Enterprise Server, your wireless service provider includes a handheld email account as part of your BlackBerry service. Enabling this account is critical for sending and receiving wireless email on your device, as well as for setting up other email accounts so you can receive their email messages on your device. To establish your handheld email account, you must create a BlackBerry Web Client account. This account is associated with your unique device and can only be accessed online using the user ID and password you provide. Of course, you can also access the account wirelessly using your BlackBerry device.

After your BlackBerry Web Client account is set up, you'll be able to begin sending and receiving email wirelessly on your device. Perhaps even more interesting is that you will be able to fine-tune email delivery, organize email messages, and send and receive messages through a web interface thanks to the BlackBerry Web Client.

▶ **NOTE**

If you are exclusively using a corporate email account with the BlackBerry Enterprise Server, you might not need the BlackBerry Web Client. You really need the BlackBerry Web Client only if you aren't using the BlackBerry Enterprise Server or have an additional POP or IMAP email account with an ISP or an account such as Hotmail. Just ask your network administrator whether you have access to the BlackBerry Enterprise Server. If you don't have a network administrator, chances are you need to be using the BlackBerry Web Client! An alternative email option involving a special desktop application called the BlackBerry Redirector can be useful for corporate email accounts that don't use the BlackBerry Enterprise Server; to learn more, see 41 **Redirect Messages with the BlackBerry Redirector**.

24 Create a BlackBerry Web Client Account

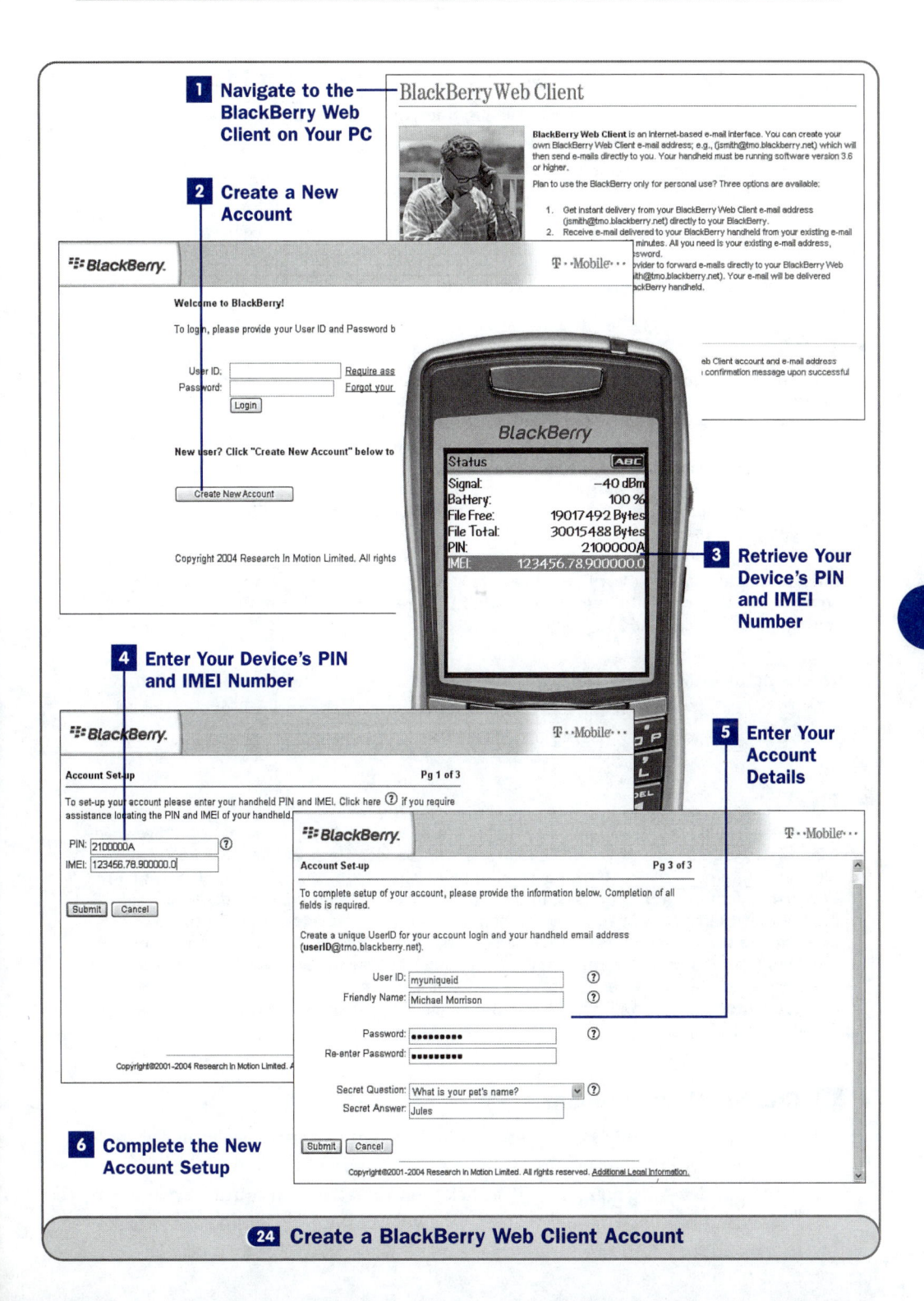

1 Navigate to the BlackBerry Web Client on Your PC

2 Create a New Account

3 Retrieve Your Device's PIN and IMEI Number

4 Enter Your Device's PIN and IMEI Number

5 Enter Your Account Details

6 Complete the New Account Setup

24 Create a BlackBerry Web Client Account

1 Navigate to the BlackBerry Web Client on Your PC

Your wireless service provider will provide you with a link to use for accessing the BlackBerry Web Client. If you don't know the exact link, go to your provider's main website using your computer's web browser and find the BlackBerry Web Client there. As an example, T-Mobile's BlackBerry Web Client is accessible from the following URL on the T-Mobile website: http://www.t-mobile.com/bwc/. You must enter your mobile phone number to gain access to the BlackBerry Web Client.

▶ **TIPS**

The BlackBerry Web Client is actually hosted on Research In Motion's BlackBerry site. In reality, your wireless provider is linking to the BlackBerry site. If you have trouble finding the BlackBerry Web Client for your wireless provider, try tinkering with the following link: https://webclient.blackberry.net/WebMail/Window.jsp?site=Rogers&locale=en. The part you're tinkering with is the word between site= and &locale, which in this case is Rogers. This word is the name of your wireless service provider—in this example, Rogers Wireless in Canada. In the case of T-Mobile in the United States, use the same link but change Rogers to tmo.

Be sure to add the BlackBerry Web Client link to your web browser favorites/bookmarks so you can easily return to it later. In Internet Explorer, select **Favorites** from the main menu and then select **Add to Favorites**.

Using the T-Mobile website as an example, after entering your phone number and clicking the little button with the arrows on it, the main BlackBerry Web Client page appears, asking for a user ID and password.

▶ **NOTE**

Some wireless service providers open the BlackBerry Web Client in a separate browser window. Newer versions of Windows (starting with Service Pack 2) include a pop-up blocker in Internet Explorer that blocks all pop-up windows by default. Although this can be a useful feature in many cases, in this particular case it can prevent you from accessing the BlackBerry Web Client. The solution is to add your provider's website as an exception to the pop-up blocker. To do this, select **Tools**, **Pop-up Blocker**, **Pop-up Blocker Settings** from the main Internet Explorer menu. In the **Pop-up Blocker Settings** window, enter the name of your wireless provider's website, like this: *.t-mobile.com. Then click the **Add** button and you will have enabled pop-ups for your wireless provider. Click the **Close** button to finish.

2 Create a New Account

Although you already have a wireless account with your service provider, the BlackBerry Web Client requires its own separate account that is associated with your device's phone number. Click the **Create New Account** button to begin creating a new account. Later, you will use the **User ID** and **Password** entry fields to log in to your newly created BlackBerry Web Client account.

24 Create a BlackBerry Web Client Account

The first **Account Set-up** page appears and requires two important pieces of information: your device's PIN and *IMEI* number. Fortunately, this information is readily available on your device.

▶ **KEY TERM**

IMEI—Stands for International Mobile Equipment Identity, which is a unique number assigned to every mobile device. This number is often used by wireless service providers to tie your device to their networks. Some software vendors also use the IMEI number to associate purchased applications with your device in an attempt to prevent piracy.

3 Retrieve Your Device's PIN and IMEI Number

To retrieve your device's PIN and IMEI number, pick up your BlackBerry device, scroll to the **Tools** icon on the **Home** screen, and click the trackwheel. The **Tools** screen appears, offering a list of tools options. Scroll to the **Settings** icon and click the trackwheel. Then scroll to the **Status** option in the list of settings and click the trackwheel. The **Status** screen opens and lists the PIN and IMEI number for your device.

▶ **TIP**

You can also retrieve the IMEI number for your device by launching the Phone application and entering *#06# as a phone number to dial; you don't have to use the **Alt** key to enter the numbers because the Phone application defaults to numeric input mode. The device returns the IMEI number instead of making a call.

With this information in hand, return your attention to the first BlackBerry Web Client **Account Set-up** page on your desktop web browser.

4 Enter Your Device's PIN and IMEI Number

In the two edit fields on the first **Account Set-up** page, enter the PIN and IMEI number exactly as they appear on your device's **Status** screen. Then click the **Submit** button to continue the account creation process.

The next **Account Set-up** page prompts you to accept the licensing agreement for the BlackBerry Web Client. Click the **I Agree** button to accept the licensing agreement and continue to the third **Account Set-up** page.

5 Enter Your Account Details

The third **Account Set-up** page prompts you to enter a user ID, friendly name, password, secret question, and secret answer. The user ID is a unique ID that you will use from here on to log in and access your BlackBerry Web Client account. The friendly name is the name that appears for you alongside your email address when messages are sent from the BlackBerry Web Client.

CHAPTER 5: Taking Control of Email with the BlackBerry Web Client

▶ **NOTE**
The user ID you choose for your BlackBerry Web Client account also serves as the basis for your handheld email account. For example, the user ID of **myuniqueid** means the T-Mobile handheld email address will be **myuniqueid@tmo.blackberry.net**. When choosing a user ID, keep in mind that it also serves as your email address. Also keep in mind that it must be unique among all other BlackBerry Web Client users, which means you might have to tack on some numbers to the end of the ID if you choose a common name or phrase.

The password is made up entirely by you and is used in conjunction with your user ID to securely log in to the BlackBerry Web Client. And finally, the secret question and answer come into play in the event that you forget your password and have to request it from Research In Motion (RIM). You will be asked the secret question and then must provide the secret answer to receive your password or have a new one issued. Be sure to choose a secret question you will remember the answer to, yet one that others don't readily know.

After entering the account information and clicking the **Submit** button, your new BlackBerry Web Client account is created. A completion page appears that notifies you of your user ID and handheld email address.

24

6 Complete the New Account Setup

Your new BlackBerry Web Client account is now set up, and you have a new handheld email address to show for it. Be sure to write down or otherwise remember this email address. Keep in mind that you can hide this Web Client email address when you send email from your device if you'd rather have another email address appear for consistency; see **29 Change the Sent from Email Address**.

25 Configure Web Client Options

✔ BEFORE YOU BEGIN	→ SEE ALSO
24 Create a BlackBerry Web Client Account	**26** Import Your Address Book
	32 Create an Email Filter

The BlackBerry Web client is a full-featured email client that provides all the expected bells and whistles you might find in a traditional email application, plus a few options tailored specifically to mobile email. It's important that you get a handle on the options available to you within the BlackBerry Web Client and tweak them to suit your particular email needs.

25 Configure Web Client Options

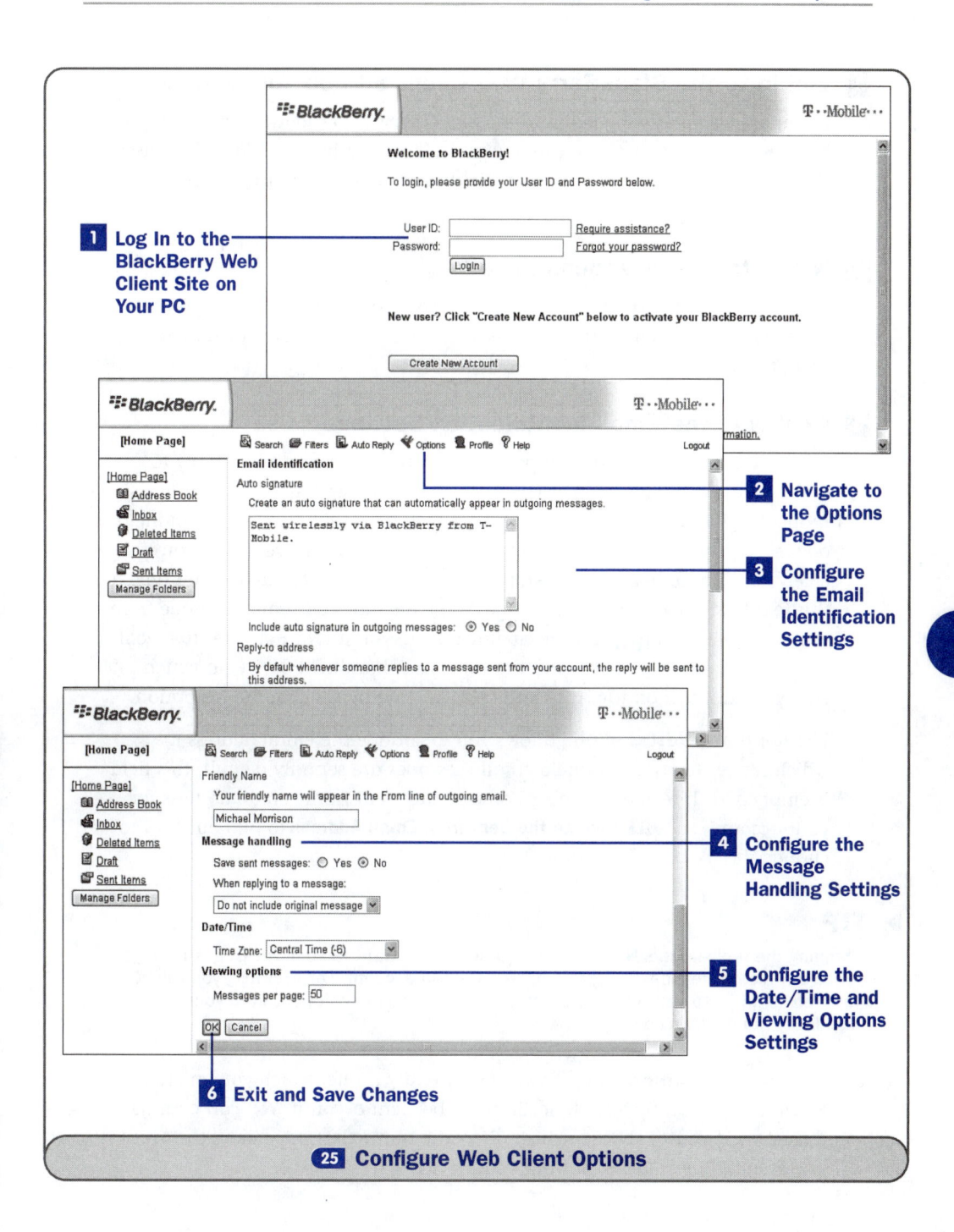

1 Log In to the BlackBerry Web Client Site on Your PC

2 Navigate to the Options Page

3 Configure the Email Identification Settings

4 Configure the Message Handling Settings

5 Configure the Date/Time and Viewing Options Settings

6 Exit and Save Changes

25 Configure Web Client Options

1 Log In to the BlackBerry Web Client Site on Your PC

If you aren't already logged in to the BlackBerry Web Client, navigate to the **BlackBerry Web Client** site using your desktop web browser. Enter your user ID and password in the appropriate fields and click the **Login** button to log in.

2 Navigate to the Options Page

Click the **Options** icon on the top BlackBerry Web Client menu to open the **Options** page, which provides access to a variety of options related to your account.

3 Configure the Email Identification Settings

The **Email identification** settings consist of an auto signature, a reply-to address, and a friendly name. The **Auto signature** setting is useful in automatically calling out in your emails that they were sent from your handheld device, as opposed to your desktop email account. In the event that you receive both handheld and desktop emails to your device, the text you type in this text box helps clarify to message recipients that you sent a message from your device. Of course, in some circumstances, you might not want to reveal that email messages are originating from your handheld device, in which case you can turn off the **Auto signature** setting by clicking the **No** option.

The **Reply-to address** setting allows you to change the email address to which replies to your handheld email messages are sent. By default, this field is empty, which results in replies going to the "sent from" email address for your account. See **29 Change the Sent from Email Address** to find out how to change the "sent from" address.

▶ **TIP**

Changing the reply-to address can be useful when you want to send messages from your device but receive responses using a different email account. For example, you might want replies to go to your primary corporate email account, as opposed to your BlackBerry handheld account.

The **Friendly Name** setting shows your friendly name, which you entered when you first set up your BlackBerry Web Client account. You can change this name if you so choose, which alters the name that appears in the **From** line of email messages sent from your device.

4 Configure the Message Handling Settings

The **Message handling** settings on the **Options** page allow you to save a copy of sent messages and include or attach the original message to message replies you send. Unless you really need a history of sent handheld emails and you don't mind cleaning up your **Deleted Items** folder on a regular basis, I recommend turning off the **Save sent messages** option. Otherwise, your email storage space can get eaten up rather quickly.

▶ **NOTE**

Allotted email storage space varies among wireless service providers; for example, T-Mobile gives you 10MB of space for your BlackBerry Web Client email messages. Although this might seem like a lot of space, when you factor in email attachments, it can still get exhausted If you aren't careful. By *careful*, I mean deleting any messages you don't need anymore, especially those with attachments.

5 Configure the Date/Time and Viewing Options Settings

The last block of settings on the **Options** page consists of **Date/Time** and **Viewing options** settings. The **Date/Time** setting simply determines the time zone used for messages sent through the BlackBerry Web Client, whereas the **Viewing options** setting specifies the maximum number of messages displayed on the Web page at a time. The **Viewing options** setting is purely up to your own tastes—I prefer scrolling through a big list of messages as opposed to clicking from page to page, so I cranked the setting up to **50**.

6 Exit and Save Changes

When you're finished configuring the BlackBerry Web Client options, click the **OK** button to finish and accept the changes. If, for some reason, you want to back out of any changes you've made, just click the **Cancel** button instead.

---

26 Import Your Address Book

✔ **BEFORE YOU BEGIN**

24 Create a BlackBerry Web Client Account

→ **SEE ALSO**

25 Configure Web Client Options
31 Add Another Email Account to the Web Client

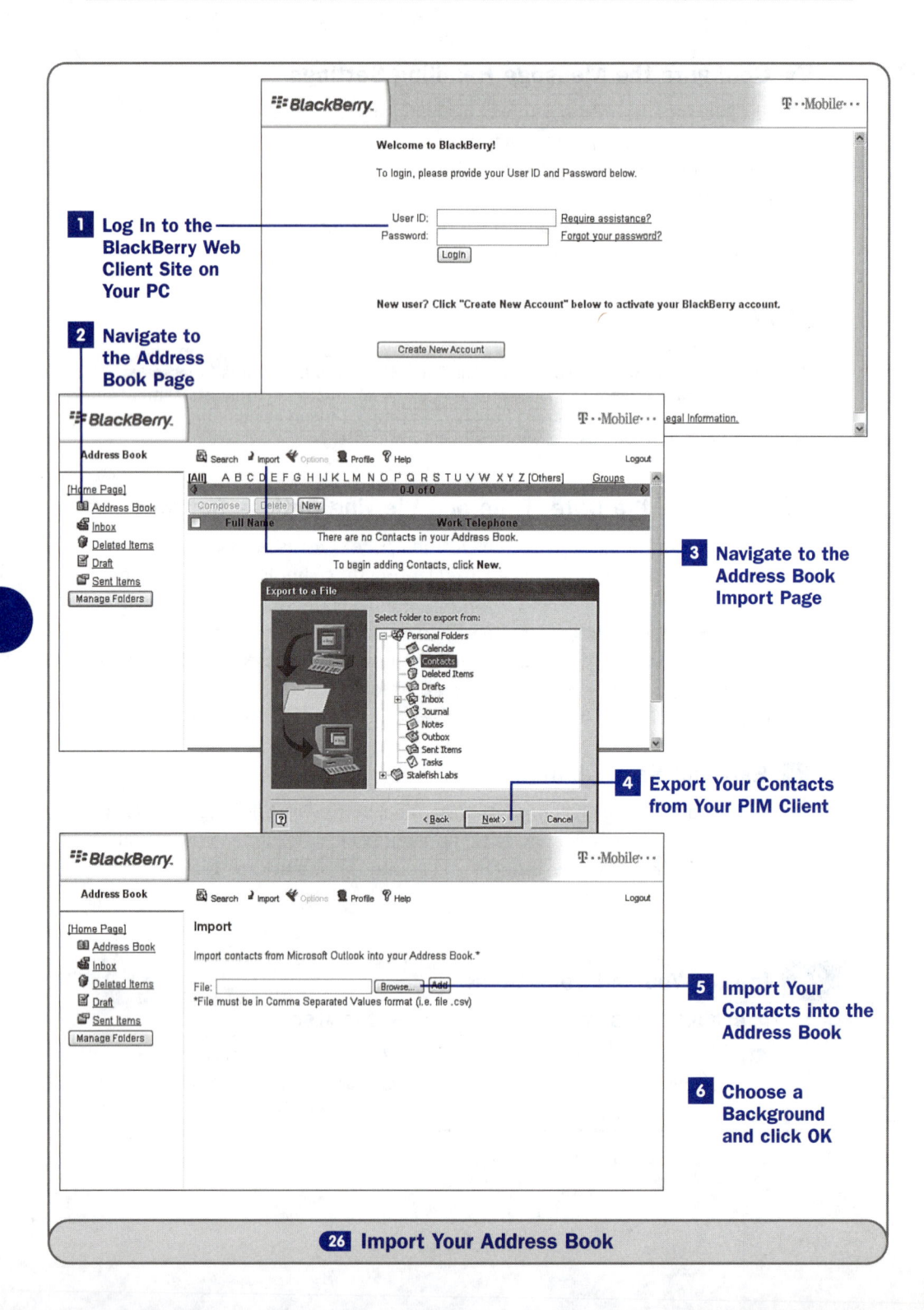

CHAPTER 5: Taking Control of Email with the BlackBerry Web Client

1 Log In to the BlackBerry Web Client Site on Your PC

2 Navigate to the Address Book Page

3 Navigate to the Address Book Import Page

4 Export Your Contacts from Your PIM Client

5 Import Your Contacts into the Address Book

6 Choose a Background and click OK

26 Import Your Address Book

26 Import Your Address Book

The cornerstone of any useful email application is the list of contacts to which you can send email messages. Although you can certainly enter an email address the slow way, it's much more efficient to simply enter it once for a particular contact and then reference that contact to send email messages. Of course, this approach requires you to enter the email addresses of all your contacts, which I suspect is a chore you've already carried out in your current email client software. Knowing this, an even more efficient approach to getting your current contact list into your BlackBerry device involves importing your existing contacts into the BlackBerry Web Client Address Book, which instantly gives you access to your full contact list without having to reenter any information.

The Web Client Address Book provides a feature for importing contacts from an email or *PIM client*—provided that you export it from the client application in the appropriate format (CSV). Assuming that your client application supports the *CSV* format, you can export and then import contacts into the BlackBerry Web Client with very little effort. Microsoft Outlook provides export functionality that works great for this task, but even if you use a different client application, you might find that it is equally capable of exporting the contacts in the CSV format.

▶ KEY TERMS

PIM client—Stands for personal information management client, an application used to access and manage personal information such as contacts, appointments, and tasks.

CSV—Stands for Comma Separated Values, a file format in which text data is listed in order and separated by commas. Many popular productivity applications such as Microsoft Outlook and Excel allow you to import and export data in CSV format.

1 Log In to the BlackBerry Web Client Site on Your PC

If you aren't already logged in to the BlackBerry Web Client, navigate to the **BlackBerry Web Client** site using your desktop web browser. Enter your user ID and password in the appropriate fields, and click the **Login** button to log in.

2 Navigate to the Address Book Page

Click the **Address Book** icon on the left side of the BlackBerry Web Client page to open the **Address Book** page, which displays the BlackBerry Web Client online Address Book.

3 Navigate to the Address Book Import Page

Click the **Import** icon on the top BlackBerry Web Client menu to open the Address Book **Import** page, which provides access to the Address Book's import feature. This feature allows you to import contact data in the CSV format.

4 Export Your Contacts from Your PIM Client

Before you can import data into the BlackBerry Web Client Address Book, you must first export it using PIM client software that supports the CSV format, such as Microsoft Outlook. In Microsoft Outlook, you export contacts by selecting **File**, **Import and Export**. The **Import and Export Wizard** appears, which allows you to export Address Book contacts in the CSV format.

▶ **TIP**

If you don't use Microsoft Outlook as your email client, check to see whether your email client supports exporting its address book as a CSV file. If not, you won't be able to import your existing address book into the BlackBerry Web Client.

Select **Export to a file** as the action to perform in the **Import and Export Wizard**; then click the **Next** button. Then select **Comma Separated Values (Windows)** as the type of file to be created, and click **Next** again. Then select **Contacts** as the only folder to export, and click **Next** again. And finally, enter the name and location of the file to contain the exported CSV data, and click **Next** once more. Click the **Finish** button on the final page of the wizard to export the data to the specified file.

Now you're ready to import contacts from the newly created CSV file into the BlackBerry Web Client Address Book. So, turn your attention back to the Address Book **Import** page.

5 Import Your Contacts into the Address Book

The Address Book **Import** page prompts you to enter the name of the CSV file that contains your contact data to be imported. Click the **Browse** button and browse your PC to find the file you created in step 4. Then click the **Add** button to import the contacts from the file and add them to the Web Client Address Book.

▶ **NOTE**

Unfortunately, the contacts in the BlackBerry Web Client Address Book are in no way synchronized with your PIM client or your BlackBerry device. So, if you want to update the contacts in the Web Client Address Book, you'll need to delete the contacts in the Web Client and reimport them from your PIM client; if you reimport without first deleting the existing contacts, you'll end up with duplicates.

27 Compose an Email Message Using the Web Client

✔ BEFORE YOU BEGIN

24 Create a BlackBerry Web Client Account

→ SEE ALSO

26 Import Your Address Book
29 Change the Sent from Email Address
34 Compose an Email Message

The BlackBerry Web Client isn't just an online repository for mobile email; it's a full-blown online email client. This means you can use it to carry out tasks common to any email client, such as composing email messages and sending them purely through the Web Client interface. What this means is that you actually have two options for sending email using your handheld email account. You can compose messages on your device and send them wirelessly through your device's data connection, or you can compose them through a web browser and the BlackBerry Web Client and send them over the Internet. Both approaches yield the same result of sending a message through your handheld email account.

Composing a message and sending it through the BlackBerry Web Client is straightforward and is the focus of this task. If you want to learn how to compose a message on your device and send it wirelessly, see **34** **Compose an Email Message**.

1 Log In to the BlackBerry Web Client Site on Your PC

If you aren't already logged in to the BlackBerry Web Client, navigate to the **BlackBerry Web Client** site using your desktop web browser. Enter your user ID and password in the appropriate fields, and click the **Login** button to log in.

2 Navigate to the Inbox Page

Click the **Inbox** icon on the left side of the BlackBerry Web Client menu to open the **Inbox** page, which shows the contents of the **Inbox** folder that contains your received email messages.

3 Start Composing a New Email Message

Click the **New** button on the **Inbox** page to begin composing a new email message. The **New – Message** page appears.

CHAPTER 5: Taking Control of Email with the BlackBerry Web Client

1 Log In to the BlackBerry Web Client Site on Your PC

3 Start Composing a New Email Message

2 Navigate to the Inbox Page

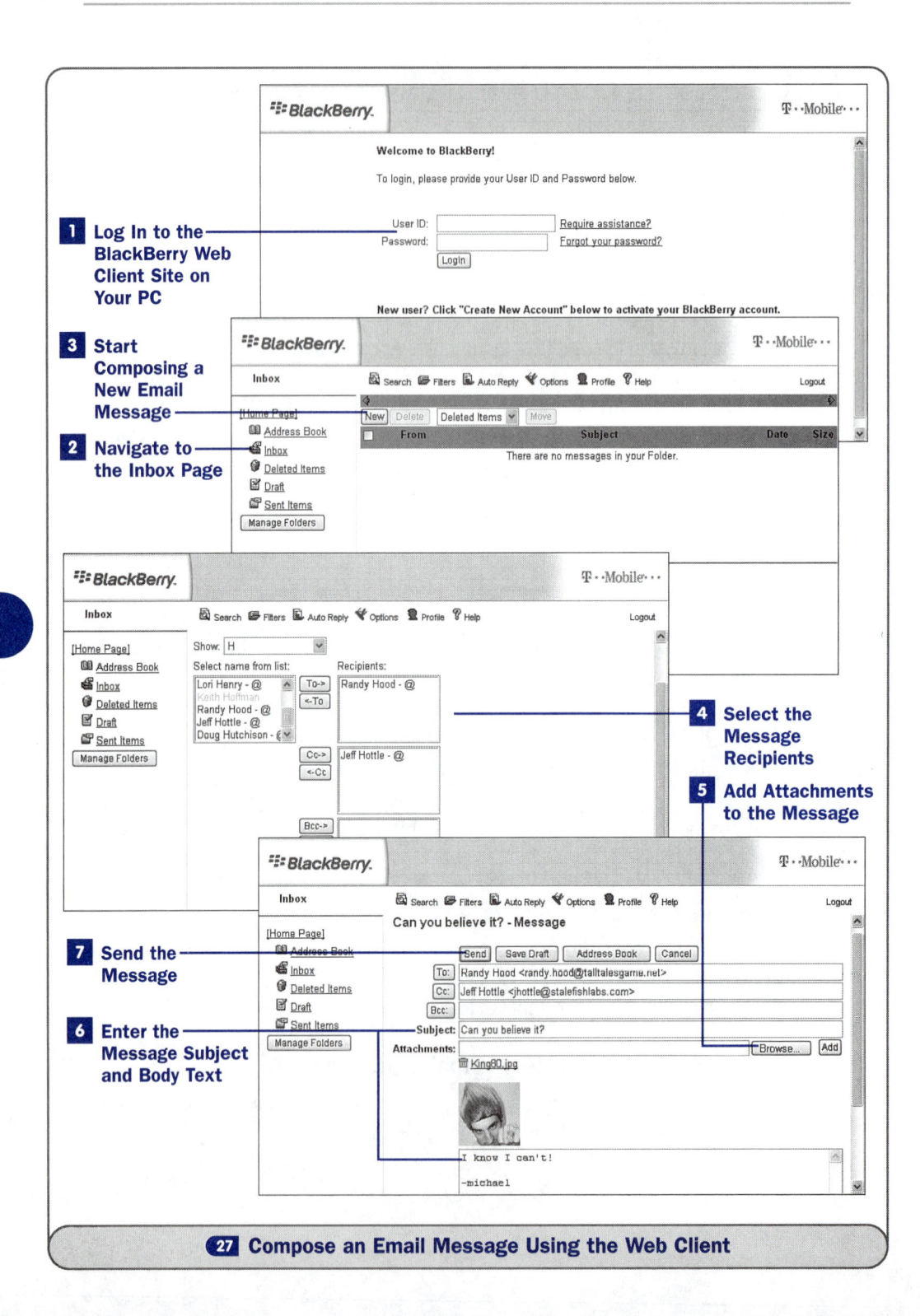

4 Select the Message Recipients

5 Add Attachments to the Message

7 Send the Message

6 Enter the Message Subject and Body Text

27 Compose an Email Message Using the Web Client

4 Select the Message Recipients

The **New – Message** page includes several fields that allow you to specify the message recipients, as well as the subject of the message, the attachments, and the message body itself. Before getting into the subject or body of the message, you need to specify exactly who is receiving the message. To do this, you can enter email addresses directly into the **To**, **Cc**, and **Bcc** fields just as you would in any other email client. If you want to make things easier on yourself, you can select the email recipients from your Address Book. For the Address Book to be useful, you should consider importing contacts from your PIM client, such as Microsoft Outlook. See **26 Import Your Address Book**.

▶ **NOTE**

Importing contacts into the Address Book isn't critical for sending email, but it is a nice convenience. However, if your PIM client doesn't allow you to export contacts in the CSV format, you'll have to settle for entering email recipients manually. (See **68 Create and Manage Contacts**.) Keep in mind that you can also create and add contacts to the Address Book in the BlackBerry Web Client independently of any contacts you import. You can then select them as email recipients just as you select contacts you imported.

To select email message recipients from your Address Book, click the **To**, **Cc**, or **Bcc** button. The **Select Names** page appears and provides access to your list of contacts as well as to each of the three types of recipient fields (**To**, **Cc**, and **Bcc**). You can easily navigate to a subset of the Address Book by selecting a letter in the **Show** drop-down list. Only contacts whose last names begin with that letter are shown. You then click a contact in the contact list to select it and then click the appropriate recipient button (**To**, **Cc**, or **Bcc**).

When you're finished selecting message recipients, click the **OK** button to return to the **New – Message** page and continue composing the message.

5 Add Attachments to the Message

You can add attachments to a message sent from the BlackBerry Web Client very easily. Just click the **Browse** button next to the **Attachments** field and browse to find the attachment. After you've located the file and accepted it, click the **Add** button to add it to the message as an attachment. For images, you'll see the name of the file along with a picture of the image. For other file types, you'll just see the name of the file. All attachments are shown with a little trash can next to the filename that allows you to delete the attachment if you change your mind about sending it.

After you've added any attachments to the message, you're ready to enter the most important information of all: the message subject and body.

6 Enter the Message Subject and Body Text

The subject of the message is entered in the **Subject** field just above the **Attachments** line. The body text of the message is entered just below the **Attachments** line in the large edit field. There really aren't any tricks or secrets associated with composing the message text—just type what you want to say!

7 Send the Message

When you're finished composing the message, you can either send it immediately or save it to continue working on later. To save the message for later, click the **Save Draft** button. The message will be available for future editing and sending by clicking the **Draft** icon on the left side of the page and viewing the **Draft** folder.

To send the message immediately, click the **Send** button. The message is sent to the specified recipient(s). If you have set your BlackBerry Web Client options to save a copy of each message sent, a copy of the message will be saved in the **Sent Items** folder. To view this folder, click the **Sent Items** icon on the left side of the page. To change the **Save Sent Items** setting, see **25 Configure Web Client Options**.

28 Create an Auto Reply Message

✔ BEFORE YOU BEGIN	→ SEE ALSO
24 Create a BlackBerry Web Client Account	29 Change the Sent from Email Address
	30 Copy Your Email Messages to Another Account

If you use your handheld email account as a distinct account separate from your primary email account, you might want to clarify to people who send messages to your handheld account that you are away and might not reply as quickly as normal. For example, you may be traveling and not have constant wireless service, in which case you won't be able to reply as readily as you might from your desktop PC. Or maybe you just aren't the kind of person to immediately reply to every mobile email when you're out and about. Either way, you can benefit from adding an auto reply message to your handheld account, which is possible in the BlackBerry Web Client. The auto reply message you set is automatically sent in response to any messages sent to your handheld email account.

28 Create an Auto Reply Message

1 Log In to the BlackBerry Web Client Site on Your PC

2 Navigate to the Auto Reply Page

3 Enter an Auto Reply Message

4 Exit and Save Changes

28 Create an Auto Reply Message

1 Log In to the BlackBerry Web Client Site on Your PC

If you aren't already logged in to the BlackBerry Web Client, navigate to the **BlackBerry Web Client** site using your desktop web browser. Enter your user ID and password in the appropriate fields, and click the **Login** button to log in.

2 Navigate to the Auto Reply Page

Click the **Auto Reply** icon on the top BlackBerry Web Client menu to open the **Auto Reply** page, which allows you to specify an auto reply message that is sent in response to messages received by your handheld email account.

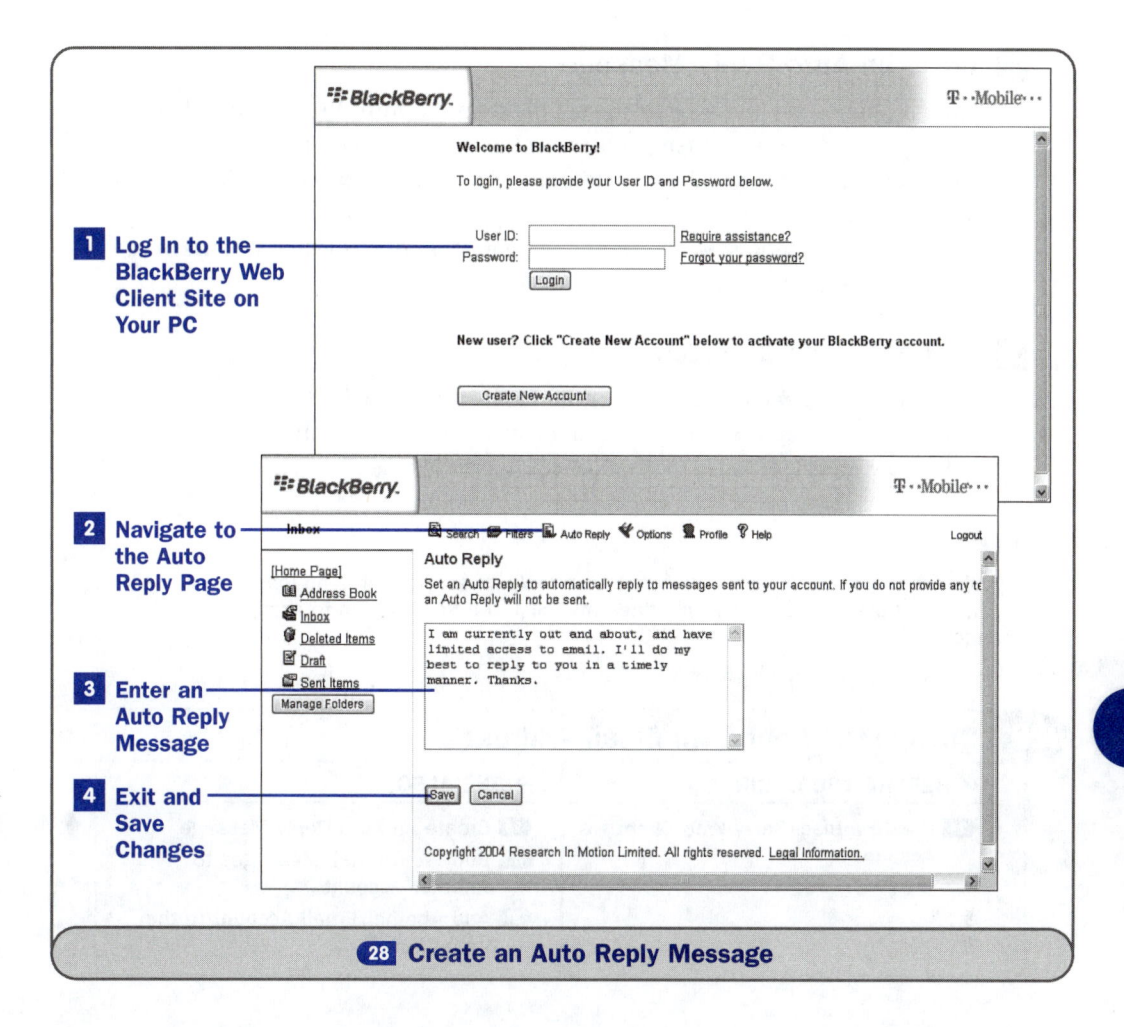

3 Enter an Auto Reply Message

Enter an auto reply message in the edit field on the **Auto Reply** page. This message is automatically sent as an email in response to all messages received by your handheld email account. If no text is provided in the auto reply message (the default setting), no auto reply message is sent. An auto reply message is a good way to notify people if you are traveling or otherwise aren't able to respond to messages in a timely manner.

4 Exit and Save Changes

When you're finished entering the auto reply message, click the **Save** button to finish and accept the changes. If, for some reason, you want to cancel the auto reply message, just click the **Cancel** button instead.

▶ **TIP**

If you'd like to get rid of a previously set auto reply message so it is no longer sent, clear out the edit field on the **Auto Reply** page and click the **Save** button to accept the change.

29 Change the Sent from Email Address

✔ BEFORE YOU BEGIN	→ SEE ALSO
24 Create a BlackBerry Web Client Account	28 Create an Auto Reply Message
	30 Copy Your Email Messages to Another Account
	31 Add Another Email Account to the Web Client

It might sound strange at first, but you might not want everyone to see the handheld email address that was provided to you when you first created your BlackBerry Web Client account. I'm not talking so much about a security issue as I am a consistency issue. You might want to present a consistent email address to the people with whom you communicate via email, regardless of whether you're sitting in front of your desk or rounding the turn on the back nine of your local golf course. In the latter example, you might not want clients to know you're on the golf course when replying to their messages. The solution is to alter the sent from email address for your device so that it looks as if the message came from your normal email account. Of course, for this effect to work, you should be sure not to include an auto signature for the BlackBerry Web Client; see 25 **Configure Web Client Options**.

29 Change the Sent from Email Address

1 Log In to the BlackBerry Web Client Site on Your PC

2 Navigate to the Profile Page

3 Navigate to the Sent from Address Page

4 Enter the Sent from Email Address

5 Exit and Save Changes

29 Change the Sent from Email Address

Changing your sent from address doesn't have to be about tricking people into thinking you're at work, however. It serves just as vital a purpose for simply not confusing people. If you set your primary email account so mail is delivered to your handheld (see **31** **Add Another Email Account to the Web Client**), there's no reason not to have that same email address shown as the sent from address when you reply to messages from your device. Otherwise, a subsequent reply to one of your handheld messages will only make it to your handheld, in which case you might miss it when you return to your desktop PC. This is one of those issues that has a great deal to do with your own personal work style and how often you move back and forth between your desktop PC and your BlackBerry device for email management.

1 Log In to the BlackBerry Web Client Site on Your PC

If you aren't already logged in to the BlackBerry Web Client, navigate to the **BlackBerry Web Client** site using your desktop web browser. Enter your user ID and password in the appropriate fields, and click the **Login** button to log in.

2 Navigate to the Profile Page

Click the **Profile** icon on the top BlackBerry Web Client menu to open the **Profile** page, which provides access to a variety of options related to your Web Client account profile.

3 Navigate to the Sent from Address Page

Click the **Sent From Address** link on the **Profile** page to access the **Sent From Address** settings. The **Sent From Address** page appears and allows you to enter a sent from email address for your account.

4 Enter the Sent from Email Address

You have some options when it comes to specifying your sent from email address. You can leave the sent from address as your handheld email address, which is the default setting. Alternatively, you can select from a list of additional email accounts to be used as the sent from address. To do this, you must have already added the email account you want to specify as your sent from address to the BlackBerry Web Client; see **31 Add Another Email Account to the Web Client**.

The third option for the sent from email address allows you to set the address to any email address of your choosing. Just click the third radio button and type the email address you want to use as the sent from address in the **Sent From Address** edit field. Keep in mind that the idea behind this address setting is to reveal to message recipients a certain address to which they can send email replies. This can be your desktop email address or even a special mobile email address like I've shown in the example. This setting is somewhat similar to the reply-to address you can set for your main handheld email account.

30 Copy Your Email Messages to Another Account

▶ **TIP**

If you have access to your main mailbox settings, you might want to create an alias for a mobile email account, such as traveling.yourname@yourdomain.com or mobile.yourname@yourdomain.com. As an example, for me, this alias could be mobile.mmorrison@stalefishlabs.com. You can then set this alias to point to your handheld email account and also set it as the sent from address in the BlackBerry Web Client. The idea with using aliases is to provide a more consistent email address that is easier to remember than the handheld email address you were given by your wireless service provider.

5 Exit and Save Changes

When you're satisfied with the sent from address setting, click the **Submit** button to finish and accept the changes. If you change your mind about altering the sent from address, just click the **Cancel** button to exit without saving the changes.

---

30 Copy Your Email Messages to Another Account

✔ **BEFORE YOU BEGIN**

24 Create a BlackBerry Web Client Account

→ **SEE ALSO**

28 Create an Auto Reply Message
29 Change the Sent from Email Address
31 Add Another Email Account to the Web Client

Depending on how you use your BlackBerry device and what kinds of email messages you send, you might find it helpful to keep a record of all the messages you send from your device. For example, if you travel and want a history of the mobile email messages you sent to customers while on the road, consider copying the messages to another email account that is used on a desktop computer to help save storage space on your BlackBerry device. The BlackBerry Web Client provides an option for sending a copy of every sent message to another account. You can easily turn the option on and off as needed, which is probably how you'll find yourself using it.

1 Log In to the BlackBerry Web Client Site on Your PC

If you aren't already logged in to the BlackBerry Web Client, navigate to the **BlackBerry Web Client** site using your desktop web browser. Enter your user ID and password in the appropriate fields, and click the **Login** button to log in.

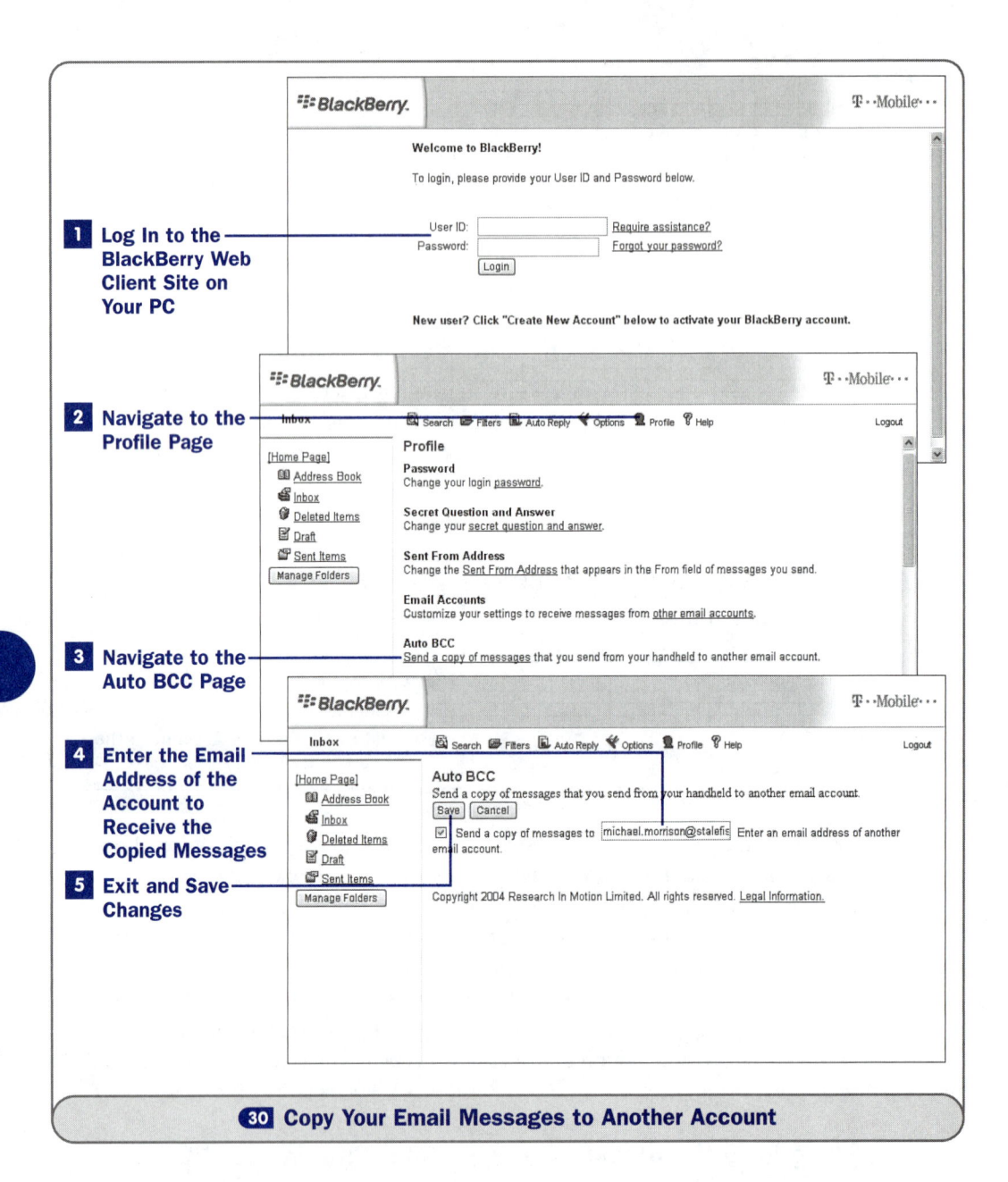

120 CHAPTER 5: Taking Control of Email with the BlackBerry Web Client

1 Log In to the BlackBerry Web Client Site on Your PC

2 Navigate to the Profile Page

3 Navigate to the Auto BCC Page

4 Enter the Email Address of the Account to Receive the Copied Messages

5 Exit and Save Changes

30 Copy Your Email Messages to Another Account

2 Navigate to the Profile Page

Click the **Profile** icon on the top BlackBerry Web Client menu to open the **Profile** page, which provides access to a variety of options related to your account profile.

31 Add Another Email Account to the Web Client

3 Navigate to the Auto BCC Page

Click the **Send a copy of messages** link under the **Auto BCC** heading on the **Profile** page to access the **Auto BCC** settings. The **Auto BCC** page appears and allows you to enter an email address to receive copied messages from the BlackBerry Web Client.

4 Enter the Email Address of the Account to Receive the Copied Messages

To send a copy of sent handheld email messages to another email account, first enable the **Send a copy of messages to** check box just under the **Auto BCC** heading on the **Auto BCC** page. Then enter the email address into the edit field just to the right of the check box. This email address will then receive a copy of any messages sent from your handheld device.

▶ **NOTE**

The **Auto BCC** setting only sends copies of messages that you send *from* your handheld; this setting does not send copies of messages sent *to* your handheld from other people. In other words, it's simply a handy way to keep a copy of messages you send from your device.

5 Exit and Save Changes

When you're finished entering the email address you want to receive copied mail, click the **Save** button to finish and accept the changes. If you want to cancel the change, just click the **Cancel** button instead.

---

31 Add Another Email Account to the Web Client

✔ BEFORE YOU BEGIN	→ SEE ALSO
24 Create a BlackBerry Web Client Account	**26** Import Your Address Book **30** Copy Your Email Messages to Another Account

---

When you first set up the BlackBerry Web Client, you were given a handheld email account that is associated with your device. When someone sends a message to your handheld email address, the message is immediately delivered to your device as well as to the BlackBerry Web Client. Although you can certainly use this email account exclusively, in all likelihood you have at least one other existing email account that you already use. It's probably safe to say you'd like to be able to incorporate this account(s) into your mobile email experience. Fortunately, adding an existing email account to the BlackBerry Web Client so that your existing email is forwarded to your device is easy.

CHAPTER 5: Taking Control of Email with the BlackBerry Web Client

1 Log In to the BlackBerry Web Client Site on Your PC

2 Navigate to the Profile Page

3 Navigate to the Email Accounts Page

4 Add a New Email Account

5 Enter the Account Details

6 Clarify How You Access the Account

7 Enter the Email Server and Port Number for the Account

8 Exit and Save Changes

31 Add Another Email Account to the Web Client

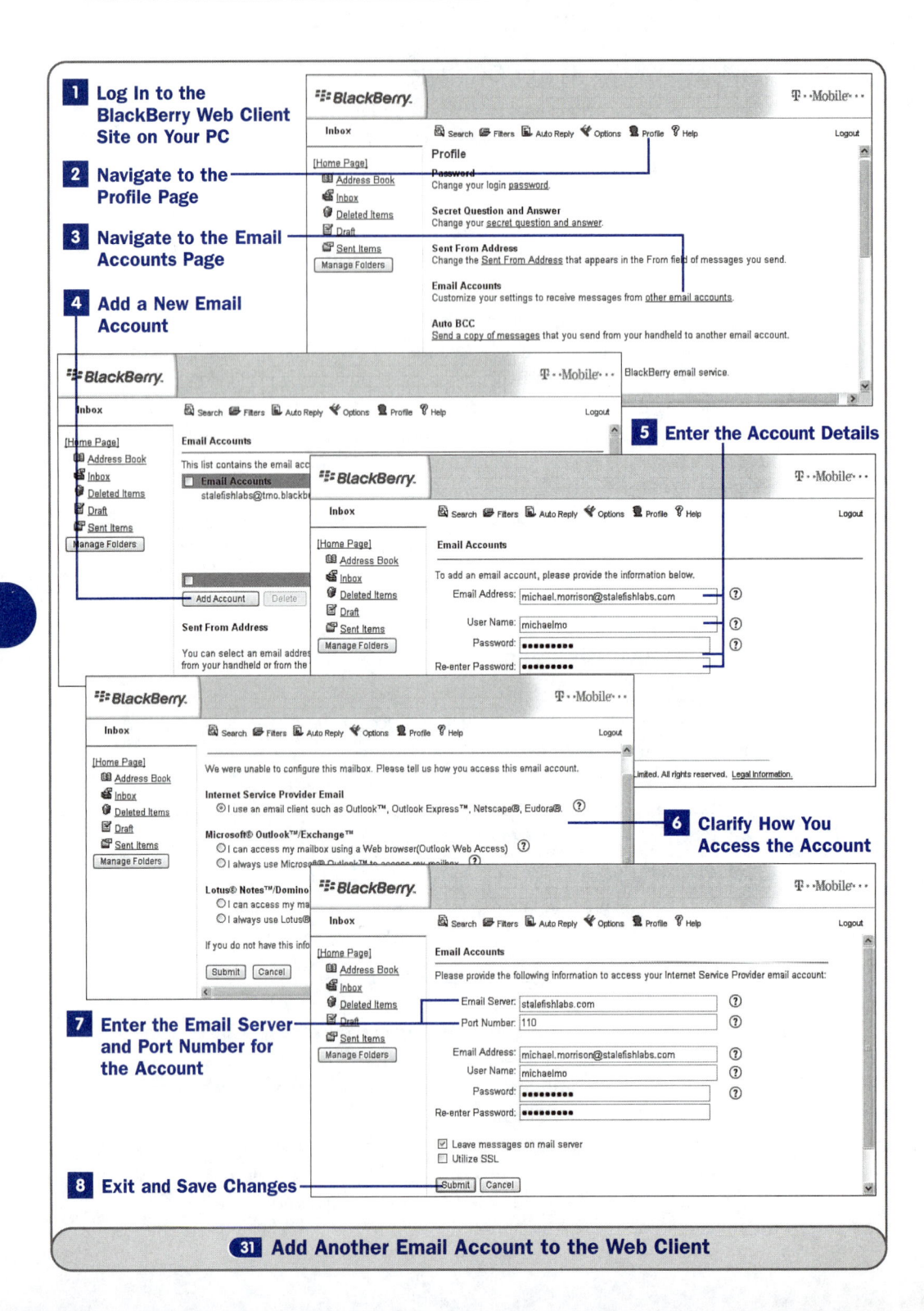

31 Add Another Email Account to the Web Client 123

It's worth pointing out that you probably don't need to add an account to the BlackBerry Web Client if you are using a corporate email account with the BlackBerry Exchange Server. In fact, you might not need the BlackBerry Web Client at all if you're using the BlackBerry Exchange Server. However, if you have a POP or IMAP email account (typically through an ISP), you'll find the multiple account feature of the BlackBerry Web Client to be incredibly useful.

▶ **NOTE**
The BlackBerry Web Client doesn't provide true email synchronization; when you delete a message from your device or through the BlackBerry Web Client, it isn't automatically deleted from your desktop email client. True email synchronization requires the BlackBerry Enterprise Server. Ask your network administrator if you aren't sure whether you're using the BlackBerry Enterprise Server. If your email is through a provider such as Earthlink, Hotmail, or Comcast, you probably are not using the BlackBerry Enterprise Server and therefore must use the BlackBerry Web Client to integrate multiple email accounts.

1 Log In to the BlackBerry Web Client Site on Your PC

If you aren't already logged in to the BlackBerry Web Client, navigate to the **BlackBerry Web Client** site using your desktop web browser. Enter your user ID and password in the appropriate fields, and click the **Login** button to log in.

2 Navigate to the Profile Page

Click the **Profile** icon on the top BlackBerry Web Client menu to open the **Profile** page, which provides access to a variety of options related to your account profile.

3 Navigate to the Email Accounts Page

Click the **other email accounts** link under the **Email Accounts** heading on the **Profile** page to open the **Email Accounts** page. The **Email Accounts** page allows you to view and modify email accounts associated with the BlackBerry Web Client.

4 Add a New Email Account

The **Email Accounts** page shows all the email accounts currently associated with the BlackBerry Web Client. Initially, the only account shown is your handheld email account. To add a new account, click the **Add Account** button. Keep in mind that you aren't creating a new handheld account; you're simply associating an existing email account with the BlackBerry Web Client so that messages sent to that account are also sent to the Web Client.

After clicking the **Add Account** button to add a new account, the page changes to allow you to enter account information for the new email account.

5 Enter the Account Details

Adding an email account to the BlackBerry Web Client involves entering the email address, username, and password for the account—you actually have to enter the password twice. Click the **Submit** button to add the email account.

If the email account is hosted by an ISP, there's a good chance the BlackBerry Web Client will need some additional information from you. If the BlackBerry Web Client needs additional information, it presents you with a page asking how you access the email account. If the Web Client doesn't ask you for any further information, proceed to step 8.

6 Clarify How You Access the Account

When prompted to specify how you access the email account, simply select one of the three options and click the **Submit** button. You are then presented with one more page asking you for the email server and port number for the account.

▶ **TIP**

When specifying how you access the email account, be sure you select the option that corresponds with how you actually check email. More specifically, if you have an email account with an ISP such as AOL, Yahoo!, MSN, or some other service that provides you with an email account, the first option is likely the best. Although the second option mentions using Microsoft Outlook, it is referring to using Microsoft Outlook with Microsoft Exchange Server, which applies mostly to corporate email accounts.

7 Enter the Email Server and Port Number for the Account

If you don't know the email server for your account, ask your network administrator; if you use an ISP, contact technical support. You should take a stab at entering just the domain name that is used in your email address. For example, my mail server is **stalefishlabs.com**. Some mail servers also include **mail.** as a prefix to the mail server's name, like this: **mail.stalefishlabs.com**. You probably don't need to change the port number unless you've been told to do so by a network administrator or tech support.

Notice the options at the bottom of the page. The first option, **Leave messages on mail server**, allows you to specify that email messages are left on your mail server when they are pulled into the BlackBerry Web Client.

32 Create an Email Filter

This is an important setting to leave enabled; if you disable it, the messages only go to the BlackBerry Web Client and are removed from the mail server before getting to your desktop email client. The second option, **Utilize SSL**, applies only if your email server requires you to use Secure Sockets Layer to access your account, which is unlikely unless you are using a corporate email account; ask your network administrator about this option before enabling it.

▶ **TIP**

Only disable the **Leave messages on mail server** option if you don't want messages to be received anywhere but the BlackBerry Web Client. Although it might sound as if I'm trying to scare you away from this setting, it can actually be useful. If you plan on being away from your desktop PC for a few days and want to check email exclusively on your BlackBerry device, you might want to disable the option. This results in messages being deleted from the mail server when you delete them on your device or on the BlackBerry Web Client. More importantly, disabling this option prevents the messages from also going to your desktop PC, which keeps you from having to sift through the same messages on your PC when you get back from your trip.

8 Exit and Save Changes

When you're done finalizing the new email account settings, click the **Submit** button to finish and accept the changes. If you want to cancel the change, just click the **Cancel** button instead.

32 Create an Email Filter

✔ **BEFORE YOU BEGIN**

24 Create a BlackBerry Web Client Account

→ **SEE ALSO**

25 Configure Web Client Options
31 Add Another Email Account to the Web Client

You might already be familiar with email filters from using them on your desktop email client. If not, you'll probably find them incredibly useful for helping to fine-tune message delivery on your BlackBerry device. Email filters allow you to set rules, or conditions, that determine how email messages are organized and delivered through the BlackBerry Web Client. For example, you can create filters to look for junk mail and automatically send them to a fiery death without you ever having to see them. Similarly, you can get more elaborate and create filters that break out email messages into separate folders based on any criteria you choose, such as work and personal messages or maybe even on a project-by-project basis.

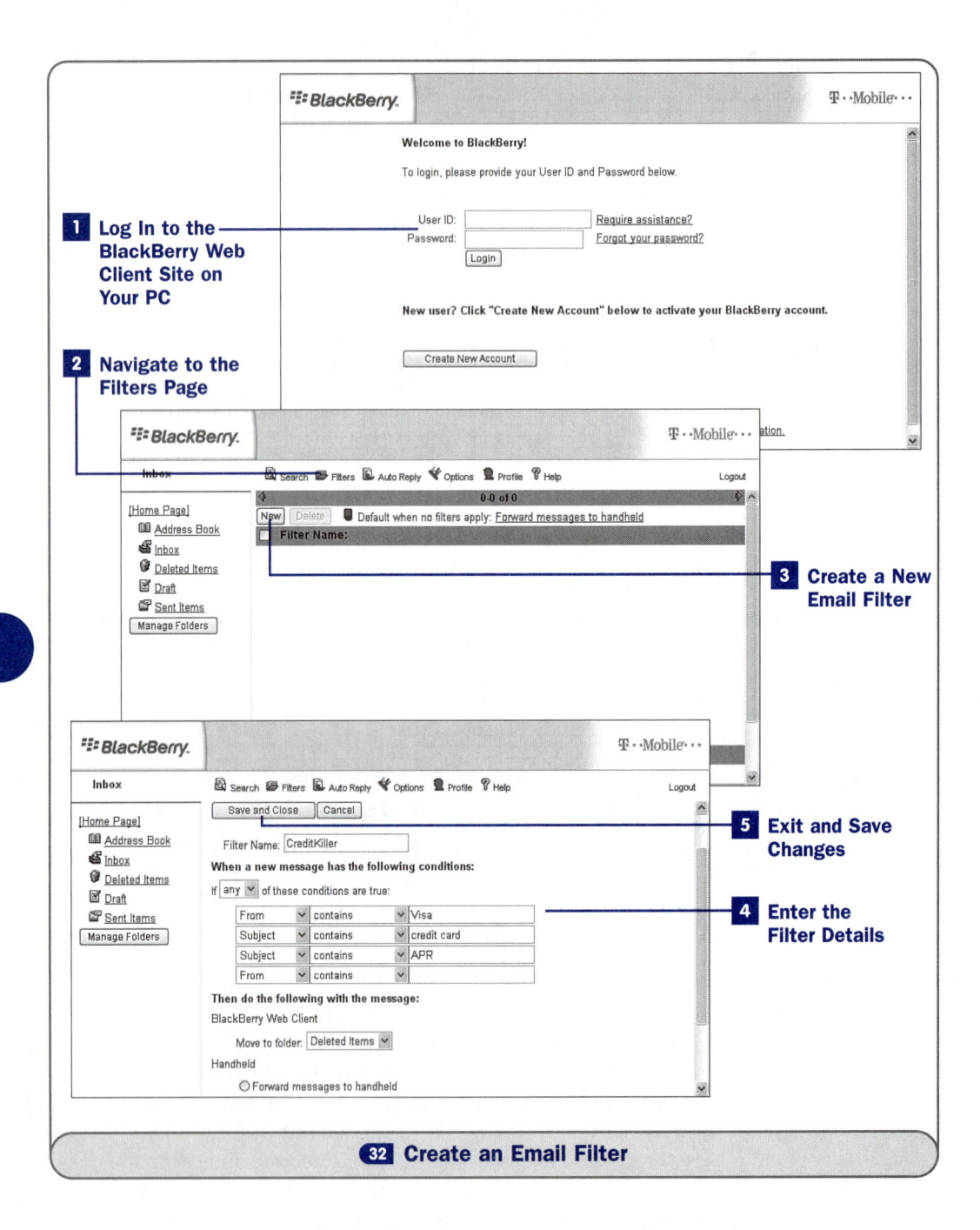

CHAPTER 5: Taking Control of Email with the BlackBerry Web Client

1 Log In to the BlackBerry Web Client Site on Your PC

2 Navigate to the Filters Page

3 Create a New Email Filter

4 Enter the Filter Details

5 Exit and Save Changes

32 Create an Email Filter

32 Create an Email Filter

The key thing to remember about filters is that they provide a great deal of flexibility in determining exactly which email messages are delivered to your device. If you've already added an email account to the BlackBerry Web Client, you might already be experiencing how annoying it can be to get overrun with email while on the go. Filters provide a good way to streamline your mobile email message flow and minimize unwanted messages being sent to your device.

1 Log In to the BlackBerry Web Client Site on Your PC

If you aren't already logged in to the BlackBerry Web Client, navigate to the **BlackBerry Web Client** site using your desktop web browser. Enter your user ID and password in the appropriate fields, and click the **Login** button to log in.

2 Navigate to the Filters Page

Click the **Filters** icon on the top BlackBerry Web Client menu to open the **Filters** page, which provides access to the email filters for your handheld email account.

3 Create a New Email Filter

Initially, no filters are set up for your account. To begin creating a new filter, click the **New** button. The **Add Filter** page appears.

4 Enter the Filter Details

Keep in mind that the purpose of an email filter is to look for certain types of email and somehow handle them differently from the rest of the email. Usually this means filtering out unwanted email and promptly sending it to the trash. A good example is credit card offers, which are much easier to stop in email form than in their traditional snail mail form. To create a filter that filters out credit card offers, you must look for certain pieces of information in the email message. But first, you must name the filter you're about to create.

▶ **NOTE**

Filter names aren't allowed to have spaces, but you can use capitalization to give them more meaningful names.

To name the new filter, enter the name in the **Filter Name** edit field. The next block of input fields is what really defines the filter. These fields allow you to specify exactly what information you are looking for and in what combinations you expect it. You are basically setting individual conditions that must be met for the message to get filtered. You can then declare whether **any** or **all** of the conditions must be met for the filtering to take place. Within the conditions, you specify a particular part of the message such as the **From**, **Sent To/Cc**, **Subject**, or **Body** part. In the second field you indicate whether it **contains** or **does not contain** the information in order to get filtered. And finally, you enter the actual text that describes the condition.

In this example, I created a filter called **CreditKiller** to filter out spam offering me new credit deals. Because this kind of spam comes in many guises, my filter has several conditions. The first condition says, in effect, that the Web Client is to search the **From** field of all incoming email; if this field contains the characters `Visa`, the filter should be activated and such email should be routed to a special folder. The other conditions of my filter look for the text `credit card` and `APR` in the **Subject** line. If any of these conditions is met by an incoming email message, the filter moves the message to the specified folder—in this case, the **Deleted Items** folder.

After entering the filter conditions, you specify where qualifying messages are to go to be filtered. The **Deleted Items** folder is the proper destination for unwanted email, although you can also create filters that separate work from personal email, for example, and route it to other folders.

The final option on the **Add Filter** page allows you to specify whether filtered messages are forwarded from the BlackBerry Web Client to your handheld. In the case of unwanted email messages, you definitely want this option set to **Do not forward messages to handheld**.

▶ **TIP**

By default, the BlackBerry Web Client forwards all unfiltered messages to your device. You typically create filters that prevent certain messages from being forwarded to your handheld. However, you can also flip the tables and use filters in an opposite manner. For example, you can click **Forward messages to handheld** on the **Filters** page to change the default behavior so that messages are *not* sent to your device when no filters apply. Then you can create filters to only let through certain messages. If you want to be more guarded about what email makes it to your device, this isn't a bad way to set up your email filters.

5 Exit and Save Changes

When you're satisfied with the new filter, click the **Save and Close** button to finish and accept the changes. If, for some reason, you want to cancel creating the filter, just click the **Cancel** button instead.

6

Digging Deeper into Email and Text Messages

IN THIS CHAPTER:

- **33** About Email and Text Messages
- **34** Compose an Email Message
- **35** View an Email Attachment
- **36** Send a PIN Message
- **37** Send an SMS Message
- **38** Organize Your Messages
- **39** Search Your Messages
- **40** Configure Email Options
- **41** Redirect Messages with the BlackBerry Redirector

CHAPTER 6: Digging Deeper into Email and Text Messages

Text messaging is what put the BlackBerry family of handheld devices on the map. Not surprisingly, text messaging is still considered the killer app for the BlackBerry 7100 series of devices, although its phone and compact form certainly add some sizzle. When you think of text messaging, one of the first things you think of is email. But your BlackBerry device is equipped to do much more in the way of text messaging than just send and receive email messages. In addition to email messages, there are also PIN and SMS messages, which can offer a simpler, more efficient alternative to email in some situations.

Not only is it important to understand how to send, receive, reply, and forward email and text messages using your BlackBerry device, it is also important to know how to organize those messages and search them intelligently. If you get in the habit of using your device to send a hefty amount of email—which is probably inevitable—you'll certainly want to know how to organize and search through old messages. It's also helpful to have a solid grasp of the email options available to you, along with why you might tweak them on your device to meet your specific messaging needs.

33 About Email and Text Messages

✔ **BEFORE YOU BEGIN**

23 About Email and the BlackBerry Web Client

→ **SEE ALSO**

34 Compose an Email Message
36 Send a PIN Message
37 Send an SMS Message

Text messaging is at the heart of everything that makes BlackBerry devices so useful, and the 7100 series of devices is no exception. Text messaging is a highly efficient method of mobile communication and in many ways is competing with voice telephony communication. It's often easier to receive a text message and reply to it at your own convenience than to answer a live voice call and deal with an issue in real time. This is the primary reason so many business users have adopted the BlackBerry platform as their mobile communication devices of choice. The BlackBerry 7100 has begun to introduce the BlackBerry name to a wider base of users, but business text messaging is still the bread and butter of the BlackBerry family of devices.

One potential source of confusion with respect to BlackBerry devices and text messages has to do with what exactly constitutes a text message. You obviously know that it must contain text, but so do Word documents and web pages, and those obviously aren't considered text messages. A *text message* is a message consisting purely of text (and possibly an attached file or files) that is sent

33 About Email and Text Messages   131

electronically over a network from one place to another. The BlackBerry 7100 series of devices supports the following primary types of text messages:

▶ **KEY TERM**

Text message—A message consisting purely of text (and possibly an attached file or files) that is sent directly over a network from one place to another.

▶ **NOTE**

Some email clients, such as Microsoft Outlook, allow you to create email messages that include HTML code similar to that found in web pages. Although HTML-based email messages are technically still considered text messages, they require special formatting to be viewed and therefore don't qualify as text messages under the more strict definition I'm applying to BlackBerry text messages.

- **Email message**—A text message addressed to an email address and sent through an email server. Email messages are sent and received through a client email application. This type of message can accept attachments.

- **PIN message**—A text message addressed to a specific mobile device and sent through a wireless service provider. *PIN* (personal identification number) messages are sent and received directly on a mobile device. This type of message can accept attachments.

- **SMS message**—A text message addressed to a phone number or special code and sent through a wireless service provider. *SMS* (short message service) messages are sent and received directly on a mobile device. This type of message cannot accept attachments.

- **Instant message**—A text message sent in the context of a live conversation between two connected parties. Instant messages are sent and received through a client instant messaging application. This type of message can accept attachments.

The most important thing to take from this list of text message types is the distinction between the first three (email, PIN, and SMS messages) and the last one (instant message). The distinction is that an instant message involves the notion of a *live connection* between two parties; the other types of messages are delivered regardless of whether anyone is on the other end to receive them when they are sent. This might seem like a minor issue, but it makes a huge difference in terms of how instant messages are handled as compared to email, PIN, and SMS messages. More specifically, the standard BlackBerry Messages application handles email, PIN, and SMS messages together in a seamless manner, while it doesn't handle instant messages at all.

To send and receive instant messages, you need an instant messaging (IM) client application. Fortunately, most BlackBerry devices ship with IM clients for AOL Instant Messenger, Yahoo! Messenger, and ICQ. If you use a different IM service, such as MSN Messenger, you should consider downloading and installing an IM client that works for that service. Alternatively, consider a unified IM client that supports multiple IM services—you must download and install this client to your device as well. For more information on BlackBerry IM, take a look at **42 About Instant Messages**.

Now that you understand the distinction between instant messages and the other three main types of text messages, it's worth taking just a moment to cover the differences between email, PIN, and SMS messages. As you might already know, email messages are routed through email servers and often traverse a variety of network and computer configurations along the way. Email messages are addressed using the familiar **name@website.com** format, with which most people are familiar. PIN and SMS messages are a bit different from email messages both in terms of how they are delivered and how they are addressed.

▶ **NOTE**

Email and PIN messages accept file attachments, whereas SMS messages do not. Email and PIN messages are limited in the kinds of attachments that can be opened on your device, although you can forward received messages with other kinds of attachments. In other words, even if your device doesn't support the opening of a particular message attachment, you can still forward the message with the attachment intact.

PIN and SMS messages are peer-to-peer messages, which means they don't go through a server in the same way that email does. Instead, they are sent directly from one device to another one, much like a phone call is made directly from one mobile phone to another one. Moreover, PIN and SMS messages are sent solely through your wireless service provider. PIN messages are more limited than SMS messages in that they can be sent only to other BlackBerry devices. Every BlackBerry device has a unique PIN, which serves as the target address for PIN messages. This means you can't send PIN messages to email addresses or other (non-BlackBerry) devices that don't have PINs. Similar to SMS and email addresses, you can store the PIN for a contact in your device's address book.

▶ **TIP**

To determine the PIN of your device, scroll to the **Tools** icon on the **Home** screen and click the trackwheel. Then scroll to the **Settings** icon on the **Tools** screen and click the trackwheel. Finally, scroll down to **Status** and click the trackwheel once more. Your device's PIN is listed along with other important device information.

▶ **NOTE**
PIN messages aren't as secure as email messages because they are not encrypted when they are delivered. Be wary of using PIN messages to communicate sensitive information.

SMS messages don't suffer from the same limitation as PIN messages—they can be sent to anyone with a mobile device that supports SMS. And currently, many mobile phones and wireless handheld communicators support SMS. Whereas a PIN uniquely identifies a device for a PIN message, your mobile phone number serves as your unique ID for SMS messaging. So, if a mobile phone or handheld is capable of SMS messaging, you can send the owner a text message by simply addressing the message to her mobile phone number. Not surprisingly, the flexibility of being able to send a quick message to a person by simply addressing the message to her mobile phone number is causing a quick rise in popularity for SMS in North America. (It is already a hit in many other parts of the world.)

All this text messaging talk converges with the Messages application on your device, which supports email, PIN, and SMS messages. The benefit of how the BlackBerry 7100 series device supports these message types is that you compose text messages the same way regardless of what type you are sending; the only thing that really distinguishes between an email, a PIN, or an SMS message is how you address it.

Before moving on to composing messages, it's worth taking a quick moment to explore the viewing of messages. You access the messages on your device by launching the **Messages** application, which is a trackwheel click away on the **Home** screen. To view a message in the main message list, just scroll to select the message and click it with the trackwheel. The message appears and can then be viewed using the following navigational techniques:

- Use the trackwheel to scroll up and down in the message, one line at a time.

- Hold down the **Alt** key while scrolling the trackwheel to move left and right within the text of the message, one character at a time.

- The **E R** and **C V** keys represent the **Home** and **End** keys on a traditional keyboard; they take you to the start and end of the message, respectively.

- The **U I** and **M** keys are equivalent to **Page Up** and **Page Down**, respectively.

- The **Backspace** key deletes the message; a confirmation window appears that prompts you before the message is actually deleted.

- The **Q W** key replies to the sender of the message, the **A S** key replies to all, and the **O P** key forwards the message.

- The **Next** key moves to the next message in the message list.

CHAPTER 6: Digging Deeper into Email and Text Messages

Similar navigational techniques apply to email message attachments, which you find out about in **35 View an Email Attachment**.

34 Compose an Email Message

✔ BEFORE YOU BEGIN	→ SEE ALSO
33 About Email and Text Messages	**27** Compose an Email Message Using the Web Client **36** Send a PIN Message **37** Send an SMS Message

Composing an email message on your device is straightforward and primarily involves getting comfortable typing on the compact BlackBerry 7100 keyboard. You can address an email message to multiple recipients and use familiar addressing options such as Cc and Bcc. The standard Messages client email application also supports email attachments, albeit somewhat limited attachments—you are only allowed to attach address book contacts to email messages. Even though you can't create a new email with an attachment other than an address book attachment, you are allowed to forward emails with other types of attachments. As an example, even though you can't compose an email message on your device and attach an image to it, you can receive an email with an image attachment and then forward it with the attachment intact. The image attachment can be forwarded even if your wireless service doesn't support the viewing of image attachments.

1 Open the Messages Screen

Scroll to the **Messages** icon on the **Home** screen and click the trackwheel. The **Messages** screen appears, displaying a list of messages that have been sent and received on your device. Initially, no messages appear if you are just starting to use email with your device.

2 Start Composing a New Message

Click the trackwheel to open the **Messages** menu and scroll to select **Compose Email**. Click the trackwheel to select the menu item and begin composing a new email message. The **Select Address** screen appears.

▶ **TIP**

An even quicker way to begin composing a new email message is to simply press the **L** key while viewing the **Messages** screen. Just be sure you then select **Email** *Recipient Name* from the menu that appears.

34 Compose an Email Message

1 Open the Messages Screen

2 Start Composing a New Message

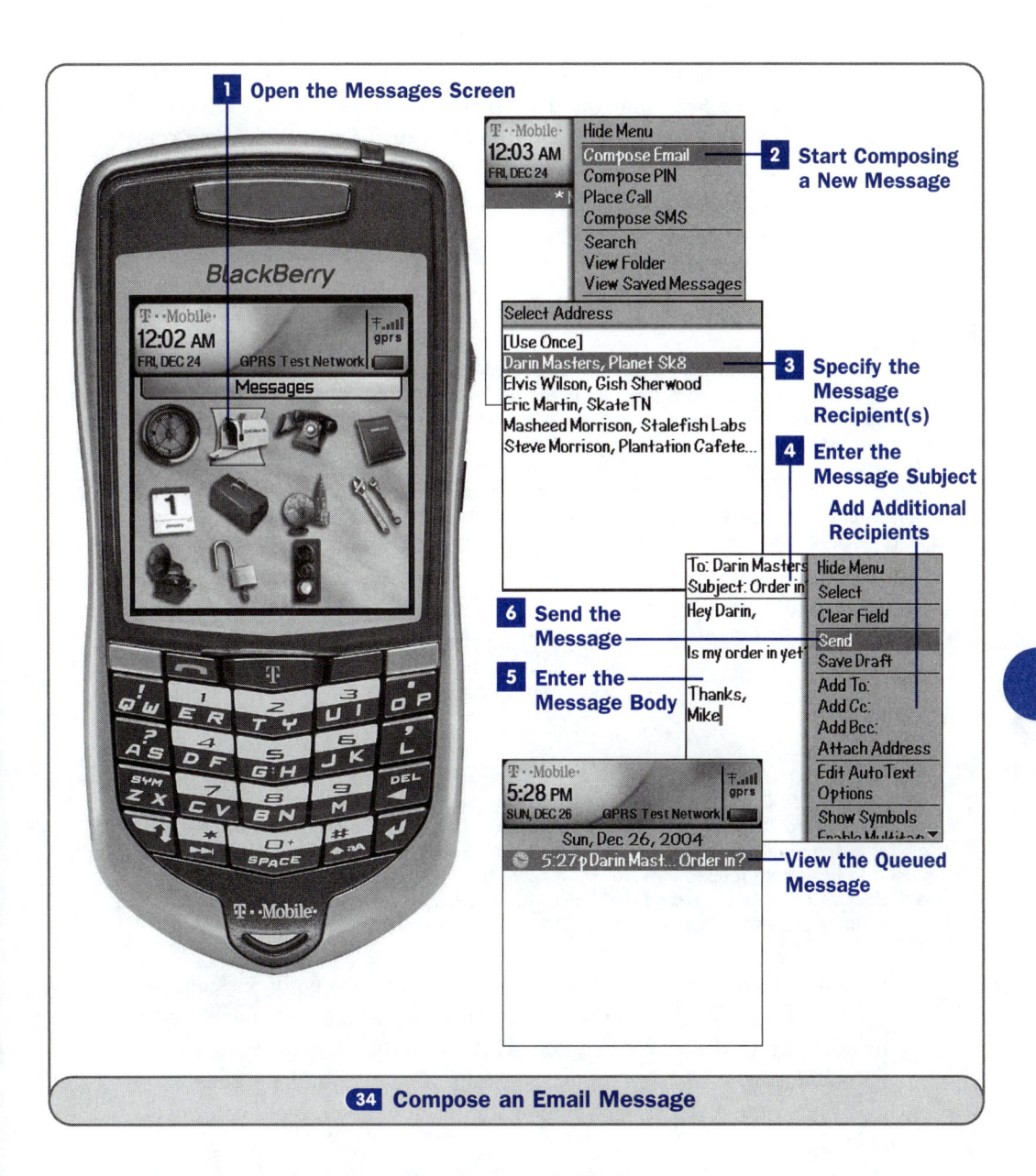

3 Specify the Message Recipient(s)

4 Enter the Message Subject

Add Additional Recipients

5 Enter the Message Body

6 Send the Message

View the Queued Message

34 Compose an Email Message

3 Specify the Message Recipient(s)

The **Select Address** screen is where you enter the email address of the message recipient(s). By default, the first entry in your Address Book is selected. Scroll with the trackwheel to select the message recipient, or select **Use Once** to enter an email address directly. The idea behind the **Use Once** designation is that you are specifying an email address you don't want to bother adding to your Address Book as a new contact. To select an existing contact, just click the trackwheel after scrolling to select it. The menu changes to show a list of options you can select from regarding the email address you've chosen—in this case, click the selected menu item (**Email Darin Masters**) to begin composing the email message. You might see other messaging options such as **SMS** *Recipient Name* or **PIN** *Recipient Name*, so be sure you select **Email** *Recipient Name* to indicate that you want to send an email message instead of an SMS or PIN message.

▶ **TIP**

If you opt to enter an email address by selecting **Use Once** when choosing the email recipient, here's a handy trick you can use to enter the @ and . characters in the email address. While typing the email address, when you get to the point in the address where the @ symbol is required, just press the **Space** key and the @ symbol is automatically inserted. As you continue entering the address, press the **Space** key again when you want to insert the . (dot) in the domain name. As an example, to enter the email address **parcells@cowboys.com**, type the name **parcells** followed by the **Space** key, then **cowboys** followed by another space, and then **com**.

You can only add a single message recipient on the **Select Address** screen when you first begin composing a new message. To add more recipients, click the trackwheel after the new message appears and then select **Add To:**, **Add Cc:**, or **Add Bcc:** from the menu.

▶ **NOTE**

The **Add To:**, **Add Cc:**, and **Add Bcc:** options for specifying new message recipients follow the standard To, Cc (carbon copy), and Bcc (blind carbon copy) email designations. The To designation applies to recipients who are directly receiving the message, and Cc is used to designate recipients who will receive the message but aren't the direct targets. Bcc is similar to Cc except that none of the other recipients can see the Bcc recipient, including any other Bcc recipients—hence, the name *blind* carbon copy.

In addition to specifying more than one recipient for the email message, you can also attach a contact to the message as an attachment. To do this, click the trackwheel with the new message visible and then select **Attach Address** from the menu. You are prompted to select a contact from the Address Book—the contact is then sent along with the email message as an attachment.

▶ **NOTE**

If you're sending a contact through the BlackBerry Enterprise Server or directly to another BlackBerry device, the contact is sent as a vCard attachment that can be easily opened and added to a contact list. If you're sending the contact to another kind of device, the contact data might get packaged into a generic data file (a **.dat** file extension) that the recipient has to open in a text editor to extract the contact information.

4 Enter the Message Subject

After specifying the message's recipients, enter the message subject, which is the text that describes the message. You can enter any text you choose. When you're satisfied with the message subject, press the **Enter** key or scroll the trackwheel down to begin entering the text of the message body.

5 Enter the Message Body

The message body is the heart of your email message and is where you enter the actual message text. You can enter any text you want as the body of the message. Just keep in mind that BlackBerry email messages are composed as raw text messages with no special formatting.

▶ **TIP**

You can use several typing shortcuts while entering text on your BlackBerry device. For example, to make the most of the *SureType* feature, type the entire word letter by letter before attempting to select from the list of corrections. If you must make a correction using the SureType pop-up window, press the **Next** key (*) or scroll the trackwheel to highlight the correction, and then click. To capitalize a letter, hold the letter key until the capitalized letter appears. To scroll through all the available characters for a given key, hold the key and scroll the trackwheel. To insert a period at the end of a sentence, press the **Space** key twice. To turn NUM LOCK on, hold down the **Shift** key (#) and press the **Alt** key; to turn NUM LOCK off, press the **Alt** key by itself. And finally, to switch between SureType and traditional multitap modes, hold down the **Next** key (*).

If you don't have time to finish entering the message body or want to wait and finish it later, you can save the message instead of sending it. To save the message without sending it, click the trackwheel, select **Save Draft** from the menu that appears, and then click once more. The message appears in the message list with a special icon next to it to indicate that it is a draft message that has yet to be sent.

6 Send the Message

When you're ready to send a message, click the trackwheel with the message open and select **Send** from the menu that appears. Click the trackwheel to flag the message for sending. I say that the message is *flagged* instead of actually being sent because the actual sending of the message depends on your device having access to the wireless network. If you have the radio turned off on your device or are out of the wireless coverage area, the message isn't sent immediately. When you turn the radio back on or regain wireless coverage, the message is automatically sent.

▶ NOTES

A message that is queued for later delivery pending network access is displayed with a small icon of a clock next to it. A small broadcast icon is shown while the message is being sent. And finally, a check mark appears next to the message after it has been successfully delivered.

You might deliberately choose to compose messages offline when you are on an airplane and then send them later. Most airlines prohibit the use of wireless radios during flight, which means you must turn off the radio on your device. However, you can still compose new messages and respond to messages; they just won't be sent until you turn the radio back on. This is a useful way to accomplish work even when you don't have wireless network access.

35 View an Email Attachment

✔ BEFORE YOU BEGIN	→ SEE ALSO
33 About Email and Text Messages	38 Organize Your Messages

34

The BlackBerry 7100 series of devices was designed with the business user in mind. For this reason, the devices are somewhat limited in the area of handling media objects through email. More specifically, 7100 devices support only a couple email attachment file types by default. You can obviously view text attachments, which is to be expected. You can also open Adobe Acrobat PDF files, Microsoft Word documents, and Microsoft Excel spreadsheets as attachments, all of which is extremely handy. However, support for file types other than these depends entirely on your wireless service provider or corporate email server (in the case of the BlackBerry Enterprise Server). In other words, there is no guarantee that your device will be able to open attachments such as GIF or JPEG images. As an example, BlackBerry 7100t devices used through T-Mobile originally didn't support image attachments at all, but now they do. Be sure to check with your provider or corporate IT department to find out whether your device supports image attachments.

I would've expected native support for viewing image attachments on all 7100 devices, but this is not the case. If your provider or corporate email server doesn't support the viewing of image attachments, you might want to look into third-party email applications that provide support for additional attachment types. For example, Reqwireless EmailViewer (http://www.reqwireless.com/emailviewer.html) and Terratial's BBImageViewer (http://www.terratial.com/products/bbimage/viewer/) both support additional attachment types; the latter application works in conjunction with the standard **Messages** application. Just to be clear, before you run out and buy a third-party messaging application, be sure to try the **Messages** application that ships standard on your device. Your wireless provider or corporate BlackBerry solution might offer plenty of flexibility in handling attachments.

35 View an Email Attachment

1 Open the Messages Screen

2 Open the Message with the Attachment

3 Open the Attachments Screen

4 Select the Attachment

5 View the Attachment

6 Close the Attachment and Message

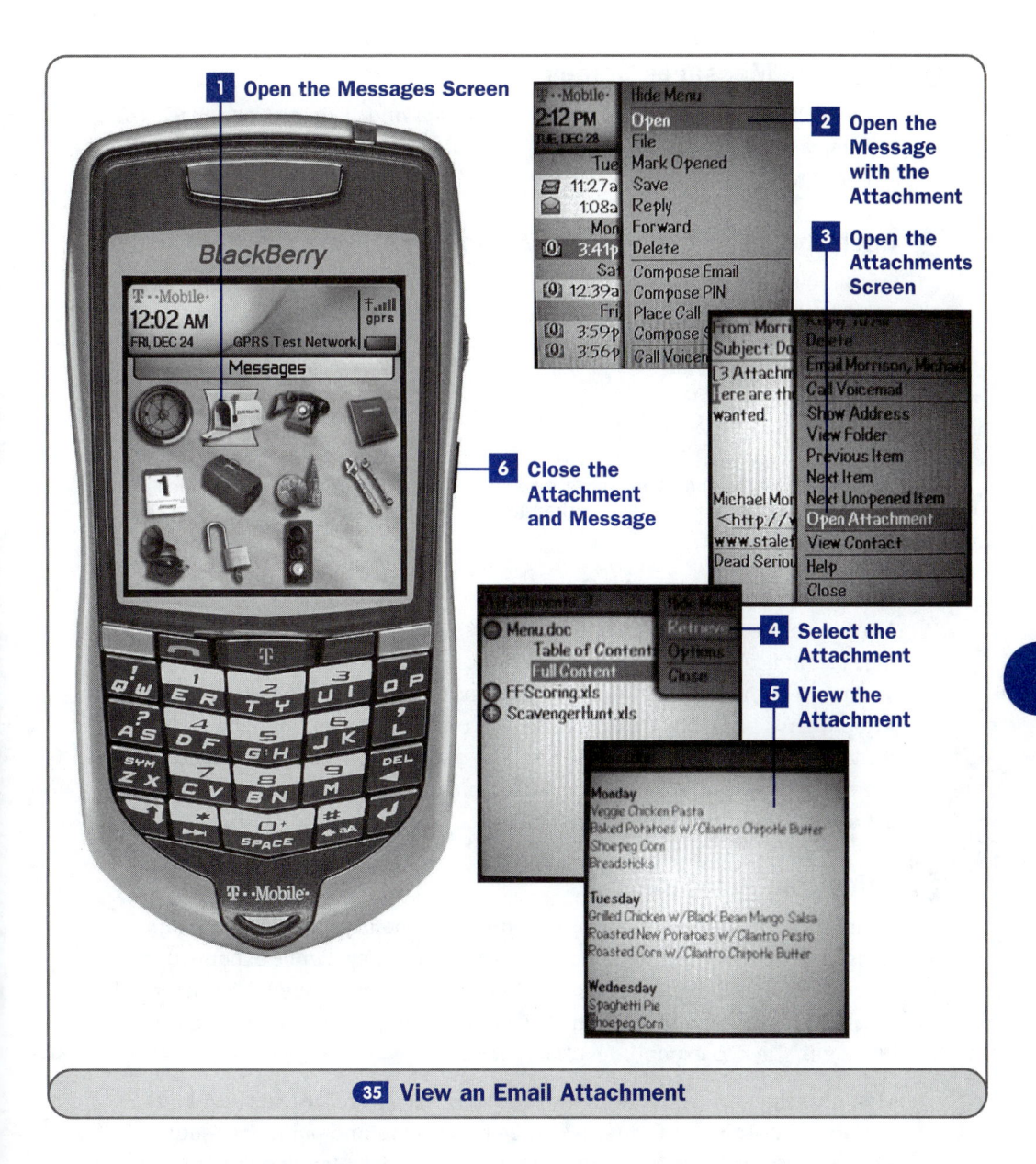

35 View an Email Attachment

▶ **WEB RESOURCE**

http://www.reqwireless.com/emailviewer.html—Reqwireless EmailViewer

http://www.terratial.com/products/bbimage/viewer/—Terratial **BBImageViewer**

Two third-party email applications that provide support for viewing additional types of attachments on your BlackBerry device.

1 Open the Messages Screen

Scroll to the **Messages** icon on the **Home** screen and click the trackwheel. The **Messages** screen appears, displaying a list of email messages that have been sent and received on your device.

2 Open the Message with the Attachment

Scroll the trackwheel to select a message from the message list and click. (Note that messages with attachments appear in the list with a paperclip icon.) Select **Open** from the menu that appears and then click to open the selected message.

▶ TIP

An even quicker way to open a message is to simply press the **Enter** key after selecting the message from the message list on the **Messages** screen.

3 Open the Attachments Screen

Aside from the paperclip icon that appears next to the message in the message list, indication that the message has attachments appears near the beginning of the message text as a word inside square brackets, such as [1 Attachment] or [3 Attachments]. To select an attachment for opening, click the trackwheel while viewing the message and then select **Open Attachment** from the menu that appears. The **Attachments** screen appears and shows all the attachments for the message.

4 Select the Attachment

Notice that the list of attachments for an email message includes plus sign icons next to the attachment files, indicating that they can be expanded to show additional information. To expand an attachment, scroll the trackwheel to select the attachment, click the trackwheel, and then select **Expand** from the menu. Click to expand the attachment.

Most attachments expand to show two items: **Table of Contents** and **Full Content**. The **Table of Contents** can be retrieved to find out more about what is contained within the attachment without downloading the full attachment content. To actually open and view the attachment itself, scroll the trackwheel to select **Full Content** and then click. Select **Retrieve** from the menu that appears and click once more.

35 View an Email Attachment

You might have to wait a few moments while the attachment is downloaded. After it is successfully retrieved, it is opened and displayed on the screen.

5 View the Attachment

You view an attachment in much the same way as you view other content on your BlackBerry device. For example, Microsoft Word and Acrobat PDF documents are navigated and viewed similarly to email messages. Microsoft Excel spreadsheets are somewhat unique in that there isn't a standard BlackBerry document type that is similar.

Here are a few useful navigational techniques to remember when viewing attachments. These techniques actually apply to all content on your BlackBerry, including email messages, but they are often required to efficiently move around within an attachment, which is typically sized for a screen much larger than your BlackBerry device:

- Use the trackwheel to scroll up and down in an attachment.
- Hold down the **Alt** key while scrolling the trackwheel to move left and right.
- The **E R** and **C V** keys represent the **Home** and **End** keys on a traditional keyboard; they take you to the start and end of an attachment, respectively.
- The **U I** and **M** keys are equivalent to **Page Up** and **Page Down**, respectively.
- For Excel spreadsheets, use the **T Y**, **B N**, **D F**, and **J K** keys to navigate up, down, left, and right, respectively.

▶ **TIP**
You must have specific server support for images to view images as attachments on your BlackBerry device. If you *can* view images, there are a few navigational tips that you'll definitely want to know about. First, you can zoom in on an image by pressing the **U I** key. You can zoom out in a similar fashion by pressing the **M** key. Optionally, you can hold down the **Shift** key and scroll the trackwheel to quickly zoom in and out on an image. Each press of the **O P** key rotates the image 90° clockwise.

6 Close the Attachment and Message

When you're finished viewing an attachment, press the **Escape** button to close the attachment. Press the **Escape** button again to exit the **Attachments** screen. Press the **Escape** button two more times to close the email message and exit the **Messages** application back to the **Home** screen. Alternatively, to bypass all those **Escape** button presses, press the **End** key once.

36 Send a PIN Message

✔ **BEFORE YOU BEGIN**

34 Compose an Email Message

→ **SEE ALSO**

37 Send an SMS Message

Email is likely your primary mode of text message communication, but it is by no means your only option. Another useful option for text messaging involves PIN messages, which are messages sent directly from one wireless device to another. Unlike email messages, which must be routed from your device through email servers and often traverse a variety of network and computer configurations along the way, PIN messages are sent solely through your wireless service provider. More importantly, PIN messages are peer-to-peer messages, which means they don't go through a server at all—they are sent directly from one device to another one, much like a phone call is made directly from one mobile phone to another one.

Because PIN message are peer-to-peer, they usually are sent much faster than email messages. So, why don't you just use PIN messages for all your text messaging needs? The reason is because PIN messages can only be sent to other BlackBerry devices. Every BlackBerry device has a unique PIN, which serves as the target address for PIN messages. This means you can't send PIN messages to email addresses or other devices that don't have PINs. Depending on how many of your co-workers, clients, and other contacts use BlackBerry devices, this might or might not be a limitation. For those people you can reach using PIN messages, you'll likely find that PIN messaging is very handy. You can enter the PIN for your BlackBerry friends and co-workers in the **PIN** field of their contact information.

▶ **NOTE**

Unlike SMS messages, which are pure text messages with no frills, PIN messages can be sent with attachments. However, the BlackBerry 7100 series devices are limited to sending only Address Book contacts as message attachments. Even so, PIN messages are more powerful than SMS messages, providing that your target recipient is accessible through PIN messaging.

1 Open the Messages Screen

Scroll to the **Messages** icon on the **Home** screen and click the trackwheel. The **Messages** screen appears, displaying a list of messages that have been sent and received on your device.

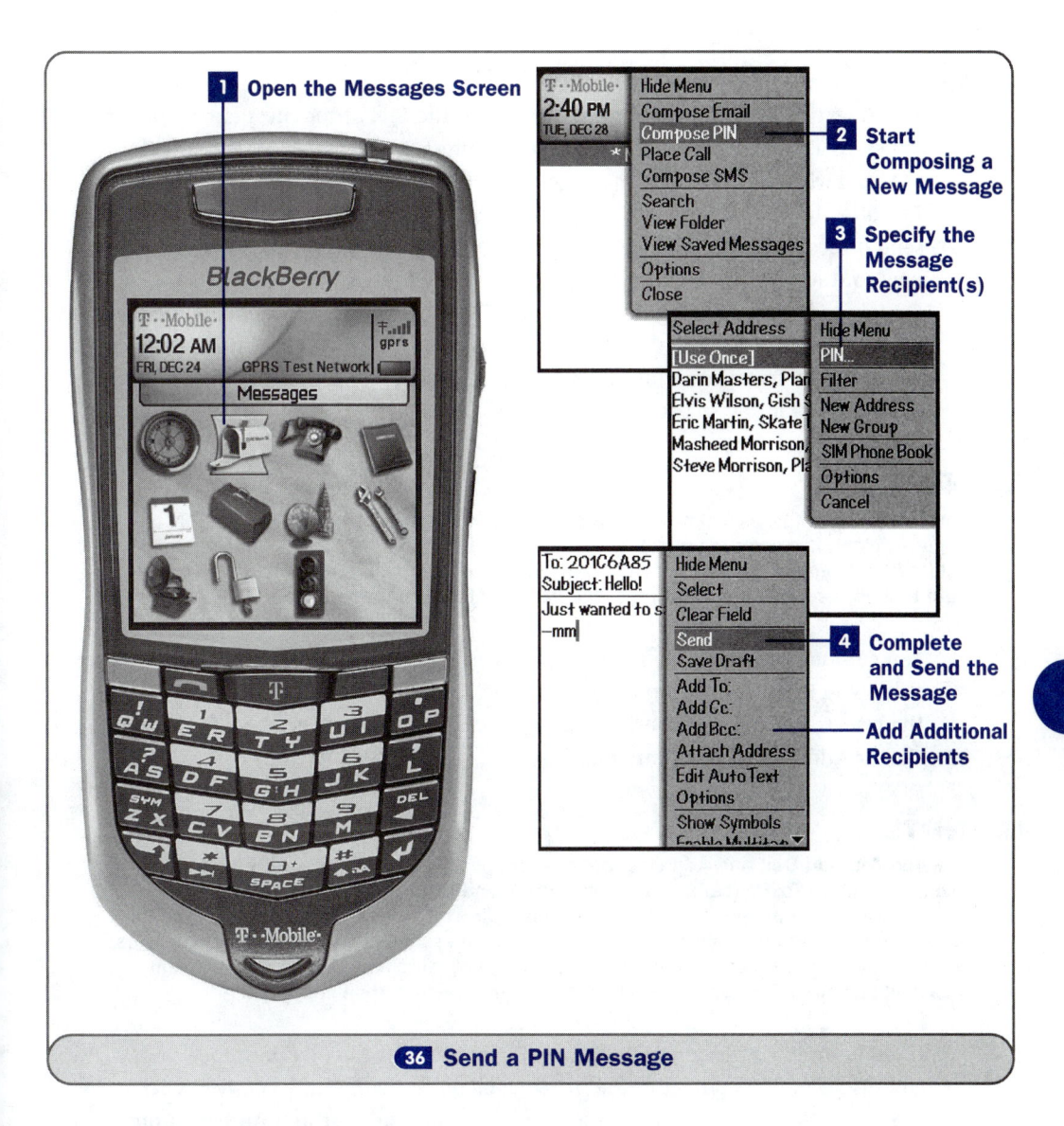

36 Send a PIN Message

1 Open the Messages Screen

2 Start Composing a New Message

3 Specify the Message Recipient(s)

4 Complete and Send the Message

Add Additional Recipients

36 Send a PIN Message

2 Start Composing a New Message

Click the trackwheel to open the **Messages** menu and scroll to select **Compose PIN**. Click the trackwheel to select the menu item and begin composing a new PIN message. The **Select Address** screen appears.

▶ **TIP**

An even quicker way to begin composing a new PIN message is to simply press the **L** key while viewing the **Messages** screen. Just be sure you then select **PIN *Recipient Name*** from the menu that appears.

3 Specify the Message Recipient(s)

The **Select Address** screen is where you enter the PIN of the message recipient(s). By default, the first entry in your Address Book is selected. Scroll with the trackwheel to select the message recipient, or select **[Use Once]** to enter a PIN directly. The idea behind the **[Use Once]** designation is that you want to send a message to a PIN you don't want to add to your Address Book as a new contact. To use a PIN once, scroll with the trackwheel to select **[Use Once]**, and click. Click again to accept **PIN** on the menu that appears, and then enter the PIN. When you're finished entering the PIN, click the trackwheel, select **Continue** from the menu that appears, and click again. Or just press the **Enter** key to accept the PIN as the message recipient.

▶ **NOTE**

You must have a PIN associated with a contact for the contact to be used as a PIN message recipient. If a contact has a PIN associated with him in his contact information, select **PIN** *Recipient Name* from the menu when you compose a new message to indicate that you are sending a PIN message instead of an email message.

You can add only a single message recipient on the **Select Address** screen when you first begin composing a new message. To add more recipients, click the trackwheel after the new message appears and then select **Add To:**, **Add Cc:**, or **Add Bcc:** from the menu.

▶ **NOTE**

The **Add To:**, **Add Cc:**, and **Add Bcc:** options for specifying new message recipients follow the standard To, Cc (carbon copy), and Bcc (blind carbon copy) email designations. The To designation applies to recipients who are directly receiving the message, and Cc is used to designate recipients who will receive the message but aren't the direct targets. Bcc is similar to Cc except that none of the other recipients can see the Bcc recipient, including any other Bcc recipients—hence the name *blind* carbon copy.

In addition to specifying more than one recipient for the PIN message, you can also attach a contact to the message as an attachment. To do this, click the trackwheel with the new message visible and select **Attach Address** from the menu. You are prompted to select a contact from the Address Book—the contact is then sent along with the PIN message as an attachment.

4 Complete and Send the Message

After specifying the message's recipient(s), enter the message subject, which is the text that describes the message. The message body comes next, which is the heart of your PIN message, and is where you enter the actual message text. You can enter any text you want as the body of the message. Just keep in mind that PIN messages are composed as raw text messages with no special formatting.

▶ TIP

You can use several typing shortcuts while entering text on your BlackBerry device. For example, to make the most of the *SureType* feature, enter an entire word letter by letter before attempting to select from the list of corrections. If you must make a correction using the SureType pop-up window, press the **Next** key (*) or scroll the trackwheel to highlight the correction and then click. To capitalize a letter, hold the letter key until the capitalized letter appears. To scroll through all the available characters on a given key, hold the key and scroll the trackwheel. To insert a period at the end of a sentence, press the **Space** key twice. To turn on NUM LOCK, hold down the **Shift** key (#) and then press the **Alt** key; to turn off NUM LOCK, press the **Alt** key by itself. And finally, to switch between SureType and traditional multitap modes, hold down the **Next** key (*).

If you don't have time to finish entering the message or otherwise want to finish it later, you can save the message instead of sending it. To save the message for later without sending it, click the trackwheel, select **Save Draft** from the menu that appears, and then click. The message will appear in the message list with a special icon (a small yellow sheet of paper) next to it to indicate that it is a draft message that has yet to be sent.

When you're ready to send a message, open the message, click the trackwheel, and select **Send** from the menu that appears. Click the trackwheel to flag the message for sending. I say that the message is *flagged* instead of being sent because the actual sending of the message depends on your device having access to the wireless network. If you have the radio turned off on your device or are out of the wireless coverage area, the message isn't sent immediately. When you turn the radio back on or regain wireless coverage, the message is automatically sent.

37 Send an SMS Message

✔ BEFORE YOU BEGIN	→ SEE ALSO
34 Compose an Email Message	36 Send a PIN Message

SMS, which stands for Short Message Service, is a text-messaging protocol that is extremely popular in Europe and Asia and is rapidly gaining in popularity in the United States. SMS is extremely user-friendly because you send text messages to someone by simply specifying the phone number of his handheld device. In this way, it's apparent that SMS grew out of a need to allow text messaging on mobile phones. What makes it useful for BlackBerry devices is that it provides a way to communicate with people who use traditional mobile phones that don't have full-blown email access. Although SMS is somewhat new to American mobile phone users, its widespread success in other parts of the world gives it a stable and interesting base of applications that are available to all SMS users.

CHAPTER 6: Digging Deeper into Email and Text Messages

1 Open the Messages Screen

2 Start Composing a New Message

3 Specify the Message Recipient(s)

4 Complete and Send the Message

37 Send an SMS Message

SMS is a standardized messaging protocol used all around the world. The protocol that allows business people to share ideas and make important business decisions is the same protocol kids use to pass notes between each other. The success of SMS has spawned some really neat applications and services that you might not have realized exist. For example, one of my favorite SMS applications is Google SMS, which allows you to carry out a Google search purely through SMS messages. This is a simple and elegant application of SMS and a great example of how to make a popular service available to mobile devices.

Send an SMS Message

▶ **TIP**

Google SMS is a useful service that allows you to quickly perform Google searches using SMS messages. To initiate a Google SMS search, send an SMS message with the form **g** *search terms* to the Google SMS address, **46645** (GOOGL). For example, if you want to search for Florida swamp land, send a message containing **g florida swamp land** to the SMS address **46645**. Google SMS returns the search results to you as SMS messages. You can perform a few special searches using Google SMS: Send an area code as the search term to find the area it covers; send a phone number to get a phone book listing; and send a business type and ZIP Code to get a listing of businesses in that area. For more information, visit the Google SMS website at http://www.google.com/sms/.

SMS messages are somewhat similar to PIN messages in that they are sent directly to another device using a unique ID that is specific to that device. Whereas a PIN uniquely identifies a device for a PIN message, your mobile phone number serves as your unique ID for SMS messaging. If a mobile phone or handheld is capable of SMS messaging, you can send the owner a message by simply addressing the message to his mobile phone number.

1 **Open the Messages Screen**

Scroll to the **Messages** icon on the **Home** screen and click the trackwheel. The **Messages** screen appears, displaying a list of messages that have been sent and received on your device.

2 **Start Composing a New Message**

Click the trackwheel to open the **Messages** menu and scroll to select **Compose SMS**. Click the trackwheel to select the menu item and begin composing a new SMS message. The **Select Address** screen appears.

▶ **TIP**

An even quicker way to begin composing a new SMS message is to simply press the **L** key while viewing the **Messages** screen. Just be sure you then select **SMS** *Recipient Name* from the menu that appears.

3 **Specify the Message Recipient(s)**

The **Select Address** screen is where you enter the SMS address of the message recipient(s). By default, the first entry in your Address Book is selected. Scroll with the trackwheel to select the message recipient (**SMS** *Recipient Name*), or select [**Use Once**] to enter an SMS address directly. The idea behind the [**Use Once**] designation is that the address you want to use for this text message is an SMS address you don't want to add to your Address Book as a new contact. To use an SMS address once, scroll with the trackwheel to select [**Use Once**] and click. Click again to accept **SMS** on the menu that appears, and then enter the SMS address. When you're finished entering the SMS address, click the trackwheel, select **Continue** from the menu that appears, and click again. Or just press the **Enter** key to accept the SMS address as the message recipient.

▶ **NOTES**

You must have an SMS address associated with a contact for the contact to be used as an SMS message recipient.

With a few exceptions, such as SMS services that use short codes, SMS addresses are typically just mobile phone numbers. A *short code* is a special SMS address that is typically a four-, five-, or six-digit number. Short codes are usually assigned to special wireless services such as Google SMS. They are also sometimes used for special promotions. For example, the television show *American Idol* has used a short code to allow viewers to vote on show participants using SMS.

You can add only a single message recipient on the **Select Address** screen when you first begin composing a new message. In fact, SMS messages allow only a single recipient.

4 Complete and Send the Message

After specifying the message's recipient, enter the message body, which is the actual message text. Unlike email and PIN messages, SMS messages don't have a message subject. You can enter any text you want as the body of the message. Just keep in mind that SMS messages are composed as raw text messages with no special formatting.

▶ **TIP**

You can use several typing shortcuts while entering text on your BlackBerry device. For example, to make the most of the *SureType* feature, enter an entire word letter by letter before attempting to select from the list of corrections. If you must make a correction using the SureType pop-up window, press the **Next** key (*) or scroll the trackwheel to highlight the correction and then click. To capitalize a letter, hold the letter key until the capitalized letter appears. To scroll through all the available characters on a given key, hold the key and scroll the trackwheel. To insert a period at the end of a sentence, press the **Space** key twice. To turn on NUM LOCK, hold down the **Shift** key (#) and press the **Alt** key; to turn off NUM LOCK, press the **Alt** key by itself. And finally, to switch between SureType and traditional multitap modes, hold down the **Next** key (*).

If you don't have time to finish entering the message body or otherwise want to finish it later, you can save the message instead of sending it. To save the message for later without sending it, click the trackwheel, select **Save Draft** from the menu that appears, and then click. The message will then appear in the message list with a special icon (a small yellow piece of paper) next to it to indicate that it is a draft message that has yet to be sent.

38 Organize Your Messages 149

When you're ready to send a message, open the draft message, click the trackwheel, and then select **Send** from the menu that appears. Click the trackwheel to flag the message for sending. I say that the message is *flagged* instead of being sent because the actual sending of the message depends on your device having access to the wireless network. If you have the radio turned off on your device or are out of the wireless coverage area, the message isn't sent immediately. When you turn the radio back on or regain wireless coverage, the message is automatically sent.

38 Organize Your Messages

✔ BEFORE YOU BEGIN	→ SEE ALSO
33 About Email and Text Messages	**39** Search Your Messages

Whether it's email, PIN, or SMS text messages, you will no doubt accumulate a fair number of messages on your BlackBerry device over time. For this reason, it's important to understand how to organize your messages. Whether you're replying to or forwarding a message, deleting a message, or saving a message for later, the BlackBerry 7100 Messages application makes manipulating your messages and keeping them all sorted simple. You might be surprised to find that you can access several message folders when organizing your messages.

1 Open the Messages Screen

Scroll to the **Messages** icon on the **Home** screen and click the trackwheel. The **Messages** screen appears, displaying a list of email messages that have been sent and received on your device.

2 Reply to a Message

You can reply to a message either from the **Messages** screen or from within the message while it is open. With the message either selected on the **Messages** screen or open, click the trackwheel and then select **Reply** from the menu that appears. Click once more to reply to the message; a new message opens with the original message inserted just below the area where you compose the new message. Now simply compose and send the message just as you would a new message; see **34** **Compose an Email Message**.

▶ **TIP**

An even quicker way to reply to an email message is to press the **Q W** key after selecting the message on the **Messages** screen. Similarly, you can reply to *all* the recipients (if there are more than one) of the currently selected message by pressing the **A S** key.

CHAPTER 6: Digging Deeper into Email and Text Messages

1 Open the Messages Screen
2 Reply to a Message
3 Forward a Message
4 Delete Unwanted Messages
5 Mark Important Messages As Unopened
7 Save Messages for Later
6 Navigate Message Folders

38 Organize Your Messages

3 Forward a Message

Similar to replying, you can forward a message either from the **Messages** screen or from within the message while it is open. With the message either selected on the **Messages** screen or open, click the trackwheel and then select

38 Organize Your Messages   151

Forward on the menu that appears. Click once more to forward the message; the **Select Address** screen appears. Now simply select recipients or type "use once" addresses just as you would when addressing a new message; see **34 Compose an Email Message**, **36 Send a PIN Message**, and **37 Send an SMS Message**. The message you send when replying to or forwarding an original message can be an email message, an SMS message, or a PIN message—make your choice from the **Select Address** screen.

▶ **TIP**

An even quicker way to forward a message is to select the message on the **Messages** screen and press the **O P** key.

4 Delete Unwanted Messages

Unwanted email, PIN, and SMS text messages are easily deleted either from the **Messages** screen or from within the message while it is open. With the message either selected on the **Messages** screen or open, click the trackwheel and select **Delete** from the menu that appears. You are prompted to confirm the deletion of the message; select and click **Delete** to follow through with the deletion or select **Cancel** if you change your mind.

▶ **TIP**

You can disable the delete confirmation so you don't have to always confirm message deletions; see **40 Configure Email Options**.

▶ **NOTE**

Unless you are synchronizing personal email folders using the BlackBerry Enterprise Server, BlackBerry messages have no concept of a trash can or recycling bin, so when you delete a message from your device it truly is gone forever unless you have saved a copy elsewhere. Knowing this, it's important to be sure that you want to delete a message before doing so.

▶ **TIP**

An even quicker way to delete a message is to select the message on the **Messages** screen and press the **Delete** key.

If your messages have a tendency to pile up and you find yourself needing to delete several messages at once, try selecting more than one message and then initiating a deletion. To do this, scroll to the first message in the range of messages to be deleted, press and hold the **Shift** key, and continue scrolling the trackwheel to select additional messages. Now initiate a deletion by pressing the **Backspace** key (or click and select **Delete** from the menu); all the selected messages are deleted in one action.

▶ **TIP**

Another way to delete a large group of messages is to delete the messages you've accumulated before a certain date. To do this, scroll with the trackwheel on the **Messages** screen and select a *date* (not a message). Click the trackwheel and select **Delete Prior** from the menu that appears. Click again, and all the messages with a date before the selected date are deleted. Be careful with this approach to deleting messages because you can easily wipe out a lot of messages at once.

5 Mark Important Messages As Unopened

When you first receive a message on your device, the message is flagged as unopened, as is evidenced by the bright yellow envelope icon that appears next to the message. After you open a message, the icon changes to a gray open envelope to indicate that you've already seen it. In some situations, you might want to change the status of an important opened message back to unopened so you remember to read it again.

To change the status of a message to unopened, either select the message on the **Messages** screen or open the message. Then click the trackwheel and select **Mark Unopened** from the menu that appears. The message is now marked unopened as if you had just received it; the new message count is even increased to reflect the new status of the message.

▶ **TIP**

Just as you can mark important opened messages as unopened, you can also mark a new, unread message as opened. Just select **Mark Opened** on the **Messages** menu and click. You can also mark an entire group of messages as opened based on a certain date. To do this, scroll with the trackwheel on the **Messages** screen and select a *date* (not a message). Click the trackwheel and select **Mark Prior Opened** from the menu that appears. Click again, and the status of all the messages with a date before the selected date is changed to opened. This technique provides a handy way to clear the new message count so you can focus on incoming new messages. Just keep in mind that you are flagging messages as opened that you haven't actually read yet.

6 Navigate Message Folders

It might come as a surprise to learn that your device actually has message folders. In fact, most of the messages on your device are organized into folders based on the type of message and the organization of folders on your desktop email client. Folders aren't just for messages, however. Your device also contains folders that store call logs and missed calls, for example.

To view all the folders for your device, click the trackwheel on the **Messages** screen and select **View Folder** from the menu that appears. Click to view the folders for your device. What you are actually doing is viewing the folder for the currently selected message. So, the folder is shown for whatever message is selected on the **Messages** screen when you select **View Folder**. In this example, the **Web Client Inbox** folder is shown because I first selected an email message that was delivered through the BlackBerry Web Client.

▶ **NOTE**

You can think of the main **Messages** screen as a view of all the message folders on your device at once. In other words, it combines all the messages currently stored on your device into a single view. You can then navigate to specific folders to limit the view to certain messages. The only messages that aren't displayed on the main **Messages** screen are saved messages, which are stored in a special **Saved Messages** folder; step 7 covers saved messages.

Notice that some of the folders have a plus (+) sign next to them, which indicates they contain subfolders. To open a folder and reveal its subfolders, scroll to select the folder and click the trackwheel. Select **Expand** from the menu that appears and click again. The same process applies to closing a folder and hiding its subfolders, except that you select **Collapse** from the menu instead. To view the contents of a folder, scroll to select the folder and click the trackwheel. Then choose **Select Folder** from the menu and click again. The folder is displayed, showing the list of messages stored within the folder. To return to the main **Messages** screen, just press the **Escape** button.

7 Save Messages for Later

A good way to organize your messages so the main **Messages** screen isn't so cluttered is to save important messages in the **Saved Messages** folder. To save a message in the **Saved Messages** folder, first select the message on the **Messages** screen or open the message. Then click the trackwheel and select **Save** from the menu that appears. A *copy* of the message is placed in the **Saved Messages** folder, which means you can delete the original message from the main **Messages** screen and access it later as a saved message.

To access saved messages in the **Saved Messages** folder, click the trackwheel on the **Messages** screen and select **View Saved Messages** from the menu that appears. Click to display the **Saved Messages** folder, which contains all your saved messages. You interact with these messages just as you would messages on the main **Messages** screen.

39 Search Your Messages

✔ BEFORE YOU BEGIN	→ SEE ALSO
33 About Email and Text Messages	**38** Organize Your Messages

As your list of sent and received text messages grows on your device, immediately accessing information within them becomes increasingly difficult. Although it's certainly possible to open every message and look for information that is of interest, this approach is woefully inefficient. Fortunately, your device has a built-in search feature that allows you to instantly search all your messages for keywords. Using this search approach, you can quickly search for and isolate messages based on a name, message subject, or message text.

1 Open the Messages Screen

Scroll to the **Messages** icon on the **Home** screen and click the trackwheel. The **Messages** screen appears, displaying a list of messages that have been sent and received on your device.

2 Open the Search Screen

Click the trackwheel and select **Search** from the menu that appears. Click once more to open the **Search** screen.

3 Enter the Search Criteria

The **Search** screen allows you to search for messages based on any combination of the following search criteria: **Name**, **Subject**, **Message**, **Folder**, **Show**, and **Type**. The **Name** criterion can consist of any name in any address field or specifically the **From:**, **To:**, **Cc:**, or **Bcc:** field; use the **In** setting to determine whether you are searching for *any* name or *within a specific field*. You can specify text for the **Subject** and **Message** criteria that is used to match text in the subject and body of the message, respectively. The **Folder** criterion allows you to specify an individual folder in which to limit the search. The **Show** criterion allows you to limit the search results to messages in the **Received**, **Sent**, **Saved**, or **Draft** folder. And finally, the **Type** criterion allows you to limit the search to a particular type of message, such as an email or PIN message. In the example shown, I've chosen to search only for messages I've received from my brother.

39 Search Your Messages 155

1 Open the Messages Screen

2 Open the Search Screen

3 Enter the Search Criteria

4 Perform the Search

39 Search Your Messages

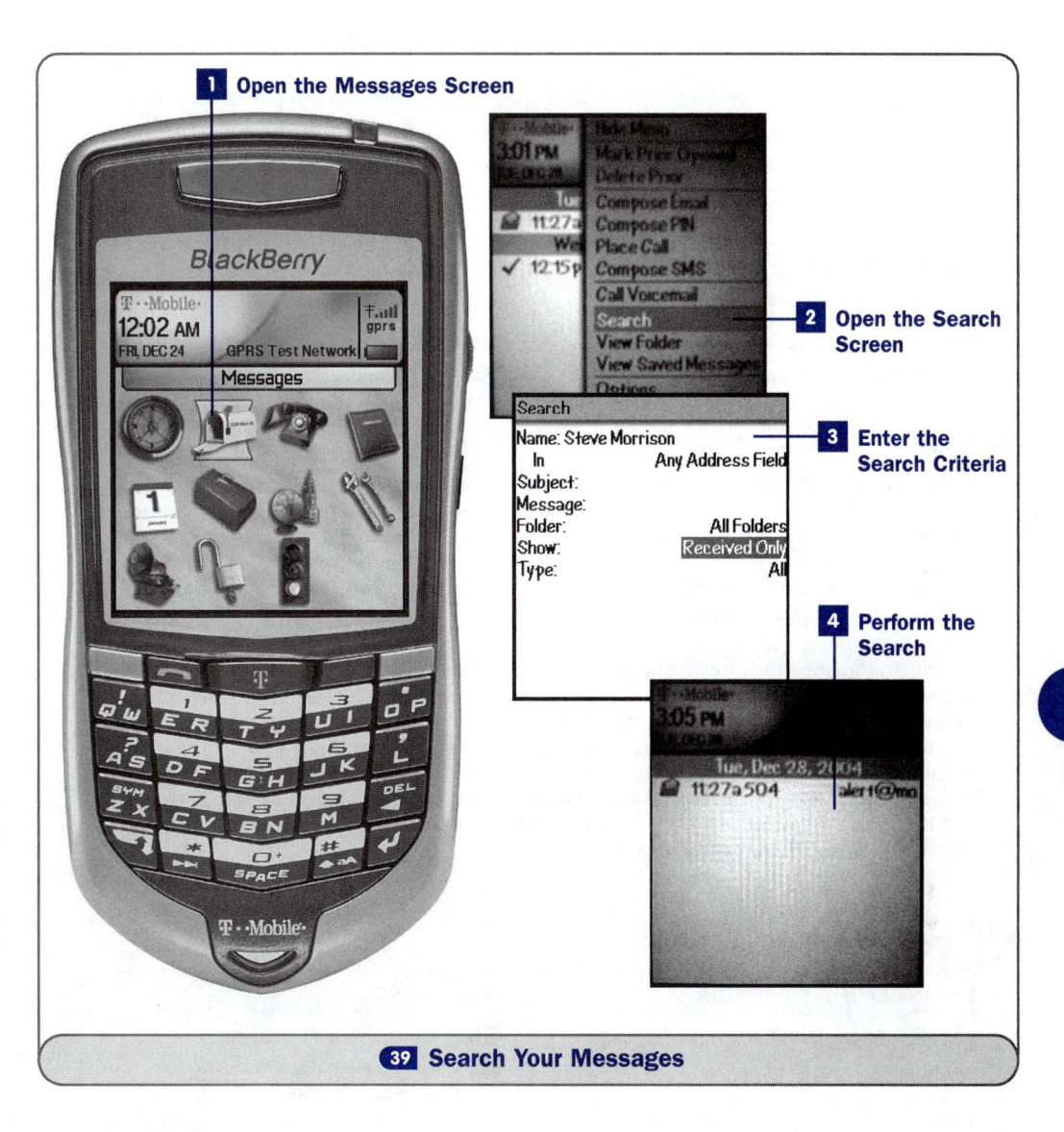

▶ **TIPS**

When entering the **Name** criterion for a message search, keep in mind that the name can be a person's name, a PIN, or a phone number (SMS address).

You can quickly perform a message search based on a particular sender or message subject by selecting a message on the **Messages** screen, clicking the trackwheel, and then selecting **Search Sender** (select **Search Recipient** if you sent the message) or **Search Subject** from the menu that appears. Click once more to instantly search your messages for the particular sender or subject.

You can enter as many or as few of the search criteria as you want. Just keep in mind that the more information you provide, the more accurate the results will be. On the other hand, if you try to get too specific, you might limit the search results too much. It all comes down to how exacting you want the search to be.

4 Perform the Search

After entering the search criteria, click the trackwheel and select **Search** from the menu that appears. Click once more to initiate the search. The results are displayed as a message list.

▶ TIPS

If you find yourself repeatedly performing a similar search, consider saving the search. After entering the search criteria on the **Search** screen, click the trackwheel and select **Save** from the menu that appears. Click once more, and then enter a title for the saved search on the **Save Search** screen; you can also create a shortcut for the search if you'd like, which is the combination of the **Alt** key plus another unused key. To save the search, click the trackwheel, select **Save** from the menu, and click again.

In addition to any of your own saved searches, consider using some built-in saved searches. To recall and issue a saved search from the **Search** screen, click the trackwheel and select **Recall** from the menu that appears. Click once more to display a list of saved searches. If a saved search has a keyboard shortcut, the key is shown in parentheses next to the search in the list; press the **Alt** key plus the letter key to initiate the search directly from the **Messages** screen. Otherwise, initiate a saved search by selecting the search from the list, clicking the trackwheel, choosing **Select Search** from the menu that appears, and clicking once more.

40 Configure Email Options

✔ BEFORE YOU BEGIN	→ SEE ALSO
33 About Email and Text Messages	38 Organize Your Messages
	41 Redirect Messages with the BlackBerry Redirector

As with most aspects of the BlackBerry 7100 series of devices, the email system is highly configurable. The default email settings will likely serve your needs just fine—especially early on—but you can tailor the email system to your own work style with a few tweaks. For example, by changing the email options, you can eliminate the delete confirmation request that appears every time you attempt to delete an email message. This is an important confirmation that helps you avoid accidentally deleting email messages, but it can also be a pain if you regularly delete messages and get tired of okaying every deletion.

40 Configure Email Options

1 Open the Messages Screen

2 Open the General Options Screen

3 Configure General Email Options

4 Configure Email Reconciliation Options

5 Exit Email Options

40 Configure Email Options

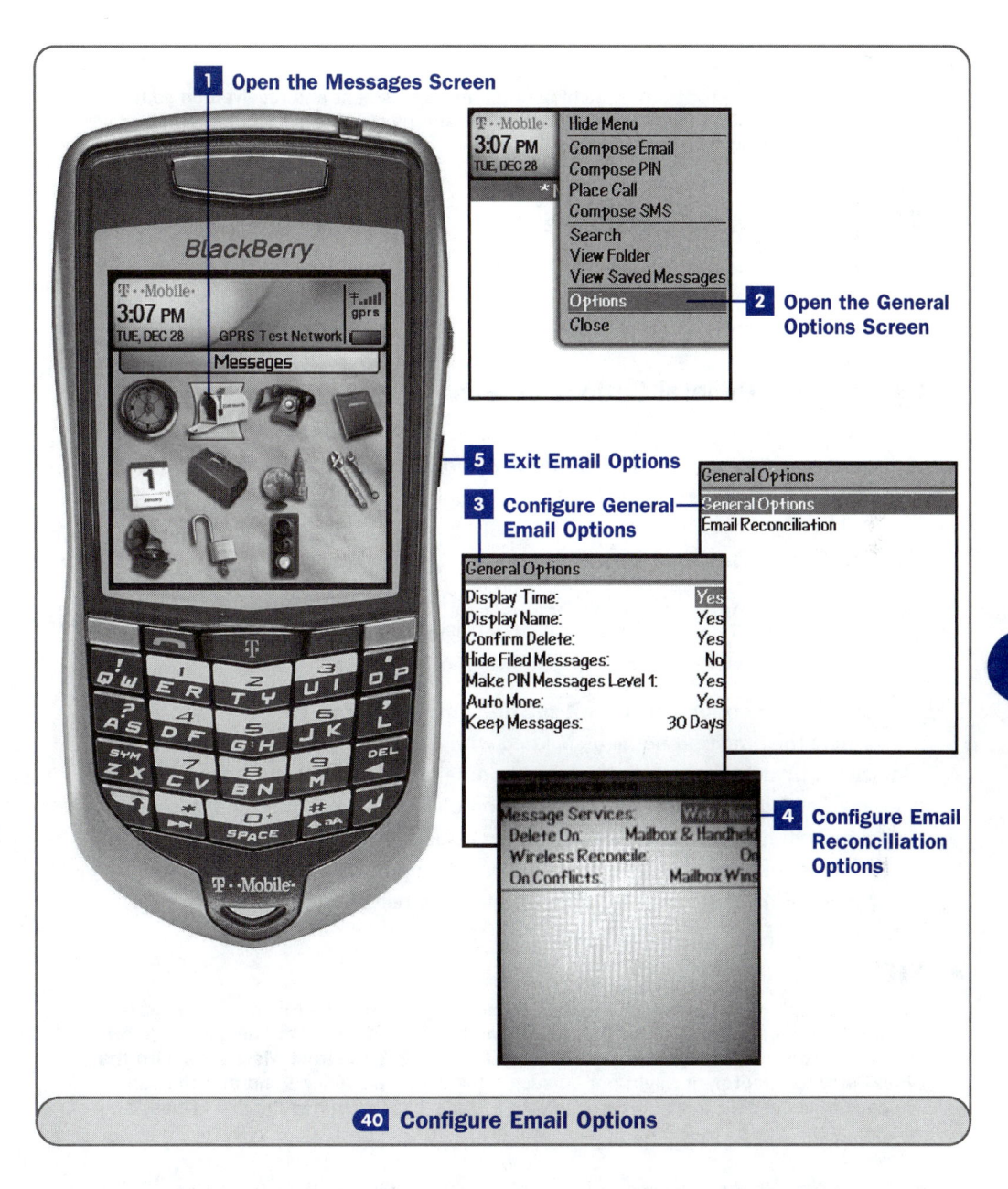

You can also change email *reconciliation* settings through the email options, although this isn't usually necessary unless you are changing your method of reconciliation. For example, if you're switching from the BlackBerry Redirector to the BlackBerry Web Client, or vice versa, changing the reconciliation options certainly makes sense. You can also specify exactly how conflicts are resolved between your device and your email mailbox during reconciliation.

▶ KEY TERM

Reconciliation—The process of matching email messages sent and received on your BlackBerry device with those that have been sent and received using another email client, such as Microsoft Outlook.

1 Open the Messages Screen

Scroll to the **Messages** icon on the **Home** screen and click the trackwheel. The **Messages** screen appears, displaying a list of email messages that have been sent and received on your device.

2 Open the General Options Screen

Click the trackwheel on the **Messages** screen and scroll to select **Options** from the menu that appears. The **General Options** screen appears and provides access to two categories of email options.

3 Configure General Email Options

To configure general email options, select **General Options** on the **General Options** screen and click the trackwheel. The second **General Options** screen appears and provides access to general email options.

The first two options, **Display Time** and **Display Name**, enable you to show or hide the time and name associated with a message on the **Messages** screen; by default, both the time and name are shown, which is generally a good setting. The **Confirm Delete** option allows you to eliminate the confirmation that appears when you delete messages. Although setting this option to **No** certainly speeds up the process of deleting messages, it removes the safeguard that prevents you from accidentally deleting a message.

▶ TIP

Unless you don't mind the risk of accidentally deleting an important message, I recommend that you leave the **Confirm Delete** option enabled. On the other hand, if you know you have a copy of messages on your desktop PC (see **41 Redirect Messages with the BlackBerry Redirector**), it might not be such a big deal. Personally, I find that the convenience of being able to zap messages with a single click overrides the risk of possibly deleting messages by accident.

The **Hide Filed Messages** option applies to email reconciliation: When enabled, the option hides files in the **Messages** list after they've been filed to a personal folder. The **Make PIN Messages Level 1** option determines the priority level of PIN messages; a level 1 message is a high-priority message, which is typically appropriate for PIN messages. The **Auto More** option applies to long messages, which are delivered to your device in sections.

When enabled, the **Auto More** option causes your device to automatically request additional pages of a long message as you read through the message. If you disable the option, you have to explicitly request each additional page of the message by opening the individual submessages. Finally, the **Keep Messages** option determines how long messages are kept around on your device before being automatically deleted. You can select a set number of days before messages are deleted or select **Forever** to never have messages automatically deleted.

▶ **TIP**

Saved messages are never automatically deleted. To prevent a message from automatically being deleted based on the value of the **Keep Messages** option, be sure to save the message; see **38 Organize Your Messages** for details on how to save a message.

After tweaking the general email options, press the **Escape** button to return to the initial **General Options** screen. If you've made changes, select **Save** in the confirmation window to confirm the changes and then click the trackwheel.

4 Configure Email Reconciliation Options

Email reconciliation allows you to keep email messages synchronized between your BlackBerry device and your desktop PC. Several options are available when it comes to reconciling email messages. From the main **General Options** screen, scroll to select **Email Reconciliation**; then click the trackwheel. The **Email Reconciliation** screen appears and provides access to options related to how your email is reconciled with an email client.

The first setting on the **Email Reconciliation** screen is **Message Services**, which enables you to select the message service whose options you want to change. For example, select **Web Client** to change the options for the BlackBerry Web Client message service, or select **Desktop** to change the options for the BlackBerry Redirector service. After selecting a message service, the options for the service appear just below the **Message Services** field. If you don't see a **Message Services** field on your device, it likely means that the only service you have installed is the **Web Client** service; the **Desktop** service is associated with the BlackBerry Redirector application.

The specific options for a message service can range from how messages are deleted to how the service handles conflicts; a conflict occurs when a message on your device doesn't match a message on your desktop or in the BlackBerry Web Client. For example, the **Delete On** option for the Web Client service determines whether a message is deleted only on the handheld, on both the Web Client mailbox and the handheld, or based on a prompt that allows you to choose for each message. The **Wireless Reconcile** option simply turns wireless reconciliation on and off. And finally, the **On Conflicts** option determines how reconciliation conflicts are resolved. This option comes into play if messages have changed on both the handheld and the Web Client before the last reconciliation. The safe setting is to allow the mailbox to win (**Mailbox Wins**), which means the handheld changes will give way to the mailbox changes.

When you're finished configuring email reconciliation options, press the **Escape** button to return to the initial **General Options** screen. If you've made changes, select **Save** in the confirmation window to confirm the changes and then click the trackwheel.

▶ **NOTE**

To reconcile messages on your device, click the trackwheel, scroll down to **Reconcile Now**, and click once more. Messages are then reconciled based on your device's email reconciliation options.

5 Exit Email Options

Press the **Escape** button to exit the initial **General Options** screen. Press the **Escape** button again to navigate back to the **Home** screen, or just press the **End** key.

41 Redirect Messages with the BlackBerry Redirector

✔ BEFORE YOU BEGIN	→ SEE ALSO
33 About Email and Text Messages	40 Configure Email Options

The BlackBerry **Redirector** application runs on your desktop PC and serves as a way of shuttling desktop email to your BlackBerry device. This application is primarily applicable to corporate email users who don't have access to the BlackBerry Enterprise Server and who can't integrate their corporate email account with the BlackBerry Web Client. The BlackBerry Redirector enters the picture in this scenario and provides a clever means of forwarding email from your desktop email client to your BlackBerry device. Because the BlackBerry Redirector simply watches your email client and forwards messages as they are received, your desktop PC must be running at all times for you to receive forwarded messages on your device. For this reason, the BlackBerry Redirector is less than ideal in some ways. But like I said, if you don't have the BlackBerry Enterprise Server or BlackBerry Web Client as options, the BlackBerry Redirector is a lifesaver!

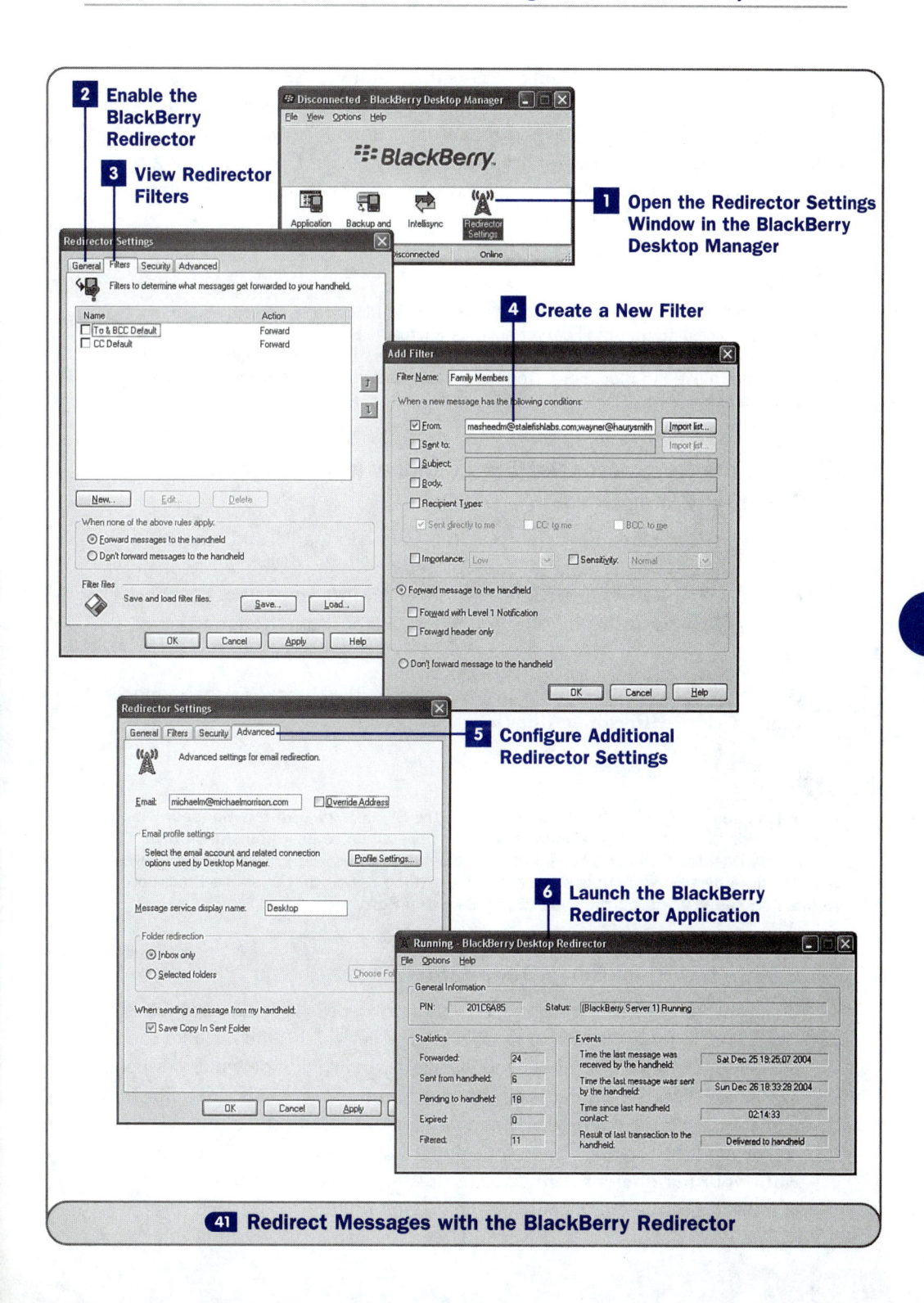

41 Redirect Messages with the BlackBerry Redirector

1 Open the Redirector Settings Window in the BlackBerry Desktop Manager

2 Enable the BlackBerry Redirector

3 View Redirector Filters

4 Create a New Filter

5 Configure Additional Redirector Settings

6 Launch the BlackBerry Redirector Application

41 Redirect Messages with the BlackBerry Redirector

CHAPTER 6: Digging Deeper into Email and Text Messages

The nice thing about the BlackBerry **Redirector** is that you can be anywhere with your device and receive wireless email. Messages are forwarded wirelessly as long as your desktop PC is on and the **Redirector** application is running. The BlackBerry **Redirector** requires a Microsoft Exchange server to work properly, so you should check to ensure that you have access to an Exchange server before attempting to use **Redirector**.

▶ **NOTE**

Although the BlackBerry Redirector doesn't require the BlackBerry Enterprise Server, it *does* require access to an email server such as Microsoft Exchange Server. If you use a POP email account through an ISP and don't have access to an Exchange server, you won't be able to use the BlackBerry **Redirector** application; use the BlackBerry Web Client instead.

🔷 41

1 Open the Redirector Settings Window in the BlackBerry Desktop Manager

With your BlackBerry device plugged in to your desktop PC and turned on, click the **Start** button on the Windows Taskbar of your desktop PC to open the main Windows system menu. Then select **All Programs**, **BlackBerry**, **Desktop Manager**. The BlackBerry Desktop Manager application window appears.

Double-click the **Redirector Settings** icon in the BlackBerry Desktop Manager window. The **Redirector Settings** window appears.

▶ **TIP**

If you don't see the **Redirector Settings** icon in the BlackBerry Desktop Manager window, you didn't install the BlackBerry Redirector application when you installed the BlackBerry Desktop Software. You'll need to reinstall the BlackBerry Desktop Software—and this time be sure you choose the email integration option that uses the BlackBerry Redirector; see **8 Install the BlackBerry Desktop Software**.

2 Enable the BlackBerry Redirector

When the **Redirector Settings** window initially appears, the **General** tab is visible. In addition to showing the PIN of your device, this tab includes check boxes that allow you to enable and disable the redirection of email messages. The **Redirect incoming messages to your handheld** option is what ultimately controls the redirection of messages; make sure this box is checked to enable email redirection. The second option, **Disable email redirection while your handheld is connected**, is used to disable redirection while your handheld is connected to your desktop PC. You usually should keep this option enabled because your device should automatically remain synchronized while connected to your desktop PC.

The **Auto Signature** field on the **General** tab allows you to set the signature that appears on outgoing messages sent from your handheld. It's up to you whether you want messages originating from your handheld to have a unique signature.

When you're finished with the **General** tab, click the **Filters** tab to view redirector filters.

3 View Redirector Filters

Filters allow you to take exacting control over the messages forwarded from your desktop email client to your BlackBerry device. By default, all messages are forwarded to your device. If you want to limit forwarded messages, select the **Don't forward messages to the handheld** option, located just under the filter list. This option changes the default action so that no messages are delivered to your handheld. Then you set up specific filters to allow the forwarding of messages that meet certain criteria.

To begin creating a new filter, click the **New** button. The **Add Filter** window appears.

4 Create a New Filter

Creating a new filter using the **Add Filter** window involves specifying the characteristics of a message that set it apart from other messages. This could be the address from which the message was sent, the address to which the message is sent, the message subject, the message body, and so on.

Start by entering a name for the filter in the **Filter Name** field. As an example, you might create a filter that identifies email from your immediate family. After entering the filter name, select the contacts for your family members by enabling the **From** check box and clicking the **Import List** button. After specifying the contacts in the **From** field, make sure the **Forward message to the handheld** option is selected as the action you want taken. Click the **OK** button and the new filter is created. You now have a filter that allows emails from your family members to be forwarded to your device. And if you enabled the **Don't forward messages to the handheld** option on the **General** tab, only the filtered family messages will be forwarded to your device. You can set up additional filters to further broaden the range of emails that are forwarded to your device.

▶ **TIP**

You should save your filters so you can easily restore them in case you ever have a problem and need to reinstall or set up the BlackBerry Redirector on another computer. To save your filters, click the **Save** button on the **Filters** tab of the **Redirector Settings** window. Then browse to the desired folder, specify a single filename for all the filters, and click **Save** to save them. You can later load filters from a file by clicking the **Load** button on the **Filters** tab of the **Redirector Settings** window.

5 Configure Additional Redirector Settings

You might want to configure a few additional redirector options before launching the **Redirector** application. I'm referring to those options found on the **Advanced** tab of the **Redirector Settings** window. Here you can change the email address that appears on messages sent from your device through the BlackBerry Redirector. You can also change the email profile used for email redirection. Email profiles are used in email clients to keep track of a set of settings and email accounts—it's unlikely that you'll change the email profile used for redirection unless you already take advantage of multiple profiles. The **Message service display name** option enables you to change the name of the message service for redirection, which is matched up in the email options on your device; see ④⓪ **Configure Email Options**.

▶ **NOTE**

Notice the **Security** tab in the **Redirector Settings** window. This tab enables you to control how encryption keys are generated for encrypting redirected messages. Unless you have a good reason for not trusting the automatic approach to encryption-key generation, there is no reason to change this setting.

Most of the options on the **Advanced** tab of the **Redirector Settings** window are unlikely to need changing, but you might find the **Folder redirection** option worthy of a closer look. This option enables you to specify individual folders for email redirection, as opposed to simply forwarding messages from the email client's **Inbox** folder. The **Inbox** folder is the most likely folder to be used for message redirection, but if you have set up filters in your email client to shuttle messages into certain folders, you might want to focus the redirection on those folders instead of the **Inbox**.

The last option in the **Advanced** tab of the **Redirector Settings** window simply determines whether copies of messages sent from your device are saved in the **Sent** folder on your device. This option is entirely up to your own personal tastes and how important you consider sent messages. Just keep in mind that, if you do keep copies of sent messages in the **Sent** folder, you'll need to visit the folder from time to time to clear out old messages and conserve space; see ③⑧ **Organize Your Messages**.

When you're finished with the **Redirector Settings** window, click the **OK** button to accept your changes or click **Cancel** if you want to exit the settings without saving. You are returned to the BlackBerry Desktop Manager.

6 Launch the BlackBerry Redirector Application

You're finally ready to launch the BlackBerry **Redirector** application and begin redirecting messages from your desktop email client to your device. Click the **Start** button on the Windows Taskbar of your desktop PC to open the main Windows system menu. Then select **All Programs**, **BlackBerry**, **BlackBerry Desktop Redirector**. The BlackBerry **Redirector** application appears and begins redirecting messages to your device.

The BlackBerry **Redirector** application provides a variety of information related to the redirection of messages. The **Statistics** area of the main window shows redirection statistics such as how many messages have been forwarded, how many have been sent from the handheld, how many are pending delivery, and how many have been filtered. Similarly, the **Events** area of the main window shows the last time a message was sent and received on the device, the last time contact was made with the device, and what happened during the last contact.

Just leave the BlackBerry **Redirector** application running to have messages continually redirected to your BlackBerry device.

▶ **NOTE**

To help minimize unnecessary message redirection, the BlackBerry Redirector doesn't forward a message if it is opened in the desktop email client while awaiting wireless delivery. In other words, redirection is cancelled if you open a message on your desktop before it actually gets redirected to your device.

7

Instant Messaging with Your BlackBerry

IN THIS CHAPTER:

- **42** About Instant Messages
- **43** Set Up Instant Messaging
- **44** Manage Your IM Contacts
- **45** Carry On an IM Conversation
- **46** About Instant Messaging Services

CHAPTER 7: Instant Messaging with Your BlackBerry

Email, **SMS**, and **PIN** messages all provide useful approaches for communicating with other people using your BlackBerry device. However, they suffer from a common problem in that they tend to have a delayed sense to them in terms of how rapidly you can carry on a dialogue with someone. Granted, **push email** messaging helps in terms of delivering messages rapidly, but for the true feel of a live conversation, look toward instant messaging as opposed to email, SMS, or PIN messaging. Instant messaging involves a live "connection" to another device to which you can send and receive messages in real time. Not only does instant messaging have a perceived effect of being faster than other messaging options, the user interface for instant messaging is typically structured more like a conversation. This chapter introduces you to instant messaging as it pertains to your BlackBerry 7100 device.

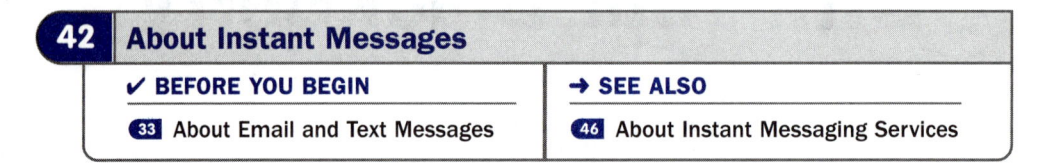

42 About Instant Messages

✔ **BEFORE YOU BEGIN**
33 About Email and Text Messages

→ **SEE ALSO**
46 About Instant Messaging Services

Instant messaging is a specific type of text messaging that focuses on a real-time conversation between two or more parties. Unlike email, PIN, and SMS messages—all of which can be sent and received using a BlackBerry device—instant messages (IMs) are considered part of an ongoing dialogue in which all the messages in a conversation are directly shown onscreen. In other words, you don't have to open an instant message to view it and there is no concept of an *inbox* for instant messages.

There is, however, the concept of a *conversation* in instant messaging. The idea is that you establish a communication link with another person or persons and then carry out a conversation by sending short text messages back and forth. In the case of BlackBerry devices, the communication link is wireless, which facilitates mobile instant messaging. As you can imagine, mobile instant messaging opens up many unique possibilities for communicating in ways that weren't previously possible with traditional wired text messaging. For example, businesspeople can quietly comment and share ideas with each other while sitting in on a presentation.

If you've used a BlackBerry device in the past, you are no doubt already familiar with sending and receiving text messages such as email, PIN, and SMS messages. However, none of those forms of text messaging have the same feel as instant messaging. Just as Nextel's two-way pager feature on its mobile phones has changed the way some people work, so does instant text messaging. There is no

42 About Instant Messages

better way to have a quick, quiet, two-way conversation with someone from any location, assuming you both you have wireless coverage.

▶ **NOTE**
Generally speaking, you must use the same instant messaging service as the person with whom you want to communicate. For example, if you want to carry on an instant messaging conversation with someone using Yahoo! Messenger, you must use the Yahoo! Messenger client application on your BlackBerry device. You also must set up an account with the instant messaging service you select, assuming you don't already have one.

Lest you think I'm completely sold on instant messaging, there *is* a downside. Similar to a phone call, an incoming instant message requires you to respond in real time—or at least that's the expectation. Unlike a phone call, where no one knows whether you're truly available to take the call, your instant message status is readily available to your circle of contacts; your status can be conveyed by an icon, text, or both. In other words, people know whether you're available for instant messaging, which isn't always a good thing. For this reason, it's important to keep close tabs on your instant messaging status and change it to **Available** only when you truly are open to receiving instant messages. Keep in mind that every instant messaging application shows a list of "buddies," who are people you've decided to keep in your circle of communication. The status of people in your buddy list constantly changes to reflect their availability. If you send a message to someone who is offline or unavailable, she won't receive the message until she gets back online or makes herself available.

Another downside to instant messaging has to do with the immediacy of the communication. One of the enormous benefits that has made email so successful is the ability it gives you to think about or otherwise research a response before replying to a message. Email is not immediate—you have time to gather your thoughts and reply at your own leisure. This is the key reason email has replaced the telephone for many professionals, especially in the tech industry. Instant messaging doesn't offer this similar comfort of having time to consider a response—it is as immediate as a phone call. This aspect of instant messaging makes it extremely handy for time-critical communication but a pain for situations in which someone is expecting an immediate answer that you don't have.

▶ **NOTE**
Instant messaging is also sometimes referred to simply as *IM*.

Because you can certainly conduct business using instant messages, you might be curious about saving conversations that take place. Unlike other types of text messages, instant messages aren't granular in the sense that you can't save an individual message. However, most IM clients allow you to save an entire conversation. This is in many ways more powerful than saving a single text message because you get to see the entire exchange of ideas as a sequence of messages within a conversation. You could argue that email has a similar sequence if you read through a series of replies to a message, but the headers and other formatting generally make the email thread tougher to follow than that of an instant message conversation.

One last point to make about instant messaging as it applies to BlackBerry devices has to with your IM account "roaming" from your desktop PC to your BlackBerry device. One of the key concepts behind instant messaging is that it keeps track of your presence at a computer—this is where your IM status comes into play. You have a status that indicates whether you are available, busy, or away, for example. Because your access to an IM service is linked with your presence at a computer, you can be logged in to an IM account on only one computer at a time. So, when you log in to an IM service on your BlackBerry device, you are automatically logged off the service on your desktop (if you were logged on). In this way, your IM account travels with you and allows you to establish an IM presence on any computer, including your BlackBerry device.

42 ▶ **NOTE**

Presence is an important aspect of instant messaging and in fact helps to further distinguish instant messaging from the other types of text messaging. Email, PIN, and SMS messages have no concept of whether you are actually available to receive a message, while instant messaging does.

43 Set Up Instant Messaging

✔ BEFORE YOU BEGIN	→ SEE ALSO
42 About Instant Messages	44 Manage Your IM Contacts
	45 Carry On an IM Conversation

Depending on your wireless service provider, you will likely have instant messaging capabilities already installed on your device by default. These instant messaging capabilities typically target one or more specific instant messaging services, such as AOL Instant Messenger or Yahoo! Messenger. In the United States, T-Mobile ships all its BlackBerry 7100t devices with standard support for AOL, Yahoo!, and ICQ instant message services. If you have an instant messaging account with any of these services, you can carry on instant messaging conversations with your T-Mobile BlackBerry device.

43 Set Up Instant Messaging 171

1 Open the Instant Messaging Screen

2 Select an Instant Messaging Service

3 Sign In to the Instant Messaging Service

4 Change Your IM Status

5 Sign Out and Exit the IM Client

43 Set Up Instant Messaging

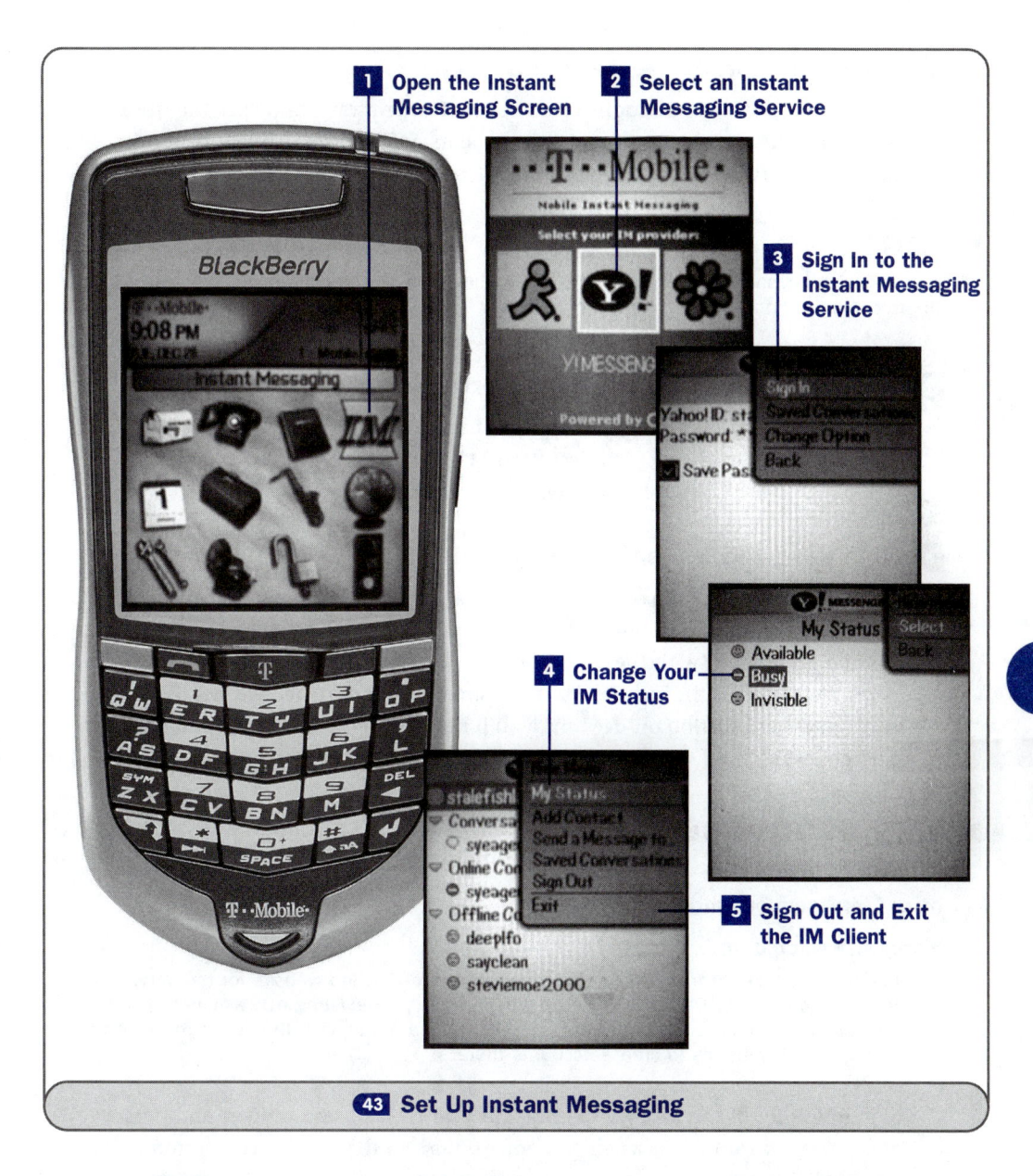

▶ **NOTE**

This task focuses on a T-Mobile 7100t device to demonstrate BlackBerry instant messaging. Your wireless carrier might support different instant messaging services by default, but the idea is still the same. Instant messaging client applications all perform roughly the same function, so it doesn't matter a great deal which service you use as long as you can access it using your device. If your wireless service provider doesn't support the instant messaging service you use, hope is not lost. Check into a third-party unified IM client; see **46 About Instant Messaging Services**.

1 Open the Instant Messaging Screen

Scroll to the **Instant Messaging** icon on the **Home** screen and click the trackwheel. The **Instant Messaging** screen appears, offering an array of instant messaging services offered by your provider from which to choose.

▶ **NOTE**
If your device doesn't include an **Instant Messaging** icon on the **Home** screen, refer to the documentation for the device to find out how to access instant messaging services.

2 Select an Instant Messaging Service

To use one of the services shown on the **Instant Messaging** screen, simply scroll with the trackwheel to select it and then click twice. In the example, I've opted to use Yahoo! Messenger.

3 Sign In to the Instant Messaging Service

Every instant messaging service requires you to sign in before you can carry on IM conversations. To sign in to an IM service, you must have already created an account with the service. If you don't currently have any IM accounts, just visit the website for the desired service and create a new account. After creating an account, you'll have a user ID (or user number) and password you'll use to sign in and use the IM service.

▶ **WEB RESOURCE**
http://www.aol.com/

http://messenger.yahoo.com/

http://www.icq.com/

Creating a new account for an IM service requires you to visit the website for the service you want to create. For AOL Instant Messenger, just use your existing AOL account. If you don't already have an AOL account and you'd like to create one, visit the AOL website. Visit the Yahoo! or ICQ websites to create accounts there.

Sign in to the IM service by entering your user ID (or user number) and password. Keep in mind that when you enter a password, your device automatically switches into multitap mode so you can more easily enter the exact characters in the password. If you want to save the password so you don't have to reenter it in the future, enable the **Save Password** option. When you're ready to sign in, click the trackwheel and scroll to select **Sign In** on the menu that appears. Click once more to sign in.

4 Change Your IM Status

After signing in, you might want to change your IM status from time to time to reflect your current availability. You can always sign out, which obviously makes you unavailable for instant messaging, but you might opt to simply change your status to busy when you don't want anyone contacting you with IM. In Yahoo! Messenger, you can choose from three statuses: **Available**, **Busy**, and **Invisible**. **Available** is the default state, which means you are available and will appear as such to anyone who has you in her IM contact list. **Busy** reflects that you are connected but currently unavailable for chatting. And finally, **Invisible** makes it appear as if you are offline but you can still monitor your own contact list. Other IM clients might have additional statuses, but these three are fairly common across all IM clients. Sometimes the names are slightly different (AOL Instant Messenger uses **Away** instead of **Busy**), but generally the same statuses apply to all IM clients.

To change your status in Yahoo! Messenger, click the trackwheel and select **My Status** from the menu that appears. Click once more to view the **My Status** screen, which allows you to choose a status. Scroll to select a status and then click the trackwheel twice to accept it.

5 Sign Out and Exit the IM Client

When you're finished using an IM service and don't want to remain available, you should sign out . To sign out of Yahoo! Messenger, click the trackwheel and select **Sign Out** from the menu that appears. Then click again to sign out and make yourself unavailable for chatting. Select **Exit** from the menu to exit the IM client. If you don't sign out, selecting **Exit** only minimizes the IM session and you remain available to receive messages.

---

44 Manage Your IM Contacts

✔ BEFORE YOU BEGIN	→ SEE ALSO
43 Set Up Instant Messaging	45 Carry On an IM Conversation

CHAPTER 7: Instant Messaging with Your BlackBerry

1 Sign In to an Instant Messaging Service

2 Create a New Contact

3 Enter the Contact's User ID

4 Delete an Existing Contact

5 Confirm the Deletion

44 Manage Your IM Contacts

Just as you have a circle of family, friends, and business acquaintances with whom you carry on conversations in the real world, you also have a list of contacts that form the basis for instant messaging conversations in the virtual world. In fact, your IM contact list is critical for instant messaging because it not only provides you with a list of people to whom you can send messages, but also provides a means of finding out whether those people are available for chatting. Unlike email, which is sent with no regard for a person's availability, instant messages are typically sent only when you know a person is available and willing to respond in a short amount of time. The immediacy of instant messaging is what makes it so useful. Assembling a list of contacts is therefore a critical part of the instant messaging equation. To add people to your IM buddy (contact) list, just find out from them what their usernames are on the IM service you plan on using.

1 Sign In to an Instant Messaging Service

Launch the desired IM client for the IM service you want to use and sign in to the service. See **43 Set Up Instant Messaging** if you haven't already set up an IM account on your device.

▶ **NOTE**

If you use an IM service other than Yahoo! Messenger, the exact steps for creating and deleting contacts might vary a bit from those listed in this task. Even so, the general approach will likely be very similar.

2 Create a New Contact

The *contact list* is the main screen in every IM client and is the place where you add new contacts. To add a new contact in Yahoo! Messenger, click the trackwheel, select **Add Contact** from the menu that appears, and click once more. The **Add Contact** screen appears and prompts you to enter the contact's user ID.

3 Enter the Contact's User ID

The **Add Contact** screen prompts you to enter the user ID for the contact, which in this case is the Yahoo! ID for the contact. Enter the contact's user ID; then click the trackwheel and select **OK** from the menu that appears. Click the trackwheel once more to add the contact to your contact list and view his current IM status. Keep in mind that people are allowed to reject their addition to your contact list; this helps IM participants prevent unwanted instant messages from people they don't know. If you're adding someone who knows you as a contact, this shouldn't be a problem.

▶ **NOTE**

Every IM client is a little different, and some might not follow the exact process outlined here. For example, in AOL Instant Messenger, you are asked whether you want to accept an IM message, not whether you want to accept being added to someone's contact list. Either way, accepting or declining a contact list addition or an IM message is as simple as saying *yes* or *no*. And keep in mind that you'll see the username of who is on the other end, so you should be able to tell immediately whether it is someone you know.

After adding a new contact, you return to the main contact list, where you might also choose to delete a contact you no longer need.

4 Delete an Existing Contact

To delete an existing contact from the contact list in Yahoo! Messenger, scroll to select the contact, click the trackwheel, select **Delete Contact** from the menu that appears, and click once more. The **Delete Contact** screen appears.

5 Confirm the Deletion

You confirm the deletion of a contact by scrolling to select **OK** on the **Delete Contact** screen, clicking the trackwheel, choosing **Select** from the menu, and clicking again; you can also double-click the trackwheel quickly. If you change your mind about deleting the contact, just select **Back** instead of **OK** on the **Delete Contact** screen.

---

45 Carry On an IM Conversation

✔ **BEFORE YOU BEGIN**

43 Set Up Instant Messaging
44 Manage Your IM Contacts

→ **SEE ALSO**

46 About Instant Messaging Services

Unlike email, PIN, and SMS messages, instant messaging takes place in real time. In this way, the sending and receiving of instant messages is referred to as an *IM conversation*. Just as you talk back and forth with a person in a normal voice conversation, you send messages back and forth in an IM conversation. What makes this unique from other types of text messages is that an IM client application shows the ongoing conversation as a list of messages that are immediately visible. In other words, you don't have to open an IM message to read it. The flow of an IM conversation as a list of immediately viewable text messages in real time is what makes instant messaging such a unique form of wireless communication.

1 Sign In to an Instant Messaging Service

Launch the desired IM client for the IM service you want to use and sign in to the service. See 43 **Set Up Instant Messaging** if you haven't already set up an IM account on your device. When you have selected the IM client you want to use, the list of clients appears; this list applies only to the service you selected.

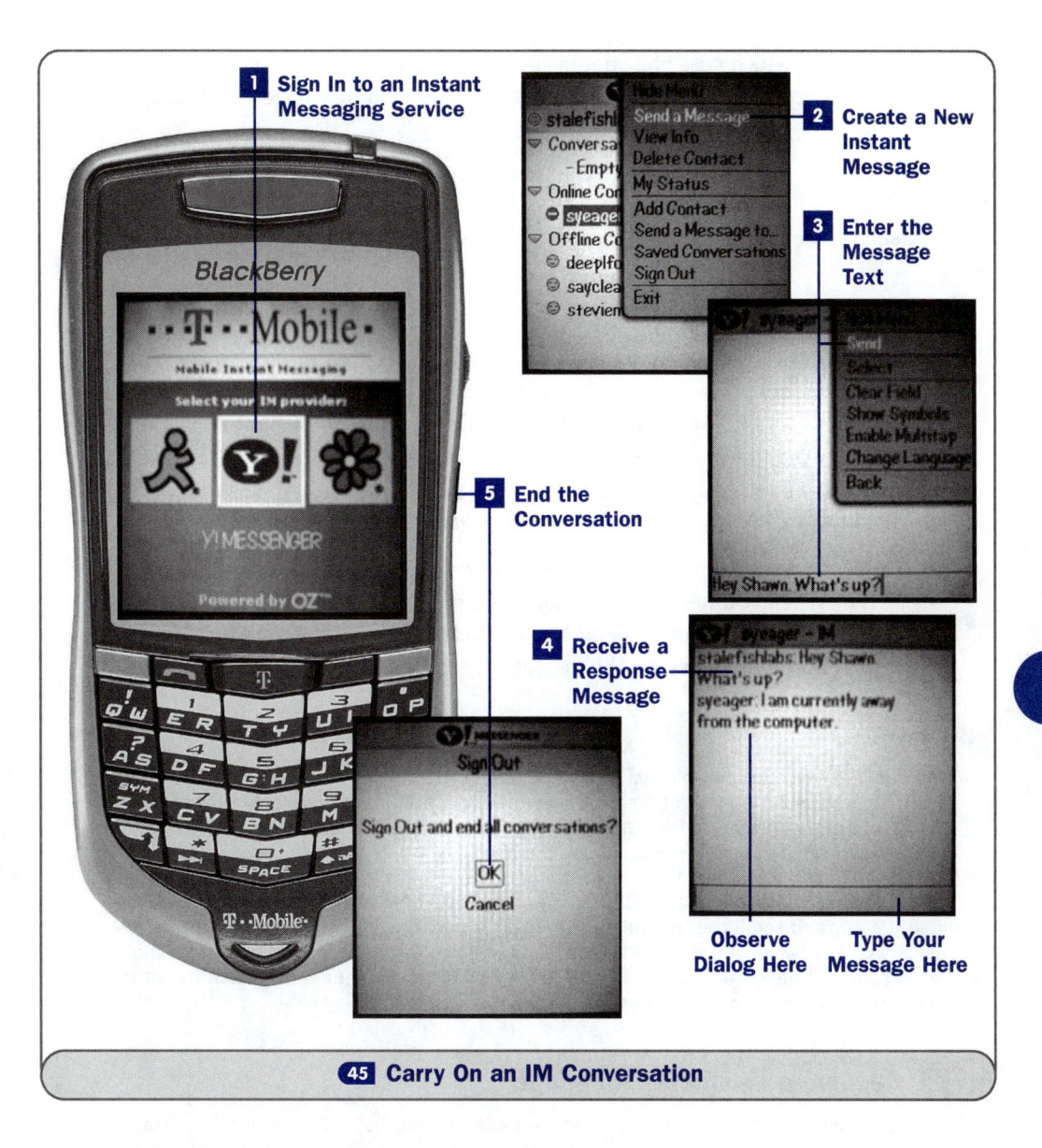

45 Carry On an IM Conversation   177

1. Sign In to an Instant Messaging Service
2. Create a New Instant Message
3. Enter the Message Text
4. Receive a Response Message
5. End the Conversation

Observe Dialog Here   Type Your Message Here

45 Carry On an IM Conversation

2 Create a New Instant Message

If you want to send a message to someone who isn't in your contact list, click the trackwheel, select **Send a Message to** from the menu that appears, and click again. You will be prompted to enter the user ID (or user number) of the person to whom you want to send the message.

Scroll to select a contact from your contact list and then click to confirm the selection. More than likely, you'll want to send a message to an existing contact, in which case you should click the trackwheel, select **Send a Message** from the menu, and click again to create a new message. A new message screen appears.

▶ **NOTE**
By creating a new instant message, you are effectively starting an IM conversation.

3 Enter the Message Text

The screen where you enter a new message is interesting in that most of the screen is blank; the area where you enter the message is just a small space along the bottom. This user interface reflects the fact that instant messages are intended to be short and sweet. Additionally, it shows how instant messaging is more about carrying on a conversation, where the back-and-forth dialogue is displayed in the main area of the screen.

Enter your instant message in the text entry field along the bottom of the screen. When you're finished, double-click the trackwheel (you're actually clicking once to display a menu and then clicking a second time to select the default menu item, **Send**.) The message is sent to the target contact.

▶ **TIP**
You can use several typing shortcuts while entering text on your BlackBerry device. For example, to make the most of the *SureType* feature, enter an entire word letter by letter before attempting to select from the list of corrections. If you must make a correction using the SureType pop-up window, press the **Next** key (*) or scroll the trackwheel to highlight the correction and then click. To capitalize a letter, hold the letter key until the capitalized letter appears. To scroll through all the available characters on a given key, hold the key and scroll the trackwheel. To insert a period at the end of a sentence, press the **Space** key twice. To turn on NUM LOCK, hold down the **Shift** key (#) and press the **Alt** key; to turn off NUM LOCK, press the **Alt** key by itself. And finally, to switch between SureType and traditional multitap modes, hold down the **Next** key (*).

4 Receive a Response Message

After sending an instant message to someone who is available for chatting, it shouldn't take long to receive a response. If the person is unavailable or otherwise unwilling to "talk," you might get a message much like the one I received in the example—my friend Shawn changed his status and stepped out just as I sent him a message! In this case, I received an automatic response message letting me know that Shawn was no longer available.

Assuming your IM conversation doesn't end as abruptly as mine did, you can continue talking as long as you want and the conversation text will continue scrolling up the screen.

46 About Instant Messaging Services

▶ **TIP**

You might find that an IM conversation is worth saving so that you can later access the information discussed. To save a conversation, click the trackwheel at any point during the conversation and select **Save** from the menu that appears. Click once more to save the conversation. You are prompted to enter a "history name" for the conversation, which is used to identify it. To view a saved conversation at a later date, click the trackwheel on the main Yahoo! Messenger screen, select **Saved Conversations** from the menu, and click again. You will see a list of saved conversations from which to choose.

5 End the Conversation

Unless you change your status, sign out, or exit the IM client, you never truly end a conversation—at least not from a technical perspective. When you finish a conversation with someone, you close the conversation screen just by pressing the **Escape** button. However, if that contact sends you another message, the same conversation screen appears and the conversation is resumed. So ending an IM conversation is really more akin to ending a conversation in the real world. If you want to make sure the conversation is over and you don't receive any more messages, change your status to **Busy** or **Invisible** or sign out altogether.

46 About Instant Messaging Services

✔ **BEFORE YOU BEGIN**

42 About Instant Messages

→ **SEE ALSO**

43 Set Up Instant Messaging

One of the biggest problems with instant messaging is the many divergent IM services, each of which requires you to use and potentially install its own unique IM client before you can communicate using that service. This might not seem like a big deal; just pick one service and stick with it, right? The problem arises when you start realizing that your friends, family, and business acquaintances all use different IM services. The only way to communicate with all of them using instant messages is to install all the IM clients, which is like having to install Internet Explorer, Firefox, Safari, and Opera on your desktop PC just so you can browse a variety of websites.

Some wireless providers have helped solve this problem by offering built-in support for several IM services. For example, T-Mobile includes standard support for AOL Instant Messenger, Yahoo! Messenger, and ICQ in its 7100t devices. Of course, this leaves many MSN Messenger/Windows Messenger users out in the cold. The problem therefore still exists to some degree because you have a variety of IM services and no way to consolidate them under one roof. Or so it might seem. Before I touch on a solution to this problem, let's quickly assess the current major IM services. Here they are

- AOL Instant Messenger (AIM)
- Yahoo! Messenger
- ICQ
- MSN Messenger (Windows Messenger)
- Jabber

There's a good chance you already have an account on one of these services, even if you've never used it. For example, if you are an AOL member, you are already capable of using AOL Instant Messenger with your AOL screen name. An even more likely scenario involves MSN Messenger and Windows Messenger, both of which are built on the .NET Messenger Service. If you've ever created a Passport account for one of Microsoft's many online services, you already have an account for use with MSN Messenger or Windows Messenger.

Regardless of which type of IM service you might or might not already use, the challenge remains that you need a good way to consolidate them under one IM client. In an ideal world, all IM services would adopt a standard protocol such as Jabber's XML-based Extensible Messaging and Presence Protocol (XMPP), which establishes a common language for instant messaging. But the world is not, in fact, ideal, so we're stuck trying to unify a handful of different instant messaging services under one umbrella. Enter unified instant messaging.

▶ **NOTE**
If you're using a T-Mobile 7100t device and your family, friends, and business acquaintances all use AOL, Yahoo!, or ICQ for instant messaging, the IM consolidation issue really isn't a problem because your device already supports these three IM services.

In *unified instant messaging*, a single IM client takes on the challenge of allowing IM conversations through more than one IM service. The default T-Mobile IM client does an adequate job of playing the role of unified IM client in that it supports AOL, Yahoo!, and ICQ instant messaging. But MSN and Jabber users are still left out in the cold. To pick up support for additional IM services, you must turn to a third-party application. Following are a few good IM client applications you might want to consider for unifying your instant messaging needs:

- **Verichat**—http://www.verichat.com/
- **Web Messenger**—http://www.webmessenger.com/
- **IM+ Mobile Instant Messenger**—http://www.shapeservices.com/eng/im/BLACKBERRY/

▶ **KEY TERM**

Unified instant messaging—A single instant messaging client that supports several instant messaging services.

Keep in mind that your ultimate goal with instant messaging on your BlackBerry device is to develop a consistent way to communicate with important contacts in a timely manner. If you are working within a closed corporate setting, you might be able to get everyone signed on to the same IM service, in which case a third-party unified IM client is unnecessary. As long as you can efficiently communicate with important contacts, it really doesn't matter which application or IM client handles the details of shuttling messages back and forth.

8

Browsing the Wireless Web

IN THIS CHAPTER:

- **47** About BlackBerry Web Browsing
- **48** Navigate to a Web Page
- **49** Create and Manage Bookmarks
- **50** Install a New Application Over-the-Air
- **51** Download New Wallpaper
- **52** Download New Ring Tones
- **53** Tweak Browser Options

Except for perhaps wireless messaging, the most exciting feature of wireless handheld devices such as the BlackBerry 7100 is the ability to browse the wireless Web. To have the entirety of the Web at your fingertips from just about anywhere is quite an empowering feeling. And unlike the vast majority of mobile phones with wireless web support, the BlackBerry 7100 has a screen large enough to make real browsing possible. Sure, you can still visit mobile-specific websites that cater to devices with limited screen sizes—and I encourage you to do so. However, you should also visit websites designed for normal desktop computers. Not all of them are a joy to view on the BlackBerry screen, but many of them are very accessible. This chapter explores the wireless Web and how you can enhance your BlackBerry experience by jacking into it.

47 About BlackBerry Web Browsing

→ **SEE ALSO**

48 Navigate to a Web Page

Although it runs on a handheld device with a relatively small screen and limited memory—at least in comparison to a desktop web browser—the BlackBerry 7100 web browser packs a fair amount of punch. Before getting into the specifics of the BlackBerry browser software, it's important to nail down a few important concepts related to mobile browsing. You've probably heard the expression *wireless web*. If so, you quite likely heard someone talk about **WAP**, even if they didn't realize it. WAP, which stands for Wireless Application Protocol and is pronounced so that it rhymes with *slap*, is a technology that enables wireless devices to receive data from the Internet and display it on their constrained displays. You can think of WAP as essentially a technology that supports a minimal web browser on wireless devices. However, as its name clearly states, WAP is not an application but a protocol.

▶ **KEY TERM**

WAP—Wireless Application Protocol, a protocol similar in concept to the popular Hypertext Transfer Protocol (HTTP). Instead, though, it's designed for delivering compact web pages over a wireless network to mobile devices.

WAP must be supported on both the client (device) and the web server, and there must also be a WAP gateway, which is an intermediary between the Internet and the device's mobile network. The WAP gateway is responsible for converting WAP requests into traditional web requests, and vice versa. Web pages for WAP are somewhat different from traditional web pages in that they are written in a special markup language called Wireless Markup Language (WML), as opposed to the familiar HTML. WML also supports a scripting language called WMLScript that is a simplified version of JavaScript.

WAP is an important part of BlackBerry web browsing because many mobile websites are designed to be viewed by WAP web browsers; many popular websites such as CNN.com offer mobile versions that use WAP. The web browser in your BlackBerry 7100 actually supports both WAP and HTTP, as well as another data service known as the BlackBerry Mobile Data Service (MDS). These facets of the BlackBerry web browser are known as *browser configurations* and are available to all BlackBerry devices. Your device might have separate icons to distinguish between the three browser configurations, but they are ultimately just variations of the same browser software.

▶ **NOTE**
I don't make a big distinction between the different browser configurations because they all operate fairly seamlessly. So, when I refer to the "BlackBerry web browser," I'm referring to the browser in general, not a specific configuration.

The BlackBerry web browser application is designed to maximize the content area in which web pages are displayed. There is a short title bar along the top of the browser screen that includes a fair amount of information, considering it is such a small space. The following information is included in the browser's title bar using text and small icons:

- **Page title**—This text is simply the title of the web page being viewed.
- **Unread messages**—The unread messages icon doesn't relate to the browser at all; instead it lets you know whether you have unread text messages waiting. Different icons identify unread text messages as opposed to "unread" voice mail messages.
- **Pending service books**—This icon lets you know whether any pending *service books* are waiting to be accepted.

▶ **KEY TERM**
Service book—Used to support a specific service on your device, such as remote address lookup for email or wireless calendar synchronization. You can add new services to your device by obtaining service books for them.

▶ **NOTE**
Service books function sort of as software plug-ins for your BlackBerry device and add support for additional services. Generally speaking, you don't have to worry about installing, removing, or configuring service books because they are managed automatically when you install new features.

CHAPTER 8: Browsing the Wireless Web

- **Connection information**—This information consists primarily of an icon to indicate whether you are connected to a wireless network.

- **Security settings**—This icon indicates whether the page you are viewing is secure. The icon is a padlock like the one that plays a similar role in desktop web browsers.

- **Network signal strength**—This icon is the same one shown on the **Home** screen, and it simply conveys the current wireless network signal strength.

You can easily hide the browser's title bar, which puts the browser into full-screen mode and provides more viewing area. To toggle between normal mode and full-screen mode, simply press the **Q W** key on the keyboard.

The BlackBerry web browser includes an application menu with a lot of commands for performing various browser operations. Most immediately familiar are the commands for navigating among web pages:

- **Home**—Navigates to the home page
- **Back**—Navigates back to the previously viewed page
- **Forward**—Navigates forward to the previously viewed page
- **History**—Views the browser history
- **Refresh**—Refreshes (reloads) the current page

These commands are all standard commands found in any web browser. The BlackBerry web browser functions just like a desktop web browser in terms of maintaining a history of visited websites and keeping track of opened pages as a sequence you can move through either forward or backward.

▶ NOTES

The BlackBerry web browser history can contain up to 20 entries. After 20 entries are reached, the oldest entry is dropped to make room for each new entry.

The BlackBerry web browser doesn't support frames, but it does display a list of frames for pages that use frames. You can then select a frame from the list and view it as an individual page if you want.

48 Navigate to a Web Page

✔ **BEFORE YOU BEGIN**
47 About BlackBerry Web Browsing

→ **SEE ALSO**
49 Create and Manage Bookmarks
53 Tweak Browser Options

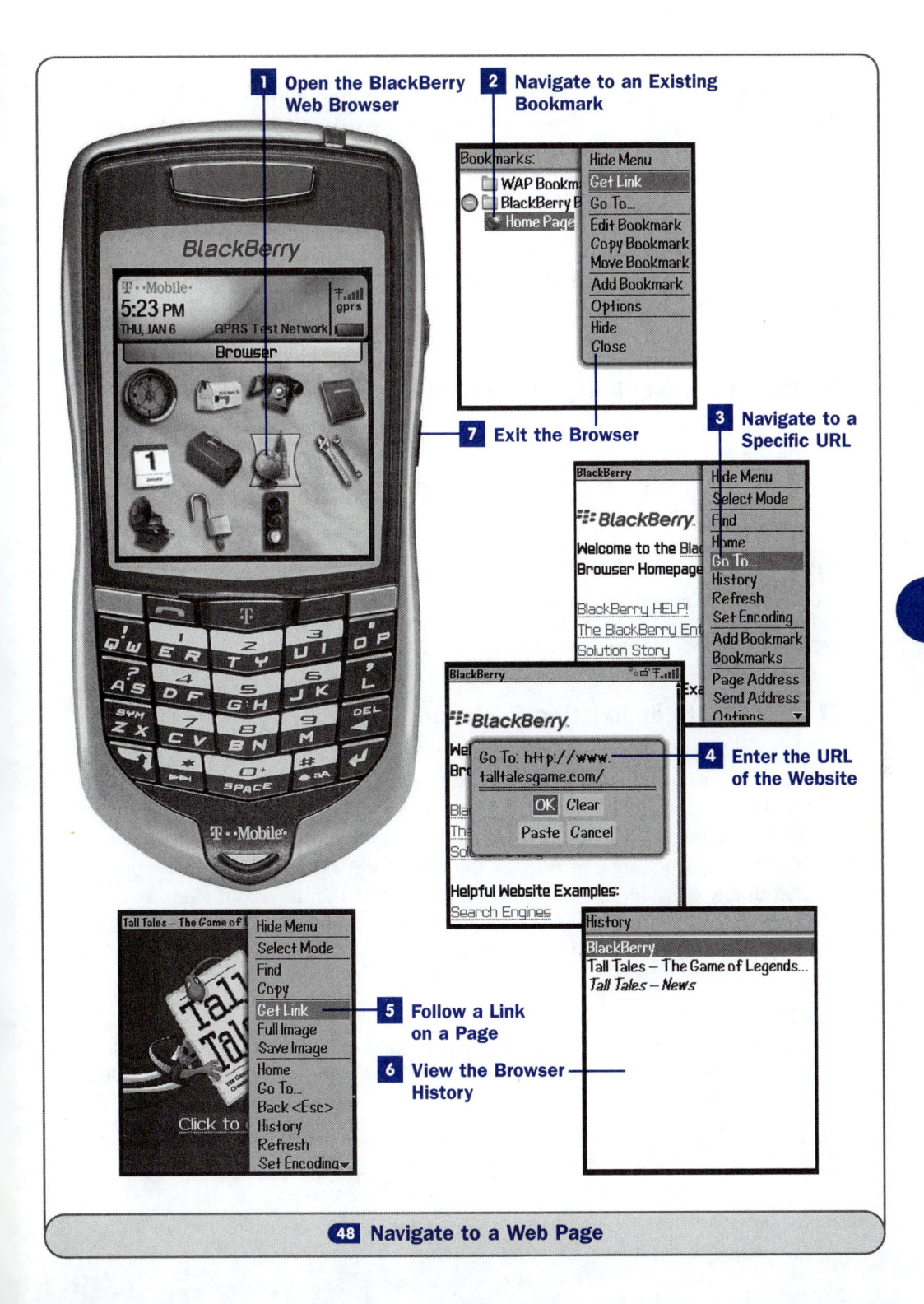

48 Navigate to a Web Page

1 Open the BlackBerry Web Browser

2 Navigate to an Existing Bookmark

3 Navigate to a Specific URL

4 Enter the URL of the Website

5 Follow a Link on a Page

6 View the Browser History

7 Exit the Browser

48 Navigate to a Web Page

The concept of a truly wireless Internet is certainly powerful, and the BlackBerry 7100 series of devices puts that power in the palm of your hand. Using the standard web browsing features in your device, you can view pages delivered through either WAP or HTTP. WAP pages are specifically designed for viewing on mobile devices, whereas HTTP web pages are designed for a full desktop web browser but in many cases can be viewed without problems on your device.

Just as with a desktop web browser, you can navigate to any web page you want by simply entering its address. You can also easily make future visits to a favorite site or page by saving a bookmark for the address; see **49 Create and Manage Bookmarks**.

1 Open the BlackBerry Web Browser

Scroll to the **Browser** icon on the **Home** screen and click the trackwheel. The **Bookmarks** screen appears and offers a list of websites you can visit using the BlackBerry web browser; in this case there is only one bookmark. Keep in mind that you can add your own bookmarked sites to this default list.

TIP

The **Convenience** key on your device also serves as a shortcut to the **Bookmarks** screen. The **Convenience** key is the large key on the top of the keyboard between the **Send** and **End** keys.

2 Navigate to an Existing Bookmark

The **Bookmarks** screen contains a list of bookmarks for existing websites that you can visit using the BlackBerry web browser. To navigate to one of the bookmarked sites, scroll the trackwheel to select a bookmark and double-click; you are actually selecting **Get Link** from the menu that appears on the first click. The website opens in the BlackBerry web browser. In this example, I'm simply accessing the default **Home** bookmark that links to the home page established by my wireless service provider. You will add your own bookmarks as you explore the wireless Web.

▶ TIPS

The **U I** and **M** keys serve as **Page Up** and **Page Down** keys while viewing a web page in the browser. Additionally, the **E R** and **C V** keys serve as **Home** and **End** keys for jumping to the top and bottom of a page.

The **Q W** key enables you to switch between normal mode and full-screen mode, which effectively hides and shows the title bar in the browser.

3 Navigate to a Specific URL

At some point, you'll want to travel beyond the predefined list of bookmarks and navigate directly to a website or web page of your own choosing. To navigate to a specific URL, click the trackwheel either from the **Bookmarks** screen or directly from the browser. Scroll the trackwheel to select **Go To** from the menu and then click. A dialog box appears and prompts you to enter the URL.

▶ **TIP**

You can quickly navigate to a new web page at any time by pressing the **O P** key.

4 Enter the URL of the Website

The **Go To** URL text-entry screen automatically begins with the expected http://, which forms the start of most URLs. Begin typing the URL for the web page you want to visit following the http:// prefix. To help make entering the URL easier, you can hold down the **Next** key for a moment to switch into multitap mode; *SureType* can make URLs more difficult to enter.

You can use a few typing tricks while entering a URL. To enter a dot (.) in a URL, press the **Space** key. The other handy symbol shortcut is the **Shift+Space** combination, which enters a forward slash (/). Forward slashes often appear in URLs, and you can quickly enter one by pressing the **Shift** key followed by the **Space** key.

▶ **TIP**

As you enter additional URLs, the **Go To** dialog box expands to show a history of recently entered URLs. Scroll the trackwheel to select one of these URLs. An even handier trick is to hold down the **Alt** key when scrolling the trackwheel, which allows you to select and edit one of the previously entered URLs.

When you finish entering the URL, scroll the trackwheel to select the **OK** button in the dialog box and click. The browser opens the website referenced by the specified URL.

▶ **TIP**

You can copy the address of a web page and even send the address as a message to someone in an email, PIN, or SMS message. Just click the trackwheel on the page and select **Page Address** from the menu that appears. Click once more, and you are presented with a dialog box that allows you to copy or send the page address. You can also select **Send Address** directly from the menu as a shortcut for sending the page address.

▶ TIP

You can save a web page to the message list so it appears alongside your text messages. This can be a helpful way to remember a page if you don't want to create a bookmark. Just click the trackwheel on the page and select **Save Page** from the menu that appears. Click once more and you are prompted to confirm the save—click the **Save** button to save the page. The page now appears as a new message on the **Messages** screen. If a page hasn't finished loading, you can save the page request instead of the completed page by clicking to open the menu and selecting **Save Request**; the page continues loading in the background and appears in the message list when it finishes. Saving a page is different from copying a page address in that you are saving the actual contents of the page, not just its URL.

5 Follow a Link on a Page

The main thing that makes the Web so great is the connectivity between pages. The browser on your device makes it easy to navigate between pages by following links. As you scroll the trackwheel and view a page, you automatically are guided from one link to the next. In other words, the browser automatically selects links for you as you view a page—image links are shown with a dotted square around them and text links are highlighted in reverse-colored text.

To follow a link on a page, select the link using the trackwheel and double-click; you are actually selecting **Get Link** from the menu that appears after the first click. You can also follow a link by just clicking the trackwheel once but also holding it down. The browser opens the page referenced by the specified link.

▶ TIPS

The **Enter** key serves as a shortcut to navigate to a page using a selected link. With the link selected, just press the **Enter** key to follow the link.

You can copy the address of a link and even send the link as a message to someone via an email, PIN, or SMS message. Just select the link with the trackwheel, click, and select **Link Address** from the menu that appears. Click once more and you are presented with a dialog box that allows you to copy or send the link address. Sending a link is similar to sending a page address, except in this case you're sending a link on a page as opposed to the URL of the page itself.

6 View the Browser History

A handy way to quickly navigate back to pages you've already visited is to use the browser's history. The browser keeps track of all the websites you visit and stores them in a list known as the *browser history*. From that list, you can revisit any of the sites. To access the browser history, click the trackwheel from within the browser and select **History**. Click to display the **History** screen.

To visit a page listed on the **History** screen, scroll the trackwheel to select the page and click. The URL of the page is displayed in a dialog box. Click the **OK** button to accept the URL and navigate to that page in the browser.

▶ **TIP**

To move to the next page in the browser's history, press the **J K** key. Similarly, press the **D F** key to move to the previous page in the browser's history.

7 Exit the Browser

Unlike most BlackBerry applications, the **Escape** button in the web browser returns you to the previously viewed page (much like the **Back** button does in a desktop web browser). However, after you back out to the first page you opened in the browser, the **Escape** button serves its expected role of exiting the browser application. You can also exit the browser at any time by clicking the trackwheel, selecting **Close** from the menu that appears, and then clicking again. You should close the browser when you're finished with it to preserve memory—this rule applies to all BlackBerry applications.

▶ **NOTE**

Selecting **Close** from the browser menu closes the browser application. If you select **Hide**, you simply hide the browser from view while keeping the current page open. When you launch the browser after hiding it, you return to the page you were last viewing. If you use the **Escape** button to exit the browser, the browser is closed as if you had selected **Close** from the menu. Use the **End** key as a shortcut for hiding the browser, as opposed to closing it.

49 Create and Manage Bookmarks

✔ BEFORE YOU BEGIN	→ SEE ALSO
48 Navigate to a Web Page	53 Tweak Browser Options

Your BlackBerry device ships with several handy web addresses that are bookmarked and ready for you to visit when you first run the web browser. These bookmarks provide the quickest option for browsing the Web from your device because you just click to visit the sites they represent. In addition to using the standard bookmarks, you can create bookmarks of your own to identify your personal favorite sites for quick visiting in the future. You also have the flexibility to create folders for bookmarks and then use the folders to organize your bookmarks so you can more easily access them.

192 CHAPTER 8: Browsing the Wireless Web

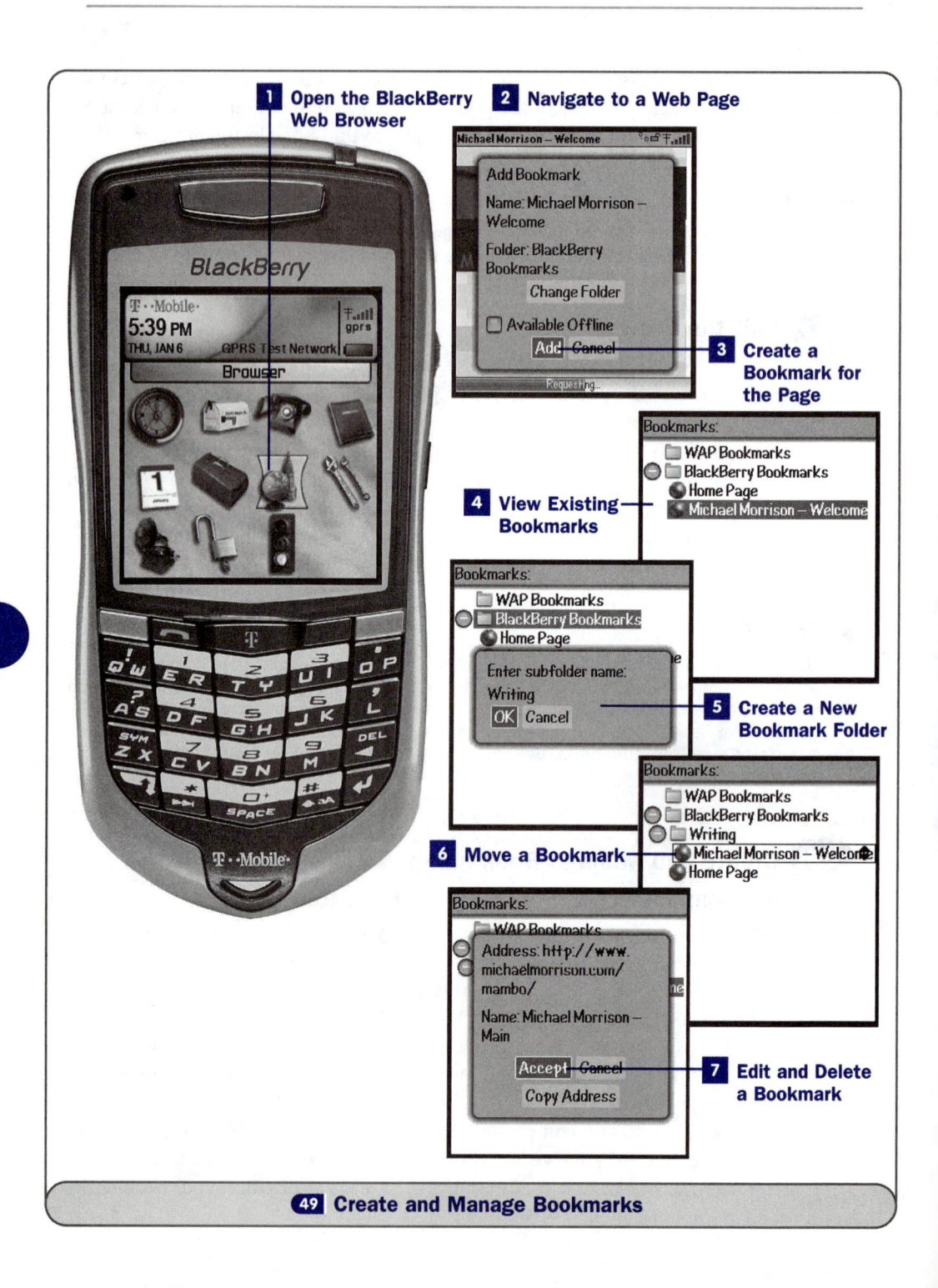

49

1 Open the BlackBerry Web Browser

2 Navigate to a Web Page

3 Create a Bookmark for the Page

4 View Existing Bookmarks

5 Create a New Bookmark Folder

6 Move a Bookmark

7 Edit and Delete a Bookmark

49 Create and Manage Bookmarks

1 Open the BlackBerry Web Browser

Scroll to the **Browser** icon on the **Home** screen and click the trackwheel. The **Bookmarks** screen appears and displays a list of websites you can visit using the BlackBerry web browser.

▶ **TIP**

The **Convenience** key on your device also serves as a shortcut to the **Bookmarks** screen. The **Convenience** key is the large key on the top of the keyboard between the **Send** and **End** keys.

2 Navigate to a Web Page

To navigate to a specific web page using a URL you type, click the trackwheel and scroll to select **Go To** from the menu that appears. Click the trackwheel; a dialog box appears and prompts you to enter the URL. Enter the URL, scroll the trackwheel to select the **OK** button in the dialog box, and click. The browser opens the website referenced by the specified URL.

▶ **TIP**

To make entering a URL easier, hold down the **Next** key for a moment to switch into multitap mode; *SureType* can make URLs more difficult to enter. To enter a dot (.) in a URL, press the **Space** key. Forward slashes often appear in URLs, and you can quickly enter one by pressing the **Shift** key followed by the **Space** key.

3 Create a Bookmark for the Page

To create a bookmark for the page you are currently viewing, click the trackwheel and select **Add Bookmark** from the menu that appears. Click again, and the **Add Bookmark** dialog box appears. This dialog box allows you to set the name of the bookmark along with the folder in which it is stored. You can count on two folders being available for storing bookmarks: **WAP Bookmarks** and **BlackBerry Bookmarks**. The **WAP Bookmarks** folder is intended to store websites that are accessed using *WAP*; the **BlackBerry Bookmarks** folder is intended to store HTTP websites. Other bookmark folders in addition to these might be provided by your wireless service provider.

The last setting in the **Add Bookmark** dialog box is the **Available Offline** option, which determines whether the bookmark's content should be made available for offline viewing. This option is useful if you want to be able to view a web page even if you don't have wireless coverage. If you choose to make a bookmarked page available offline, the content on the page is kept current from when you last viewed the page in the browser.

▶ **TIP**

If you've previously copied a web page address, the **Add Bookmark** dialog box includes a **Paste** button that allows you to create a bookmark based on the address. You can copy any bookmark by selecting the bookmark, clicking, and then selecting **Copy Bookmark** from the menu that appears.

To finish creating the new bookmark, click the **Add** button in the **Add Bookmark** dialog box. You return to the browser, where the page is still in view.

4 View Existing Bookmarks

At any time, you can view all the bookmarks on your device by clicking the trackwheel in the browser, selecting **Bookmarks**, and then clicking again. The **Bookmarks** screen is displayed and shows a list of bookmarks and folders used to store bookmarks. Depending on your specific wireless service provider and device configuration, you might have several bookmark folders. For example, most T-Mobile devices include folders named **T-Zones Links** and **Web Links** in addition to the standard **WAP Bookmarks** and **BlackBerry Bookmarks** folders.

▶ **NOTE**

It's worth pointing out that you typically aren't allowed to delete bookmarks that are pre-installed on your device. This is admittedly somewhat of a strange limitation, but it's one you'll have to live with.

Bookmark folders help you organize bookmarks and navigate through them more easily. You can expand and collapse folders by double-clicking them with the trackwheel. You can visit any bookmarked site by opening a bookmark folder and selecting the desired bookmark. Double-click the bookmark to open it in the browser.

5 Create a New Bookmark Folder

Although the standard bookmark folders are useful, you will likely want to create your own bookmark folders. You can only create subfolders within the standard **WAP Bookmarks** and **BlackBerry Bookmarks** folders. To create a subfolder, scroll the trackwheel to select the desired parent folder and click. Select **Add Subfolder** from the menu that appears, and click again. A dialog box appears that prompts you to enter the subfolder name.

▶ **TIP**

If you create a lot of bookmarks and want to organize them hierarchically, you can nest subfolders within each other. Just select a subfolder as the parent when creating a new subfolder. The hierarchical directory of bookmark folders is logically similar to the directory of file folders on your desktop PC hard drive.

You can name a bookmark subfolder just about anything you want, but be sure it accurately describes a collection of bookmarks. After entering the name of the bookmark subfolder, click the **OK** button to accept it and create the folder.

If you change your mind about a bookmark folder after you've created it, you can easily rename or delete the folder. Scroll the trackwheel to select the folder, and then click. Select **Delete Folder** to delete the folder or **Rename Folder** to rename the folder; then click again.

6 Move a Bookmark

As you create bookmark folders and take more control over the organization of your bookmarks, you might want to move the bookmarks around a bit. Moving a bookmark can mean either changing its position within a folder or moving it to a different folder entirely. To move a bookmark, scroll the trackwheel to select the bookmark and click. Select **Move Bookmark** from the menu that appears and click again. The bookmark now has a box around it; you can move the boxed bookmark by scrolling the trackwheel. Notice that you can easily drag the bookmark to a different folder. When you finish moving the bookmark, click the trackwheel to accept the new location. If you change your mind about the new position before clicking the trackwheel, cancel the move by pressing the **Escape** button.

7 Edit and Delete a Bookmark

In some instances, you might want to edit a bookmark, such as when the URL for a bookmark changes. To edit a bookmark, scroll the trackwheel to select the bookmark and click. Select **Edit Bookmark** from the menu that appears, and click again. A dialog box appears that enables you to edit the address (URL) and name of the bookmark. After modifying the address or name for the bookmark, click either the **Accept** button to accept the changes or the **Cancel** button to cancel. You can also copy the address of the bookmark by clicking the **Copy Address** button. A copied bookmark address can be used to create a new bookmark. More specifically, when you add a new bookmark, you'll see a **Paste** button that enables you to paste in the address of a copied bookmark (refer to step 3).

In some cases, editing a bookmark might not be enough to salvage it, in which case you might opt to simply delete the bookmark altogether. To delete a bookmark, scroll to select the bookmark and click the trackwheel. Select **Delete Bookmark** from the menu that appears, and click once more. Click **Delete** to confirm the deletion; the bookmark is deleted and removed from the bookmark list.

CHAPTER 8: Browsing the Wireless Web

▶ **NOTE**

If **Delete Bookmark** doesn't appear on the menu when you click a bookmark, it means that the bookmark is a default bookmark and cannot be deleted. Unfortunately, your device comes with several of these permanent bookmarks preinstalled.

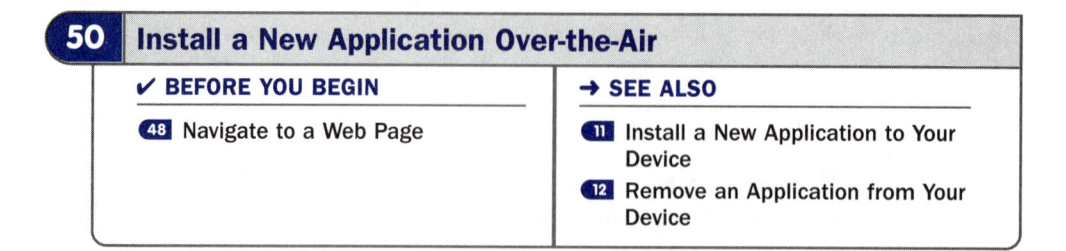

50 Install a New Application Over-the-Air

✔ BEFORE YOU BEGIN	→ SEE ALSO
48 Navigate to a Web Page	11 Install a New Application to Your Device
	12 Remove an Application from Your Device

The standard approach to installing a new application on your BlackBerry device is to transfer the application to your device from your desktop PC using the BlackBerry Desktop Manager. Although this approach works great, it requires the assistance of your desktop PC, which isn't ideal. Besides, the idea of using a BlackBerry device is to accomplish more of your electronic tasks while on the go. You shouldn't have to be tethered to your desktop PC any time you want to install a new application to your device. This is where over-the-air application installation enters the picture.

Over-the-air (OTA) application installation involves downloading and installing an application directly to your device wirelessly. Your desktop PC and the BlackBerry Desktop Manager are eliminated from the installation equation entirely. The obvious upside to this approach to application installation is that you can do it from anywhere you have wireless coverage. Because you sometimes might be traveling and have limited access to your desktop PC, OTA application installation is useful and can in fact be a necessity. Ideally, all applications would be installed OTA, but we don't live in an ideal world—many applications simply aren't available for OTA installation.

▶ **KEY TERM**

Over-the-air (OTA)—This refers to the type of application installation that takes place over a wireless network connection to an application provider. The application is being installed wirelessly "over the air," as opposed to using a direct connection with a desktop PC.

1 Open the BlackBerry Web Browser

Scroll to the **Browser** icon on the **Home** screen and click the trackwheel. The **Bookmarks** screen appears and displays a list of websites you can visit using the BlackBerry web browser.

50 Install a New Application Over-the-Air

1 Open the BlackBerry Web Browser

2 Navigate to the Application Web Page

3 Follow the Link to Access the Application

4 Follow the Link to Download the Application

5 Launch the Application

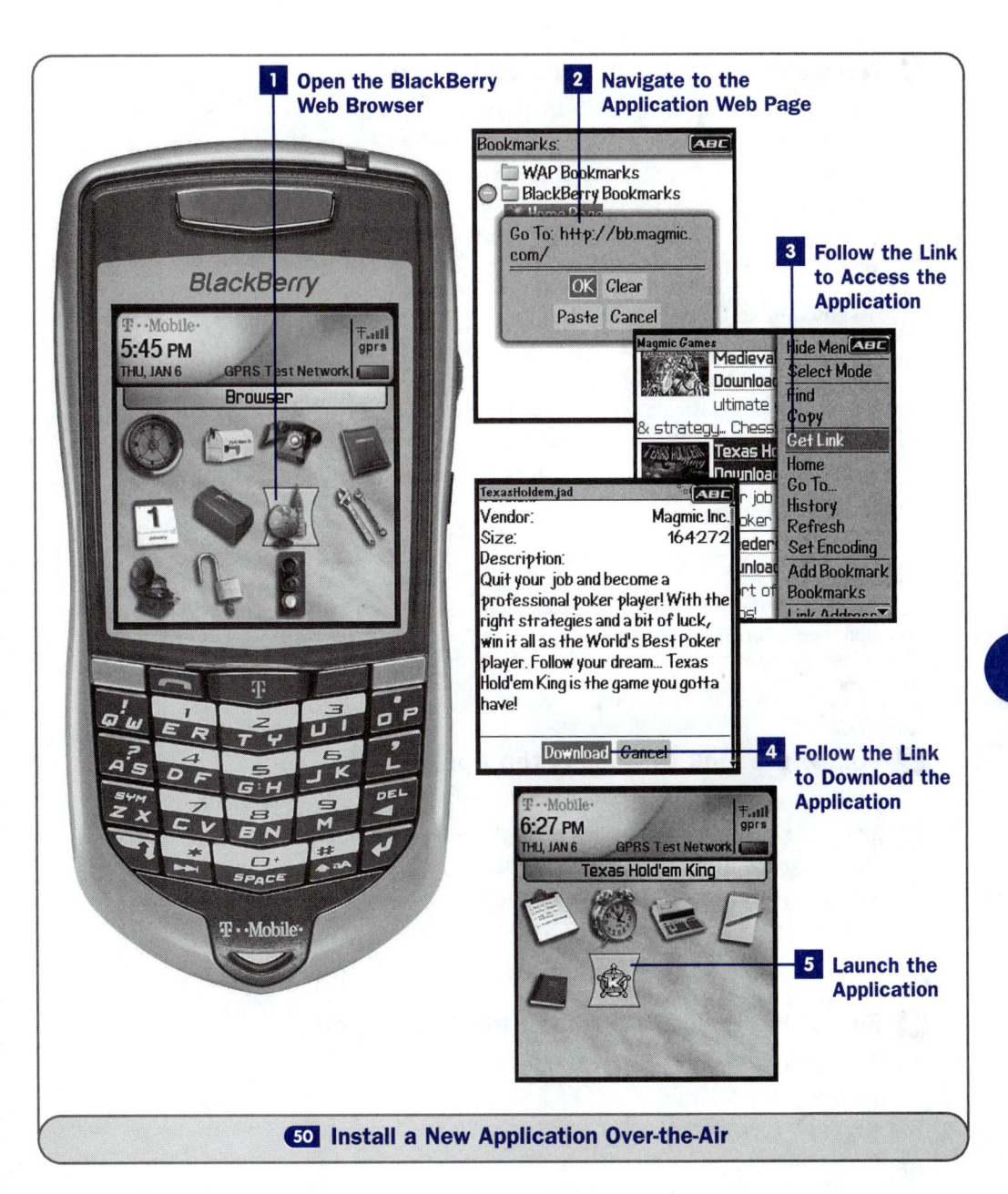

50 Install a New Application Over-the-Air

▶ **TIP**

The **Convenience** key on your device also serves as a shortcut to the **Bookmarks** screen. The **Convenience** key is the large key on the top of the keyboard between the **Send** and **End** keys.

2 Navigate to the Application Web Page

You might already have a website in mind from which you want to download BlackBerry applications OTA. If not, I have a good suggestion to try for games. A company called Magmic develops games for wireless devices, and I like its site because it offers a variety of games, each of which is available in a trial format as an OTA download. The URL for the site is http://bb.magmic.com/.

To navigate to the Magmic web page, click the trackwheel and scroll to select **Go To** from the menu that appears. Click the trackwheel; a dialog box appears and prompts you to enter the URL. Because **http://** is already provided, type **bb.magmic.com**, scroll the trackwheel to select the **OK** button in the dialog box, and click. The browser opens the Magmic website, where several games are available for OTA download. Scroll around to find a game you like.

▶ **TIP**

To make entering a URL easier, hold down the **Next** key for a moment to switch into multitap mode; *SureType* can make URLs more difficult to enter. To enter a dot (.) in a URL, press the **Space** key. Forward slashes often appear in URLs, and you can quickly enter one by pressing the **Shift** key followed by the **Space** key.

3 Follow the Link to Access the Application

After selecting the game (or other application) you want to download, click the trackwheel, select **Get Link** from the menu that appears, and click again. Another page appears that provides more details about the application, including links for either downloading a trial version or purchasing the full version. In the example, I've selected the poker card game Texas Hold'em King.

4 Follow the Link to Download the Application

To download the trial version of the game, scroll the trackwheel down the page to select **Download Trial** (or a similar link provided on the screen for the application you want to download) and click. Select **Get Link** from the menu that appears, and click again. One more page appears, this time with specific information about what you are downloading, including the size of the file. To download the game, scroll to select the **Download** button and click. The application begins downloading.

51 Download New Wallpaper　　199

▶ **NOTE**

If you later choose to purchase a game from the Magmic website, you'll be prompted to enter contact information, credit card information, and your BlackBerry PIN. Then you can download the full version of the game OTA to your device. The good news is that mobile games tend to cost less than their desktop counterparts.

When the download finishes, you are prompted with a dialog box that lets you know the download and installation are complete. Just click the **OK** button. The application (the game in this case) is now installed on your device and ready to run.

5 Launch the Application

To try the application, close or hide the browser (click the trackwheel, select **Close** from the menu, and click again) and open the **Applications** folder—press the **End** key, scroll to the **Applications** icon, and click the trackwheel. You see the icon for the newly installed application, which in this example is Texas Hold'em King. Scroll to select the application icon and click to launch it.

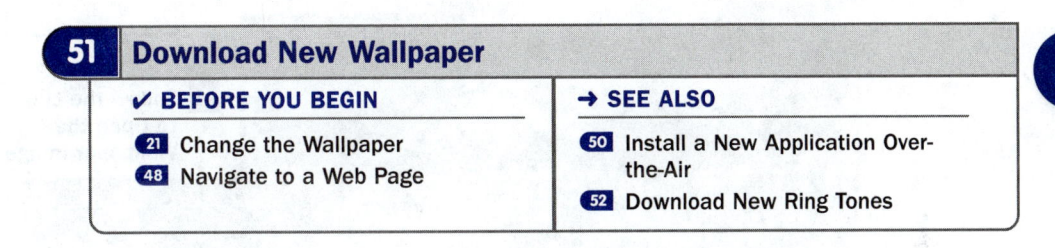

---

51 Download New Wallpaper

✔ **BEFORE YOU BEGIN**

- **21** Change the Wallpaper
- **48** Navigate to a Web Page

→ **SEE ALSO**

- **50** Install a New Application Over-the-Air
- **52** Download New Ring Tones

Even if you aren't the type to watch home decorating shows, you might still dream of a BlackBerry device makeover beyond the limited set of default wallpaper images included on your device. Fortunately, you can easily download new wallpaper images and install them onto your device. Unfortunately, however, you have to perform this process through a website by downloading images from a link to your device—there is currently no way to directly transfer an image from your desktop PC to your device. So, if you have an image you want to use as wallpaper on your device, you have to host it online somewhere and open the link through the browser on your device. You learn a trick for making image hosting a bit easier as you work through this task.

200   CHAPTER 8:   Browsing the Wireless Web

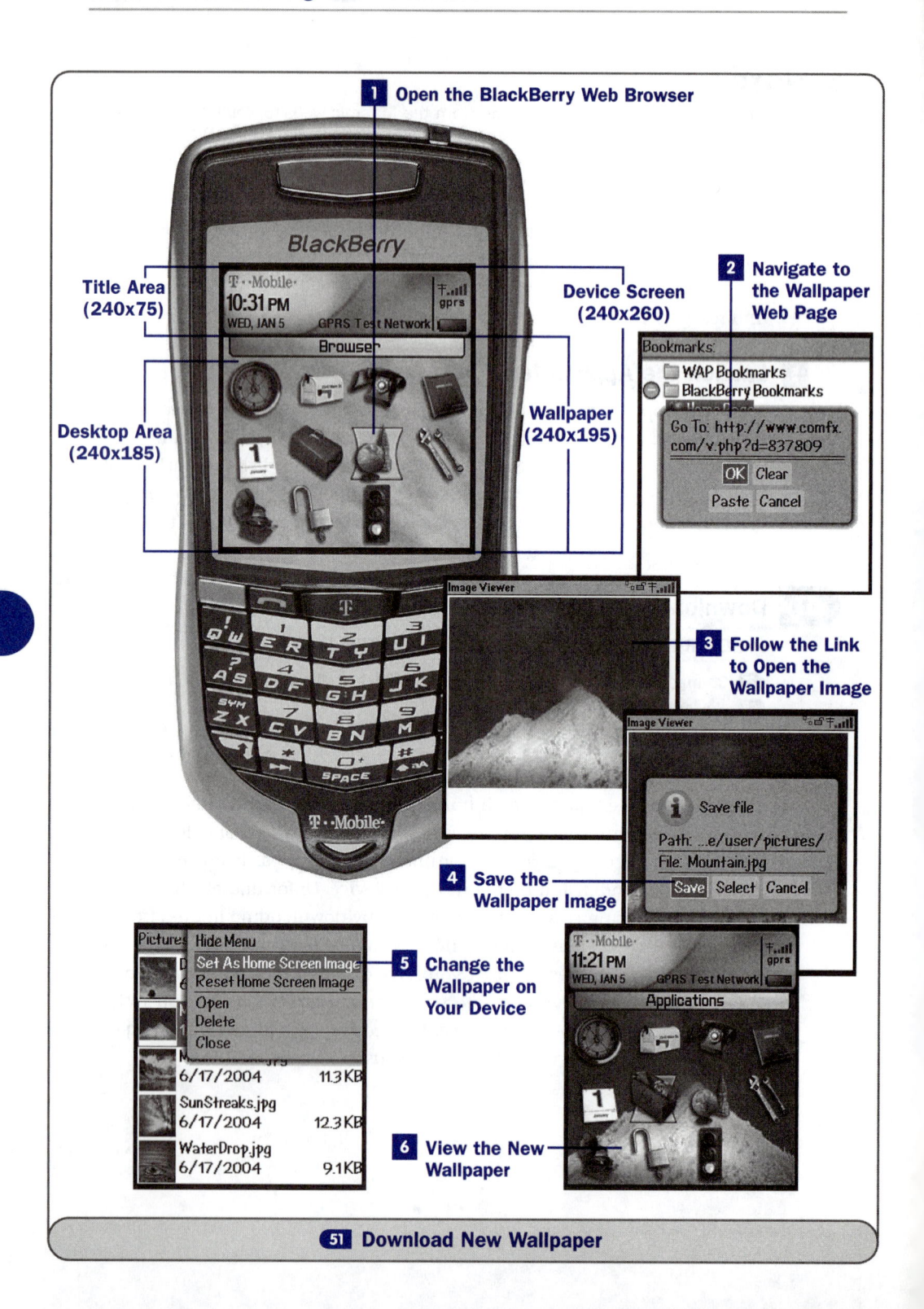

1 Open the BlackBerry Web Browser

Title Area (240x75)

Desktop Area (240x185)

Device Screen (240x260)

Wallpaper (240x195)

2 Navigate to the Wallpaper Web Page

3 Follow the Link to Open the Wallpaper Image

4 Save the Wallpaper Image

5 Change the Wallpaper on Your Device

6 View the New Wallpaper

51 Download New Wallpaper

Before getting into the steps for downloading new wallpaper, it's worth pointing out the physical dimensions of the BlackBerry screen and desktop area in case you're thinking about creating your own custom wallpaper. As you might already know, the BlackBerry 7100 screen is 240 pixels wide and 260 pixels tall. However, a standard title area along the top of the **Home** screen takes up a lot of space. Specifically, the title area is 75 pixels in height, which reduces the visible wallpaper area to 185 pixels in height. However, some themes (such as the standard T-Mobile theme) allow the wallpaper to show through just a bit on the right and left sides of the lower part of the title area. If you want the wallpaper to extend up and be visible on these sides, tack on 10 pixels to the height, making the final target size for BlackBerry 7100 wallpaper 240×195.

1 Open the BlackBerry Web Browser

Scroll to the **Browser** icon on the **Home** screen and click the trackwheel. The **Bookmarks** screen appears, displaying a list of websites you can visit using the BlackBerry web browser.

▶ **TIP**

The **Convenience** key on your device also serves as a shortcut to the **Bookmarks** screen. The **Convenience** key is the large key on the top of the keyboard between the **Send** and **End** keys.

2 Navigate to the Wallpaper Web Page

Your device might already include bookmarks for wallpaper you can purchase and download—or possibly download free. If so, I encourage you to follow one of these links to a web page that contains wallpaper images. As an example, T-Mobile users have access to a bookmark called **Download Fun** that includes links to categorized wallpaper images. I created and uploaded my own custom wallpaper image to a hosting site where I could download it to my device. Regardless of where you go to find wallpaper images, you use the browser on your device to follow a link and open a page with one or more images.

▶ **WEB RESOURCE**
http://www.comfx.com/g.php

A website called ComFX offers a free image-hosting service for BlackBerry wallpaper that is extremely handy. The service allows you to upload an image from your desktop PC; the site then provides you with a link to the image you can visit using your BlackBerry device. The image hosting is temporary (images are cleared off weekly), but you have to access an image only once with your device to download it and use it for wallpaper. Follow the instructions on the ComFX website and then use the URL they provide to go to the page containing your newly uploaded image.

3 Follow the Link to Open the Wallpaper Image

If you're following a link directly to an image, the image opens immediately in the browser. Otherwise, you might have to navigate through a list of images, select the image you want, and click the trackwheel. Then select **Get Link** from the menu that appears, and click again. The image downloads and opens in the browser.

4 Save the Wallpaper Image

With the wallpaper image open and in view in the browser, you're ready to save it to your device so you can select it as wallpaper. Click the trackwheel and scroll to select **Save Image** from the menu that appears. Click once more, and you are prompted to enter a name for the image. Be sure you enter an appropriate image name with the correct file extension (**.gif** for GIF images or **.jpg** for JPEG images); a sufficient image name might be automatically provided for you. When you finish entering the image name, click the **Save** button to finish and save the image.

5 Change the Wallpaper on Your Device

To change the wallpaper on your device, you must first close or hide the browser by pressing the **End** key. Next scroll to the **Applications** icon on the **Home** screen and click the trackwheel. Then scroll to the **Photo Album** application icon and click the trackwheel. The Photo Album appears with a list of pictures and their thumbnails. Scroll the trackwheel through the list of pictures, and click the picture you downloaded. In the menu that appears, scroll to **Set As Home Screen Image** and click to set the picture as the wallpaper.

▶ **NOTE**

For a more detailed explanation of how to set the wallpaper on your device, see **21 Change the Wallpaper**.

6 View the New Wallpaper

With your wallpaper successfully changed, you're ready to view it in all its splendor. Press the **End** key to immediately jump back to the **Home** screen where the wallpaper is clearly visible in the background behind the icons.

52 Download New Ring Tones

✔ BEFORE YOU BEGIN

- 18 Tweak the Profiles
- 48 Navigate to a Web Page

→ SEE ALSO

- 50 Install a New Application Over-the-Air
- 51 Download New Wallpaper

No teenager's mobile phone is complete without a custom Top 40 ring tone. Although your BlackBerry device is likely used for more than chatting during homeroom, you still might want to personalize your ring tones. If nothing else, BlackBerry profiles offer enough different event notifications that you can experiment with downloaded ring tones just to better differentiate between events.

To install a new ring tone on your device, you must download it from a website. Fortunately, numerous websites offer ring tones—some free and some for a small fee. Whether you download free or purchased ring tones, the process is the same: You follow a link on a web page to download a ring tone to your device and then access the ring tone by editing the profiles for your device. Currently, you can't download a ring tone directly from your desktop PC to your device, which is why you must always go through a website from your device's browser to download new ring tones.

Many websites offer ring tones and, unfortunately, some of them want to charge you for the tones. That might be fine for you, but I personally don't put an enormous amount of financial value on the ring tone for my device. I found a few free ring tone sites you might want to consider:

- **Partners in Rhyme**—http://www.partnersinrhyme.com/midi/
- **3gWiz**—http://www.3gwiz.com/
- **Smart Phone Depot**—http://www.smartphonedepot.com/media/

Keep in mind that your wireless service provider has likely provided some default bookmarks to sites that offer both free and for-pay ring tones, so consider looking through the default bookmarks as well. T-Mobile offers numerous ring tones through its standard Download Fun bookmark.

1 Open the BlackBerry Web Browser

Scroll to the **Browser** icon on the **Home** screen and click the trackwheel. The **Bookmarks** screen appears, showing a list of websites you can visit using the BlackBerry web browser.

CHAPTER 8: Browsing the Wireless Web

1 Open the BlackBerry Web Browser

2 Navigate to the Ring Tone Web Page

3 Follow the Link to Play the Ring Tone

— Menu Button

4 Save the Ring Tone

5 Change a Device Profile to Use the Ring Tone

52 Download New Ring Tones

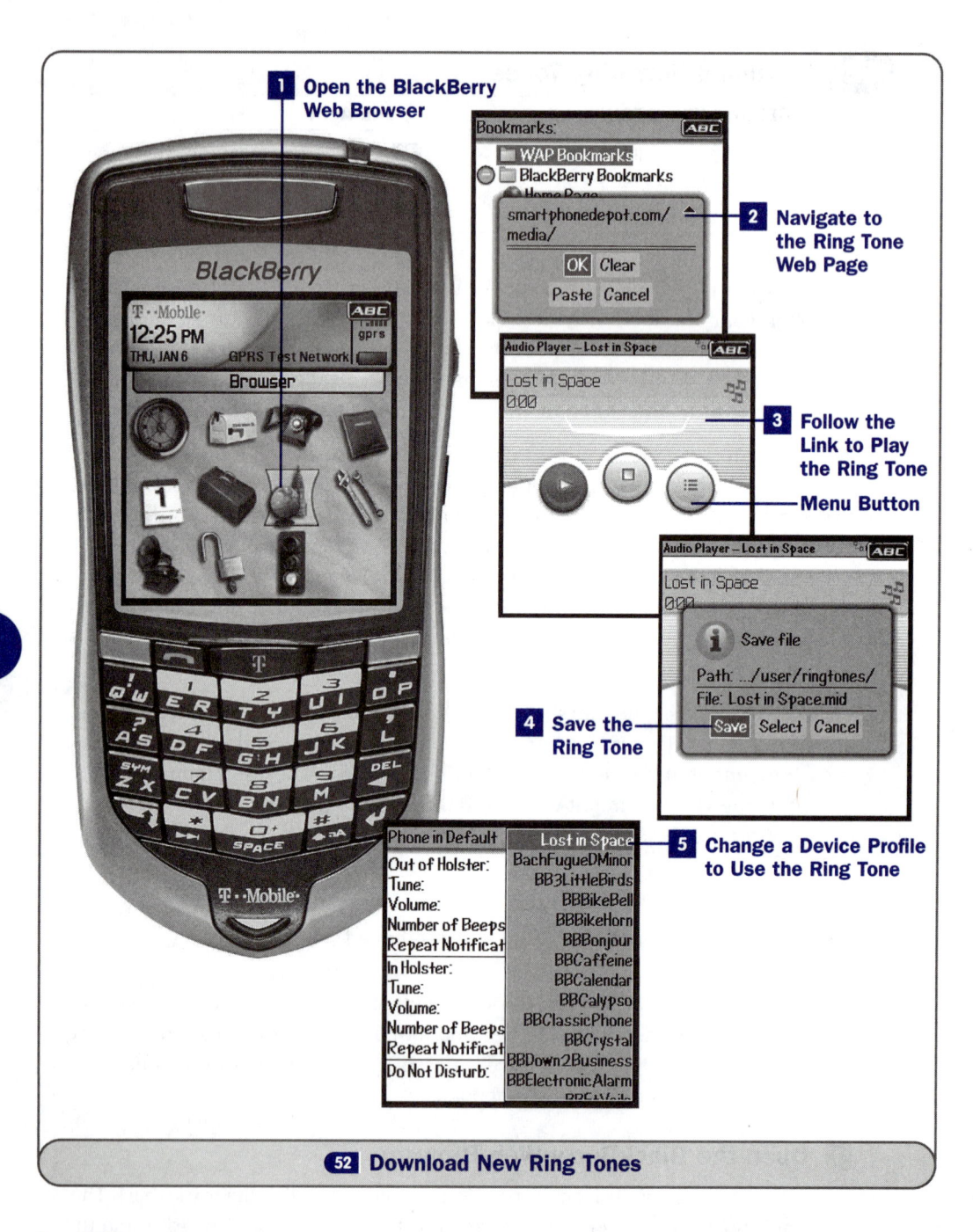

▶ **TIP**

The **Convenience** key on your device also serves as a shortcut to the **Bookmarks** screen. The **Convenience** key is the large key on the top of the keyboard between the **Send** and **End** keys.

2 Navigate to the Ring Tone Web Page

To navigate to the web page containing the ring tones in which you are interested, click the trackwheel and scroll to select **Go To** from the menu that appears. Click the trackwheel; a dialog box appears and prompts you to enter the URL. Enter the URL of the website, scroll the trackwheel to select the **OK** button in the dialog box, and click. The browser opens the website, where you'll likely find several ring tones available for download. Scroll around to find a ring tone you like.

▶ **TIP**

To make entering a URL easier, hold down the **Next** key for a moment to switch into multitap mode; *SureType* can make URLs more difficult to enter. To enter a dot (.) in a URL, press the **Space** key. Forward slashes often appear in URLs, and you can quickly enter one by pressing the **Shift** key followed by the **Space** key. Some URLs work without entering the **www.** prefix. You might want to try entering a URL without the **www.** to save some typing.

3 Follow the Link to Play the Ring Tone

If you're following a link directly to a ring tone, the ring tone automatically opens in the browser's audio player and begins playing. Otherwise, you might have to navigate through a list of ring tones, select the tone you want, and click the trackwheel. Next, select **Get Link** from the menu that appears, and click again. The ring tone downloads and begins playing in the browser's audio player.

4 Save the Ring Tone

If you like the ring tone and want to keep it for use in a device profile (see **18 Tweak the Profiles**), scroll the trackwheel to select the **Menu** button in the audio player; the **Menu** button is the far right button next to the **Stop** button. Click the **Menu** button, scroll to select **Save** from the menu, and click the trackwheel. A dialog box appears that prompts you to enter a name for the ring tone; the default name will suffice in most cases. When you finish entering the ring tone name, click the **Save** button to finish and save the ring tone.

5 Change a Device Profile to Use the Ring Tone

To use the ring tone on your device, you set it as the tune for an event notification profile, such as the **Phone** event notification in the **Default** device profile. To change a profile, you must first close or hide the browser—press the **End** key. Then, scroll to the **Profiles** icon on the **Home** screen and click the trackwheel. The **Profiles** screen appears, displaying a list of profiles from which to choose. If you want the ring tone you just downloaded to play whenever you have an incoming phone call, edit the **Phone** notification within the **Default** profile and set its **Tune** field to the newly downloaded ring tone.

▶ **NOTE**

For a more detailed explanation of how to set the **Tune** field for a profile notification on your device, see **18 Tweak the Profiles**.

---

53 Tweak Browser Options

✔ BEFORE YOU BEGIN	→ SEE ALSO
47 About BlackBerry Web Browsing	**48** Navigate to a Web Page
	49 Create and Manage Bookmarks

Similar to the web browser on your desktop PC, you can fine-tune the BlackBerry web browser to operate exactly as you want it to. In fact, in some ways it is more important to tweak the configuration of your mobile web browser because it has more critical limitations than its desktop counterpart. For example, you might opt to forego viewing images on web pages so the pages load faster; this is an option you can set for the mobile browser. You can also control other important browser features such as whether scripts are allowed to run, whether style sheets are supported, and what type and size of default font is used when displaying web pages. All these options affect the speed and security associated with web pages in varying degrees.

1 Open the BlackBerry Web Browser

Scroll to the **Browser** icon on the **Home** screen and click the trackwheel. The **Bookmarks** screen appears, showing a list of websites you can visit using the BlackBerry web browser.

▶ **TIP**

The **Convenience** key on your device also serves as a shortcut to the **Bookmarks** screen. The **Convenience** key is the large key on the top of the keyboard between the **Send** and **End** keys.

53 Tweak Browser Options

1 Open the BlackBerry Web Browser

2 Open the Browser Options Screen

3 Configure Browser Configuration Options

4 Configure General Browser Property Options

5 Clear Browser Caches

6 Exit Browser Options

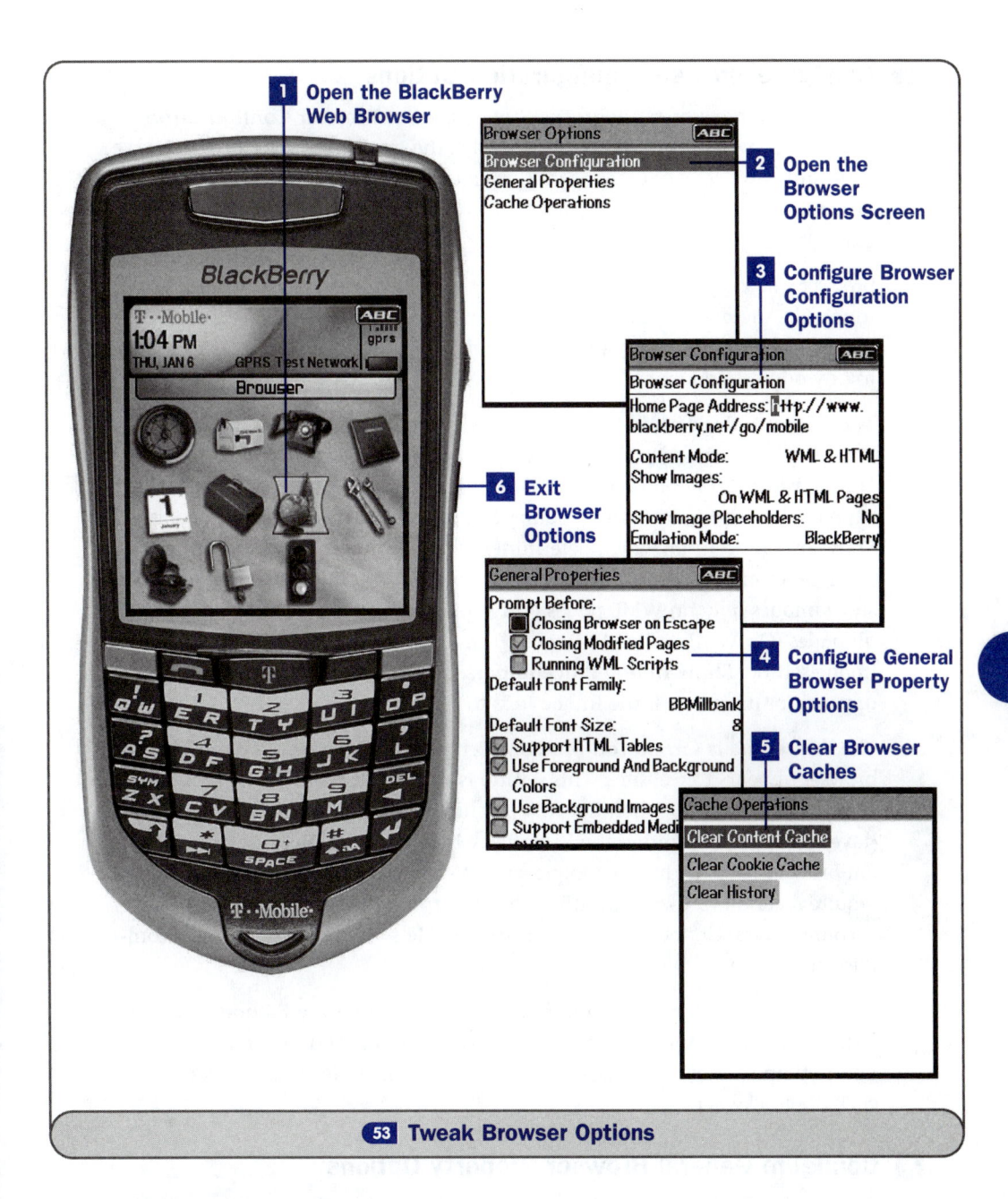

2 Open the Browser Options Screen

Click the trackwheel to open the browser menu, select **Options** from the menu, and click again. The **Browser Options** screen appears and provides access to a variety of browser options.

3 Configure Browser Configuration Options

To configure browser configuration options, select **Browser Configuration** from the **Browser Options** screen and click the trackwheel. The **Browser Configuration** screen appears and provides access to several configuration options.

The first option, **Home Page Address**, is where you set the address of the browser's home page—this is the page opened in the browser by default, much like the home page on your desktop browser. Your wireless service provider has likely already provided a suitable home page, but you can set it to any address you want.

The **Content Mode** setting is used to restrict the type of content allowed for browsing. More specifically, you can limit content to just WML pages (**WML Only**) or just HTML pages (**HTML Only**). The default setting, **WML & HTML**, supports both types of content. Somewhat related to the content mode is the **Show Images** setting, which determines whether images are displayed. Possible settings for **Show Images** allow you to turn off images entirely (**No**), show images only on WML pages (**On WML Pages Only**), or show images on all pages (**On WML & HTML Pages**). The last setting is the default. The other image setting, **Show Image Placeholders**, determines whether a placeholder appears for an image if the image fails to load.

The last setting is **Emulation Mode**, which determines how the BlackBerry browser appears to websites. This setting is important because websites often analyze your browser when figuring out how to present content. You might have a reason for wanting the BlackBerry browser to disguise itself as a different browser (such as Internet Explorer or Netscape). For example, some banks require a certain browser (usually Internet Explorer or Netscape) for online account access. Changing the **Emulation Mode** setting allows you to accomplish this trickery.

After tweaking the browser configuration options, press the **Escape** button to return to the **Browser Options** screen. If you've made changes, a confirmation pop-up window appears—select **Save** to confirm the changes and then click the trackwheel.

4 Configure General Browser Property Options

From the main **Browser Options** screen, scroll to select **General Properties** and click the trackwheel. The **General Properties** screen appears and provides access to a variety of options related to how the browser handles web content.

The first setting on the **General Properties** screen is a series of **Prompt Before** options, which control how you are prompted when performing various browsing tasks. For example, you can control whether you must be prompted before the browser allows a script to run. If you recall, pressing the **Escape** button while viewing the first page opened in the browser causes the browser to exit. You can change this behavior so you are prompted before the browser exits.

The **Default Font Family** and **Default Font Size** settings determine the default font used for pages displayed in the browser. You can decrease the font size to pack more content on the browser screen.

▶ **NOTE**
Many websites—especially those with HTML pages as opposed to WML—specify their own font families and font sizes, in which case the default font settings you select on the **General Properties** screen might have no effect.

The remaining general browser properties relate to enabling or disabling a variety of browser features. Generally speaking, you should leave the default settings of allowing HTML tables, allowing foreground and background colors, and using background images. If you need to access pages that use Flash and SVG for multimedia, consider enabling the **Support Embedded Media** option. Many web pages take advantage of JavaScript, which is why JavaScript is supported by default; because pop-ups can be a huge annoyance, JavaScript pop-ups are disabled by default. However, there are certainly legitimate, necessary uses of JavaScript pop-ups, and if you need them, enable the **Allow JavaScript popups** setting.

You will likely want to keep style sheets enabled because they are commonly used across the Web and pose no security risks. Style sheets are used in concert with web pages to apply fonts, colors, and other visual properties to pages. If you keep the default **Support Style Sheets** option enabled, it brings into question what the **Style sheets media type** setting controls. This setting determines how the browser processes browser-specific style sheet information. Style sheets can be divided into styles that apply solely to handheld browsers and styles that apply solely to desktop browsers. The default value of **Handheld** for the **Style sheets media type** setting results in the browser processing only browser-specific styles that target handheld browsers.

The last setting on the **General Properties** screen, **Repeat Animations**, determines how many times an animated GIF image on a web page animates. The default setting (**100 times**) causes all animated GIFs to run through their animations 100 times before they stop. Other possible options include **Never**, **Once**, **10 times**, and **As Many As Image Specifies**. The last option is a reasonable change to make for the **Repeat Animations** setting in that it allows animated GIF images to run as many times as they were originally intended.

When you're finished configuring the general browser properties, press the **Escape** button to return to the **Browser Options** screen. If you've made changes, a pop-up confirmation window appears—select **Save** to confirm the changes and then click the trackwheel.

5 Clear Browser Caches

If you've already visited some web pages, you'll see a third entry in the list on the **Browser Options** screen, called **Cache Operations**. To access the browser's cache operations, select **Cache Operations** from the **Browser Options** screen and click the trackwheel. The **Cache Operations** screen appears and gives you a chance to clear the various browser caches. Browser caches store recently browsed content for faster access. For privacy purposes, you might consider clearing the browser caches from time to time.

▶ **NOTE**

If you don't see all three of the buttons on the **Cache Operations** screen (**Clear Content Cache**, **Clear Cookie Cache**, and **Clear History**), it simply means that you haven't browsed enough to add anything to the missing caches.

The **Cache Operations** screen contains three buttons that allow you to clear the following browser caches: content, cookies, and history. (Technically, the browser history isn't really a cache, but for the purposes of this discussion it is handled just like the two real caches.) To clear any of the caches, scroll to select the button with the trackwheel and click. The cache is immediately emptied, and the button disappears from the **Cache Operations** screen.

▶ **NOTE**

Although your wireless service provider can alter the default setting, BlackBerry 7100 devices have a default 2MB content cache for caching web pages.

6 Exit Browser Options

Press the **Escape** button to exit the **Browser Options** screen. Press the **Escape** button again to navigate back to the **Home** screen, or just press the **End** key.

9

BlackBerry As the Ultimate Mobile Phone

IN THIS CHAPTER:

- **54** About the BlackBerry Phone
- **55** Make and Receive Phone Calls
- **56** Make a Conference Call
- **57** Forward Calls
- **58** Manage the Speed Dial List
- **59** Take Advantage of Smart Dialing
- **60** Work with Call Logs
- **61** Tweak Phone Options
- **62** Access a 411 Phone Directory

The BlackBerry 7100 series of devices represents an important shift in the way BlackBerry devices are used and perceived. The 7100 series devices add mobile phone functionality in a slim form factor to the already popular text-messaging features of the BlackBerry product line. Text messaging and tight email integration have long been the strong suit of all BlackBerry devices, but it's only with the 7100 series that users can now forego carrying around two devices for mobile phone and text-messaging features.

Because the BlackBerry 7100 series devices are designed with relatively large screens and a full-featured graphical user interface, the phone facet of the devices is in many ways more advanced than that of single-purpose mobile phones. The BlackBerry 7100 manages to carefully walk the line between handheld computer and mobile phone and does a decent job in the process. You would perhaps expect the device to be weak on phone features because its legacy is text messaging, but I've found the BlackBerry phone to be intuitive. And being able to use synchronized contacts from Microsoft Outlook to initiate calls is a real luxury.

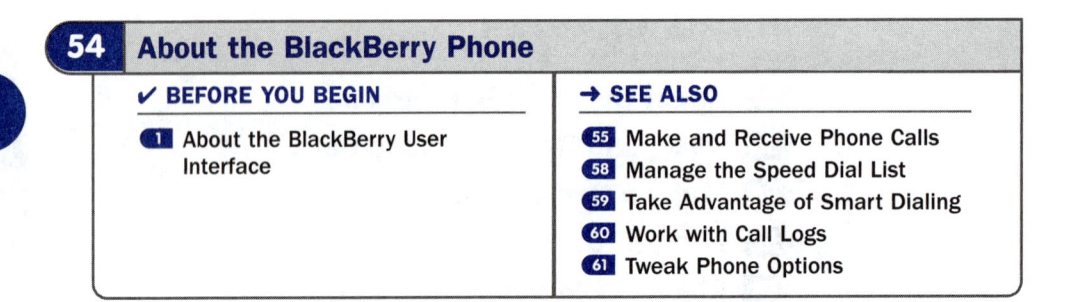

54 About the BlackBerry Phone

✔ BEFORE YOU BEGIN

1 About the BlackBerry User Interface

→ SEE ALSO

55 Make and Receive Phone Calls
58 Manage the Speed Dial List
59 Take Advantage of Smart Dialing
60 Work with Call Logs
61 Tweak Phone Options

The BlackBerry 7100 series device is designed from the ground up to supplement BlackBerry's robust text-messaging features with mobile phone features that rival—and in some ways surpass—popular mobile phones. Although there are a few notably missing ingredients in the BlackBerry phone, such as voice dialing and Bluetooth synchronization support, the mobile phone features of the 7100 still make it an incredibly useful multipurpose device that is as much handheld computer as it is mobile phone.

What sets the 7100 apart from most other mobile phones and handheld computers is its form factor, which rests clearly in the middle of these two ends of the mobile divide. The screen is considerably larger than that of most mobile phones yet smaller than most handheld computers; although it has a less-than-full QWERTY keyboard, it has more keys than a typical numeric phone keypad. Some of the hardware phone aspects of the 7100 are conveniently hidden to help streamline the device. For example, the handset speaker is cleverly concealed under the shiny chrome metal piece along the top front of the device and the microphone is hidden from view in the keyboard.

About the BlackBerry Phone 54

▶ **NOTE**
Even though the BlackBerry 7100 keyboard is not a full QWERTY keyboard, it simulates a full keyboard with its predictive *SureType* typing technology.

A few other hardware features fit into the compact form factor of the 7100 device and help give it the feel of a traditional mobile phone. More specifically, there are familiar **Send** and **End** keys for making and ending phone calls. The trackwheel and **Escape** button also enter the picture with the 7100 phone by allowing you to change the volume (scroll the trackwheel) and navigate through software phone screens (the **Escape** button backs out of a screen). Additionally, a large speakerphone speaker is located on the back of the device that drives the speakerphone feature of the device, as well as a headphone jack along the upper-left edge of the device for plugging in a wired headset.

The compact form factor of the BlackBerry 7100 series device allows it to play the role of mobile phone without feeling too big and clunky.

After you are comfortable with the hardware design of the BlackBerry 7100 series device, you can move on to assessing the software it uses. The phone in the 7100 device is a software application that functions much like any of the other standard BlackBerry applications. The **Phone** application is launched directly from the **Home** screen and is easily identifiable on most 7100 series devices thanks to its telephone icon.

You use familiar screens, menus, and other BlackBerry user interface components to set phone options and use the **Phone** application. In fact, one of the most interesting aspects of the 7100 device is that you can use other applications on the device while talking on the phone. So, if you need to reference a text message or perhaps the calendar while on a call, you can simply jump over to the **Messages** application or the **Calendar** application. To do this, you must first navigate from the phone back to the **Home** screen by clicking the trackwheel, selecting **Home Screen** from the menu that appears, and clicking again. From there, you're free to do anything you would normally do with your device when not on a call—while still staying connected with your call.

▶ **NOTE**
Although you can compose messages while you're talking on the phone, the messages won't actually be delivered until the call ends.

When not on a call, you can query the device to find the current phone status, which consists of your mobile phone number, the amount of time spent in the previous call, and the total amount of call time the device has experienced. To view the phone status, click the trackwheel in the **Phone** application, select **Status** from the menu that appears, and click once more. The **Phone Info** screen is displayed and shows the current phone status.

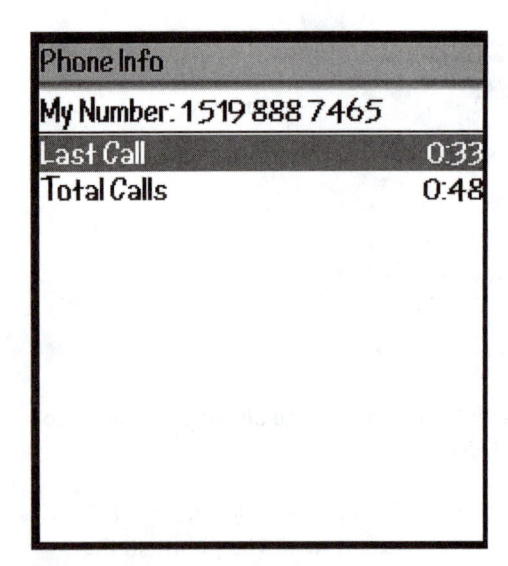

```
Phone Info
My Number: 1 519 888 7465
Last Call                    0:33
Total Calls                  0:48
```

*The **Phone Info** screen allows you to view your phone number, the duration of the last call, and the total call minutes.*

The call timers displayed on the **Phone Info** screen can be reset so you can track phone usage from a particular point in time. To reset the call timers, open the **Phone Info** screen by clicking the trackwheel in the **Phone** application, selecting **Status** from the menu that appears, and clicking once more. Click again to open the **Status** screen menu, select **Clear Timer** or **Clear All Timers** from the menu that appears, and click once more. The **Clear Timer** menu command clears only the selected timer; **Clear All Timers** clears both call timers. After clearing the timers, click the trackwheel, select **Save** from the menu, and click again to save the changes.

▶ **NOTE**

You can feasibly use the main call timer (**Total Calls**) to track phone usage as a business expense. I realize that mobile phone bills typically itemize the minutes in phone usage, but you could make expense reports a bit easier to manage by clearing the main call timer when you embark on a business trip. Think of it as a trip odometer for your phone.

Although clearing a call timer might not be something you need to do often, there is another feature of the BlackBerry 7100 I hope you never have to use. I'm referring to the ability of the phone to make emergency calls. What is interesting about this feature is that your phone is equipped to make emergency phone calls regardless of whether the **SIM card** is inserted or the wireless radio is turned on. If the keyboard is unlocked, you can simply dial the emergency number (911, for example) and press the **Send** key. If the keyboard is locked, click the trackwheel, select **Emergency Call** from the menu that appears, and click again. Then click **Yes** to confirm that you want to make an emergency call.

▶ **NOTE**

The idea behind the emergency call feature on your phone is to allow you or someone else to use the phone in an emergency, even if the phone is locked to prevent access. As an example, if you are in an accident and are unable to use your phone, a passerby could use your phone to make an emergency call and assist you.

One last phone feature worth pointing out is voice mail—or at least how to access it. Every wireless provider is free to implement its own specific voice mail system. However, regardless of how your specific voice mail system works when you access it, connecting to voice mail from your device is consistent across all 7100 devices. Just hold down the 1 key (**E R** key) from the **Home** screen or from within the **Phone** application, and you will be connected to voice mail.

55 Make and Receive Phone Calls

✓ BEFORE YOU BEGIN

54 About the BlackBerry Phone

→ SEE ALSO

56 Make a Conference Call
57 Forward Calls
58 Manage the Speed Dial List
59 Take Advantage of Smart Dialing
68 Create and Manage Contacts

Sure, it sounds like something a toddler should be able to master in a few minutes, but there's more to it than you might think. I'm referring to making and receiving phone calls on your BlackBerry 7100 device. Although your device certainly serves as a traditional mobile phone that isn't difficult to use, it is more advanced than many mobile phones in terms of how you make and receive calls. For example, you can either dial a number manually or dial a contact from the address book. You can also put a call on hold and mute a call, not to mention switch between the handset, speakerphone, and an optional Bluetooth headset or car kit. These features are all reasonably intuitive, but you'll find that some handy shortcuts allow you to make and receive calls using the BlackBerry phone with the utmost efficiency.

1 Open the Phone Screen

Scroll to the **Phone** icon on the **Home** screen and click the trackwheel. The **Phone** screen appears, displaying a dialing area and a list of recently made and received phone calls.

▶ **TIP**

You can quickly jump to the **Phone** screen from any location on your phone by simply pressing the **Send** key.

2 Dial a Number Manually

To manually dial a number from the **Phone** screen, press the desired number keys on the keyboard to enter the number into the BlackBerry phone. To insert a wait when typing the number, press the **Q W** key. A *wait* results in the phone waiting for you to enter numbers. This can be helpful if you want to dial a security code of some sort after the initial number is dialed. Similarly, insert a pause into the number by pressing the **L** key. A *pause* waits a brief amount of time and continues dialing any other numbers you've specified. And finally, to insert a + in the number—necessary in making an international call—hold down the **Space** key (**0** key). When you finish entering the number, press the **Send** key to dial it and initiate a phone call.

55 Make and Receive Phone Calls

- Wait/Mute (During Call)
- **1** Open the Phone Screen
- **2** Dial a Number Manually
- **3** Dial a Contact from the Address Book
- Volume
- **8** End the Call and Exit
- **4** Hold and Resume the Call
- Toggle Speakerphone/Handset
- Pause
- **5** Mute the Call
- **6** Activate the Speakerphone or Headset
- Wait to Dial Extension
- Hold for +
- **7** Answer or Ignore a Call

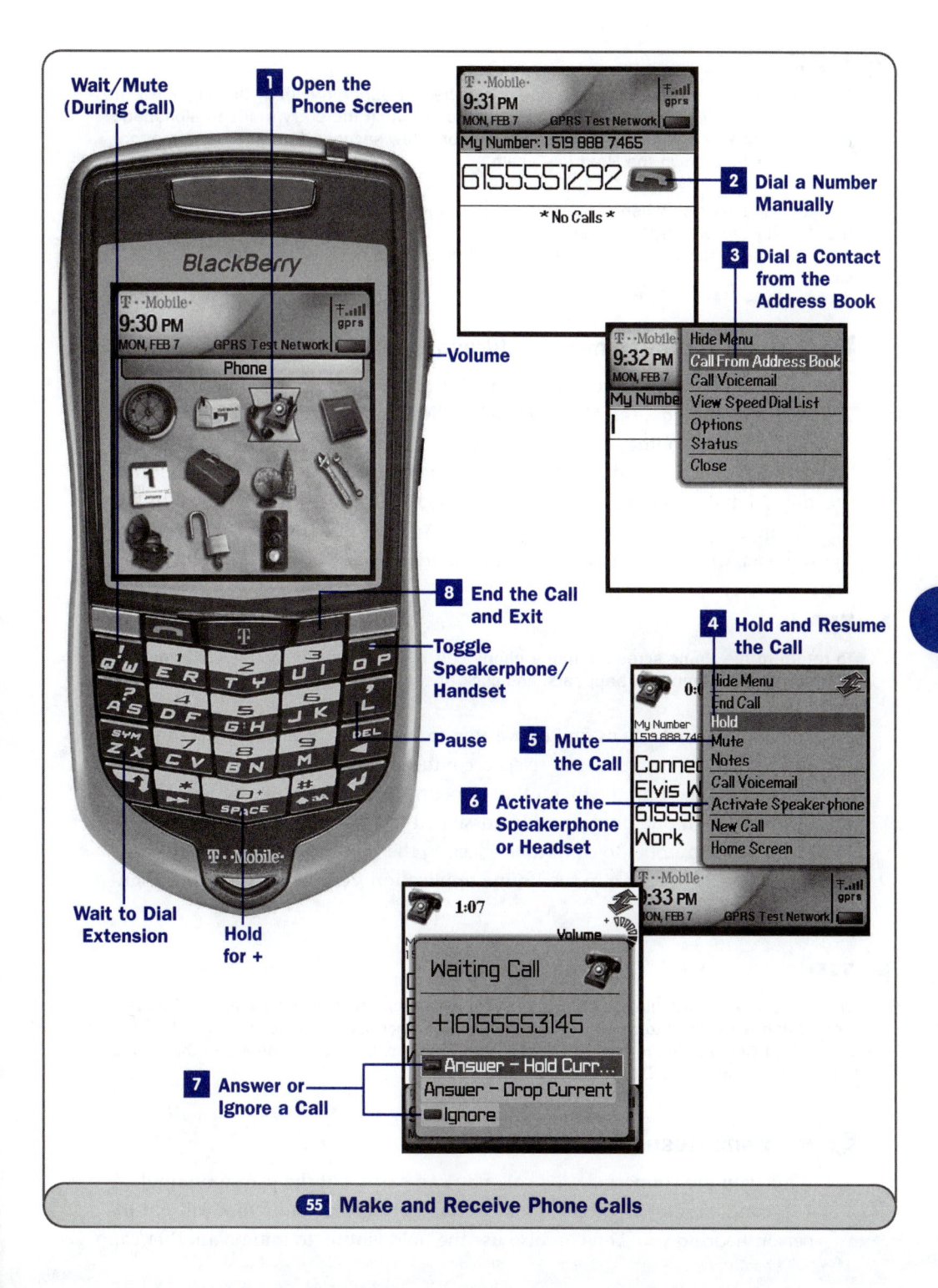

55 Make and Receive Phone Calls

▶ TIPS

You can type letters while dialing a phone number (or during a call) by holding down the **Alt** key while typing the letters. Optionally, you can switch the entry mode to alphabetic multitap mode by holding down the **Next** key for a few seconds. To return to numeric input mode, hold down the **Next** key again.

To enter an extension when dialing a phone number, enter the number and then press the **Z X** key followed by the extension. The number is dialed; when the call is connected, your BlackBerry device waits for a specified amount of time and then dials the extension.

3 Dial a Contact from the Address Book

If you've synchronized contacts from a desktop client application such as Microsoft Outlook (see **10 Synchronize PIM Data with Your PC**) or have manually entered contacts into the BlackBerry address book, you'll find it handy to dial contacts directly from the address book, as opposed to dialing manually. To dial a contact from the address book, click the trackwheel within the **Phone** application and select **Call From Address Book** from the menu that appears. Click once more to open the address book.

▶ TIP

To return to the **Home** screen during a phone call, click the trackwheel, select **Home Screen** from the menu that appears, and click again.

The address book opens and allows you to select any of the contacts in the contact list. After scrolling to select a contact, click the trackwheel, select **Call Contact Name** from the menu that appears, and click again. If the contact has more than one phone number assigned to him, you are prompted to select which number to call. After selecting the number and clicking the trackwheel, you return to the **Phone** application from which the call is then made.

▶ TIP

You can call a contact directly from the address book without ever opening the **Phone** application. Just scroll to select a contact in the contact list, click the trackwheel, and select **Call Contact Name** from the menu that appears. Click once more and the phone opens to initiate the call.

4 Hold and Resume the Call

While you are connected on a call, you can easily put the person on hold. This can be useful if you must take a moment to carry out a task without the person hearing you. You can also use the hold feature to initiate another call

55 Make and Receive Phone Calls

and ultimately join the two people for a conference call (see **56** **Make a Conference Call**). To put a call on hold, click the trackwheel, select **Hold** from the menu that appears, and click again. The current call is placed on hold, and you can carry out other BlackBerry tasks without the person on the call hearing what you're doing.

▶ **TIP**
To change the volume during a call, simply scroll the trackwheel.

To resume a call you've placed on hold, click the trackwheel, select **Resume** from the menu that appears, and click once more. The call is resumed and the person on the other end can hear you again.

5 Mute the Call

If you want to prevent the person on the other end of a call from hearing you but still be able to hear him, you can mute a call instead of putting the call on hold. Muting a call simply mutes your side of the conversation but otherwise keeps the call active. You can mute and unmute calls as you see fit to prevent yourself from being heard. This comes in handy if you need to cough, sneeze, or generally prevent noises on your end of the conversation from being heard on the other end. To mute the call, click the trackwheel, select **Mute** from the menu that appears, and click again.

▶ **NOTE**
Be very careful to make sure that mute is on if you intend to make noises you don't want heard on the other end of the conversation. I personally heard a recorded call from a call center agent in which the agent thought mute was turned on and handled the tech support call in the restroom. It's fairly standard for call centers to record calls for quality assurance purposes, but this particular agent became infamous for his accidental misuse of the mute feature.

Unmuting a call is as simple as clicking, selecting **Turn Mute Off** from the menu, and clicking once more.

▶ **TIP**
To quickly turn mute on and off during a call, press the **Q W** key. And don't forget, you can adjust the call volume by scrolling the trackwheel.

6 Activate the Speakerphone or Headset

The speakerphone feature on the BlackBerry 7100 series of devices is useful in that it allows you to carry on a conversation without having to hold the device up to your ear. To switch from the handset to the speakerphone, click the trackwheel, select **Activate Speakerphone**, and click again. You can switch back to the handset by clicking, selecting **Active Handset**, and clicking again.

▶ **TIP**

To quickly switch between the speakerphone and handset during a call, press the **O P** key.

If you have a Bluetooth headset or car kit, you also have an option on the **Phone** menu for activating the headset or car kit. Bluetooth headsets and car kits enable you to carry on a hands-free conversation without any wires between the headset/car kit and your device. See **63 About Bluetooth** and **65 Pair Up with a Bluetooth Headset or Car Kit** to find out more about using a Bluetooth device with your BlackBerry 7100.

7 Answer or Ignore a Call

The other side of the BlackBerry phone equation involves answering calls you receive on your device. When a call is received, your device typically alerts you by vibrating and playing an alert tune; this action depends on the profile you currently have set (see **18 Tweak the Profiles**). If your device isn't in the holster, the incoming phone number is displayed on the screen, along with the name of the caller (if the number matches a contact in the address book). To answer the call, press the **Send** key. If you're already on a call, you can scroll the trackwheel to select whether you want to hold the current call or drop the current call to answer the new call. If you'd rather ignore the call, just press the **End** key.

8 End the Call and Exit

To end the call, simply press the **End** key. There is also an **End Call** command on the **Phone** menu, but the **End** key is more convenient. Press the **Escape** button to exit the phone and return to the **Home** screen.

56 Make a Conference Call

✔ BEFORE YOU BEGIN	→ SEE ALSO
55 Make and Receive Phone Calls	57 Forward Calls
	58 Manage the Speed Dial List
	59 Take Advantage of Smart Dialing
	68 Create and Manage Contacts

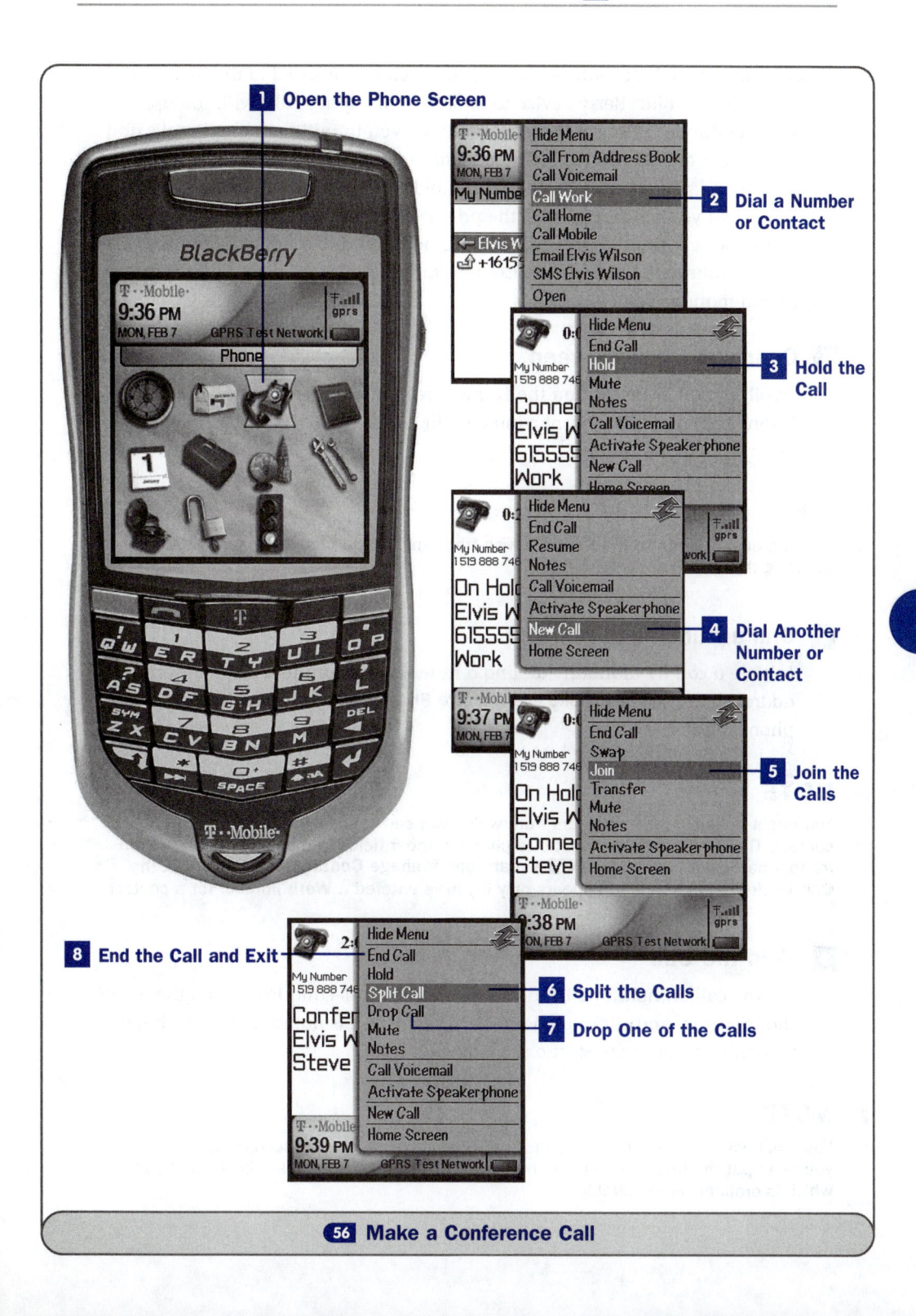

56 Make a Conference Call

1 Open the Phone Screen

2 Dial a Number or Contact

3 Hold the Call

4 Dial Another Number or Contact

5 Join the Calls

6 Split the Calls

7 Drop One of the Calls

8 End the Call and Exit

56 Make a Conference Call

CHAPTER 9: BlackBerry As the Ultimate Mobile Phone

If you've never used the feature before, you might be surprised to find out that you can use your BlackBerry device to establish conference calls with multiple parties. The standard **Phone** application allows you to initiate multiple calls and then join them together for a conference call. Additionally, you can split an individual call and put the conference call on hold while you talk to one person in private. When you're finished with the private conversation, you can quickly join the person back with the conference call. Although many mobile phones support conference calling, the BlackBerry user interface makes it particularly intuitive to set up and manage conference calls.

1 Open the Phone Screen

Scroll to the **Phone** icon on the **Home** screen and click the trackwheel. The **Phone** screen appears, displaying a dialing area and a list of recently made and received phone calls.

▶ **TIP**

You can quickly jump to the **Phone** screen from any location on your phone by simply pressing the **Send** key.

2 Dial a Number or Contact

Initiate a call by manually dialing a number or selecting a contact from the address book. See **55 Make and Receive Phone Calls** for more details on phone dialing.

▶ **NOTE**

You might notice several numbers from which you can choose when dialing a particular contact. These numbers correspond to phone number fields in the contact information for that particular contact (see **68 Create and Manage Contacts**). For example, the **Call Work** menu command appears only if you've entered a **Work** number for a contact.

3 Hold the Call

Put the call on hold by clicking the trackwheel, selecting **Hold** from the menu that appears, and clicking again. The current call is put on hold, which gives you an opportunity to start a second call.

▶ **NOTE**

You don't actually have to put the first call on hold to initiate the second call. However, if you don't put the first call on hold, the person will hear as you make the second call, which is probably not desirable.

▶ **TIP**

To resume a call that has been placed on hold, click the trackwheel, select **Resume** from the menu, and click once more.

4 Dial Another Number or Contact

To start the second call, click the trackwheel and select **New Call** from the menu that appears. Now you can manually dial a number or select a contact from the address book to make the second call.

5 Join the Calls

After the second call is connected, you'll see that the first call is on hold while the second call is active. To join the two calls into a conference call, click the trackwheel, select **Join** from the menu that appears, and click again. The two people are joined together into a three-way conversation with you. You can continue initiating new calls and joining them with the conversation to expand the conference call with additional people. When doing so, you put the entire conference call on hold to call a new person.

▶ **NOTE**

Although you can add multiple people to a conference call, you can never have more than one conversation on hold at any given time. In other words, you always have at most two conversations going on: an active conversation and a hold conversation. Keep in mind that a "conversation" can include multiple people. The **New Call** menu option disappears after you have two conversations underway. To initiate a new call, you must join the two conversations by adding the active person to the conversation on hold. Then you're free to call a new person and repeat the process to grow the conversation.

▶ **TIP**

You don't have to dial a number or contact to establish a conference call. Instead, you can just as easily have people call you and then join them together into a conference call as you answer the individual calls.

6 Split the Calls

To split an individual call out from a conference call, click the trackwheel, select **Split Call** from the menu that appears, and click again. You are prompted to select which call to split (select the appropriate phone number), which is the call that becomes active after the split. The split call is removed from the conference call and made active, while the original conference call is placed on hold. Splitting a call is a good way to pull a person aside from a conference call and hold a private discussion. To swap the conversation and return to the conference call, click the trackwheel, select **Swap** from the menu, and click again. You can then join the split call back into the conference call if you want. Note that if you are the person who did the joining of the conversations, you have control over whom you can split out from and rejoin to the main conversation.

▶ **TIP**

If you have an active call and a call on hold, you can swap between the calls at any time by clicking the trackwheel, selecting **Swap** from the menu, and clicking again. Alternatively, just press the **Send** key to quickly swap calls.

7 Drop One of the Calls

Just as you can add people to a conference call, you can also drop them. To drop a person from a conference call, click the trackwheel, select **Drop Call** from the menu, and click once more. You are prompted to select which call to drop; select the call and click to end that call and remove that person from the conference call.

8 End the Call and Exit

To end the conference call, simply press the **End** key. There is also an **End Call** command on the phone menu, but the **End** key is more convenient. Press the **Escape** button to exit the phone and return to the **Home** screen.

57 Forward Calls

✔ BEFORE YOU BEGIN	→ SEE ALSO
55 Make and Receive Phone Calls	56 Make a Conference Call
	58 Manage the Speed Dial List
	59 Take Advantage of Smart Dialing
	68 Create and Manage Contacts

The great thing about mobile phones is that they allow us to receive calls just about any time we choose. The problem is that there are some times when we'd ideally choose not to receive calls on our mobile phones. Although you can certainly turn off your device or mute the ringer, I'm talking about situations in which you might want to forward calls you receive on your BlackBerry device to another number entirely. Maybe you're spending the day at a customer's site and want to take calls at a temporary office number. Or maybe you're working at home and prefer using your home phone line instead of eating up minutes on your mobile phone. Regardless of your motive, sometimes forwarding calls to another number can be useful. The BlackBerry phone provides a few options for fine-tuning the forwarding of calls to your BlackBerry device.

57 Forward Calls

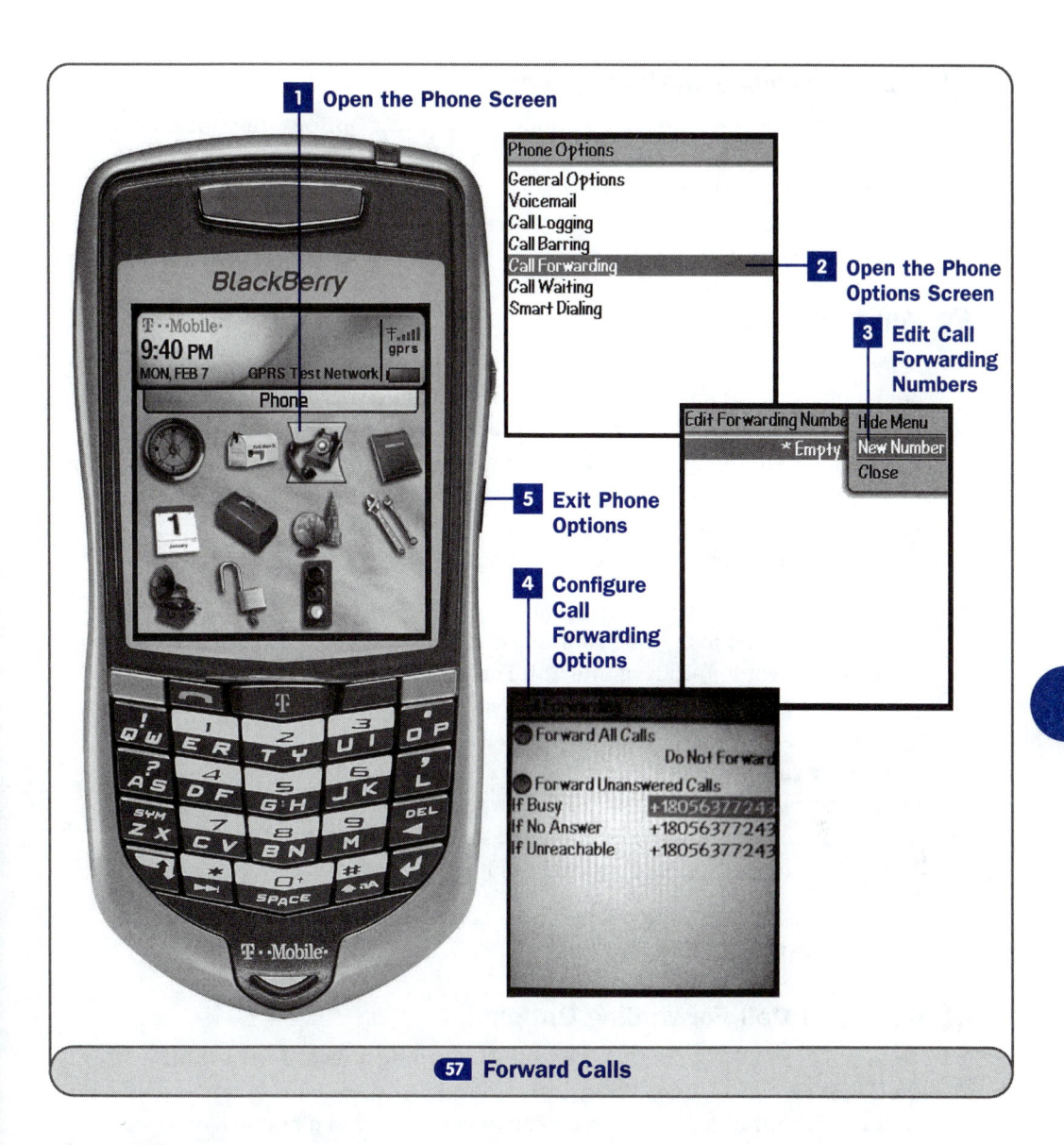

1 Open the Phone Screen

Phone Options
General Options
Voicemail
Call Logging
Call Barring
Call Forwarding
Call Waiting
Smart Dialing

2 Open the Phone Options Screen

3 Edit Call Forwarding Numbers

Edit Forwarding Number | Hide Menu
*Empty | New Number
        | Close

5 Exit Phone Options

4 Configure Call Forwarding Options

Forward All Calls
                 Do Not Forward
Forward Unanswered Calls
If Busy   +18056377243
If No Answer   +18056377243
If Unreachable +18056377243

57 Forward Calls

1 Open the Phone Screen

Scroll to the **Phone** icon on the **Home** screen and click the trackwheel. The **Phone** screen appears, displaying a dialing area and a list of recently made and received phone calls.

▶ **TIP**

You can quickly jump to the **Phone** screen from any location on your phone by simply pressing the **Send** key.

2. Open the Phone Options Screen

Click the trackwheel to open the **Phone** menu, select **Options** from the menu, and click again. The **Phone Options** screen appears and provides access to a variety of phone options. To configure call forwarding options, select **Call Forwarding** from the **Phone Options** screen and click the trackwheel. The **Call Forwarding** screen appears.

3. Edit Call Forwarding Numbers

Before you find out about setting call forwarding options, it's important to point out that your phone probably already includes your voice mail number as a forwarding number. This means you can forward your calls to your voice mail number. To use other numbers for call forwarding, you must enter them as forwarding numbers. To add a new forwarding number, click the trackwheel, select **Edit Numbers** from the menu that appears, and click again. The **Edit Forwarding Numbers** screen appears and displays a list of forwarding numbers.

Any number you add to the forwarding number list becomes available as an option for forwarding calls on the **Call Forwarding** screen. To add a forwarding number, click the trackwheel, select **New Number** from the menu that appears, and click again. You are prompted to enter the number, after which you simply click to accept it and add it to the list. To delete a forwarding number, scroll to select it, click the trackwheel, and select **Delete** from the menu that appears. Click once more and then select **Delete** in the confirmation dialog box to finish deleting the number.

When you're finished editing forwarding numbers, press the **Escape** button to return to the **Call Forwarding** screen.

4. Configure Call Forwarding Options

There are two main options on the **Call Forwarding** screen: **Forward All Calls** and **Forward Unanswered Calls**. The **Forward All Calls** option is pretty dramatic in that it forwards *every* call to your device to a number you specify. The **Forward Unanswered Calls** option is the one you will use more often; it allows you to specify individual numbers to which you want calls to be forwarded under certain conditions (such as if the device is busy, if there is no answer, or if you are unreachable—out of service or the device is turned off).

If you want to forward all calls to your device to another number, select the **Forward All Calls** option and double-click. Then scroll down to the setting just below the option and specify the number to which you want all your calls forwarded. The **Do Not Forward** setting results in the calls not being forwarded at all. Your phone probably includes your voice mail number as the other possible setting, along with any forwarding numbers of your own that you created.

▶ **TIP**
The **Forward All Calls** option is useful if you want to pass all your mobile phone calls along to another number, such as if you want mobile calls routed to your office number. Just don't forget to turn off the option when you're finished forwarding calls.

The second option on the **Call Forwarding** screen is **Forward Unanswered Calls**, which causes only unanswered calls to be forwarded. You might not realize it, but this option is likely already set for your device by default. This setting is necessary because your voice mail works by forwarding unanswered calls to your voice mail number. There are three different scenarios under which your phone doesn't answer a call, and they correspond to individual settings under the **Forward Unanswered Calls** option: **If Busy**, **If No Answer**, and **If Unreachable**. You can assign a different forwarding number to each of these scenarios; the default setting is to forward the call to your voice mail number in each scenario. To change one of the numbers, select the number, click the trackwheel, select **Change Number** from the menu that appears, and click again. Then scroll to select the number and click once more.

▶ **NOTE**
Be careful when making changes to the **Forward Unanswered Calls** setting. If you set the forwarding number to a number other than your voice mail number, the caller won't be given a chance to leave a voice mail message under the given scenario. For example, setting a forwarding number for the **If No Answer** option results in all calls being forwarded to that number when you don't answer your phone, effectively bypassing your voice mail.

After tweaking the call forwarding options, press the **Escape** button to return to the **Phone Options** screen. If you've made changes, a confirmation pop-up window appears—select **Save** to confirm the changes and then click the trackwheel.

5 **Exit Phone Options**

Press the **Escape** button to exit the **Phone Options** screen. Press the **Escape** button again to navigate back to the **Home** screen, or just press the **End** key.

58 Manage the Speed Dial List

✔ BEFORE YOU BEGIN
- 55 Make and Receive Phone Calls

→ SEE ALSO
- 56 Make a Conference Call
- 57 Forward Calls
- 59 Take Advantage of Smart Dialing
- 68 Create and Manage Contacts

Although the address book makes dialing a phone number fairly easy, for the utmost in dialing efficiency you should consider using the speed dial list. The speed dial list is a list of phone numbers mapped to the number keys on the BlackBerry keyboard. To dial a speed dial number, you simply hold down the appropriate number key. Fortunately, there is a highly intuitive user interface for assigning numbers to the speed dial list and shuffling the numbers around to get the assignments just like you want them. You'll likely find yourself relying heavily on the speed dial list to dial common numbers after you get the hang of how to set up and manage it.

▶ **NOTE**
By default, your voice mail number is initially assigned to the **1** key, although you are free to move this voice mail number to a different speed dial number if you want.

1 Open the Phone Screen

Scroll to the **Phone** icon on the **Home** screen and click the trackwheel. The **Phone** screen appears, displaying a dialing area and a list of recently made and received phone calls.

▶ **TIP**
You can quickly jump to the **Phone** screen from any location on your phone by simply pressing the **Send** key.

2 Open the Speed Dial List

To access the speed dial list, click the trackwheel and select **View Speed Dial List** from the menu that appears. Click again to open the speed dial list, which shows all the assignments for the number keys (**1–9**) on your device's keyboard.

58 Manage the Speed Dial List

1 Open the Phone Screen

2 Open the Speed Dial List

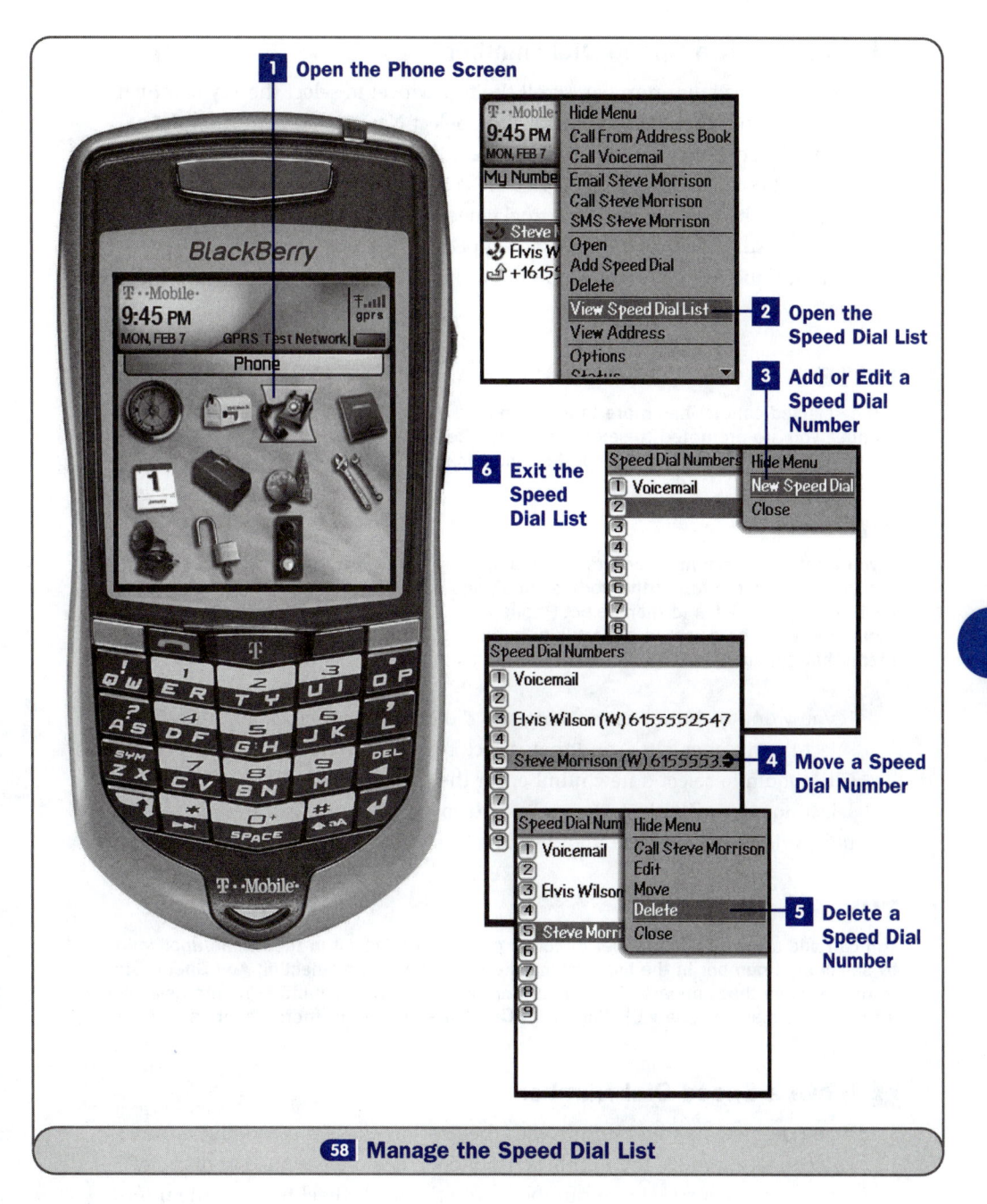

3 Add or Edit a Speed Dial Number

4 Move a Speed Dial Number

5 Delete a Speed Dial Number

6 Exit the Speed Dial List

58 Manage the Speed Dial List

3 Add or Edit a Speed Dial Number

To add a speed dial number, scroll the trackwheel to select the key to which you want to add the number and click. Select **New Speed Dial** from the menu that appears, and click once more. You are immediately taken to the address book, where you can select the contact for the speed dial number—just select the contact, click the trackwheel, and select **Add Speed Dial To Contact Name** from the menu that appears. Click once more, and the contact's number is added to the speed dial list as the specified speed dial number.

▶ **NOTE**

If the selected contact has more than one phone number when editing a speed dial number, you are prompted to select which number you want to use as the speed dial number. Just scroll to select the number and click the trackwheel.

▶ **TIP**

If you want to enter a number directly as a speed dial number, as opposed to selecting a contact, scroll to the top of the address book and select **[Use Once]** in the contact list. Click the trackwheel, and then select **Phone** from the menu that appears. Click once more, and you'll be given an opportunity to enter the number. Click **Continue** on the menu that appears, and the number is added as the speed dial number.

If you want to change an existing speed dial number, scroll the trackwheel to select the number, click, and then select **Edit** from the menu that appears. Click again to select a new number for the speed dial key. The process for selecting a new number when editing a speed dial entry is the same as initially adding a new speed dial number.

▶ **TIP**

You can add a speed dial number directly from the *call log* list in the **Phone** application by selecting a number in the list, clicking the trackwheel, and selecting **Add Speed Dial** from the menu that appears. Click once more and confirm the number before assigning it to a speed dial key. See **60 Work with Call Logs** to find out more about call logs.

4 Move a Speed Dial Number

If you decide you aren't happy with the assignment of a speed dial number, you can easily move the numbers around so they are assigned to different keys. To move a speed dial number, scroll the trackwheel to select the number, click, and select **Move** from the menu that appears. Click once more and the number is highlighted to indicate that it can be moved by scrolling the trackwheel. When you settle on a new location for the number, click the trackwheel, and the number is moved. If there is already a number in the new location, you are prompted to replace the number or cancel the move; you can't swap numbers on the speed dial list.

5 Delete a Speed Dial Number

Just as you can add new speed dial numbers and edit existing numbers, you can also delete existing numbers, which simply means you're clearing the speed dial key so it doesn't dial any number. To delete the selected speed dial number, click the trackwheel, select **Delete** from the menu that appears, and click again. You are prompted to confirm the deletion of the speed dial number; click **Delete** to continue with the deletion or **Cancel** if you've changed your mind.

▶ **NOTE**

Deleting a speed dial number removes the number assignment only from the specified speed dial key. The associated contact in the address book is completely unaffected by the speed dial deletion.

6 Exit the Speed Dial List

Press the **Escape** button to exit the speed dial list. Press the **Escape** button again to navigate back to the **Home** screen, or just press the **End** key.

---

59 Take Advantage of Smart Dialing

✔ **BEFORE YOU BEGIN**

55 Make and Receive Phone Calls

➔ **SEE ALSO**

56 Make a Conference Call
57 Forward Calls
58 Manage the Speed Dial List
68 Create and Manage Contacts

If you've ever run into problems dialing a phone number that requires you to specify an extension, you'll want to take a look at smart dialing on your BlackBerry device. Smart dialing is a feature that allows you to specify exact dialing parameters such as your country code prefix, area code, and national number length, as well as how long to wait when dialing an office phone extension. In fact, you can specify a different wait time for dialing extensions in your own office as compared to other offices. Smart dialing is a feature that can serve you just fine if you cruise along with the default settings. Or you could find it critical to alter the smart dialing settings to suit your own unique calling needs.

CHAPTER 9: BlackBerry As the Ultimate Mobile Phone

1 Open the Phone Screen

2 Open the Phone Options Screen

3 Configure Smart Dialing Options

4 Exit Phone Options

59 Take Advantage of Smart Dialing

1 Open the Phone Screen

Scroll to the **Phone** icon on the **Home** screen and click the trackwheel. The **Phone** screen appears, displaying a dialing area and a list of recently made and received phone calls.

▶ **TIP**

You can quickly jump to the **Phone** screen from any location on your phone by simply pressing the **Send** key.

59 Take Advantage of Smart Dialing   233

2 Open the Phone Options Screen

Click the trackwheel to open the **Phone** menu, select **Options** from the menu, and click again. The **Phone Options** screen appears and provides access to a variety of phone options.

3 Configure Smart Dialing Options

To configure smart dialing options, select **Smart Dialing** on the **Phone Options** screen and click the trackwheel. The **Smart Dialing** screen appears and provides access to the various settings associated with the smart dialing feature.

The first block of smart dialing options allows you to tweak general dialing settings for your device, including your originating **Country Code**, **Area Code**, and **National Number Length**. Your wireless service provider has likely already provided correct default settings for these options, but you are certainly allowed to change them if your dialing specifics have changed.

▶ **NOTE**
The national number length is a count of the characters in a full phone number (including area code) in your country, excluding the country code. As an example, the U.S. national number length is 10, which consists of a 3-digit area code and a 7-digit number. Here's an example of a 10-digit number, just to make things clear: 615-555-1234.

The last two blocks of options on the **Smart Dialing** screen determine how extensions are dialed when you make a call to an office phone number with an extension. More specifically, you can specify a single phone number in the **Number** field that has a unique wait time and extension length; this setting depends entirely on your specific office phone system. To specify these unique settings, enter the main number and then choose a wait setting for the **Wait For** option, as well as an extension length for the **Extension Length** option. Most office phone systems use extensions with 2–4 digits, but the **Extension Length** option allows you to specify an extension length up to 6 digits.

▶ **TIP**
To enter an extension when dialing a phone number, enter the number and then press the **Z X** key followed by the extension. The main number is dialed; when the call is connected, your BlackBerry device waits for a specified amount of time and then dials the extension; this amount of time is determined by the **Wait For** setting on the **Smart Dialing** screen.

The settings you enter for the second block of options on the **Smart Dialing** screen apply to the single office number you specified in the **Number** field.

All extensions you dial for other numbers are subject to a general wait time that is specified in the second **Wait For** field. Unless you have problems dialing extensions, the default setting of **2 seconds** is probably sufficient.

After tweaking the smart dialing options, press the **Escape** button to return to the **Phone Options** screen. If you've made changes, a confirmation pop-up window appears—select **Save** to confirm the changes and then click the trackwheel.

4 Exit Phone Options

Press the **Escape** button to exit the **Phone Options** screen. Press the **Escape** button again to navigate back to the **Home** screen, or just press the **End** key.

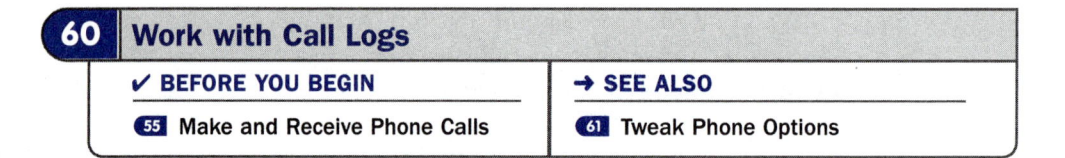

60 Work with Call Logs

✔ BEFORE YOU BEGIN	→ SEE ALSO
55 Make and Receive Phone Calls	61 Tweak Phone Options

Just as your web browser maintains a history of all the sites you've visited, your BlackBerry device maintains a list of all the phone calls you've made and received. Not only does this call history provide a useful way to keep close tabs on your phone habits and mobile communications, it can also serve as a constantly changing speed dial list. Additionally, you can use the call history to access the contact associated with a phone number.

The call history to which I'm referring is actually a list of call *logs*. Each unique phone number is given its own call log, which is a history of the calls made to or received from that particular number. By default, all calls are logged, so you can go back and see exactly when you last talked to a person at a certain number. In addition, you can also look at other calls made to or received from that same number, along with how long the calls lasted. You can even write text notes and assign them to individual calls in a call log.

In some ways, you can think of the call logs on your device as keeping up with your phone activity a bit too well. Just keep in mind that you can easily delete call logs if you want to get rid of the remnants of your recent mobile conversations.

1 Open the Phone Screen

Scroll to the **Phone** icon on the **Home** screen and click the trackwheel. The **Phone** screen appears, displaying a dialing area and a list of recently made and received phone calls (call logs).

60   Work with Call Logs

1 Open the Phone Screen

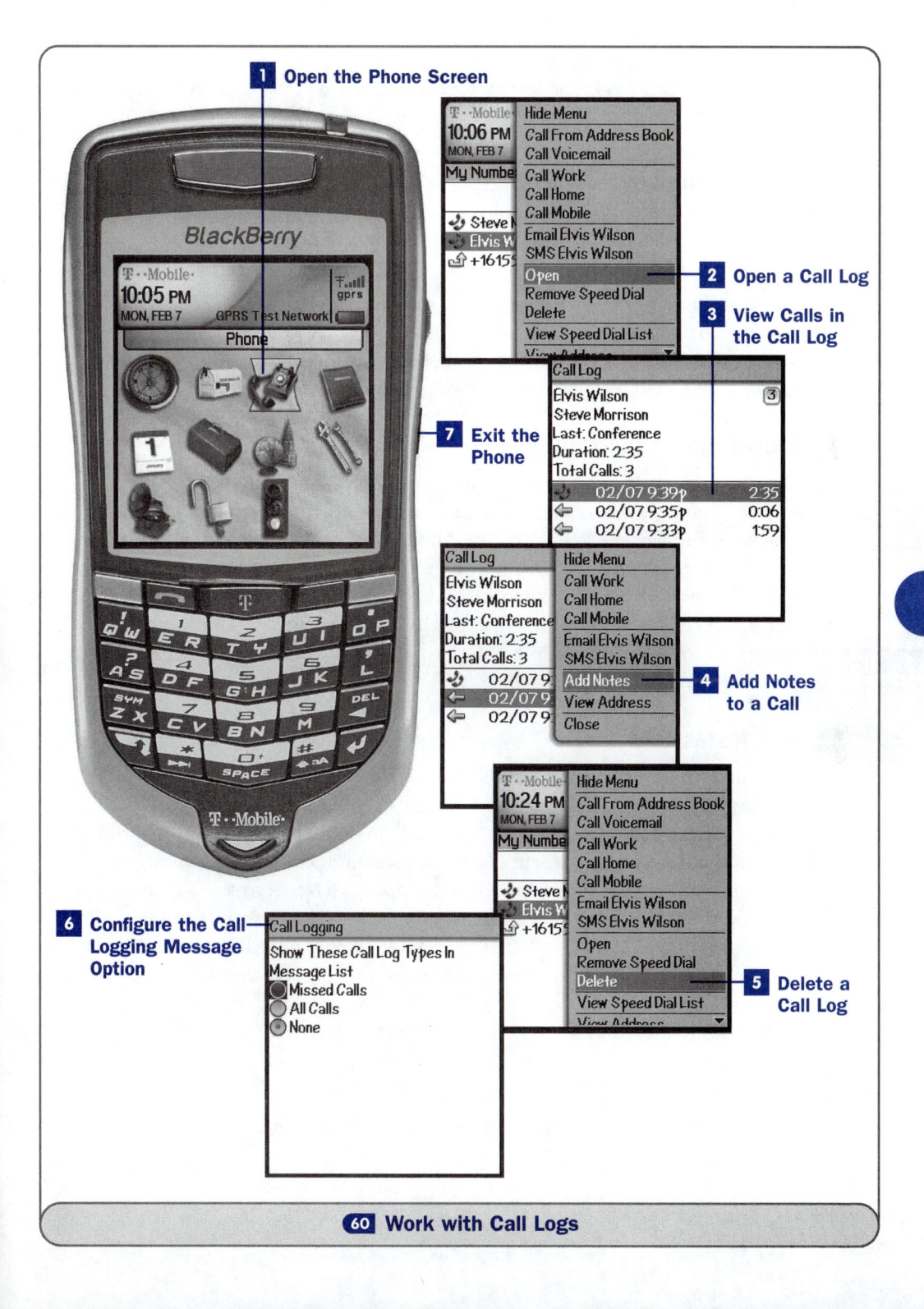

2 Open a Call Log

3 View Calls in the Call Log

4 Add Notes to a Call

5 Delete a Call Log

6 Configure the Call Logging Message Option

7 Exit the Phone

60   Work with Call Logs

▶ TIP

You can quickly jump to the **Phone** screen from any location on your phone by simply pressing the **Send** key.

2 Open a Call Log

The lower portion of the **Phone** screen consists of a list of calls that were made, received, or missed. This list of calls is really a list of call logs. Notice that no number appears more than once in the call log list because all the calls associated with that number are accessed by opening the call log for the number. To open a call log, scroll the trackwheel to select a number, click, and select **Open** from the menu that appears. Click once more, and the call log for the selected number is displayed.

3 View Calls in the Call Log

The **Call Log** screen shows all the calls made to or received from a specific number, along with the date, time, and length of each call. You can tell whether a call was made to or received from the number by the little arrow icon that appears to the left of the entry in the call log; a left arrow means you called them, a right arrow means they called you, and two little phone receivers means it was a conference call. Unanswered calls are shown with an arrow that turns upward from left to right. Conference call logs list all the people who participated in a call.

4 Add Notes to a Call

The call log feature on your BlackBerry device allows you to add notes to each call in a call log. This feature can be useful if you need to make notes related to a particular call for later reference. To add notes to a call in the call log, scroll the trackwheel to select the call, click, and select **Add Notes** from the menu that appears. Click once more to open the **Notes** screen, which allows you to enter text notes about the call. When you finish entering the notes, click the trackwheel, select **Save** from the menu, and click again. A small note icon appears next to the call in the call log to indicate that it has a note attached to it. To open the note for viewing or editing, click the trackwheel, select **Edit Notes** from the menu, and click again.

▶ TIP

To delete a note that is attached to a call log, just edit the note and delete all its text.

5 Delete a Call Log

You can easily erase the call history for a particular phone number by deleting the call log for that number. You cannot delete individual calls within a call log, however. To delete an entire call log, first return to the main **Phone** screen by pressing the **Escape** button. Then scroll the trackwheel to select the call log in the **Phone** screen (the main call log list), click, select **Delete** from the menu that appears, and click once more. You are presented with a confirmation dialog box; click **Delete** to follow through with the call log deletion or click **Cancel** if you change your mind.

6 Configure the Call Logging Message Option

An important call logging option relates to how calls are shown in the **Messages** application. You can use this option to have calls displayed alongside your email and other text messages in the main message list. This feature is particularly handy for viewing missed calls without having to open the **Phone** application.

To configure call logging options, click the trackwheel to open the **Phone** menu, select **Options** from the menu, and click again. The **Phone Options** screen appears and provides access to a variety of phone options. Select **Call Logging** on the **Phone Options** screen and click the trackwheel. The **Call Logging** screen appears, providing access to the call logging message option.

The only option on this screen allows you to determine whether calls are displayed in the main message list. The following settings are available to control the calls that are displayed: **Missed Calls**, **All Calls**, and **None**. The first option, **Missed Calls**, results in only missed calls appearing in the message list (it's the most useful option in my opinion). The **All Calls** option results in all calls being displayed in the message list (it can be a bit overwhelming when call logs begin to eclipse your text messages). The last option prevents any calls from being shown in the text message list (which is a viable option if you aren't as concerned about keeping track of every missed call). The benefit to including calls in the message list is that they appear right there alongside your messages. From the message list, you can quickly return a call by selecting the call, clicking the trackwheel, and clicking **Call** *Name* on the menu that appears.

▶ **NOTE**

Keep in mind that call logs are still readily available in the **Phone** application's call log list, regardless of how you set the call logging message option.

After setting the call logging option, press the **Escape** button to return to the **Phone Options** screen. If you've made changes, a confirmation pop-up window appears—select **Save** to confirm the changes and then click the trackwheel. Press **Escape** again to return to the main **Phone** screen.

7 Exit the Phone

Press the **Escape** button to exit the **Phone** application and return to the **Home** screen, or just press the **End** key.

---

61 Tweak Phone Options

✔ BEFORE YOU BEGIN	→ SEE ALSO
55 Make and Receive Phone Calls	60 Work with Call Logs

Like most applications on your BlackBerry device, the **Phone** application is customizable, which means you can fine-tune the phone's functionality to suit your own particular needs. You can control several subtle phone behaviors by tweaking the general phone options, such as whether the phone ever auto-answers calls and whether it auto-ends calls when you put your device in the holster. You can also restrict your identity so your phone number doesn't appear in the caller ID of phones you call. If you're really guarded about your privacy, you can even change a setting so your phone number doesn't even appear on your own device. Other handy options include changing the default call log list on the **Phone** screen so it displays the most commonly dialed numbers in the order of how frequently they are dialed.

1 Open the Phone Screen

Scroll to the **Phone** icon on the **Home** screen and click the trackwheel. The **Phone** screen appears, displaying a dialing area and a list of recently made and received phone calls.

▶ **TIP**

You can quickly jump to the **Phone** screen from any location on your phone by simply pressing the **Send** key.

2 Open the Phone Options Screen

Click the trackwheel to open the **Phone** menu, select **Options** from the menu, and click again. The **Phone Options** screen appears and provides access to a variety of phone options.

61 Tweak Phone Options 239

1 Open the Phone Screen

2 Open the Phone Options Screen

3 Configure General Options

4 Configure Voice Mail Options

5 Enable and Disable Call Waiting

6 Exit Phone Options

61 Tweak Phone Options

3 Configure General Options

To configure general phone options, select **General Options** on the **Phone Options** screen and click the trackwheel. The **General Options** screen appears, providing access to several general phone options.

The first option on the **General Options** screen is **Auto Answer Calls**, which causes the device to automatically answer a call when the phone is out of its holster. Because I like to see who is calling before answering, I personally am not a big fan of enabling this option. So, I always set it to **Never**. However, I'm a huge fan of the next option, **Auto End Calls**, which automatically ends a call when you place the device in the holster. I set this second option to **Into Holster**. I've found that enabling this option is extremely important to ensure that calls are ended when I place my device in the holster. Otherwise, I might put the device in the holster without pressing the **End** button and inadvertently stay on a call.

The **Confirm Delete** option is used to keep you from deleting call logs without a confirmation. If you want to be able to delete call logs without a confirmation, set this option to **No**. Keeping it set to the default value of **Yes** is the safer setting because it ensures that you won't inadvertently delete a call log by accidentally hitting the wrong key.

Speaking of safe settings, the **Restrict My Identity** option is used to keep you anonymous on the caller ID of phones you call. This option is truly a personal option and depends on how guarded you are about people knowing you are calling. I generally don't mind people knowing I'm calling, so I leave the option set to **No** on my device. An even more guarded option is the **Show My Number** option, which determines whether your phone number is displayed on your device (on the main **Phone** screen). If you have a reason for keeping your phone number ultraprivate, you might want to set this option to **No**. Of course, your phone number is still accessible by viewing the *SIM Card* settings (see **88 Secure the SIM Card**).

The **Phone List View** option is one of the most useful options on the **General Options** screen. It determines what kind of call information is displayed in the list on the main **Phone** screen. By default, the **Phone List View** option is set to **Call Log**, which results in the call log list being displayed. Although this view is certainly useful for seeing the exact history of recent calls, you might prefer to set it to **Most Used** so you can easily access commonly dialed numbers. Other possible settings include **Most Recent** and **Name**, which you might also find useful depending on how you plan to use the main phone list. In the case of the **Name** setting, the names of people you have called or received calls from are listed in alphabetical order; numbers that don't have names associated with them are listed in numerical order after the names.

▶ **TIP**

The **Most Used** setting for the **Phone List View** option isn't important if you've set up commonly dialed numbers in the speed dial list. See **58 Manage the Speed Dial List** to find out how to quickly access numbers you use often.

The last option on the **General Options** screen is **Default Call Volume**, which determines the default volume of calls. Although you can set this value to a specific percentage of the maximum volume—including **25%**, **50%**, **75%**, and **100%**—the default value of **Previous** proves to be the most valuable option by far. This default option results in the phone adopting the volume of the previous call (which you set using the trackwheel as the volume control knob). The **Previous** setting is ideal because you might need to adjust the volume based on your surroundings, connection quality, and so on.

After tweaking the general phone options, press the **Escape** button to return to the **Phone Options** screen. If you've made changes, a confirmation pop-up window appears—select **Save** to confirm the changes and then click the trackwheel.

4 Configure Voice Mail Options

To access voice mail options, select **Voicemail** on the **Phone Options** screen and click the trackwheel. The **Voicemail** screen appears, providing access to a couple settings where you can change the voice mail phone number and any other numbers required to access your voice mail.

The first option on the **Voicemail** screen, **Access Number**, contains the phone number used to access your voice mail service. This number is likely already set correctly on your device by your wireless service provider, but if you have to change it, you can do so through the **Access Number** option. The second voice mail option, **Additional Numbers**, is one you're more likely to change because it enables you to enter additional numbers that are required to access your voice mail. Whatever you enter in this option is dialed after you connect to your voice mail number, so it is ideally suited for specifying a special extension or password, if required.

▶ **TIP**

By default, the **1** key on speed dial is set to dial your voice mail number. To access your voice mail, just hold down the **1** key from the **Home** screen or the **Phone** application.

After tweaking the voice mail options, press the **Escape** button to return to the **Phone Options** screen. If you've made changes, a confirmation pop-up window appears—select **Save** to confirm the changes and then click the trackwheel.

5 Enable and Disable Call Waiting

To enable/disable call waiting, select **Call Waiting** on the **Phone Options** screen and click the trackwheel. The **Call Waiting** screen appears.

By default, call waiting is likely enabled on your device, which means you are notified when a new call comes in and you are already connected to a call. If you don't want to be notified of new calls while you are on a call, set the **Call Waiting Enabled** option to **No**. Unless you have a serious aversion to call waiting, it's probably a good idea to leave this option set to **Yes** so you can use the call waiting feature.

Press the **Escape** button to return to the **Phone Options** screen. If you've made changes to call waiting, a confirmation pop-up window appears—select **Save** to confirm the changes and then click the trackwheel.

6 Exit Phone Options

Press the **Escape** button to exit the **Phone Options** screen. Press the **Escape** button again to navigate back to the **Home** screen, or just press the **End** key.

62 Access a 411 Phone Directory

✔ **BEFORE YOU BEGIN**
- 11 Install a New Application to Your Device
- 50 Install a New Application Over-the-Air
- 55 About the BlackBerry Phone

→ **SEE ALSO**
- 47 About BlackBerry Web Browsing
- 55 Make and Receive Phone Calls

It's hard to argue the usefulness of a phone book when you don't know or can't remember a phone number. The popular 411 information feature serves as a quick way to obtain a phone number when you don't have access to a physical paper phone book. You might find it even more useful to use a third-party BlackBerry application that takes the 411 concept to another level. I'm referring to Berry 411, an application developed by Phillip Bogle that carries out searches to help you retrieve commonly sought information such as the phone numbers of individuals and businesses, as well as movie times, shopping information, and Google search results. The idea is that you enter a small amount of information into Berry 411 and it dispatches you to a browser search that finds and displays the information you're looking for. Although many websites can find all the same information, Berry 411 pulls it together into a clean user interface that allows you to quickly retrieve information.

62 Access a 411 Phone Directory

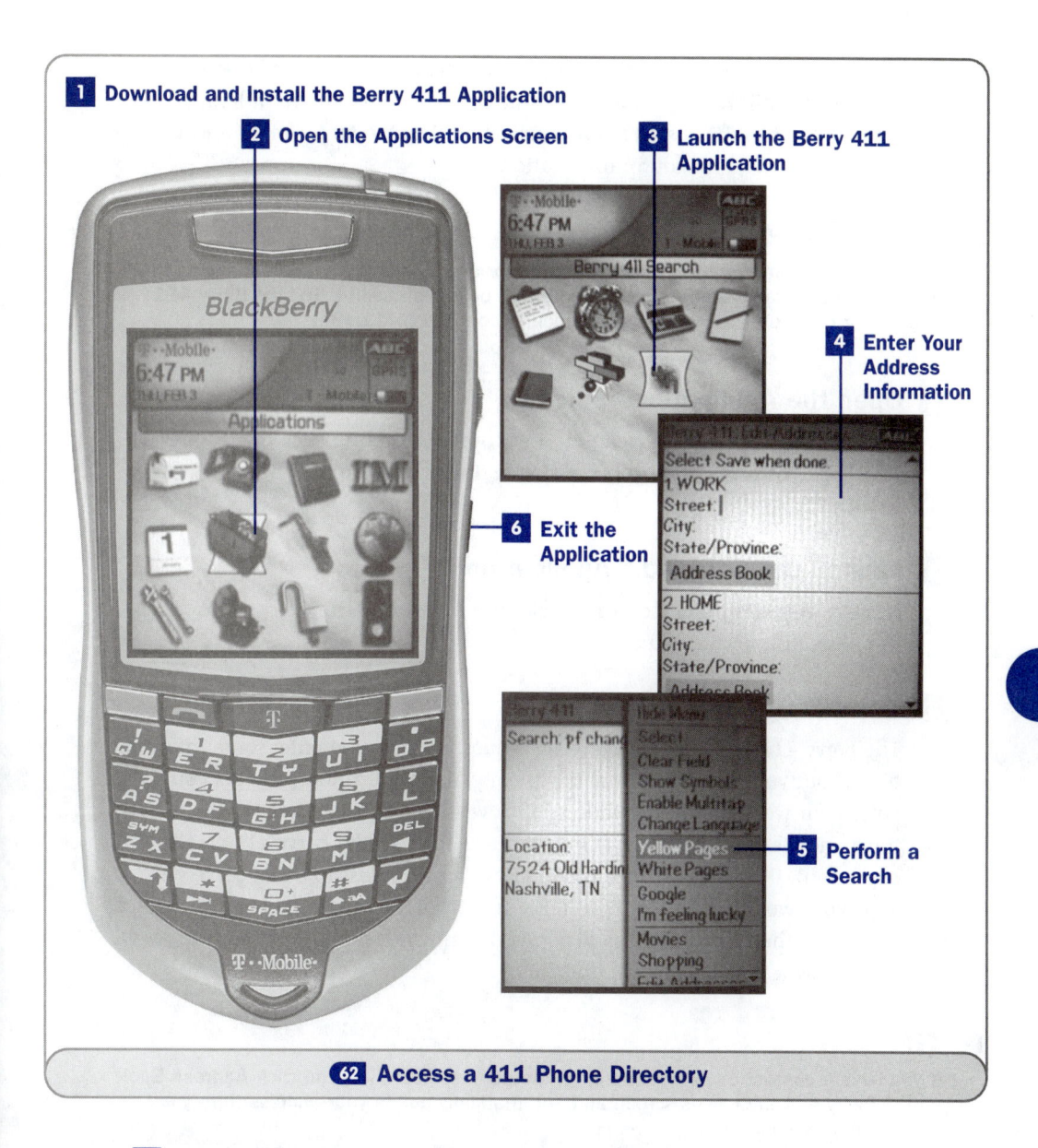

1 Download and Install the Berry 411 Application

2 Open the Applications Screen

3 Launch the Berry 411 Application

4 Enter Your Address Information

5 Perform a Search

6 Exit the Application

62 Access a 411 Phone Directory

1 Download and Install the Berry 411 Application

The Berry 411 application is available free directly from Phillip Bogle's website at http://www.thebogles.com/Berry411.htm. To obtain Berry 411, you download a file to your desktop PC and then install the application to your BlackBerry device. After installing Berry 411 to your device, an icon is added to the **Applications** screen, from which you can launch the application. For more information about downloading and installing an application using the Desktop Manager, see **11 Install a New Application to Your Device**. You can also install the application over-the-air (OTA) directly from the Berry 411 website; refer to **50 Install a New Application Over-the-Air** for more information about OTA application installation.

▶ **NOTE**

Even though the Berry 411 application is free for downloading, Mr. Bogle requests that you make a charitable donation if you find the application useful. See the Berry 411 website for more details: http://www.thebogles.com/Berry411.htm.

2 Open the Applications Screen

Scroll to the **Applications** icon on the **Home** screen and click the trackwheel. The **Applications** screen appears, displaying a list of applications you can launch.

3 Launch the Berry 411 Application

Scroll to the **Berry 411** icon and click the trackwheel. The Berry 411 application launches and appears.

4 Enter Your Address Information

The Berry 411 application begins by requesting that you enter some information about your location. More specifically, the application prompts you to enter your work and home addresses, as well as a third address if you have one. Because most of the information obtained by Berry 411 is locale-dependent, the application needs to know your address to better serve you. Type your work address in the **WORK** section of the screen and your home address in the **HOME** section. When you're finished entering addresses, scroll the trackwheel to select **Save** and click.

▶ **TIP**

If you have a contact entry for yourself in the address book, you can click **Address Book** on the Berry 411 addresses screen and automatically pull in your address from your contact information.

5 Perform a Search

After entering your addresses, the Berry 411 application displays the main application screen, which consists of a search field and the address to use for the search. Enter the text you want to search for in the **Search** field, and then scroll to select the appropriate location in the **Location** field. At this point, it's worth taking a moment to look more closely at the various kinds of searches you can perform in Berry 411.

Berry 411 supports the following search types: yellow pages (business phone numbers), white pages (residential phone numbers), Google, movies, and shopping. These searches are accessed from the menu that displays when you click the trackwheel after entering search text. For example, if I wanted to search for the phone number of the restaurant P.F. Chang's, I would enter **pf changs** in the search field, click the trackwheel, scroll to select **White Pages** on the menu, and click again. The search begins in the BlackBerry browser, and the results are shown after a few moments.

▶ **TIP**

If you want to search based on a temporary location, as opposed to from one of your specified addresses—such as when you're traveling—include the ZIP Code or city and state along with the search text. For example, a temporary P.F. Chang's sample search for Scottsdale, Arizona, would be formatted like this: **pf changs 85251**.

Each of the search types expects slightly different search text. For **Yellow Pages** searches, specify the business name or category to obtain a list of matches. For **White Pages** searches, provide the name of the person. **Google** searches can include any search text you want. In fact, Google has an additional search option called **I'm feeling lucky** that carries out a Google search and immediately links you to the top search result. A **Movies** search requires you to enter the name of the movie you want to find. And finally, a **Shopping** search consists of the item you're shopping for; the Google shopping search engine, Froogle, is used to carry out shopping searches.

▶ **TIP**

Berry 411 allows you to carry out searches in the popular communal online encyclopedia, Wikipedia. To do so, simply precede the search text with the letters **wk** and then perform a Google search. To search Wikipedia for the legendary investor Warren Buffet, enter **wk warren buffet** and do a Google search.

After performing a search, press the **Escape** button to close the browser and return to the 411 application, where you can carry out another search. Alternatively, press **Alt+Escape** to return to the 411 application without closing the browser.

6 Exit the Application

Press the **Escape** button to exit the application. You return to the **Applications** screen. Press the **Escape** button again to navigate back to the **Home** screen, or just press the **End** key once.

10

Using Bluetooth for Short-range Wireless Networking

IN THIS CHAPTER:

- **63** About Bluetooth
- **64** Turn Bluetooth On and Off
- **65** Pair Up with a Bluetooth Headset or Car Kit
- **66** Tweak Bluetooth Options
- **67** About Bluetooth Security

CHAPTER 10: Using Bluetooth for Short-range Wireless Networking

I remember five or six years ago when technology experts first started talking about the wireless revolution. For several years in a row, the revolution was predicted to take place, but for one reason or another it never seemed to materialize. It's a few years late, but I think it's now safe to say that the wireless revolution is officially underway. Although you can certainly point to long-range wireless phone networks and mid-range Wi-Fi networks as playing large roles in the wireless revolution, a significant piece of the puzzle is now being revealed in short-range wireless networking. A technology called Bluetooth is solving the problem of unwiring devices for up-close communication.

Your BlackBerry 7100 device takes a fairly conservative approach to supporting Bluetooth in that it allows you to use Bluetooth only to wirelessly connect a headset or hands-free car kit. To fully exploit Bluetooth, the folks at Research In Motion (RIM) might have included Bluetooth support for sharing files with other devices and synchronizing with a desktop PC. But these types of Bluetooth connections bring with them added security concerns that simply aren't present with headsets and hands-free kits. So, in the name of security, you are stuck with limited Bluetooth support in your BlackBerry device. Even so, you'll likely find that using a Bluetooth headset or hands-free car kit is incredibly handy.

63 About Bluetooth

→ **SEE ALSO**

- **64** Turn Bluetooth On and Off
- **65** Pair Up with a Bluetooth Headset or Car Kit
- **66** Tweak Bluetooth Options
- **67** About Bluetooth Security

Bluetooth is a wireless communication standard geared toward removing the wires between computers and their peripherals. For example, you can purchase a Bluetooth keyboard, mouse, and printer to eliminate the wires that typically connect these peripherals to your desktop or notebook PC. Similarly, Bluetooth has become popular in the mobile realm for allowing people to use a mobile headset or hands-free car kit to communicate with a mobile phone. This is the Bluetooth application currently supported in BlackBerry 7100 devices.

▶ **NOTE**

The name *Bluetooth* is derived from Harald Bluetooth, who was king of Denmark in the late 900s (that's correct, the tenth century). Along with simply having an unusual and unique name, Bluetooth is named after the Danish king because King Bluetooth is known for unifying the previously warring tribes of Denmark, Norway, and Sweden. Bluetooth is considered to be somewhat of a unifying technology between devices that otherwise have no means of communicating with each other wirelessly.

Bluetooth effectively allows you to operate a wireless personal area network (PAN), which is a series of networked devices limited to a very small area (usually up to 10 meters, or 32 feet) around you. In the case of a BlackBerry device using Bluetooth, the "network" consists of your BlackBerry device and a Bluetooth headset or hands-free car kit. The two Bluetooth devices communicate over a 2.45 gigahertz (GHz) radio connection similar to the one used by baby monitors, garage door openers, and cordless phones. For this reason, it is technically possible to experience interference if you operate a Bluetooth headset with your BlackBerry device in the same area in which you use other wireless equipment. Although interference is certainly possible, the specific design of the Bluetooth communication protocol helps to alleviate the problem.

The Bluetooth specification defines three classes of devices, each of which offers a varying level of wireless signal strength and therefore a varying operating distance (see Table 10.1).

TABLE 10.1 Classes of Bluetooth Devices

Device Class	Signal Strength	Range
Class 1	100 milliwatts	Up to 100 meters (328 feet)
Class 2	2.5 milliwatts	Up to 10 meters (32 feet)
Class 3	1 milliwatt	Well under 10 meters (32 feet)

The BlackBerry 7100 series devices are Class 2 Bluetooth devices, so you can expect a Bluetooth headset to give you a range of around 10 meters, or 32 feet. This is assuming, of course, that the headset is also a Class 2 device. If it is a Class 3 device, expect a reduced range. Keep in mind that I'm talking about the distance between your BlackBerry device and the Bluetooth headset—generally speaking, you'll likely keep the two devices in very close proximity to one another, so the 10-meter limit is unlikely to present a serious problem.

▶ **NOTE**

The only immediate competitor to Bluetooth is Infrared Data Association (IrDA), which is the infrared technology often found on notebook and handheld computers that enables you to communicate wirelessly with another computer or printer. Although IrDA currently enjoys a much larger install base than Bluetooth, the tide is rapidly turning. The major drawback to IrDA is that it requires a clear line of sight and a distance of no greater than about a meter between the two devices that are communicating. Compare this to Bluetooth, which requires no line of sight and a communication distance typically in the 10-meter range.

CHAPTER 10: Using Bluetooth for Short-range Wireless Networking

▶ **NOTE**
On the very near horizon is a competitor to Bluetooth that could ultimately render Bluetooth obsolete: Wireless USB (WUSB). WUSB is a wireless technology based on the popular USB communication standard. Similar to Bluetooth, WUSB is a short-range wireless technology geared toward connecting devices in close proximity to one another. However, WUSB is much faster than Bluetooth, which could be its killer feature. WUSB is slated to have transfer speeds in the neighborhood of 60MB per second, while Bluetooth supports much slower speeds of 1.5MB per second. Intel is putting a lot of marketing muscle behind WUSB, but it will be tough to shun the wave of new devices that support Bluetooth, including your BlackBerry device. It should be interesting to see how WUSB unfolds and whether Bluetooth can survive against it.

Every Bluetooth device is responsible for supporting one or more profiles, which describe the Bluetooth applications available for use with the device. Following are some examples of Bluetooth profiles:

- Headset Profile
- Hands-free Profile
- Fax Profile
- LAN Access Profile
- File Transfer Profile
- Human Interface Device Profile
- Audio Video Remote Control Profile
- Serial Port Profile
- Basic Printing Profile

Before you get too excited, allow me to temper your enthusiasm just a bit and explain that BlackBerry 7100 devices support only three of these profiles: Headset Profile, Hands-free Profile, and Serial Port Profile. The idea is that some of the more powerful profiles (LAN Access Profile, for example) introduce an unnecessary security risk for BlackBerry devices when most users simply want to use Bluetooth for the convenience of wireless headsets and hands-free car kits. This idea is certainly valid, but it sure would've been nice to allow BlackBerry devices to communicate with other devices for sharing contacts and synchronizing with desktop PCs. The upside to this limitation is that you don't have to worry about many of the security issues that have been publicized in regard to people hacking into Bluetooth mobile devices and stealing information. See **67 About Bluetooth Security** for more information on Bluetooth security issues and why your BlackBerry device is safe and secure.

Speaking of Bluetooth limitations on the BlackBerry 7100, I have to point out another incredibly useful Bluetooth device that currently isn't an option for use with your BlackBerry device: Portable Bluetooth keyboards fold open and allow you to type on a full QWERTY keyboard through a wireless Bluetooth connection. Of course, such keyboards require a device that supports the Human Interface Device Profile, which the BlackBerry 7100 unfortunately does not. I'm not pointing out this limitation just to show you what you can't have. There's hope that a BlackBerry operating system upgrade might introduce additional Bluetooth profiles, including the Human Interface Device Profile. Keep your fingers crossed!

▶ **NOTE**

In 2004, Bluetooth started appearing as standard equipment in some automobiles, which means you can operate your mobile phone hands free while the phone is still tucked away in your pocket or briefcase. A few of the vehicle makes and models that were early adopters of Bluetooth include the BMW 3 Series and 5 Series, Lexus LS 430, Acura TL, and Toyota Prius.

Another other important topic worth covering is the version of Bluetooth supported in the BlackBerry 7100 series devices. As you shop for Bluetooth headsets and hands-free car kits, you might run across a version number for their Bluetooth support. Although Bluetooth is currently up to version 2.0, the majority of Bluetooth accessories currently available are designed for Bluetooth version 1.1. Fortunately, BlackBerry 7100 devices are designed around Bluetooth 1.1, so you have a wide range of Bluetooth headsets and hands-free devices from which to choose. Newer versions of Bluetooth include version 1.2 and version 2.0, both of which are backward compatible with version 1.1. So, you shouldn't encounter any compatibility problems when it comes to buying headsets and hands-free devices for your BlackBerry 7100.

▶ **NOTE**

Bluetooth 1.0 had several design flaws that made it difficult to implement reliably across a variety of devices and accessories. Consequently, Bluetooth 1.1 is generally considered the first stable version of Bluetooth in widespread use.

I want to wrap up the Bluetooth discussion by tackling a common source of confusion associated with Bluetooth: how it differs from the popular Wi-Fi (802.11a/b/g) wireless networking technologies. First, Bluetooth and Wi-Fi are not competing technologies and are designed to solve uniquely different problems. The fundamental goal of both technologies is to eliminate wires between devices, but the scope of the wires they are intended to eliminate differ. Bluetooth focuses on low-power short-range connections between devices, such as the connection between a mouse and a PC. Wi-Fi addresses network connections between computer systems, such as the Ethernet cable between a computer and a router. To some degree, each

CHAPTER 10: Using Bluetooth for Short-range Wireless Networking

technology overlaps the other from time to time. As an example, both Wi-Fi and Bluetooth adapters are available for wireless printing. To help understand the relationship between Bluetooth and Wi-Fi, think of Bluetooth as the wireless equivalent of USB, while Wi-Fi is the wireless equivalent of Ethernet. This is not an exact analogy, but from a high-level perspective, it is reasonably accurate.

64 Turn Bluetooth On and Off

✔ BEFORE YOU BEGIN	→ SEE ALSO
63 About Bluetooth	65 Pair Up with a Bluetooth Headset or Car Kit
	66 Tweak Bluetooth Options
	67 About Bluetooth Security

Bluetooth enables you to connect wireless headsets and hands-free car kits to your BlackBerry device for the utmost in flexible wireless mobile communications. Similar to the main radio on your device that can be turned on and off to control voice and data wireless connectivity, your device's Bluetooth radio can also be turned on and off to control Bluetooth connectivity. All BlackBerry devices default to having their Bluetooth radios off, so you must turn it on before you can access your Bluetooth accessories. Even if you use a Bluetooth headset or hands-free car kit, you might want to turn off Bluetooth under some circumstances because it adds an unnecessary drain on your BlackBerry device's battery when not in use. If you don't plan on using a Bluetooth accessory with your BlackBerry device for more than an hour, for example, you might as well turn off Bluetooth and conserve some battery power.

1 Open the Tools Screen

Scroll to the **Tools** icon on the **Home** screen and click the trackwheel. The **Tools** screen appears, displaying a list of tool options.

2 Open the Settings Screen

Scroll to the **Settings** icon and click the trackwheel. A list of options for which you can change the settings appears.

> ▶ **TIP**
>
> Depending on your specific device, you might see a **Bluetooth** icon (looks kind of like a horizontal antenna on a blue background) on the **Tools** screen that provides direct access to enabling and disabling Bluetooth. This icon appears normal if Bluetooth is enabled; it has a no sign (a circle with a slash) around it if Bluetooth is disabled. If your device has this icon, ignore the remaining steps in this task and just click the icon with the trackwheel to enable and disable Bluetooth on your device.

64 Turn Bluetooth On and Off

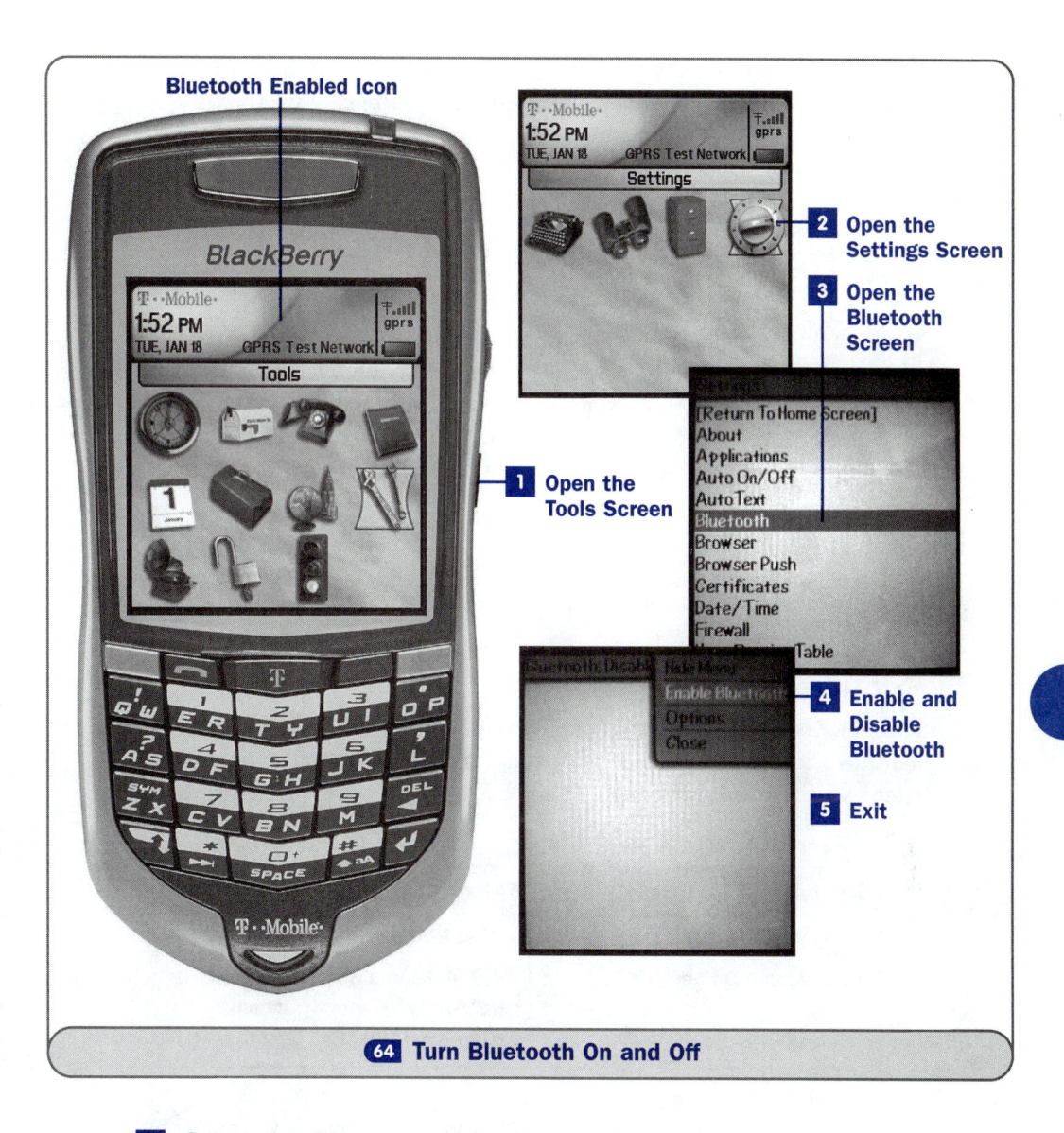

3 Open the Bluetooth Screen

Scroll to the **Bluetooth** option in the list of settings and click the trackwheel. The **Bluetooth** screen opens.

4 Enable and Disable Bluetooth

The top of the Bluetooth screen reveals the current status of Bluetooth: **Enabled** or **Disabled**. To enable Bluetooth, click the trackwheel and select **Enable Bluetooth** from the menu that appears. Click once more to enable

Bluetooth. The status at the top of the screen changes to show that Bluetooth is now enabled; any paired devices appear on the screen. If you haven't paired up with any other Bluetooth devices yet, the list is empty.

▶ **TIP**

See **65 Pair Up with a Bluetooth Headset or Car Kit** to find out how to pair your BlackBerry device with a Bluetooth headset or hands-free car kit.

Keep in mind that Bluetooth puts an additional strain on your device's batteries, so you should leave it on only if you actually plan to use it frequently. Otherwise, it's probably a good idea to turn it on and off as needed. To disable Bluetooth, click the trackwheel and select **Disable Bluetooth** from the menu that appears. Click again to disable Bluetooth.

▶ **NOTE**

You can easily tell whether Bluetooth is enabled because a small blue Bluetooth icon appears along the top of the **Home** screen when Bluetooth is turned on.

5 Exit

Press the **Escape** button to exit the **Bluetooth** screen. You return to the **Settings** screen. Press the **Escape** button twice more to navigate back to the **Home** screen, or just press the **End** key once.

---

65 Pair Up with a Bluetooth Headset or Car Kit

✔ BEFORE YOU BEGIN	→ SEE ALSO
64 Turn Bluetooth On and Off	**55** Make and Receive Phone Calls
	66 Tweak Bluetooth Options
	67 About Bluetooth Security

Bluetooth can dramatically change the manner in which you use your BlackBerry 7100 series device. For example, a Bluetooth hands-free car kit allows you to leave your device in a briefcase, purse, console, or glove box while carrying on a conversation wirelessly. Similarly, a Bluetooth headset enables you to use a discrete wireless earpiece to carry on a conversation while your BlackBerry device is tucked safely away in a pocket. Thanks to the relative simplicity of Bluetooth technology, you can easily connect a Bluetooth headset or hands-free car kit to your BlackBerry device with minimal effort and then repeatedly connect it from then on with no effort. This effectively makes a Bluetooth headset or hands-free car kit even easier to use than their wired counterparts.

65 Pair Up with a Bluetooth Headset or Car Kit

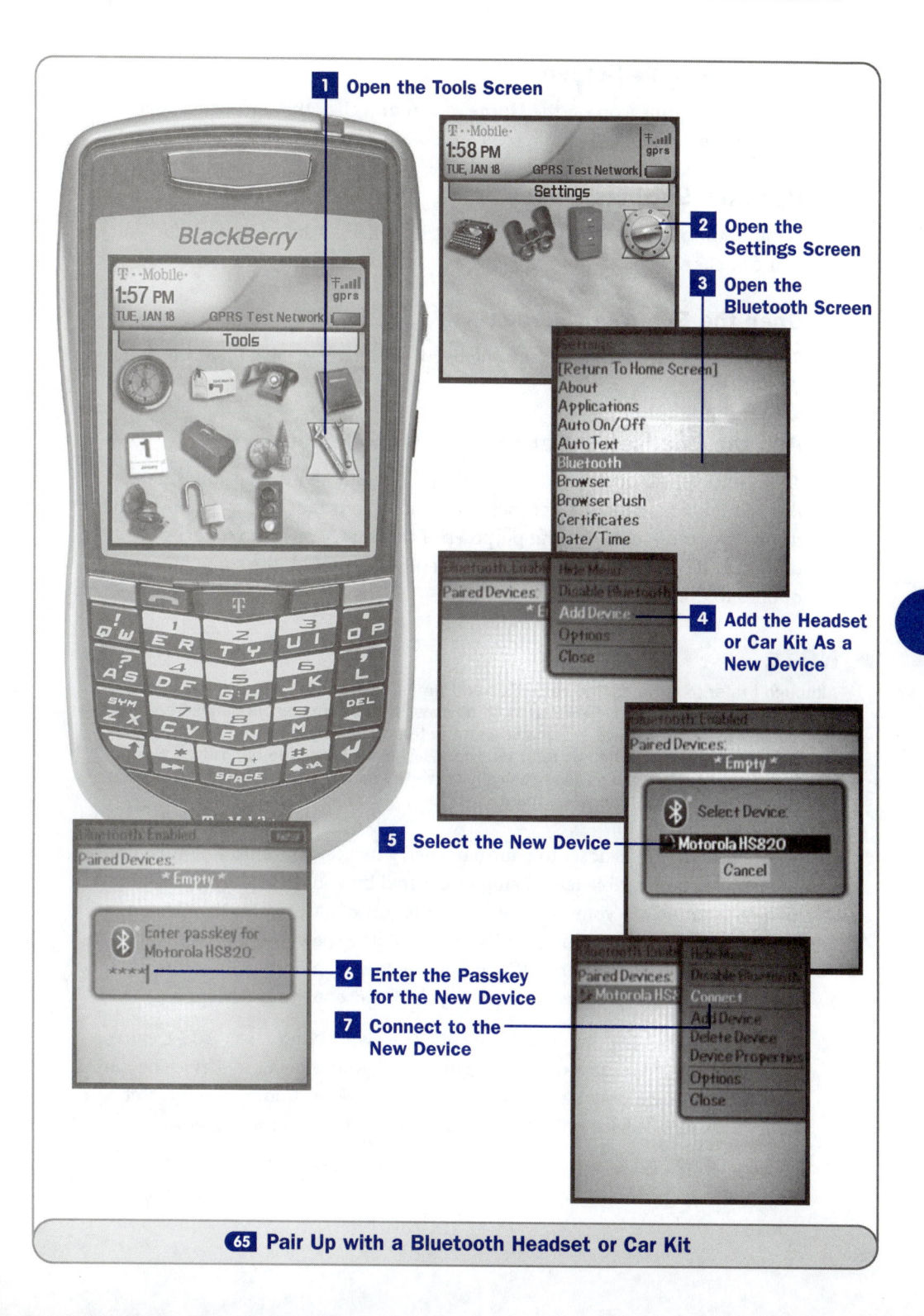

1 Open the Tools Screen

2 Open the Settings Screen

3 Open the Bluetooth Screen

4 Add the Headset or Car Kit As a New Device

5 Select the New Device

6 Enter the Passkey for the New Device

7 Connect to the New Device

65 Pair Up with a Bluetooth Headset or Car Kit

1 Open the Tools Screen

Scroll to the **Tools** icon on the **Home** screen and click the trackwheel. The **Tools** screen appears, showing a list of tool options.

2 Open the Settings Screen

Scroll to the **Settings** icon and click the trackwheel. A list of options for which you can change the settings appears.

3 Open the Bluetooth Screen

Scroll to the **Bluetooth** option in the list of settings and click the trackwheel. The **Bluetooth** screen opens.

4 Add the Headset or Car Kit As a New Device

To pair up your BlackBerry device with a Bluetooth headset or hands-free car kit, you must first add the headset or car kit to your BlackBerry device so your device knows about it. For the purposes of this task, I'm going to focus on adding and connecting to a Bluetooth headset, although the same process applies to a hands-free car kit.

▶ **NOTE**

Although I refer to a hands-free car kit several times throughout this task, you might run across other kinds of hands-free Bluetooth devices, such as a portable hands-free device that doesn't necessarily have to be used in an automobile. However, for the sake of keeping the distinction obvious, I refer to a hands-free car kit as the hands-free alternative to a headset. All these devices basically serve the same purpose, so there isn't any real reason to distinguish between them.

Before adding the headset to your BlackBerry device, you must first turn on the headset and enable it for being discovered by your device. This enabling process is unique to your particular headset. I use a Motorola HS820 headset, which requires me to hold down its multifunction (power) button for 5 seconds to make it discoverable. When your headset is powered on and ready for discovery, you can proceed with adding the headset to your device.

To add a headset to your device, click the trackwheel and select **Add Device** from the menu that appears. Click again, and your BlackBerry device begins searching for available Bluetooth devices to add. After finding the headset, your BlackBerry device prompts you to select the headset for addition.

65 Pair Up with a Bluetooth Headset or Car Kit   257

▶ **TIP**

If your BlackBerry device doesn't find the headset, first check to ensure that Bluetooth is enabled on your device; see **64** **Turn Bluetooth On and Off**. If Bluetooth is already enabled on your device, double-check that you have properly set the headset so it can be discovered. On my Motorola headset, it took a few tries before I realized how long the multifunction button had to be held down before it entered "discovery" mode. If, for some reason, your BlackBerry device locks up while searching for a Bluetooth device, perform a soft reset by removing the battery and reinserting it.

5 Select the New Device

After successfully locating a new Bluetooth device, your BlackBerry device displays a dialog box showing the Bluetooth headset. Click the name of the headset to accept it as a new Bluetooth device.

6 Enter the Passkey for the New Device

Every Bluetooth device has an associated *passkey*, which serves as a PIN code that is required for your BlackBerry device to pair up with the Bluetooth device. In the case of peripheral devices such as headsets that don't really have security implications, the passkey is typically just **0000**. Enter the passkey for your headset and click the trackwheel.

▶ **KEY TERM**

Passkey—A short password similar to a PIN code used to gain access to a Bluetooth device. Most Bluetooth peripherals have a default passkey of **0000**.

▶ **NOTE**

If you are unsure of the passkey for your headset, refer to the headset manual. If you're the kind of person who avoids reading manuals at all costs, give **0000** a try; this is the passkey typically used for most Bluetooth headsets and hands-free car kits.

After successfully entering the passkey for the headset, the headset is added to the Bluetooth device list where you can now connect to it for wireless telephony communications.

7 Connect to the Headset or Car Kit

To connect to the Bluetooth headset from your BlackBerry device, click the trackwheel and select **Connect** from the menu that appears. Click again and your device connects to the headset. Try checking your voice mail (hold down the **E R** key in the **Phone** application) or making a phone call to confirm that the headset works; see **55** **Make and Receive Phone Calls**.

▶ **TIP**

If you have difficulty connecting to your headset, make sure that it is turned on and within range of your BlackBerry device. This means the headset should be no further than 32 feet (10 meters) from your device. If you still can't connect, try going outside to avoid any radio interference from other electronic devices that might be causing problems indoors.

▶ **NOTE**

Unfortunately, the BlackBerry 7100 series devices don't support voice dialing, which means you still have to access your phone to dial—even if you have a hands-free car kit. It's really unfortunate that RIM didn't include voice dialing in the 7100 series devices because it is necessary to truly get the most out of hands-free Bluetooth accessories.

If your Bluetooth headset isn't automatically activated after being connected, you can easily activate it during a phone call by clicking the trackwheel, selecting **Activate** *Device Name* from the menu that appears, and clicking again. In fact, you use this same approach to select between the handset, speakerphone, and any Bluetooth headsets or hands-free car kits connected to your BlackBerry device.

▶ **TIP**

Using your BlackBerry device, you can configure a Bluetooth headset or hands-free car kit so it automatically connects with your device when they get within range of each other; see **66 Tweak Bluetooth Options** to find out how to configure this setting.

66 Tweak Bluetooth Options

✔ BEFORE YOU BEGIN	→ SEE ALSO
63 About Bluetooth	64 Turn Bluetooth On and Off
	65 Pair Up with a Bluetooth Headset or Car Kit
	67 About Bluetooth Security

As with virtually every aspect of your BlackBerry device, Bluetooth is a feature you can customize to a certain degree. Although a couple of settings are available for configuring general Bluetooth options for your BlackBerry device, the real flexibility in customizing Bluetooth is on a device-by-device basis. More specifically, you can identify individual Bluetooth devices, such as your favorite headset, as being trusted and therefore removed from the connection confirmation process involved in a typical Bluetooth connection. In other words, the device is automatically connected whenever it is found. You can also change the name of a Bluetooth device as it appears on your BlackBerry device, which can help make it easier to distinguish between similar devices. Additionally, you can enable encryption of the wireless Bluetooth connection between the two devices to add a measure of security.

66 Tweak Bluetooth Options

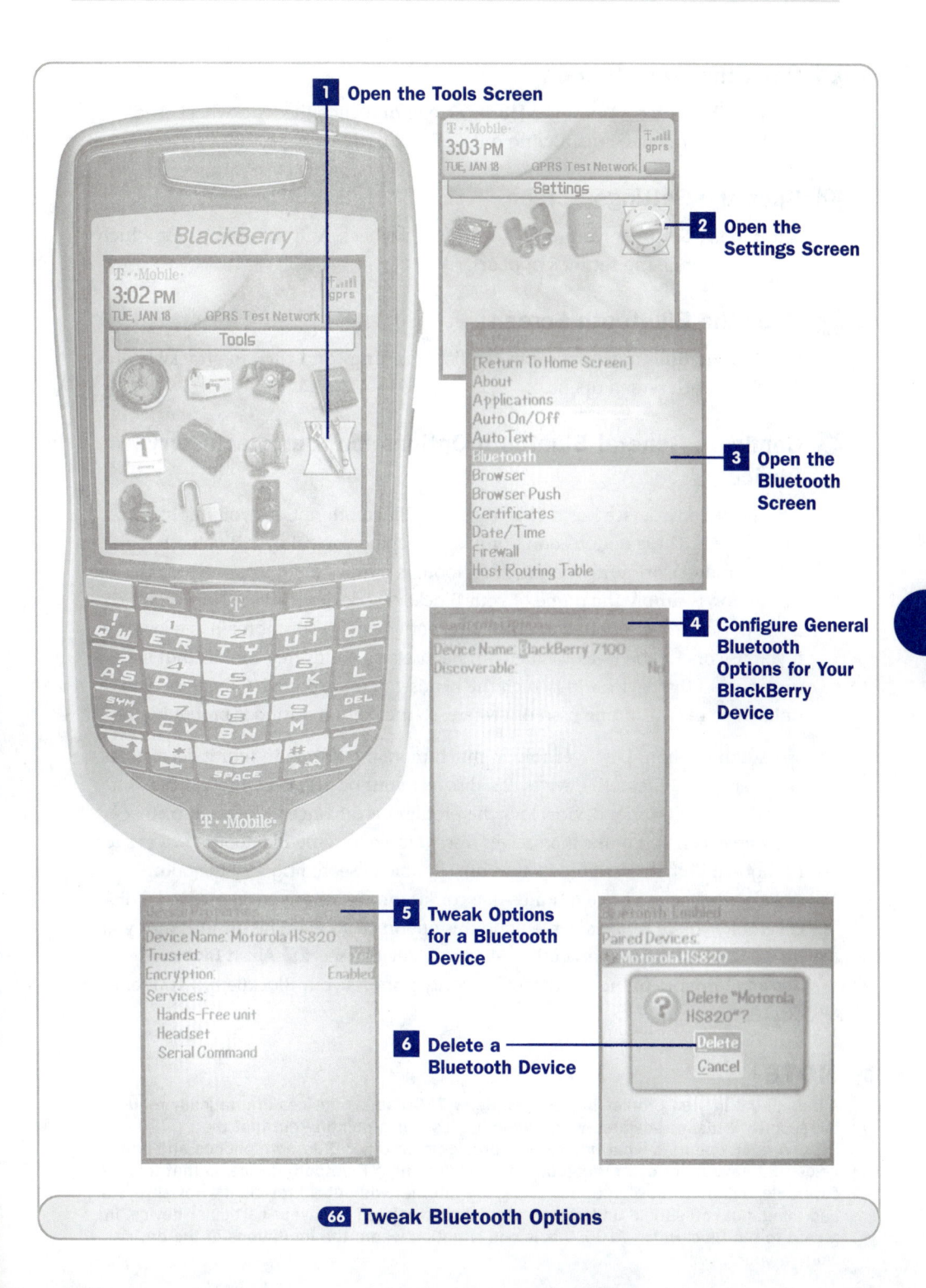

1 Open the Tools Screen

2 Open the Settings Screen

3 Open the Bluetooth Screen

4 Configure General Bluetooth Options for Your BlackBerry Device

5 Tweak Options for a Bluetooth Device

6 Delete a Bluetooth Device

66 Tweak Bluetooth Options

1 Open the Tools Screen

Scroll to the **Tools** icon on the **Home** screen and click the trackwheel. The **Tools** screen appears, displaying a list of tool options.

2 Open the Settings Screen

Scroll to the **Settings** icon and click the trackwheel. A list of options for which you can change the settings appears.

3 Open the Bluetooth Screen

Scroll to the **Bluetooth** option in the list of settings and click the trackwheel. The **Bluetooth** screen opens.

4 Configure General Bluetooth Options for Your BlackBerry Device

Your BlackBerry device has a couple general Bluetooth options you might be interested in. These options don't provide sweeping control over Bluetooth features, but that's primarily because Bluetooth is a fairly automatic technology. The first option is simply the name of your BlackBerry device (**Device Name**), which is the device name reported to other Bluetooth devices. This name has relevance if you use one of the fancier Bluetooth headsets or hands-free car kits that lists the name of the device with which the headset or kit is paired. Otherwise, you're unlikely to see this name used anywhere, so the default setting is probably fine.

The second option, **Discoverable**, is much more interesting in that it determines whether other Bluetooth devices can discover your device. Even though the BlackBerry 7100 series devices lack the profiles for advanced Bluetooth connections, they can still make themselves discoverable to some Bluetooth devices such as high-end hands-free car kits that are capable of searching for Bluetooth phones. Unless you have a hands-free car kit that requires your device to be discoverable, you're much safer leaving this option set to **No**. This ensures that your device can't be seen by any other Bluetooth devices; see **67 About Bluetooth Security** for more on how Bluetooth security impacts your BlackBerry 7100 series device.

▶ **NOTE**

Although the limited profiles in the BlackBerry 7100 series devices dramatically reduce the security issues associated with Bluetooth, it's worth pointing out that the **Discoverable** option is what has caused problems on other Bluetooth phones and handhelds that have more open Bluetooth support. Setting a Bluetooth device so that it is discoverable is somewhat akin to accessing the Internet without a firewall. It's not always a bad thing, but you should understand the risks associated with your particular device. In regard to the BlackBerry 7100, this is one situation where the limitations of the device work in your favor.

When you finish setting the Bluetooth options for your BlackBerry device, press the **Escape** button. If you've made any changes and want to save them, click **Save** in the confirmation pop-up window that appears; otherwise, click **Cancel**.

5 Tweak Options for a Bluetooth Device

Each Bluetooth device you use with your BlackBerry device has its own set of options you can configure using your BlackBerry device. To change the options for a paired Bluetooth device, scroll the trackwheel to select the device in the paired device list, and click. Select **Device Properties** from the menu that appears, and click once more. The **Device Properties** screen appears.

In the example, the Motorola HS820 device has only three properties you can change: **Device Name**, **Trusted**, and **Encryption**. The **Device Name** property allows you to change the device name, which is the name that appears in the Bluetooth device list. Unless the name of your headset or hands-free car kit is cryptic or otherwise makes the device difficult to identify, the default device name is probably fine.

The **Trusted** option determines whether your BlackBerry device considers the Bluetooth device to be trusted. *Trusted* simply means your BlackBerry device doesn't require you to confirm the Bluetooth device each time it is connected. More specifically, by setting a Bluetooth device as trusted, you allow it to automatically connect with your BlackBerry device as soon as the two devices are powered on and in range of each other. There aren't any security implications to declaring a handset or hands-free car kit as trusted, so I recommend changing the **Trusted** option to **Yes** for these types of devices simply as a convenience.

Where security does enter the picture with a Bluetooth headset or hands-free car kit is in the data transmitted between them and your BlackBerry device. Fortunately, the **Encryption** option provides an easy way to alleviate the problem by encrypting the data sent between your device and headset/car kit. Just make sure that the **Encryption** option is set to **Enabled**, and you'll be fine.

In addition to the three options just mentioned, you might also see a list of services made available by the Bluetooth device. These services indicate the profiles supported by the device, such as the Headset Profile and the Hands-free Profile. If you see profiles in addition to these two, your device might have additional Bluetooth features you'll want to find out about—check with your wireless service provider to find out more.

After setting the Bluetooth options for your headset or hands-free car kit, press the **Escape** button. If you've made any changes and would like to save them, click **Save** in the confirmation pop-up window that appears; otherwise, click **Cancel**.

6 Delete a Bluetooth Device

You will eventually have to delete a Bluetooth device from your BlackBerry device—whether you lose your headset or upgrade to a new one. To delete a Bluetooth device, you must first disconnect it. To disconnect a device, scroll the trackwheel to select the device in the paired device list and click. Select **Disconnect** from the menu that appears, and click once more. The device is disconnected, which allows you to continue and delete it.

To delete a disconnected Bluetooth device from your BlackBerry device, scroll the trackwheel to select the device in the paired device list and click. Select **Delete Device** from the menu that appears, and click again. The device is deleted and disappears from the paired device list. Your BlackBerry device will no longer make an automatic attempt to pair up with the deleted device.

66 ▶ NOTE

If you change your mind about deleting a Bluetooth device, you can always pair it up with your BlackBerry device again; see **65 Pair Up with a Bluetooth Headset or Car Kit** for details.

67 About Bluetooth Security

✔ **BEFORE YOU BEGIN**

- 63 About Bluetooth

→ **SEE ALSO**

- 64 Turn Bluetooth On and Off
- 65 Pair Up with a Bluetooth Headset or Car Kit
- 66 Tweak Bluetooth Options

There have been some concerns in the mobile community about Bluetooth security as more and more devices ship with support for Bluetooth. The concerns primarily have to do with the fact that Bluetooth is capable of opening up a notebook PC, handheld, or mobile phone to wireless attacks. Part of the problem is that some users don't realize that, by enabling Bluetooth on their devices, they might be opening a gateway for unwanted communications, much like accessing the Internet without a firewall. Another part of the problem concerns a few faulty Bluetooth implementations that expose several models of mobile phones to attack.

In reality, Bluetooth is a sophisticated technology that addresses security very seriously. Bluetooth connections require acceptance by the user and are capable of using 128-bit encryption in conjunction with other security protocols. The real concern with Bluetooth security isn't so much the technology itself as it is the manner in which people use it. As an example, the front door of your house doesn't pose a security risk unless you leave it unlocked. The door offers security by virtue of the lock, but you must take some responsibility in shutting and securing the lock after you pass through the door. Similarly, Bluetooth requires some responsibility on the part of the user if it is to offer maximum security.

To better understand your responsibility in keeping your BlackBerry device secure from Bluetooth attackers, it's important to understand the types of attacks that can be launched against a Bluetooth device. The simplest and least dangerous form of Bluetooth attack is known as **Bluejacking**, which is really more of an annoyance than a true security attack. In Bluejacking, another Bluetooth user sends an unsolicited message (usually as an electronic business card) through a Bluetooth connection to your device. You certainly have the option of rejecting the message, but just the fact that you are prompted by it, unsolicited, is a hassle. To send you a Bluejack message, of course, the other person has to be within 10 meters (32 feet) of your device, but this can be easily accomplished with anonymity in a crowded area.

▶ **KEY TERM**

Bluejacking—A minor Bluetooth security attack in which another user sends you an unsolicited message using a Bluetooth connection. The term doesn't refer to hijacking, but instead originated with a person named Jack who anonymously sent the Bluetooth message "Buy Ericsson" to a Nokia phone user while waiting in line at a bank.

It's important to understand that Bluejacking doesn't put your device at risk in any way. Both parties in a Bluejack communication are in complete control of their devices, and the Bluejacker has no way of extracting any information from your device. That's why I refer to Bluejacking as more of an annoyance than a true security attack. Even so, some people are shocked to receive an unsolicited message or, in the case of some phones, an image or a sound. They wrongly assume that someone has attacked their phone or given them a virus. Quite the contrary; some people have turned Bluejacking into a more positive experience by using it as a way to meet new people. To learn more about Bluejacking and view the official Bluejack Code of Ethics, visit http://www.bluejackq.com/.

A much more serious Bluetooth security attack is known as **Bluesnarfing**, which involves another Bluetooth user gaining access to your device data and literally stealing information from your device. The at-risk data can include your contact list, text messages, memos, and anything else stored on your BlackBerry device.

Although Bluesnarfing has certainly taken place in the past, it relied on a hole in the Bluetooth implementations on certain specific mobile phones, and not on a weakness with Bluetooth itself. In other words, the Bluetooth technology is secure enough to prevent Bluesnarfing, assuming that device manufacturers implement Bluetooth properly on their devices. Fortunately, there are no reported security problems with the Bluetooth implementation on BlackBerry 7100 series devices.

▶ **KEY TERM**

Bluesnarfing—A very serious Bluetooth security attack in which another user gains access to the data on your device using a Bluetooth connection.

Another topic closely related to Bluetooth security is **Bluetooth sniping**, which involves using specially modified equipment to send and receive Bluetooth signals over a long range, currently up to 1 mile. When combined with Bluesnarfing, Bluetooth sniping presents an extremely dangerous opportunity for hackers to breach Bluetooth devices from a long distance. So far, Bluetooth sniping has been used primarily as a way of simply exploring the limits of the Bluetooth technology. It does open up the prospect of attackers operating from afar, assuming that they've figured out a way to access your device.

▶ **KEY TERM**

Bluetooth sniping—The process of using specially modified equipment to send and receive Bluetooth signals over a much longer range than intended. Currently, the longest successful Bluetooth snipe is about 1 mile.

Now that you understand what is at risk with Bluetooth from a technological level, it's important to explain your side of the security equation. As with many technologies, it turns out that the Bluetooth technology is surprisingly secure and the real weak link is us humans. Bluetooth is obviously a communication technology that allows you to connect devices wirelessly. The key to keeping your BlackBerry device secure is ensuring that only devices you want connected to it are indeed connected to it. This involves some vigilance on your part to ensure that you don't inadvertently allow someone else to connect to your device. How can this happen?

Let's start with the biggest Bluetooth issue of them all—making your device discoverable. Your BlackBerry device can be set as discoverable or invisible, with the former option allowing any other Bluetooth device to see your device. Although seeing is different from connecting, by making your device discoverable you significantly increase the chances of someone attempting a security attack against you. It's just too easy to fish for devices in a crowded area and take a stab at breaching one of them. As I've already said, Bluetooth is pretty solid in terms

67 About Bluetooth Security

of its security, but remaining invisible is significantly safer than being discoverable—at least if you're a Bluetooth device. And keeping your device invisible is the best defense against Bluejacking.

On the other hand, the discoverable feature is built in to Bluetooth devices for a reason. For example, your car's hands-free Bluetooth system might require your BlackBerry device to be discoverable to connect, or at least connect more quickly. In this example, it might be advantageous to keep your device discoverable when driving to aid in connecting to your car's hands-free system. You might find that there is a reasonable tradeoff in terms of keeping your device discoverable some of the time and then setting it to invisible when you're in crowded areas where an anonymous attacker might be more apt to strike.

Another area in which many BlackBerry devices are potentially at risk is pairing. When you pair your device with another device, each device is added to the other's device list and given the capability of connecting to the other. In most cases, this arrangement is fine because you *want* to initiate a connection with a device. But if someone can secretively pair her device with yours, she could feasibly connect to your device without your knowledge. For this reason, most Bluetooth device users have to be careful about allowing other people to borrow their devices.

Because BlackBerry 7100 series devices have support for only a few, limited device profiles (headset and hands-free), this risk is all but eliminated. It's unlikely that someone would figure out a way to use a headset or hands-free car kit to violate the security of your device. Even so, for good measure, I recommend initially pairing your device with your headset or hands-free car kit in a private area (a safe distance away from other potential Bluetooth users) and then being very careful about allowing others to tinker with your device.

To summarize, here are a few tips to help maximize Bluetooth security with your BlackBerry device:

- Only make your device discoverable when absolutely necessary.
- Only pair up with new devices in private, out of range of other potential Bluetooth users.
- Don't allow anyone else to tinker with your BlackBerry device.
- Don't respond to unsolicited messages you receive.

If you follow these guidelines, you should be able to safely enjoy the benefits of Bluetooth with minimal worries about your device's security.

PART III

Getting Productive with Your BlackBerry 7100

IN THIS PART:

CHAPTER 11	Using the Address Book to Never Lose a Contact	269
CHAPTER 12	Managing Your Time with the Calendar	285
CHAPTER 13	Organizing Your To-Do List with Tasks	303
CHAPTER 14	Getting the Most out of Helper Applications	315
CHAPTER 15	Securing Your BlackBerry Device	339

11

Using the Address Book to Never Lose a Contact

IN THIS CHAPTER:

- **68** Create and Manage Contacts
- **69** Create and Manage Mailing Lists
- **70** Apply Categories to Contacts
- **71** Tweak Address Book Options
- **72** Access the SIM Phone Book

CHAPTER 11: Using the Address Book to Never Lose a Contact

One of the fundamental roles your BlackBerry device plays on a daily basis is that of an electronic Rolodex. The notion of carrying around all your contacts within the handy confines of a mobile device is not necessarily new, but that doesn't take anything way from its inherent usefulness. The **Address Book** application serves as a contact manager that keeps track of all your contacts, including their respective email addresses, phone numbers, snail mail addresses, and any other information you'd like to associate with them. Although you can populate the address book solely by creating contacts on your device, you should synchronize contacts from a desktop contact manager such as Microsoft Outlook—assuming that you already use such a manager. Regardless of how you build your contact list, the **Address Book** application gives you plenty of flexibility in managing contacts—and more importantly, carrying out communications with them.

68 Create and Manage Contacts

→ **SEE ALSO**

- 10 Synchronize PIM Data with Your PC
- 69 Create and Manage Mailing Lists
- 70 Apply Categories to Contacts
- 71 Tweak Address Book Options

The **Address Book** application on your device is in many ways a simple database, and the data it stores is contact information for people with whom you want to interact using your device. This interaction can be a phone call, an email message, a **PIN** message, or an **SMS** message—all these forms of communication are linked with the BlackBerry address book. Not surprisingly, creating and managing contacts is an important part of communicating using your device. Creating a new contact is as simple as entering the contact information for a person you'd like to add to the address book. You can get as detailed as you want when it comes to entering information about the person's name, company, job title, and home and work addresses (snail mail and email) and phone numbers. You can also categorize contacts, which aids in navigating the contact list because you can filter the list according to categories.

1 Launch the Address Book Application

Scroll to the **Address Book** icon and click the trackwheel. The **Address Book** application is launched and displayed on the screen. If you haven't created any contacts yet, the contact list is likely empty. However, if you've synchronized contacts with your desktop PC, you might see some contacts in the list.

68 Create and Manage Contacts   271

1 Launch the Address Book Application

2 Create a New Contact

3 Enter the Contact Details

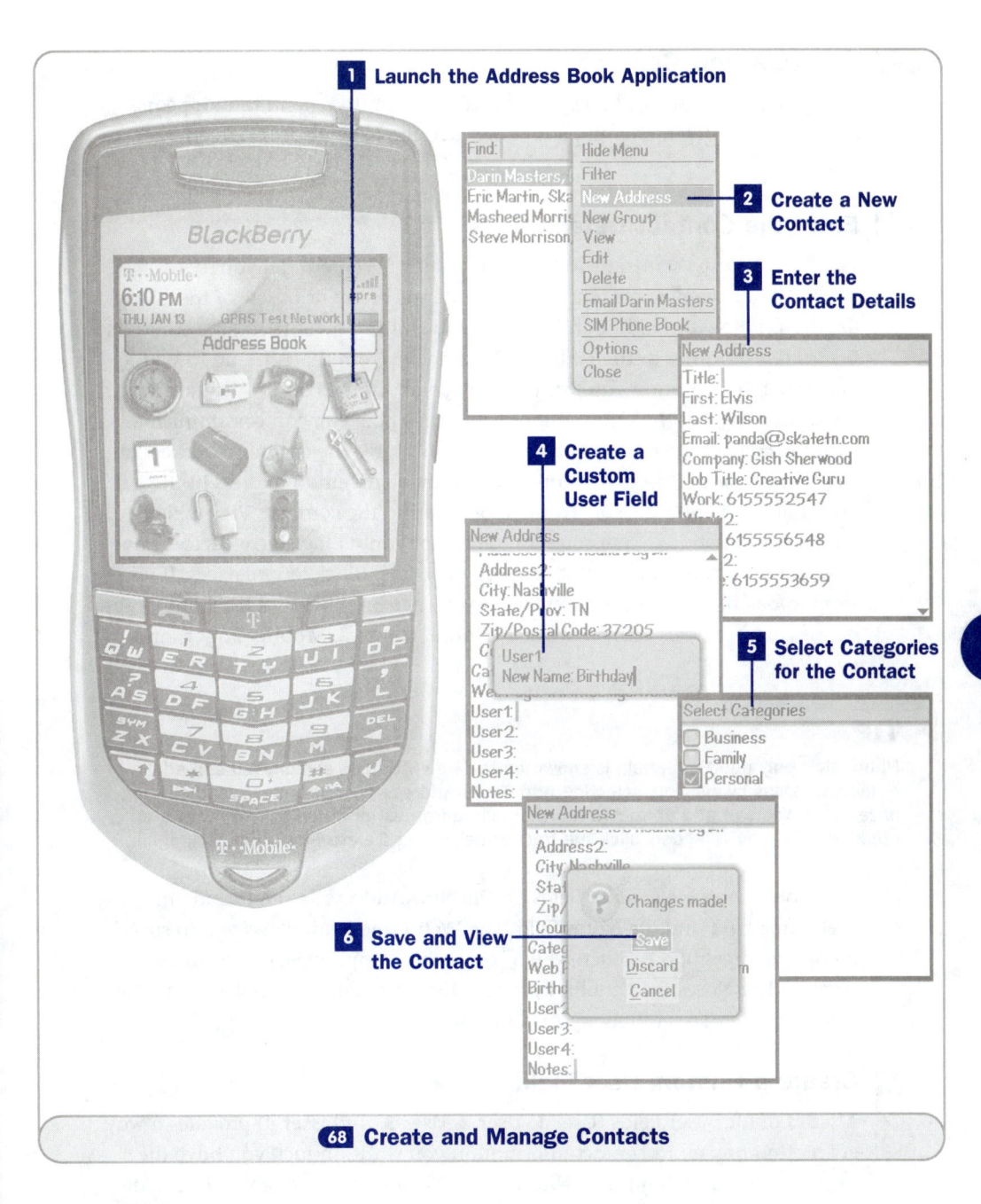

4 Create a Custom User Field

5 Select Categories for the Contact

6 Save and View the Contact

68 Create and Manage Contacts

▶ **TIP**

If you already use an address book in a personal information management (PIM) client such as Microsoft Outlook, consider synchronizing PIM data between your BlackBerry device and your desktop PC using the BlackBerry Desktop Manager software. See **10** **Synchronize PIM Data with Your PC** to find out how.

2 Create a New Contact

Click the trackwheel and select **New Address** from the menu that appears. Click again to begin creating a new contact; the **New Address** screen appears.

3 Enter the Contact Details

The **New Address** screen includes several fields for entering a variety of details about the new contact. You can enter as many or as few of these details as you want, although I recommend starting by entering the contact's first and last names in the **First** and **Last** fields. From there, it's up to you how much information you want to provide about the contact. Just keep in mind that some of the information determines how you can communicate with the contact later. For example, you won't have the option to address an email message to the contact unless you provide an email address in the **Email** field. There is also a **PIN** field for entering the contact's PIN, which allows you to send PIN messages to the person; only BlackBerry devices have PINs, and PIN messages can be sent only between BlackBerry devices. If you want to be able to make a phone call to the person, fill out at least one of the phone number fields (**Work**, **Work 2**, **Home**, **Home 2**, **Mobile**, **Pager**, and **Fax**).

▶ **TIP**

Notice that only one **Email** field is shown on the **New Address** screen. You can add email addresses by clicking, selecting **Add Email Address** from the menu, and clicking once more. You can add up to two more email addresses for a contact. To remove an email address you've added, click the trackwheel, select **Delete Field**, and click again.

A few other notable contact fields on the **New Address** screen include the **Web Page** field and the **Notes** field. The **Web Page** field allows you to specify the web address of a contact, which can be his company website or personal website. The **Notes** field enables you to enter any additional notes about the contact, which are entirely up to your discretion.

4 Create a Custom User Field

A series of four user fields (**User 1**, **User 2**, **User 3**, and **User 4**) provides a way of entering any extra contact information you want. In fact, you have the flexibility of renaming these fields across all contacts to accommodate additional information such as the birthday or anniversary of each contact. To change the name of a user field, click the field, select **Change Field Name** on the menu that appears, and click again. A dialog box appears that allows you to enter the new field name.

One of the most common uses of the custom user fields in the address book is to add a birthday field for all your contacts. Nothing quite makes a statement like remembering a client's birthday and sending him a quick note or card. To create a birthday field, enter **Birthday** as the name of the user field in the **Change Field Name** dialog box. The field name changes to **Birthday** on the **New Address** screen, where you can then enter the contact's birthday.

▶ **TIP**

Other possibilities for custom fields include fields for a contact's anniversary, spouse's name, children's names, and hobbies, to name a few. If you manage a sales force, you might consider creating a custom sales quota field.

5 Select Categories for the Contact

In addition to custom user fields, an important organizational property named **Categories** allows you to categorize the contact. When you double-click the **Categories** field, the **Select Categories** screen appears and enables you to select one or more categories for the contact. Categorizing your contacts is a handy way to organize them. I selected **Personal** as the category for the contact in the example shown because my friend Elvis has no connection to my work. You might opt to create detailed categories to further distinguish between different types of work contacts; see 70 **Apply Categories to Contacts**.

6 Save and View the Contact

When you finish editing the new contact, click the trackwheel, select **Save** from the menu that appears, and click again. The new contact is saved and added to the address book. The contact is now ready to be used as the recipient of email messages, PIN messages, SMS messages, and phone calls.

▶ **TIPS**

To send a text message or call a contact, click the contact's name in the contact list; select **Email** *Contact Name*, **PIN** *Contact Name*, **Call** *Contact Name*, or **SMS** *Contact Name* from the menu that appears; and click once more. Some of these commands might not be available depending on whether you've specified an appropriate address for the contact. For example, if you haven't specified a PIN for a contact, you won't see **PIN** *Contact Name* on the menu when you click the contact.

If your address book grows to fill more than one screen of data, you can quickly scroll up and down the contact list a screen of data at a time by holding down the **Alt** key while scrolling the trackwheel.

69 Create and Manage Mailing Lists

✔ BEFORE YOU BEGIN	→ SEE ALSO
68 Create and Manage Contacts	10 Synchronize PIM Data with Your PC
	71 Tweak Address Book Options

Individual contacts aren't the only kinds of contacts you can use in the **Address Book** application. You can also create *mailing lists*, which are groups of contacts you interact with as if they are a single entity. In other words, you can send an email message to an entire group of people by simply addressing the message to a mailing list. Mailing lists are limited to only email addresses, so you can add only those contacts who have email addresses. Mailing lists on your device are also referred to as *groups*, which is an accurate name when you consider that a mailing list is really just a group of contacts. If you have a group of people to whom you regularly send emails, you'll find that creating a group for them can save you a lot of time in addressing messages.

▶ **KEY TERM**

Mailing list—A group of contacts with whom you interact as if they were a single entity; you can send an email message to an entire group of people by simply addressing the message to a single mailing list.

1 Launch the Address Book Application

Scroll to the **Address Book** icon and click the trackwheel. The **Address Book** application is launched and displayed on the screen.

2 Create a New Group

Click the trackwheel and select **New Group** from the menu that appears. Click again to begin creating a new group; the **New Group** screen appears.

3 Enter the Group Name

The **New Group** screen includes a single field along the top of the screen for entering the group name, followed by a list of the contacts (email addresses) who belong to the group; the list is initially empty. Before adding any contacts to the group, enter a name for the group in the **New Group** edit field.

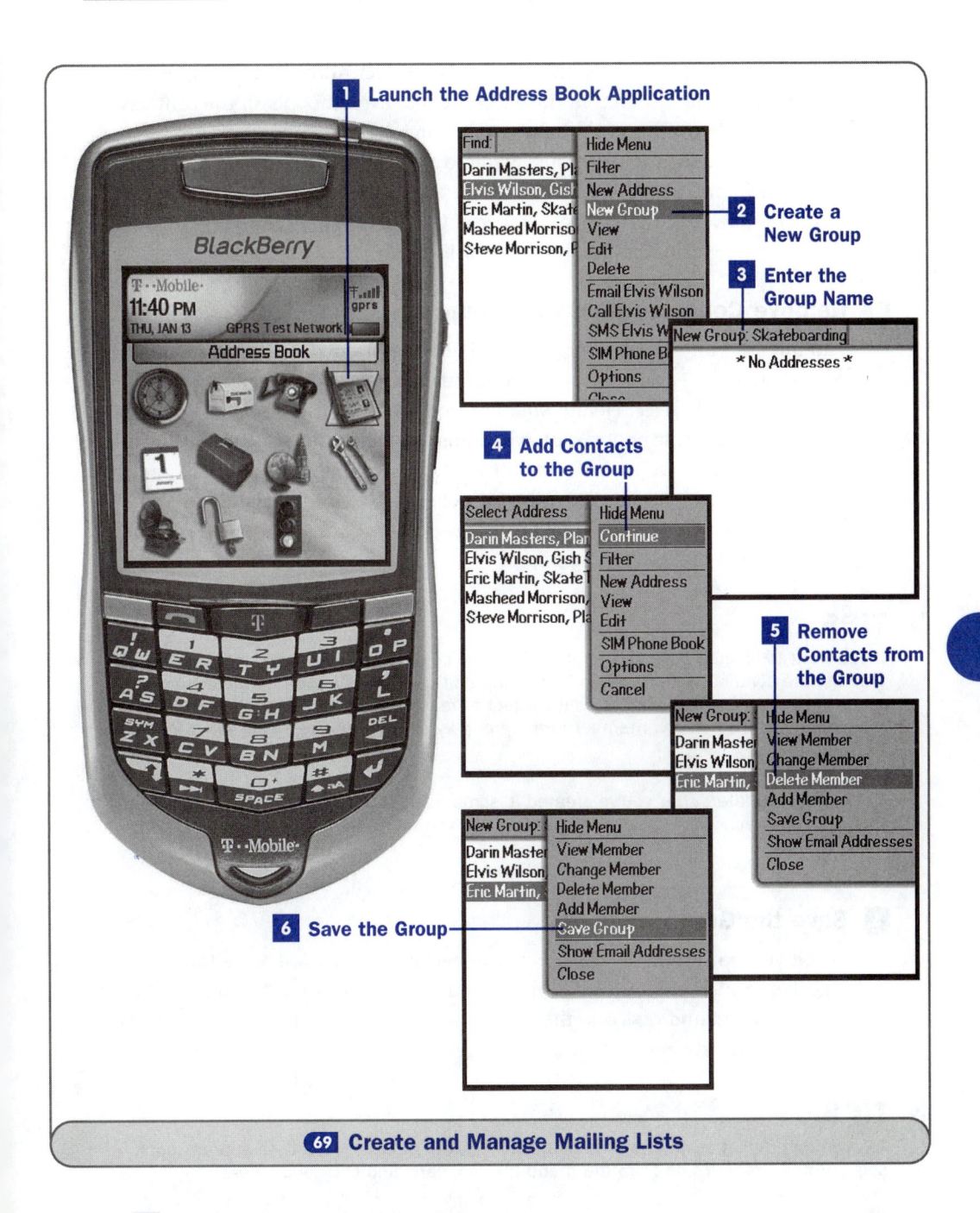

69 Create and Manage Mailing Lists

1 Launch the Address Book Application

2 Create a New Group

3 Enter the Group Name

4 Add Contacts to the Group

5 Remove Contacts from the Group

6 Save the Group

69 Create and Manage Mailing Lists

4 Add Contacts to the Group

Adding contacts to the new group is as simple as selecting them from the contact list. To add a contact, click the trackwheel, select **Add Member** from the menu that appears, and click again. The **Select Address** screen appears and shows all the contacts in the address book. Even though all the contacts are listed, only contacts for whom you've entered an email address are allowed to be added to the group. Scroll to select the desired contact, click the trackwheel, and select **Continue** from the menu. Click once more to add the contact to the group as a new member of the group. The contact appears in the group as part of the group's member list.

5 Remove Contacts from the Group

Mailing lists can change over time, and you might have to remove members on occasion. To remove a contact from the group, select the contact with the trackwheel, click, select **Delete Member** from the menu that appears, and click again. A confirmation dialog box appears that prompts you to confirm the deletion; click **Delete** to delete the contact from the group or click **Cancel** to cancel the deletion. It's important to note that deleting a contact from a group does not delete the contact from the address book; it only removes the contact as a member of the group.

▶ TIPS

If you want to change a group member from one contact to another, as opposed to deleting the contact, you can do so by clicking and selecting **Change Member** from the menu. You can then select a different contact to replace the selected contact in the group. You can also view a member in the group by clicking and selecting **View Member** from the menu.

To edit a group later, after you've created it, scroll to select the group in the contact list and click the trackwheel. Select **Edit Group** from the menu that appears and click once more.

6 Save the Group

When you finish adding contacts to the new mailing list, click the trackwheel, select **Save Group** from the menu that appears, and click again. The group is saved and added to the contact list. The mailing list is now ready to be used as the recipient of email messages.

▶ TIPS

To send an email message to a mailing list, click the group name in the address book, select **Email** *Group Name* from the menu that appears, and click once more.

If you want, you can view the mailing list as a list of email addresses instead of names. First scroll to select the group in the contact list and click the trackwheel. Then select **View Group** from the menu that appears and click once more. Finally, with the group list in view, click and select **Show Email Addresses** from the menu, and then click a final time.

70 Apply Categories to Contacts

✔ BEFORE YOU BEGIN

68 Create and Manage Contacts

→ SEE ALSO

71 Tweak Address Book Options

Categories are used throughout the BlackBerry personal information management system to help you organize address book contacts, tasks, and memos. Within the **Address Book** application, you use categories to identify and distinguish between contacts. For example, you might want to separate personal and business contacts by categorizing them differently. You can then use categories to filter the main contact list according to a certain category. The **Address Book** application provides the ability to create new categories, delete existing categories, and assign categories to contacts.

1 Launch the Address Book Application

Scroll to the **Address Book** icon and click the trackwheel. The **Address Book** application is launched and displayed on the screen.

2 Open the Select Category Screen

Click the trackwheel and scroll to select **Filter** from the menu that appears. Click once more to open the **Select Category** screen, which displays a list of categories from which you can select.

3 Create and Delete Categories

To create a new category, click the trackwheel, select **New** from the menu that appears, and click again. A dialog box appears that prompts you for the name of the category. Enter the name and click the trackwheel to create the new category.

▶ **NOTE**

Although category names can be mixed case, they aren't distinguishable by case. In other words, you can't have two categories named **Personal** and **PERSONAL**; they are considered duplicate categories.

To delete a category, scroll the trackwheel to select the category, click, select **Delete** from the menu that appears, and click again. You are prompted to confirm the category deletion—click **Delete** to follow through with the deletion or click **Cancel** to cancel the deletion.

CHAPTER 11: Using the Address Book to Never Lose a Contact

1 Launch the Address Book Application

2 Open the Select Category Screen

3 Create and Delete Categories

4 Select the Categories for Filtering

5 View All the Contacts Again

70 Apply Categories to Contacts

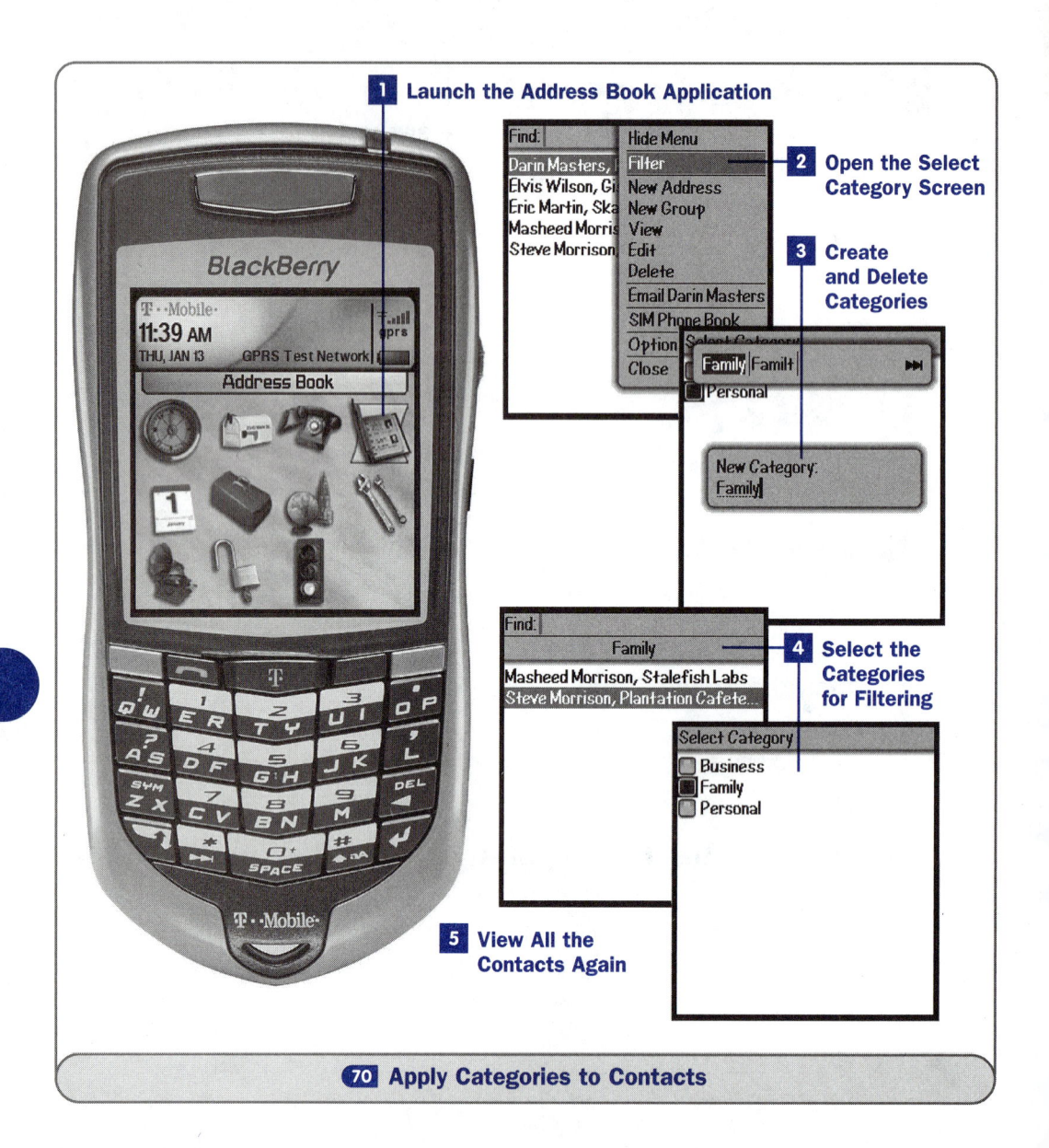

▶ **NOTES**

If you delete a category that is already assigned to a contact, the category is removed from the contact but the contact itself is not deleted.

Categories don't just apply to contacts. They are shared among address book contacts, tasks, and memos. When you add or delete a category from the **Address Book** application, you are changing the categories for contacts, tasks, and memos as well.

When you finish creating and deleting categories, use the **Select Category** screen to filter contacts so that only contacts assigned to a particular category are shown in the contact list; see **68 Create and Manage Contacts** if you need a refresher on how to assign categories to contacts.

4 Select the Categories for Filtering

By default, the contact list that appears in the **Address Book** application shows all the contacts you've created, regardless of how they are categorized. A useful technique for isolating contacts in a smaller view is to filter the contact list based on categories. For example, if you select a category for filtering, only the contacts set to that category are displayed in the contact list. If you carefully categorize your contacts, this filtering technique provides a quick way to pare down the contact list to those of particular interest to you at the time.

To filter the contact list from the **Select Category** screen, just scroll to select a category and double-click the trackwheel. You immediately return to the contact list, which now has a heading above the contacts that shows on which category the contacts are being filtered. In this example, I'm filtering contacts based on the new **Family** category, which I've already assigned to a couple of contacts. The result is that only family contacts are displayed in the contacts list.

5 View All the Contacts Again

To restore the full list of contacts, click the trackwheel, select **Filter** from the menu that appears, and click again. In the **Select Category** screen, double-click the selected category to deselect it; the main contact list appears with all the contacts again in view.

---

71 Tweak Address Book Options

✔ **BEFORE YOU BEGIN**

68 Create and Manage Contacts

The **Address Book** application includes a few options that give you control over how contacts are displayed and manipulated. For example, the options made available by the **Address Book** application allow you to do away with the delete confirmation prompt that appears whenever you delete a contact. Although doing away with this prompt can be a timesaver, it does make it easier to accidentally delete contacts. Another option determines the order in which the contacts are displayed in the contact list. In addition to providing access to option settings, the **Address Book** application provides a quick and easy way to determine how many contacts you have stored away on your device.

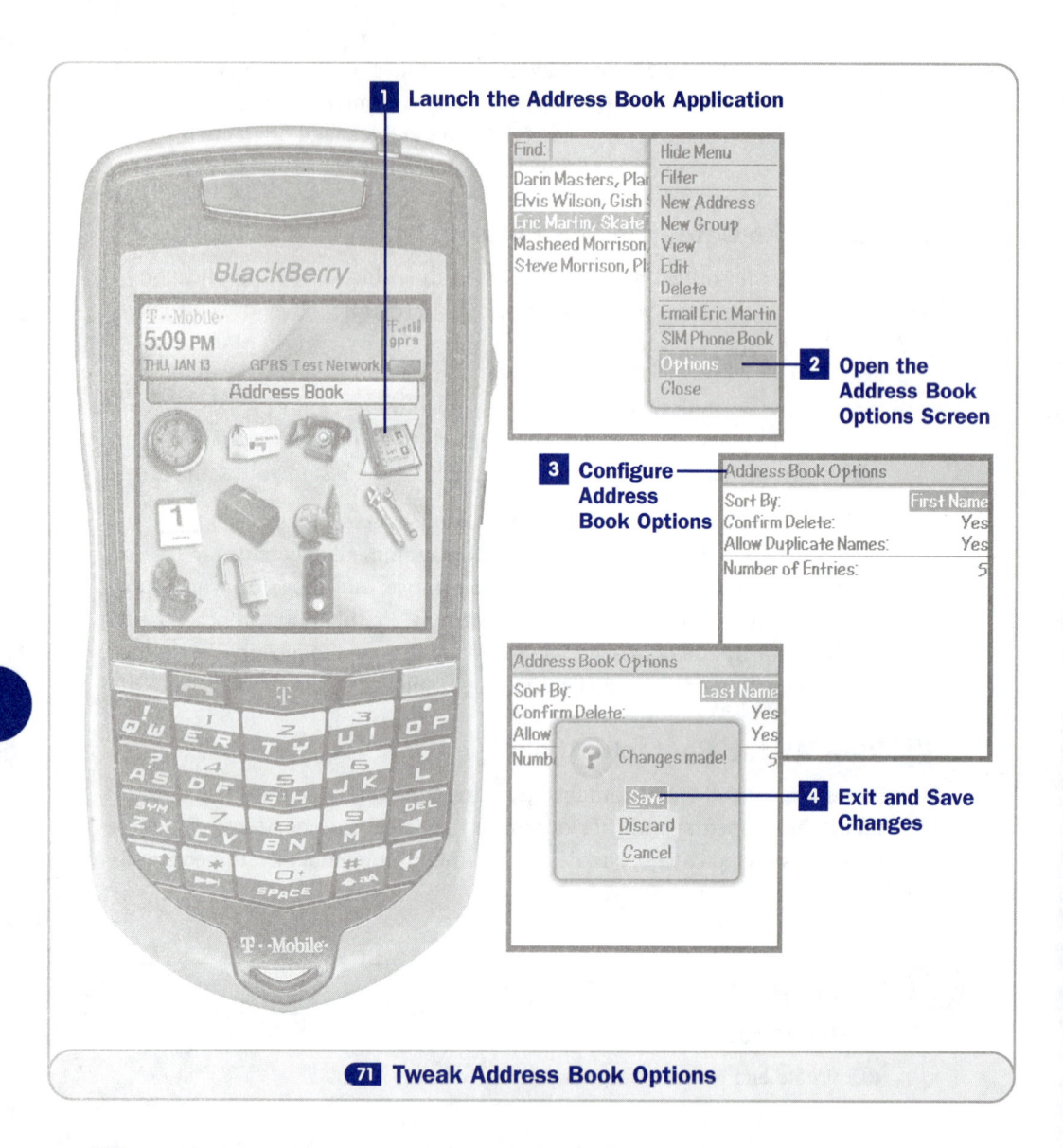

CHAPTER 11: Using the Address Book to Never Lose a Contact

1 Launch the Address Book Application

2 Open the Address Book Options Screen

3 Configure Address Book Options

4 Exit and Save Changes

71 Tweak Address Book Options

1 Launch the Address Book Application

On the **Home** screen, scroll to the **Address Book** icon and click the trackwheel. The **Address Book** application is launched and displayed on the screen.

2 Open the Address Book Options Screen

Click the trackwheel and select **Options** from the menu that appears. Click once more to open the **Address Book Options** screen.

3 Configure Address Book Options

The **Address Book Options** screen includes several options that control how contacts are displayed and interacted with in the contact list. The first option, **Sort By**, determines how the contacts are sorted in the contacts list. You can set this option to one of the following values: **First Name**, **Last Name**, or **Company**. Not only does the **Sort By** option determine the order of the contacts, but it also determines what piece of information is displayed first for a contact. As an example, if you select **Company** for this option, each contact is listed with her company name first, followed by her last and first names. Although **First Name** is the default value for the **Sort By** option, I find **Last Name** to be the most useful setting for sorting contacts.

The **Confirm Delete** option on the **Address Book Options** screen controls whether you are prompted to confirm the deletion of a contact. The default value of this setting is **Yes**, which requires you to agree to a prompt before deleting a contact. Unless you don't mind the risk of accidentally deleting a contact, I recommend keeping the default setting.

The **Allow Duplicate Names** option determines whether the address book allows more than one instance of the exact same name (first and last name). The default setting is **Yes**, which allows you to have duplicate names.

The last field in the address book options, **Number of Entries**, isn't an option but instead provides you with the total number of contacts on your device. This information might or might not be helpful to you, but at the very least it can let you know how many people you care about regularly coming into contact with electronically.

4 Exit and Save Changes

When you finish configuring address book options, press the **Escape** button. If you made changes to any of the options, you are prompted to save. Click **Save** to keep the changes or click **Discard** to ignore the changes.

---

72 Access the SIM Phone Book

✔ BEFORE YOU BEGIN	→ SEE ALSO
Just jump right in!	68 Create and Manage Contacts
	88 Secure the SIM Card

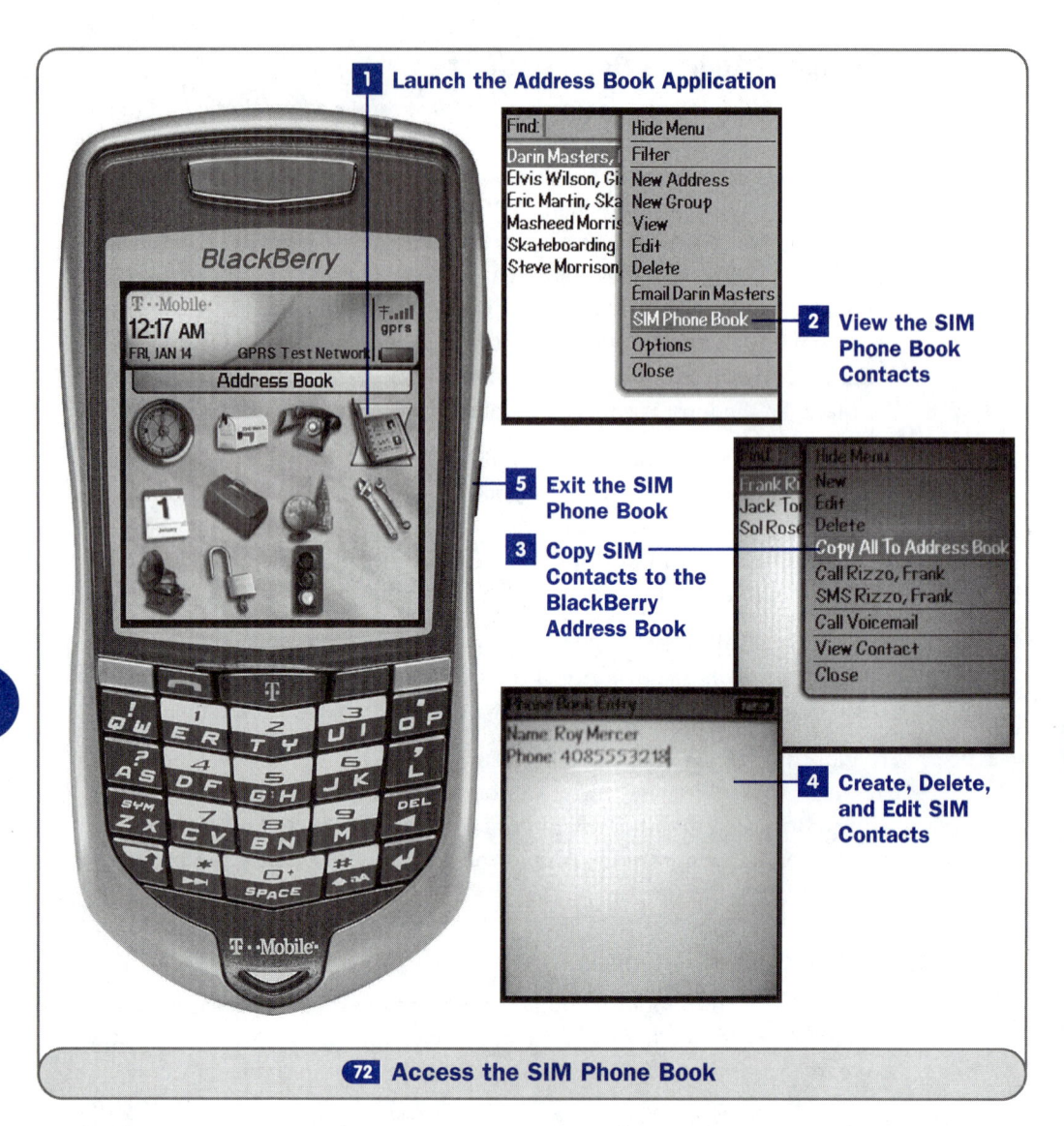

CHAPTER 11: Using the Address Book to Never Lose a Contact

1 Launch the Address Book Application

2 View the SIM Phone Book Contacts

5 Exit the SIM Phone Book

3 Copy SIM Contacts to the BlackBerry Address Book

4 Create, Delete, and Edit SIM Contacts

72 Access the SIM Phone Book

Like most mobile phones, your BlackBerry 7100 device includes a subscriber identity module (SIM) card whose primary purpose is to securely store the key that uniquely identifies you to your wireless service provider. In addition to storing your wireless subscriber key, the SIM card in your device also contains storage space for text messages and a phone book. The phone book storage area in your SIM card is known as the **SIM Phone Book**. This phone book is completely separate from the BlackBerry address book of contacts you normally access using the **Address Book** application. The **SIM Phone Book** is more limited than the BlackBerry address book in that it stores only name/number combinations.

72 Access the SIM Phone Book

You might never find a need to use the **SIM Phone Book** on your BlackBerry device. On the other hand, if you carried over a SIM card from a previous mobile phone, you might want to access the contacts you stored on the SIM card from your previous phone. Regardless of your motive in using the **SIM Phone Book**, it's important to know how to access it and interact with the contacts it contains.

1 Launch the Address Book Application

You might be surprised to find that you access the **SIM Phone Book** through the standard **Address Book** application. On the **Home** screen, scroll to the **Address Book** icon and click the trackwheel. The **Address Book** application is launched and displayed on the screen.

2 View the SIM Phone Book Contacts

Click the trackwheel and select **SIM Phone Book** from the menu that appears. Click once more to open the **SIM Phone Book** contacts; these contacts are displayed in the **Address Book** contact list, temporarily replacing the normal BlackBerry address book contacts.

▶ **NOTE**

The contacts listed in the **SIM Phone Book** can be one of two types: abbreviated dialing number (ADN) or service dialing number (SDN). ADN contacts correspond to the contacts you create and enter on your device, including those you might have created on the SIM card using a previous mobile phone. SDN contacts correspond to special service phone numbers installed on your SIM card by your wireless service provider; these numbers might allow you to contact your wireless service provider directly. ADN contacts are shown in the **SIM Phone Book** in plain text, whereas SDN contacts are shown in bold text.

▶ **TIP**

To call a contact or send an SMS message to a contact in the **SIM Phone Book**, click the contact, select **Call** *Contact Name* or **SMS** *Contact Name*, and click once more.

3 Copy SIM Contacts to the BlackBerry Address Book

The first thing you should consider doing with the **SIM Phone Book** is to copy SIM contacts over to the main BlackBerry address book. You have the option of adding individual contacts or copying all of them at once. To copy all the contacts at once, open the **SIM Phone Book**, click the trackwheel, select **Copy All To Address Book** from the menu that appears, and click again. All the **SIM Phone Book** contacts are copied over to the main BlackBerry address book. You are free to edit the contacts in the address book and fill out additional details. (Remember that all that is copied from the

SIM Phone Book to the BlackBerry address book is a name and phone number.) To add a single SIM contact to the main BlackBerry address book, scroll to select the contact, click the trackwheel, select **Add To Address Book** from the menu that appears, and click once more.

4 Create, Delete, and Edit SIM Contacts

You might decide that it's worthwhile to keep the **SIM Phone Book** contacts as a backup of important contacts, or in case you move the SIM card to another device and want to carry the contacts with you. Regardless of your motive for managing SIM contacts, the **SIM Phone Book** allows you to create, edit, and delete contacts. To create a new SIM contact, open the **SIM Phone Book**, click the trackwheel, select **New** from the menu that appears, and click again. A dialog box appears that prompts you to enter the name and phone number of the new contact. After entering this information, press the **Escape** button and then click **Save** in the confirmation prompt that appears to save the new contact.

Deleting a contact from the **SIM Phone Book** is as easy as scrolling the trackwheel to select the contact, clicking, selecting **Delete** from the menu, and clicking again. You are prompted to confirm the deletion—just click **Delete** to carry out the deletion or **Cancel** if you change your mind.

Editing a SIM contact involves scrolling the trackwheel to select the contact, clicking, selecting **Edit** from the menu, and clicking again. You are given an opportunity to edit the contact name and phone number, after which you press the **Escape** button to exit the **Phone Book Entry** screen. Click **Save** in the confirmation prompt to save the changes you made, click **Discard** to discard the changes, or click **Cancel** to continue editing the contact.

5 Exit the SIM Phone Book

Press the **Escape** button to exit the **SIM Phone Book** and return to the main BlackBerry address book contact list.

12

Managing Your Time with the Calendar

IN THIS CHAPTER:

- **73** About the Calendar
- **74** Navigate in the Calendar
- **75** Create and Manage Appointments
- **76** Tweak Calendar Options

CHAPTER 12: Managing Your Time with the Calendar

The BlackBerry calendar application is the central software component for scheduling events on your device. *Events* are appointments, meetings, and anything else you might want to keep track of that requires your time. The key thing to understand here is that the calendar is designed to help you manage your time. If an activity can be expressed as a block of time, you can create an appointment in the calendar to help you remember when the activity takes place and how long it lasts. How far you go in scheduling your life in the calendar is up to you, but at the very least, you will find it handy for scheduling important business meetings and appointments you'd like to be reminded of, in which case the calendar will alert you with a reminder.

73 About the Calendar

✔ **BEFORE YOU BEGIN**

3 Set the Date and Time

The BlackBerry **Calendar** offers a useful approach to scheduling appointments and meetings and generally keeping track of your time. If you're already familiar with using a similar software calendar in a personal information software client such as Microsoft Outlook, you'll be right at home with the BlackBerry calendar. In fact, you will likely find it beneficial to synchronize calendar data on your device with calendar data on your desktop PC. You can easily accomplish this by connecting your device to your desktop PC and using the BlackBerry Desktop Manager to synchronize the data; see 10 **Synchronize PIM Data with Your PC** for more details.

Depending on whether your company supports the feature, you might have the option of taking calendar synchronization to another level entirely. The BlackBerry calendar has the capability to be wirelessly synchronized with calendar data on your desktop PC. Wireless calendar synchronization is an option on the BlackBerry Enterprise Server. If you have access to the BlackBerry Enterprise Server, you should check with your network administrator to see whether wireless calendar synchronization is enabled. If so, the calendar on your device will suddenly take on an entirely new level of importance and sophistication because you will be constantly in sync with appointments and meetings. If a co-worker reschedules a meeting or changes the time, you will immediately receive the request wirelessly and be given an opportunity to accept or decline. If you're new to BlackBerry devices, you'll find that wireless calendar synchronization is one of the series' killer mobile features.

Even if you don't have access to wireless calendar synchronization, the **Calendar** application is still a useful tool. One of the things that makes the calendar so useful is its flexibility in providing you with different views on dates and times. More specifically, the BlackBerry calendar offers four calendar formats, which are just different ways of viewing a period of time:

- **Day**—Shows the hours in a day, including appointment and meeting details for that day

- **Week**—Shows the days in a week, including a glimpse at appointments and meetings for each hour

- **Month**—Shows the days and weeks in a month, including a glimpse at appointments and meetings for each day

- **Agenda**—Shows upcoming appointment and meeting details across multiple dates

All the calendar formats provide a view based on the currently selected time period. This time period is typically an hour or half-hour period that is initially set to the current date and time when you first open the calendar. The default calendar format is **Day** format, which shows a list of hours in the current day in one-hour increments.

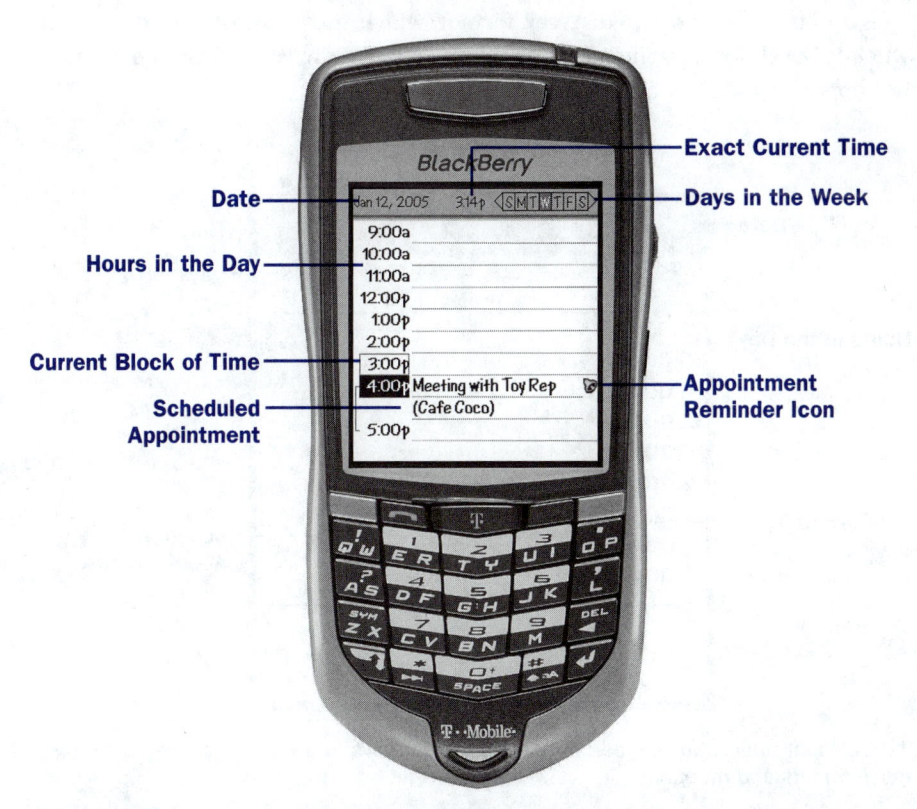

*The **Calendar** application's **Day** format shows the hours in a day, including appointment and meeting details.*

The calendar's **Day** view shows a day as a sequence of hours listed vertically down the screen. The current time is highlighted with a box around the most recent hour. Appointments and meetings are prominently displayed immediately next to the time at which they are scheduled to start. A small line extends down from the left of the time for a scheduled appointment to show how long the appointment is scheduled to last. This provides a visual cue in regard to how your time is allocated for the day.

Along the upper-right edge of the **Day** view is a series of boxes that shows the current week as a list of days arranged horizontally. As you navigate through days in the **Day** view, the small week graphic changes to indicate the day of the week.

▶ **NOTE**
To find out exactly how to navigate through the views in the **Calendar** application, see **74 Navigate in the Calendar.**

If you imagine zooming out of **Day** format to view the current week as a table of dates and times, you arrive at **Week** format, which shows the days in a week. To switch to **Week** format, click the trackwheel, select **View Week** from the menu that appears, and click again.

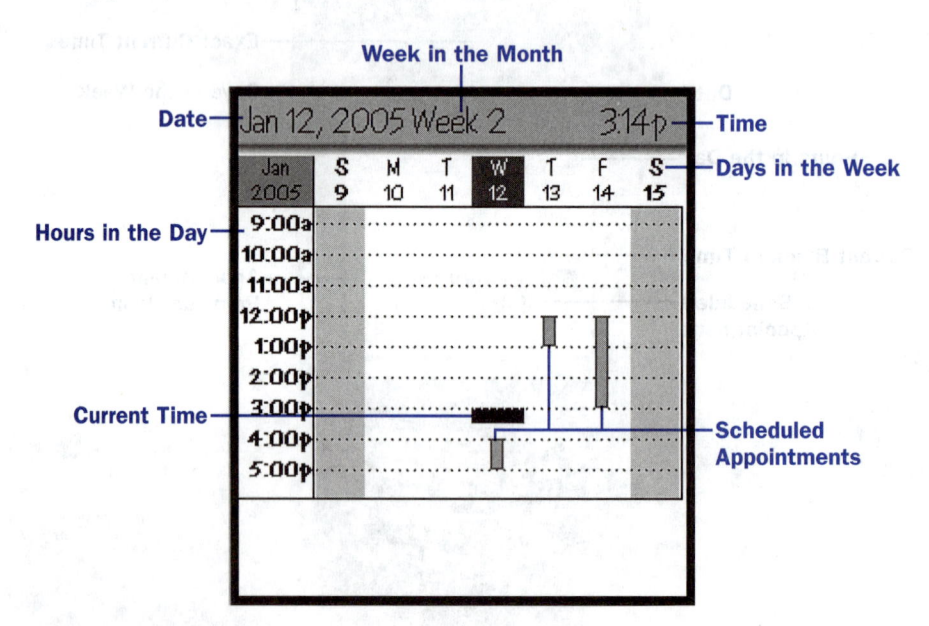

The **Calendar** application's **Week** format shows the days in a week, including a glimpse at appointments and meetings.

73 About the Calendar

Week format expands on **Day** format by showing a list of days across the screen to form a complete week. The hours in the day are still shown, but they are very small and therefore can contain only small markers that indicate appointments and meetings, as opposed to details such as the subject, location, and exact time of an appointment. Even with the compressed view of hours in a day, **Week** format in many ways provides an even better view of your scheduled time than **Day** view. This is primarily due to how appointments are shown as little vertical bar graphs to indicate how much time they take up.

As you continue to zoom out of the calendar, the next format is **Month** format, which looks a lot like a traditional month view on a print calendar.

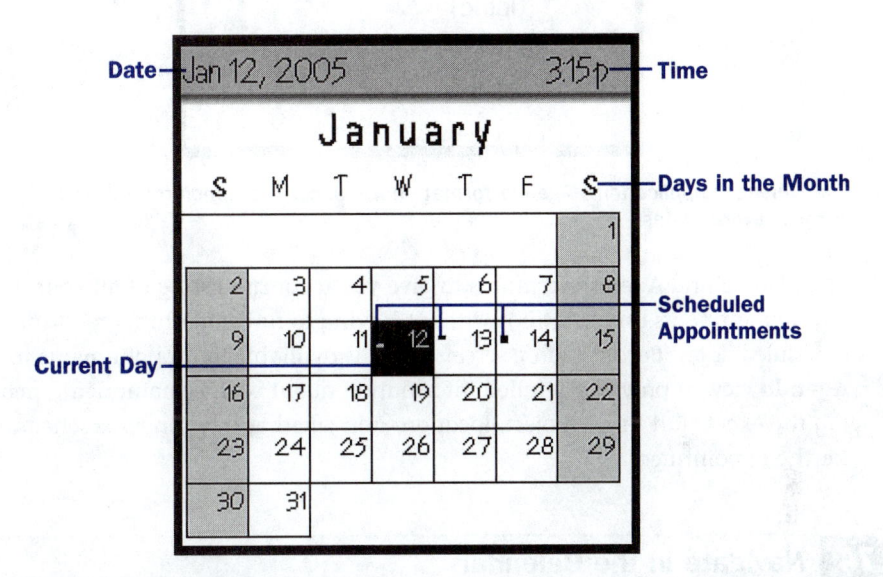

*The **Calendar** application's **Month** format shows the days and weeks in a month, including a glimpse at appointments and meetings.*

The calendar's **Month** view is more of what you expect of a software calendar in terms of being organized as weeks flowing horizontally to show a full month of days. **Month** view allows for even less detail in terms of conveying appointments and meetings, but you can still see tiny icons that do a fair job of showing how much time is scheduled for a particular day.

The last format available in the **Calendar** application is **Agenda** format, which departs from the other views by not focusing on a particular period of time. Instead, **Agenda** format focuses on upcoming appointments and meetings, even if they are spread out across several dates.

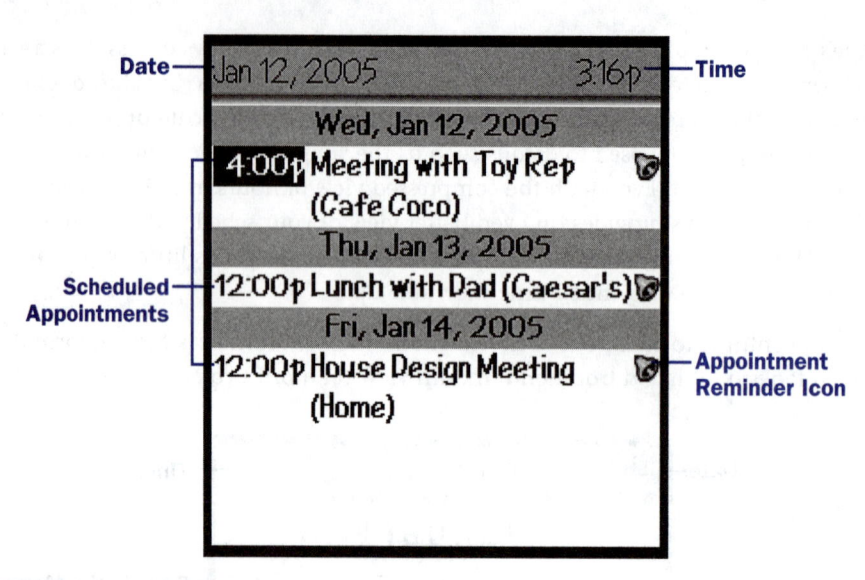

290   **CHAPTER 12:**   **Managing Your Time with the Calendar**

Calendar screenshot showing:
- Date — Jan 12, 2005
- Time — 3:16p
- Wed, Jan 12, 2005
  - 4:00p Meeting with Toy Rep (Cafe Coco)
- Thu, Jan 13, 2005
  - 12:00p Lunch with Dad (Caesar's)
- Fri, Jan 14, 2005
  - 12:00p House Design Meeting (Home)
- Scheduled Appointments
- Appointment Reminder Icon

*The **Calendar** application's **Agenda** format shows upcoming appointments and meetings across several dates.*

73

The idea behind **Agenda** format is to give you a concise listing of all your upcoming appointments and meetings without having to navigate through all the scheduled dates. Because more screen space is available for appointments in the **Agenda** view, it provides detailed information about each appointment, including the exact start time, subject, location, and whether a reminder is scheduled for the appointment.

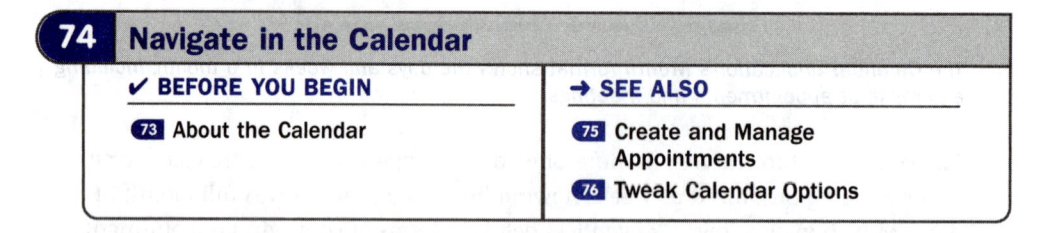

---

74 Navigate in the Calendar

✔ BEFORE YOU BEGIN	→ SEE ALSO
73 About the Calendar	**75** Create and Manage Appointments
	76 Tweak Calendar Options

The **Calendar** application is a flexible tool for analyzing and interacting with dates and times. Along with simulating a printed calendar by providing static information such as days, weeks, months, and years, the calendar also supports the creation of appointments and meetings that span lengths of time that are readily visible within the calendar's views. In fact, a thorough understanding of the calendar's views is required before you can successfully use the calendar as a scheduling assistant. Fortunately, navigating through the calendar and zooming in and out on specific dates and times is a straightforward process.

74 Navigate in the Calendar

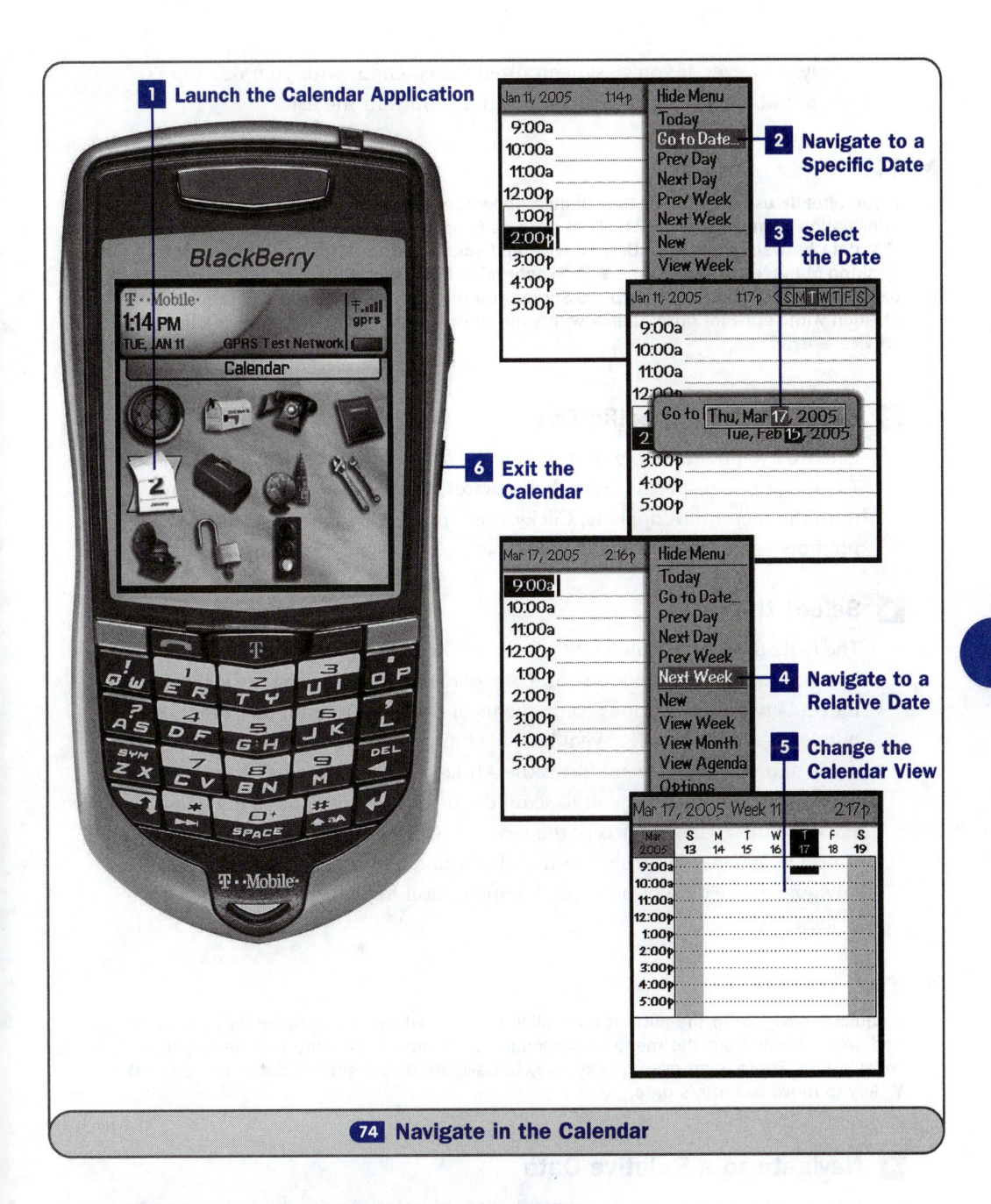

1 Launch the Calendar Application

2 Navigate to a Specific Date

3 Select the Date

4 Navigate to a Relative Date

5 Change the Calendar View

6 Exit the Calendar

74 Navigate in the Calendar

1 **Launch the Calendar Application**

On the **Home** screen, scroll to the **Calendar** icon and click the trackwheel. The **Calendar** application is launched and displayed on the screen. If you haven't yet created any appointments or meetings, your schedule is likely empty. However, if you've synchronized the calendar with your desktop PC, you might see some appointments and meetings in the list.

▶ **TIP**

If you already use a calendar to schedule appointments and meetings in a personal information management (PIM) client such as Microsoft Outlook, consider synchronizing PIM data between your BlackBerry device and your desktop PC using the BlackBerry Desktop Manager software. See **10 Synchronize PIM Data with Your PC**. If your company uses the BlackBerry Enterprise Server, you might have access to wireless synchronization with your PIM data. Check with your network administrator to see whether this service is available.

2 Navigate to a Specific Date

One way to navigate to a date within the calendar is to specify an exact date. To navigate to a specific date, click the trackwheel and select **Go to Date** from the menu that appears. Click once more to view a dialog box that prompts you to select the date.

3 Select the Date

The **Date Selection** dialog box is a bit confusing at first if you don't know how to modify the individual date components. Scrolling the trackwheel moves between the various components of the date (month, day, and year) but doesn't immediately reveal how to change the values. To change the value of a date component, press the **Alt** key on the keyboard. A small window pops up and allows you to scroll the trackwheel to change the value. Click the trackwheel to accept the new value or press the **Escape** button to cancel it. When you finish selecting the desired date, click the trackwheel to navigate to the date or press the **Escape** button to cancel the navigation request.

▶ **TIP**

To quickly navigate to the current date, click the trackwheel in the **Calendar** application and select **Today** from the menu that appears. Click once more, and you are taken to today's date. There is an even quicker way to navigate to the current date—press the **Q W** key to move to today's date.

4 Navigate to a Relative Date

Just as you can navigate to a specific date by selecting the date, you can also navigate to a relative date. You do so by simply stepping through dates either a day at a time or a week at a time. For example, to navigate to the day after the currently viewed day, click the trackwheel, select **Next Day** on the menu, and click again. Similarly, you can select **Prev Day** to navigate to the previous day. If moving through dates one day at a time isn't quick enough for you, select **Next Week** or **Prev Week** from the menu to move forward and back through the calendar a week at a time.

▶ **TIP**

You can use a few shortcut keys to navigate to a relative date. Press the **T Y** and **B N** keys to move to the previous and next hour (**Day** and **Week** formats) or week (**Month** format). Similarly, the **D F** and **J K** keys move to the previous and next day in all the calendar views.

This description of navigating to a relative date assumes that you are currently viewing the calendar in **Day** format. If you change to a different format (see step 5), the available menu commands change. For example, there are no **Next Day** and **Prev Day** commands when you are in **Week** or **Month** format. In fact, **Month** format doesn't have the **Next Week** and **Prev Week** commands, either. However, **Month** format adds commands for navigating months and years at a time (**Next Month**, **Prev Month**, **Next Year**, and **Prev Year**). **Agenda** format just has the **Next Day** and **Prev Day** commands.

5 Change the Calendar View

Unlike a traditional print calendar—which typically provides just a month view—the **Calendar** application provides several formats for viewing the calendar. The calendar defaults to showing you **Day** format, which contains a list of hours in the current day. You change the format of the calendar by clicking the trackwheel and selecting the format from the menu. To switch to **Week** format, for example, select **View Week** from the menu and click the trackwheel. The calendar view changes to show the currently selected date and time in **Week** format.

The other menu commands for changing the calendar format include **View Day**, **View Month**, and **View Agenda**. All the calendar formats operate on the currently selected date and time. In a way, you can think of the formats as zooming in and out on the currently selected date and time. **Agenda** format is the only exception to this line of thinking in that it provides an alternative way to view your appointments and meetings in one list, organized by date and time. If you have no appointments for a given day, the day isn't listed in the **Agenda** format.

▶ TIP

In **Month** format, scrolling the trackwheel moves the selection across the days of the month horizontally. To move vertically through the days, hold down the **Alt** key while scrolling the trackwheel. A similar shortcut applies to the **Week** view, where scrolling the trackwheel moves through the hours of a day, whereas holding down the **Alt** key and scrolling the trackwheel moves through the days. If you continue moving through the days past those shown in the current view, the days in the view scroll.

6 Exit the Calendar

When you finish using the **Calendar** application, press the **Escape** button to exit it and return to the **Home** screen.

---

75 Create and Manage Appointments

✔ BEFORE YOU BEGIN	→ SEE ALSO
74 Navigate in the Calendar	10 Synchronize PIM Data with Your PC
	76 Tweak Calendar Options

Appointments are used in conjunction with the **Calendar** application to provide a way of scheduling events that require your time. Appointments are tightly linked to the BlackBerry calendar because they must have a period of time associated with them. Therefore, appointments can be shown visually in the calendar as taking up a chunk of time in your day, week, or month. Creating an appointment is simply a matter of specifying the subject, the location, the start time, the end time, and a few other parameters you might use to describe an appointment or meeting.

Speaking of meetings, if you have access to the BlackBerry Enterprise Server, you can create a meeting by first creating an appointment and then inviting attendees. Beyond managing attendees for meetings, the **Calendar** application handles appointments and meetings in exactly the same manner regardless of whether you are using the BlackBerry Enterprise Server.

1 Launch the Calendar Application

On the **Home** screen, scroll to the **Calendar** icon and click the trackwheel. The **Calendar** application is launched and displayed on the screen. If you haven't created any appointments or meetings yet, your schedule is likely empty. However, if you've synchronized the calendar with your desktop PC, you might see some appointments and meetings in the list.

75 Create and Manage Appointments

1 Launch the Calendar Application

2 Create a New Appointment

3 Enter the Appointment Details

4 Save and View the Appointment

5 Invite Attendees to the Meeting

6 Delete an Appointment/Meeting

75 Create and Manage Appointments

▶ **TIP**

If you already use a calendar to schedule appointments and meetings in a personal information management (PIM) client such as Microsoft Outlook, consider synchronizing PIM data between your BlackBerry device and your desktop PC using the BlackBerry Desktop Manager software. See **10 Synchronize PIM Data with Your PC**. If your company uses the BlackBerry Enterprise Server, you might even have access to wireless synchronization with your PIM data. Check with your network administrator to see whether this service is available.

2 Create a New Appointment

Click the trackwheel and select **New** from the menu that appears. Click again to begin creating a new appointment; the **New** screen appears.

▶ **TIP**

Press the **O P** key as a shortcut to create a new appointment or meeting. If the **Enable Quick Entry** option is enabled, there is an even quicker shortcut for entering a new appointment. Make sure you are in the **Day** format and scroll the trackwheel to select the start time of the appointment. Begin typing to enter the subject of the appointment, followed by the location of the appointment in parentheses. To change the end time of the appointment, just scroll the trackwheel. You can also change the start time by holding down the **Shift** key and scrolling the trackwheel. Click the trackwheel when you're finished to save the new appointment. See **76 Tweak Calendar Options** for details on how to disable the **Quick Entry** option.

▶ **NOTE**

The only difference between an appointment and a meeting is that a meeting has attendees. So, when I refer to *creating an appointment*, all the same rules apply to meetings—you just invite attendees to turn an appointment into a meeting. Unfortunately, you can't create meetings on your device unless you are using the BlackBerry Enterprise Server. Without the BlackBerry Enterprise server, you won't see an option to invite attendees to an appointment, which would effectively turn it into a meeting.

3 Enter the Appointment Details

The **Subject** field is the first piece of information you must enter when creating a new appointment or meeting. This field describes the appointment and ideally is descriptive enough to immediately set the appointment apart from other appointments you schedule. In the example, I named the appointment **Teeth Cleaning** as a reminder for my next dental appointment. The **Location** of the appointment describes where the appointment takes place; you can enter any text you want in this field. In the example, I simply specified the dentist's office.

The timing of appointments and meetings is important, so pay close attention to the date and time when entering a new appointment. If the

75 **Create and Manage Appointments**

appointment is scheduled to last all day, check the **All Day Event** option. Otherwise, leave the option unchecked and move on to specifying the start and end times for the appointment. Use the trackwheel to scroll through the **Start** and **End** fields and set the exact date and time for when the appointment starts and ends; hold down the **Alt** key to scroll through each date/time component. The duration of the appointment is automatically calculated from the start and end time, but you can set the **Duration** field directly, and the **End** field will change accordingly. Every appointment has a time zone associated with it, and you can change this field to reflect the time zone of the appointment location. The **Time Zone** field defaults to the time zone you set for your device; see **3** **Set the Date and Time**.

An important part of creating an appointment or a meeting is establishing a reminder for it. You don't have to set a reminder for every appointment, but it is usually a good idea to do so. To set a reminder for the appointment, select an amount of time in the **Reminder** field before the start time of the appointment. For example, I opted to be reminded a day in advance of my teeth cleaning so I won't forget the appointment.

▶ **NOTE**
If you set a reminder for an appointment and then turn off the power on your device, the device does not power on to issue the reminder unless you have your device set to automatically power itself on and off. See **16** **Automatically Turn Your Device On and Off** to learn more about this option.

The **Recurrence** field allows you to create an appointment that recurs on a regular schedule. A good example of a recurring appointment is a weekly status meeting in which you meet with co-workers to get up-to-date on the status of current projects. To set the meeting as a recurring meeting, change the **Recurrence** field from **None** to **Daily**, **Weekly**, **Monthly**, or **Yearly**. Based on this setting, additional fields appear that enable you to get more specific about the appointment or meeting recurrence. You can get very detailed with the recurrence of an appointment. For example, you can select **Weekly** in the **Recurrence** field and then select **1** in the **Every** field that appears, meaning that the appointment occurs every week; a value of **2** in the **Every** field results in an appointment that occurs every other week. Then select **F** as the day for the recurring meeting, and the meeting will take place every Friday.

The **Mark as Private** option on the **New Appointment** screen allows you to flag the appointment as a private appointment. Private appointments can't be seen by anyone else, even if they have permission to access your PIM folders.

The last piece of information you can enter for a new appointment or meeting is a text note that is stored in the **Notes** field. This can be any text you want that provides additional details about the appointment or meeting.

4 Save and View the Appointment

When you finish entering the details for the new appointment, click the trackwheel, select **Save** from the menu that appears, and click again. The new appointment is saved and added to the calendar. Depending on the current date you have selected and the calendar format you are viewing, the appointment appears on the screen. Any reminders you set for the appointment are activated.

▶ TIPS

If you don't immediately see the new appointment in the current calendar view, click the trackwheel, select **Agenda View**, and click again. The off format shows all upcoming appointments and meetings, so you won't miss it in that view.

If you need to change an appointment, scroll the trackwheel to select the appointment, click the trackwheel, and select **Open** from the menu that appears; if this is a recurring appointment, select **Open the series** or **Open this occurrence** to open the entire series or just the one occurrence of the appointment, respectively. Click once more, and the **Appointment Details** screen appears, allowing you to edit all the appointment's properties. If you change a meeting, you are prompted to inform the attendees who were invited to the meeting (see step 5). This is usually a good idea because they might not otherwise know about the meeting change.

5 Invite Attendees to the Meeting

If you use the BlackBerry Enterprise Server, you have the option of inviting attendees to an appointment, which turns the appointment into a meeting. Inviting attendees to a meeting is similar to specifying recipients of an email message in that you use the address book on your device to select the attendees. To invite attendees to the new meeting you created, click the trackwheel and select **Invite Attendee** from the menu that appears. Click once more, and the **Select Address** screen appears.

To select attendees for the meeting, scroll the trackwheel to select the attendee, click, and select **Invite** from the menu that appears. Click once more, and the attendee is added to the meeting. Repeat these steps to invite additional people to the meeting. When you're finished, click the trackwheel and select **Save** from the menu. Click again and invitations are sent to the meeting attendees. These invitations are either sent directly through the BlackBerry Enterprise Server as appointment requests or as email messages if you or the invitee aren't using the BlackBerry Enterprise Server.

76 Tweak Calendar Options

▶ **TIP**

You don't have to invite yourself to a meeting that you create; you are already associated with the meeting as the person who created it.

▶ **NOTE**

In addition to being able to create meetings and invite attendees, you can also receive meeting invitations if you're using the BlackBerry Enterprise Server. You can respond to a meeting invitation by accepting, accepting with comments, declining, or declining with comments. The meeting request appears as a message within the **Messages** application. If you delete a meeting invitation (message) before responding to it, the meeting request is deleted from your device and you won't be able to respond to it. You can also receive meeting requests in traditional email messages, even if you aren't using the BlackBerry Enterprise Server.

6 Delete an Appointment/Meeting

Appointments and meetings often get cancelled, in which case you might need to delete them from the calendar. To delete an appointment, scroll the trackwheel to select the appointment, click the trackwheel, and select **Delete** on the menu that appears; for a recurring appointment, you can delete the entire series (**Delete the series**) or just the selected occurrence (**Delete this occurrence**). Click once more and you are prompted to confirm the deletion. Click **Delete** to delete the appointment or **Cancel** to cancel the deletion.

▶ **TIP**

If you delete a meeting, you are prompted to inform the attendees who were invited to the meeting. This is usually a good idea because they might not otherwise know about the meeting cancellation. The attendees will receive the meeting cancellation as a message in the **Messages** application.

76 Tweak Calendar Options

✔ **BEFORE YOU BEGIN**

75 Create and Manage Appointments

The **Calendar** application includes options that give you a fair amount of control over how appointments and meetings are displayed and manipulated. For example, the options made available by the **Calendar** application allow you to do away with the delete confirmation prompt that appears whenever you delete an appointment. Although doing away with this prompt can be a time-saver, it does make it easier to accidentally delete appointments. In addition to offering several useful option settings, the **Calendar** application provides a quick and easy way to determine how many upcoming appointments and meetings you have scheduled.

CHAPTER 12: Managing Your Time with the Calendar

1 Launch the Calendar Application

2 Open the Calendar Options Screen

3 Configure Calendar Options

4 Exit and Save Changes

76 Tweak Calendar Options

1 **Launch the Calendar Application**

On the **Home** screen, scroll to the **Calendar** icon and click the trackwheel. The **Calendar** application is launched and displayed on the screen.

2 **Open the Calendar Options Screen**

Click the trackwheel and select **Options** from the menu that appears. Click once more to open the **Calendar Options** screen, which offers several options for fine-tuning the management of appointments and meetings in the **Calendar** application.

3. Configure Calendar Options

The **Calendar Options** screen includes several options that control the appearance of the calendar view, as well as how appointments and meetings are accessed and manipulated. The first option, **Initial View**, determines the initial calendar format in view when you first launch the **Calendar** application. The default **Day** setting results in the **Day** format showing up initially. If you prefer seeing a different calendar format initially, change the setting to **Week**, **Month**, **Agenda**, or **Last**; the **Last** setting results in the last-shown view being displayed, which can vary.

The **Enable Quick Entry** option turns quick entry mode on and off. Quick entry mode allows you to create new appointments and meetings directly on the **Day** view by simply selecting a time and typing. If you regularly create new appointments, it's not a bad idea to keep the default setting of the **Enable Quick Entry** option, which is **Yes**.

The **Default Reminder** option determines the default amount of time used for appointment reminders. You can set the reminder time for appointments to anything you want when you create an appointment, but the default reminder establishes an initial time for all new appointments that you create. In other words, this time-saving feature is helpful if you prefer a common reminder time for most of your appointments, such as a day in advance of the appointment.

The **Start Of Day**, **End Of Day**, and **First Day Of Week** options determine the specifics of how days are handled in the calendar. More specifically, the **Start Of Day** and **End Of Day** options establish the hours of the day for use in the calendar, which are typically standard business hours (9:00 a.m. to 5:00 p.m.). However, you can change these hours to represent a full 24-hour day or somewhere in between if you want. The **First Day Of Week** option tells the calendar which day you want to signify the start of your week. If your work week starts on a Tuesday, for example, you can change the **First Day Of Week** option to **Tuesday**.

The **Confirm Delete** option on the **Calendar Options** screen controls whether you are prompted to confirm the deletion of an appointment. The default value of this setting is **Yes**, which requires you to agree to a prompt before deleting an appointment. Unless you don't mind the risk of accidentally deleting an appointment, I recommend keeping the default setting.

The **Number of Entries** field on the **Calendar Options** screen isn't an option but instead provides you with the total number of appointments and meetings on your device. This piece of information can help you figure out how busy your upcoming schedule is.

4 Exit and Save Changes

When you finish configuring calendar options, press the **Escape** button. If you made changes to any of the options, you are prompted to save. Click **Save** to keep the changes or **Discard** to ignore the changes.

13

Organizing Your To-Do List with Tasks

IN THIS CHAPTER:

- **77** Create and Manage Tasks
- **78** Apply Categories to Tasks
- **79** Tweak Task Options

As you probably already realize, a major functional aspect of your BlackBerry 7100 series device is to serve as a personal information manager (PIM). An important part of any good PIM is tasks, which are used to keep track of well, tasks. To put it more casually, a *task* is something you need to accomplish. A task can be as simple as mowing the yard or as daunting as completing your first novel. Both projects share in common the need to be completed, hopefully within a certain predetermined time frame.

Your BlackBerry device provides the capability to manage and keep track of tasks efficiently. Not only is it helpful from an organization perspective to create a list of tasks, but the **Tasks** application on your device can remind you when a task is due and help you along the way to completing your tasks. If you're already accustomed to using tasks in a PIM client such as Microsoft Outlook, you'll be right at home using tasks on your device. You'll now have the added benefit of being able to take your task list with you everywhere you go.

77 Create and Manage Tasks

→ **SEE ALSO**

- **10** Synchronize PIM Data with Your PC
- **78** Apply Categories to Tasks
- **79** Tweak Task Options

Creating a new task on your BlackBerry device is as simple as naming the task and filling in some details regarding when the task is due, how important the task is, and so on. You can get surprisingly detailed in how you schedule tasks. For example, you can create recurring tasks that occur at a specific date and time or on certain days of the week. The **Tasks** application provides a great deal of flexibility in the scheduling of tasks. The task list within the **Tasks** application provides you with a quick glimpse at the status of tasks thanks to the small icons that appear to the left of each task. As you start and complete tasks, you'll change the status of the tasks and see their respective icons change in the task list.

1 Open the Applications Screen

Scroll to the **Applications** icon on the **Home** screen and click the trackwheel. The **Applications** screen appears, offering a list of applications, including the **Tasks** application.

77 Create and Manage Tasks

1 Open the Applications Screen

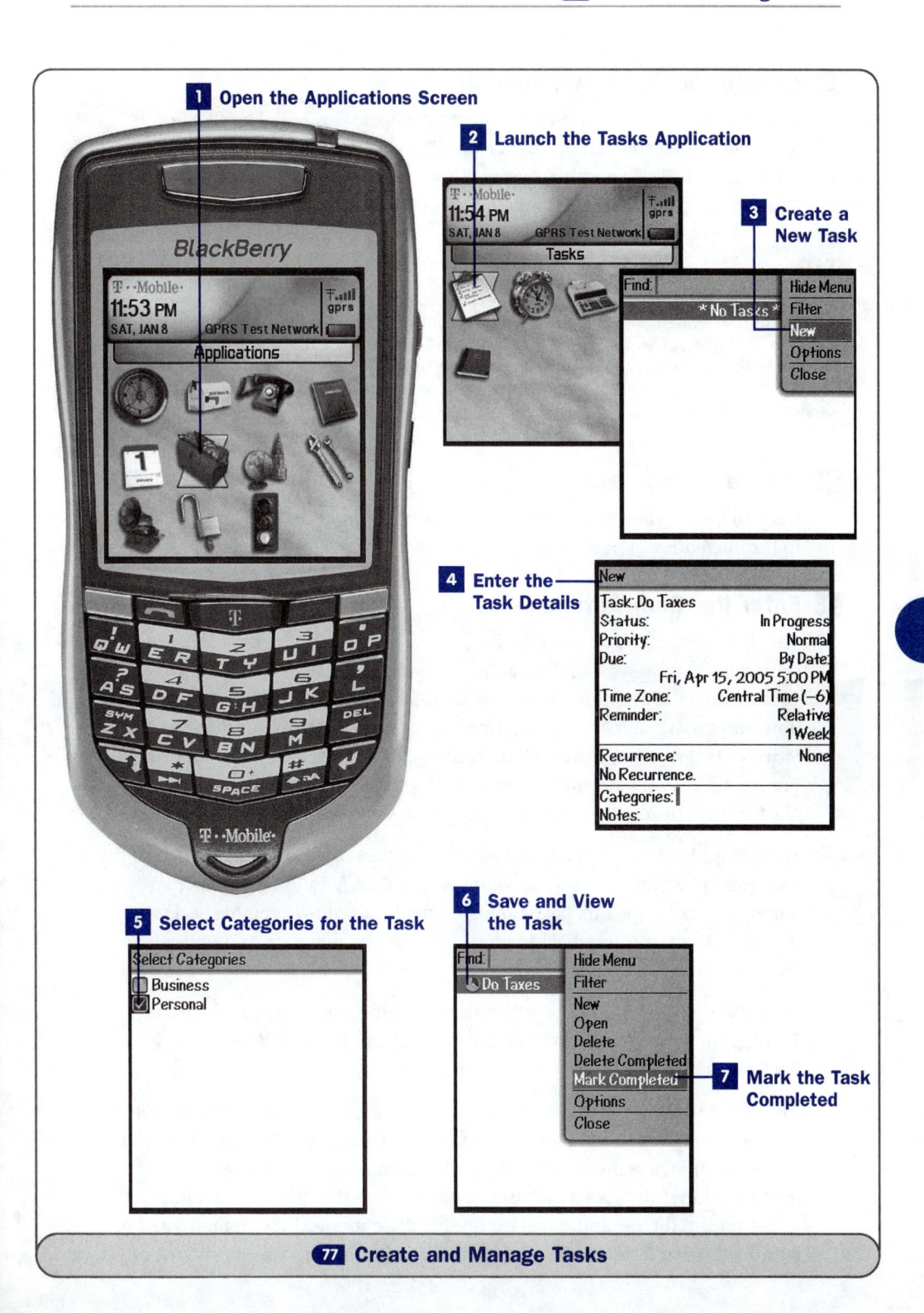

2 Launch the Tasks Application

3 Create a New Task

- Hide Menu
- Filter
- New
- Options
- Close

No Tasks

4 Enter the Task Details

New
Task: Do Taxes
Status: In Progress
Priority: Normal
Due: By Date:
 Fri, Apr 15, 2005 5:00 PM
Time Zone: Central Time (−6)
Reminder: Relative
 1 Week
Recurrence: None
No Recurrence.
Categories:
Notes:

5 Select Categories for the Task

Select Categories
☐ Business
☑ Personal

6 Save and View the Task

- Do Taxes
- Hide Menu
- Filter
- New
- Open
- Delete
- Delete Completed
- Mark Completed
- Options
- Close

7 Mark the Task Completed

77 Create and Manage Tasks

2 Launch the Tasks Application

Scroll to the **Tasks** icon and click the trackwheel. The **Tasks** application is launched and displayed on the screen. If you haven't created any tasks yet, the task list is likely empty. However, if you've synchronized tasks with your desktop PC, you might see some tasks in the list.

▶ **TIP**

If you already use tasks in a *PIM* client such as Microsoft Outlook, consider synchronizing PIM data between your BlackBerry device and your desktop PC using the BlackBerry Desktop Manager software. See **10 Synchronize PIM Data with Your PC**. If your company uses the BlackBerry Enterprise Server, you might have access to wireless synchronization with your PIM data. Check with your network administrator to see whether this service is available.

3 Create a New Task

Click the trackwheel and select **New** from the menu that appears. Click again to begin creating a new task; the **New** screen appears.

4 Enter the Task Details

The first field you must enter for a new task is the name of the task, which should be concise yet descriptive. In the example, I named the task **Do Taxes** as a reminder of when my taxes are due. The **Status** of the task indicates how far you are along in completing the task. Possible options include **Not Started**, **In Progress**, **Completed**, **Waiting**, and **Deferred**. Every task has a priority that is set with the **Priority** field. A task's priority can be set to **Low**, **Normal**, or **High**, with **Normal** being the default setting.

Some tasks have a specific due date, while others are more open-ended. If the task you are creating has a due date, set the **Due** field to **By Date**. After doing so, a date appears below the **Due** field that allows you to specify the due date. Use the trackwheel to scroll through the due date and set the exact date and time for the task.

Regardless of the due date, every task has a time zone associated with it. The **Time Zone** field defaults to the time zone you set for your device; see **3 Set the Date and Time**.

An important part of creating a task is establishing a reminder for it. Not every task requires a reminder, but many do. Decide whether you want to be reminded on a specific date or relative to the due date of the task. I recommend the latter approach because, if you change the due date at some point in the future, the reminder will automatically change. To set a relative reminder, select **Relative** in the **Reminder** field and choose an amount of time before the due date for the reminder. To set a reminder for a specific date, select **By Date** for the **Reminder** field and then select a date.

The **Recurrence** field enables you to create a task that recurs on a regular schedule. A good example of a recurring task is an expense report you must file once a month. To set the task as a recurring task, change the **Recurrence** field from **None** to **Daily**, **Weekly**, **Monthly**, or **Yearly**. Based on this setting, additional fields appear that enable you to get more specific about the task recurrence. You can get very detailed with the recurrence of a task. For example, you can select **Weekly** in the **Recurrence** field and then select **2** in the **Every** field that appears. Then select **M** and **F** as the days for the recurring task, and the task will take place every other Monday and Friday.

▶ **NOTE**
When you create a recurring task, only one instance of the task appears until you complete the task; make sure you don't mark the task completed until after you finish creating it. At that point, the completed task is shown with a completion icon next it, while the next occurrence of the task immediately appears as a new task.

The last two properties of the new task allow you to categorize the task and add extra notes about it. Extra notes are entirely up to your discretion and whether you have extra information to enter about the task. The **Categories** field enables you to choose categories for the task, which can be helpful in organizing tasks. When you double-click the **Categories** field, the **Select Categories** screen appears. You have complete control over these categories and can create and delete them as part of the organization of PIM data, including tasks.

5 Select Categories for the Task

The **Select Categories** screen enables you to select one or more categories that apply to the task. This is a handy way to organize tasks. For example, I selected **Personal** as the category for the **Do Taxes** task to indicate that this is a personal task that has nothing to do with work. You might opt to create detailed categories to further distinguish between different types of work tasks; see **78 Apply Categories to Tasks**.

6 Save and View the Task

When you finish editing the new task, click the trackwheel, select **Save** from the menu that appears, and click again. The new task is saved and added to the task list. Any reminders you set for the task are activated.

7 Mark the Task Completed

When you create a task, it appears in the task list with a small icon to the left of it that indicates its current status. You can easily distinguish between completed versus not-started or in-progress tasks by looking at their icons; you can also double-click a task to see all its details. By double-clicking and editing a task, you can access the **Status** field and change it to update the status of the task. There is also a shortcut for marking tasks as **Completed**—just click the task, select **Mark Completed** from the menu that appears, and click again.

▶ TIPS

You can also reverse the status of a completed task back to **In Progress** by clicking the task, selecting **Mark In Progress** from the menu that appears, and clicking again.

To delete a task regardless of its status, click the task, select **Delete** from the menu that appears, and click again. A pop-up confirmation window appears—just click **Delete** to confirm the deletion. If the task is a recurring task, you'll be prompted to **Delete All Events**, **Delete First Event**, or **Cancel** the deletion. You can also delete all completed tasks at once by clicking anywhere in the **Tasks** application, selecting **Delete Completed**, and clicking again.

78 Apply Categories to Tasks

✔ BEFORE YOU BEGIN	→ SEE ALSO
77 Create and Manage Tasks	70 Apply Categories to Contacts 79 Tweak Task Options

Categories are used throughout the BlackBerry personal information management system to help you organize address book contacts, tasks, and memos. Within the **Tasks** application, you use categories to identify and distinguish between tasks. You can then use categories to filter the main task list according to a certain category. The **Tasks** application provides the capability to create new categories, delete existing categories, and assign categories to tasks.

1 Open the Applications Screen

Scroll to the **Applications** icon on the **Home** screen and click the trackwheel. The **Applications** screen appears, displaying a list of applications, including the **Tasks** application.

78 Apply Categories to Tasks

1 Open the Applications Screen

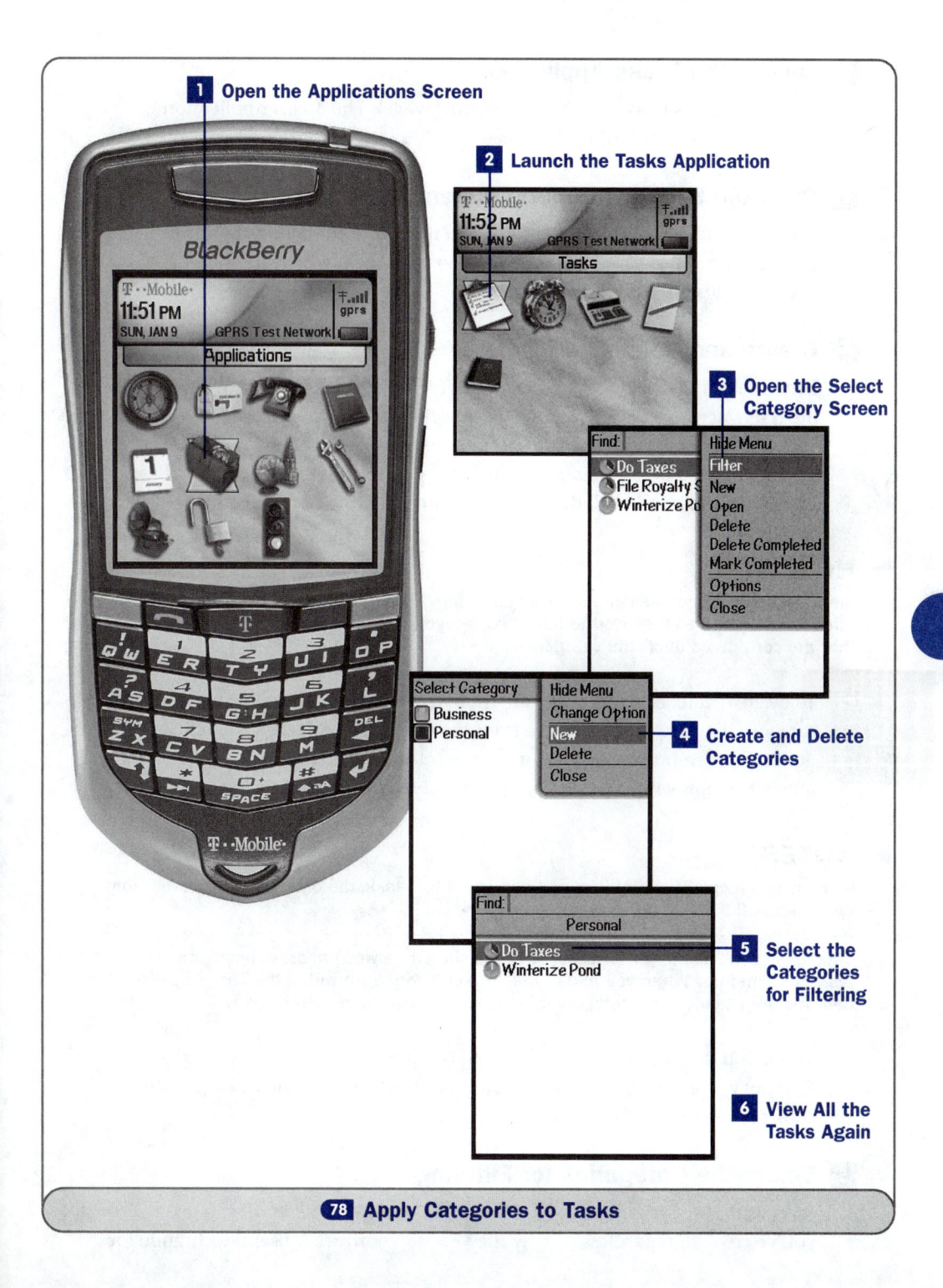

2 Launch the Tasks Application

3 Open the Select Category Screen

4 Create and Delete Categories

5 Select the Categories for Filtering

6 View All the Tasks Again

78 Apply Categories to Tasks

2 Launch the Tasks Application

Scroll to the **Tasks** icon and click the trackwheel. The **Tasks** application is launched and displayed on the screen.

3 Open the Select Category Screen

Click the trackwheel and scroll to select **Filter** from the menu that appears. Click once more to open the **Select Category** screen, which shows a list of categories from which you can select.

4 Create and Delete Categories

Before selecting a category or categories for the task, you might want to create a few new categories or delete an existing one. To create a new category, click the trackwheel, select **New** from the menu that appears, and click again. A dialog box appears that prompts you for the name of the category. Enter the name and click the trackwheel to create the new category.

▶ **NOTE**

Although category names can be mixed case, they aren't distinguishable by case. In other words, you aren't allowed to have two categories named **Business** and **BUSINESS**; they are considered duplicate categories.

To delete a category, just scroll the trackwheel to select the category in the category list, click, select **Delete** from the menu that appears, and click again. You are prompted to confirm the category deletion—click **Delete** to follow through with the deletion or **Cancel** to cancel the deletion.

▶ **NOTES**

If you delete a category that is already assigned to a task, the category is removed from the task but the task itself is not deleted.

Categories don't just apply to tasks. They are shared between address book contacts, tasks, and memos. When you add or delete a category from within the **Tasks** application, you are changing the categories for contacts, tasks, and memos as well.

When you finish creating and deleting categories, you can use the **Select Category** screen to filter tasks so that only the tasks assigned to a particular category are shown in the task list.

5 Select the Categories for Filtering

By default, the task list shown in the **Tasks** application lists all the tasks you've created, regardless of how they are categorized. A useful technique for isolating tasks in a smaller view is to filter the task list based on categories. For example, if you select a category for filtering, only the tasks set to that category are displayed in the task list.

To filter the task list from the **Select Category** screen, scroll to select a category and double-click the trackwheel. You immediately return to the task list, which now has a heading above the tasks that shows on which category the tasks are being filtered. In the example, I'm filtering tasks based on the **Personal** category so only personal tasks are displayed in the task list.

6 View All the Tasks Again

To restore the full list of tasks, click the trackwheel, select **Filter** from the menu that appears, and click again. In the **Select Category** screen, double-click the selected category to deselect it; the main task list appears with all the tasks again in view.

79 Tweak Task Options

✔ **BEFORE YOU BEGIN**

77 Create and Manage Tasks

→ **SEE ALSO**

78 Apply Categories to Tasks

The **Tasks** application includes a few options that enable you to fine-tune the manner in which the application displays tasks. The options made available by the **Tasks** application also allow you to do away with the delete confirmation prompt that appears whenever you delete a task. Although doing away with this prompt can be a time-saver, it does make it easier to accidentally delete tasks. In addition to offering a couple of useful option settings, the **Tasks** application provides a quick and easy way to determine how many tasks you have active.

1 Open the Applications Screen

Scroll to the **Applications** icon on the **Home** screen and click the trackwheel. The **Applications** screen appears, showing a list of applications, including the **Tasks** application.

2 Launch the Tasks Application

Scroll to the **Tasks** icon and click the trackwheel. The **Tasks** application is launched and displayed on the screen.

CHAPTER 13: Organizing Your To-Do List with Tasks

1 Open the Applications Screen

2 Launch the Tasks Application

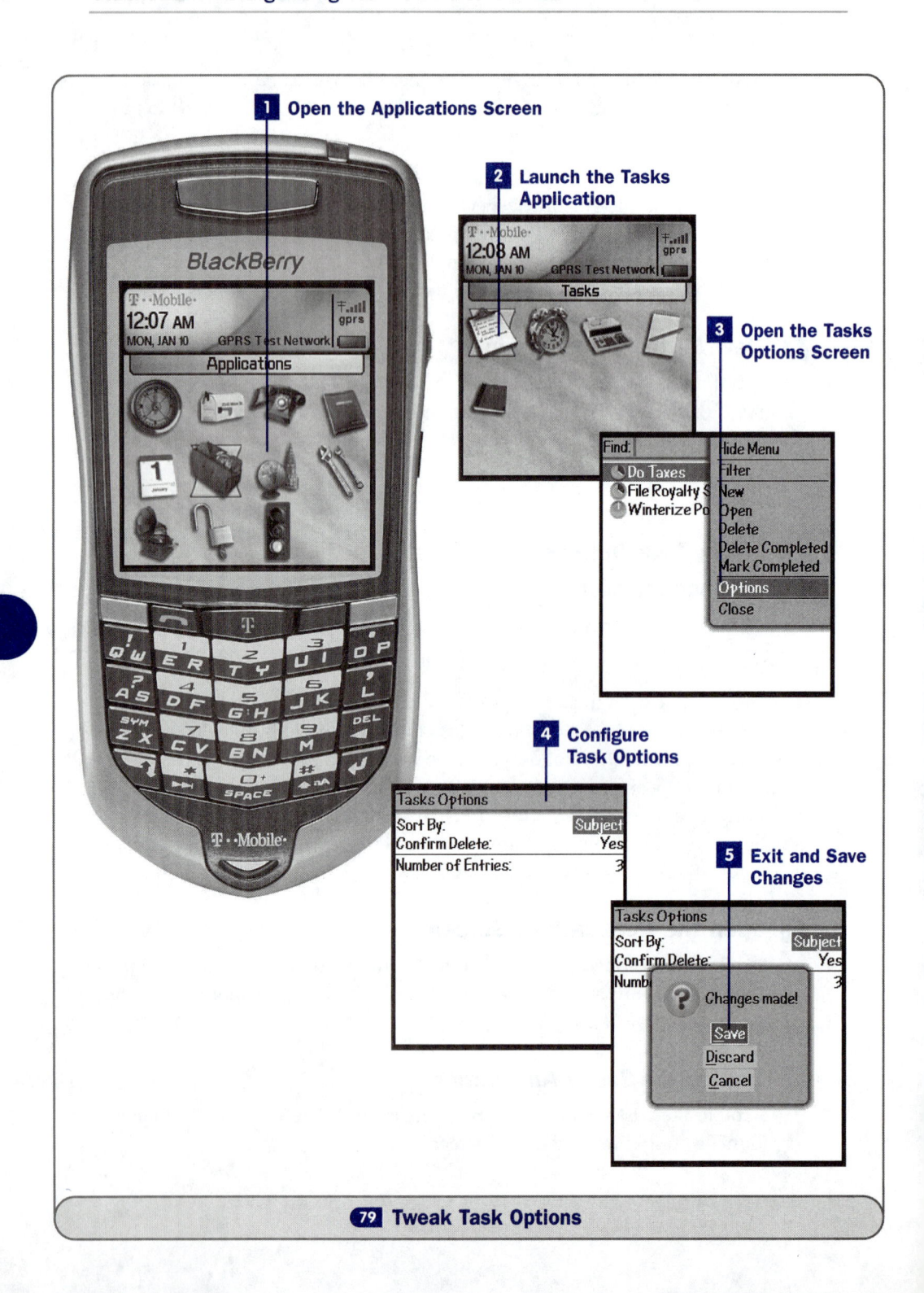

3 Open the Tasks Options Screen

4 Configure Task Options

5 Exit and Save Changes

79 Tweak Task Options

3 Open the Tasks Options Screen

Click the trackwheel and select **Options** from the menu that appears. Click once more to open the **Tasks Options** screen.

4 Configure Task Options

The **Tasks Options** screen includes a couple options that control how tasks are displayed and how they are deleted, as well as a purely informational statistic about how many tasks you currently have active. The first option, **Sort By**, determines the order in which tasks are displayed in the task list. You can use the **Sort By** field to sort tasks by **Subject**, **Priority**, **Due Date**, or **Status**.

▶ **TIP**

The **Sort By** setting is obviously up to your own personal needs, but I find that sorting tasks by **Due Date** is typically the most helpful because it allows me to see the tasks in chronological order. Alternatively, if you want to get a feel for where each task lies in terms of completion, sort by **Status**.

The **Confirm Delete** option is the other option on the **Tasks Options** screen, and it controls whether you are prompted to confirm the deletion of a task. The default value of this setting is **Yes**, which requires you to agree to a prompt before deleting a task. Unless you don't mind the risk of accidentally deleting a task, I recommend keeping the default setting.

The **Number of Entries** field on the **Tasks Options** screen isn't an option but instead provides you with the total number of tasks on your device. This piece of information can help you get a handle on how much work you have ahead of you in terms of a total task count.

5 Exit and Save Changes

When you're finished configuring task options, press the **Escape** button. If you made changes to any of the options, you are prompted to save them. Click **Save** to keep the changes or **Discard** to ignore the changes.

14

Getting the Most Out of Helper Applications

IN THIS CHAPTER:

- **80** Stay on Schedule with an Alarm
- **81** Make Notes with the MemoPad
- **82** Crunch Numbers with the Calculator
- **83** Manage Pictures with the Photo Album
- **84** Monitor Traffic and Surveillance Remotely
- **85** Use Your Device As a Flashlight and Mirror
- **86** Use Your Device As a High-tech Golf Scorecard

CHAPTER 14: Getting the Most Out of Helper Applications

There is no arguing that the bread-and-butter applications on the BlackBerry 7100 series of devices are text messaging, the mobile phone, and browsing the wireless Web. In some ways, everything else on 7100 devices comes secondary to these primary applications. However, that doesn't mean there aren't some useful BlackBerry applications for you to take advantage of and benefit from. Whether you use a built-in application already installed on your device or you purchase and download a third-party application, there is a lot to be said for expanding your device's usefulness through helper applications.

Some of the handy built-in applications you should consider using include the Alarm, MemoPad, Calculator, and Photo Album applications. You might want to look into the many third-party add-on applications available, depending on your specific needs and interests. A few popular applications I've found to be interesting include a live traffic and video surveillance monitor, an application that turns your device into a flashlight, and an electronic golf scorecard application. These applications are covered in detail in the remaining tasks in this chapter.

▶ **WEB RESOURCE**
www.handango.com

www.rimroad.com
Handango and Rim Road are a couple of my favorite online places to find BlackBerry applications.

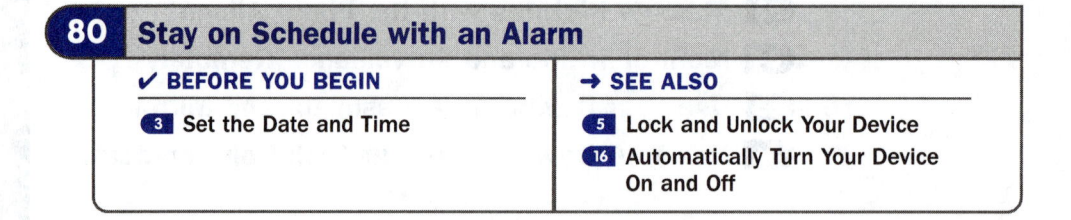

80 Stay on Schedule with an Alarm

✔ **BEFORE YOU BEGIN**
③ Set the Date and Time

→ **SEE ALSO**
⑤ Lock and Unlock Your Device
⑯ Automatically Turn Your Device On and Off

I don't travel a great deal, but when I do I've noticed that it's a pain to have to pack and carry an alarm clock that usually gets used only once or twice on the trip. Of course, when I do travel, I'm often staying in hotels, so I can rely on a wake-up call from the front desk to replace an alarm clock of my own. However, I'm one of those people who likes to get several chances at waking up, and it's tough to negotiate snooze calls from a hotel. So, I'm back to needing an alarm clock because I want a snooze feature. Thankfully, my BlackBerry device includes a handy little alarm clock that does a great job filling in for a traditional, portable alarm clock. And most importantly, it includes a snooze feature!

80 Stay on Schedule with an Alarm 317

1 Open the Applications Screen

2 Launch the Alarm Application

3 Set the Alarm Time and Frequency

4 Set the Alarm Tune and Volume

5 Dismiss the Alarm

80 Stay on Schedule with an Alarm

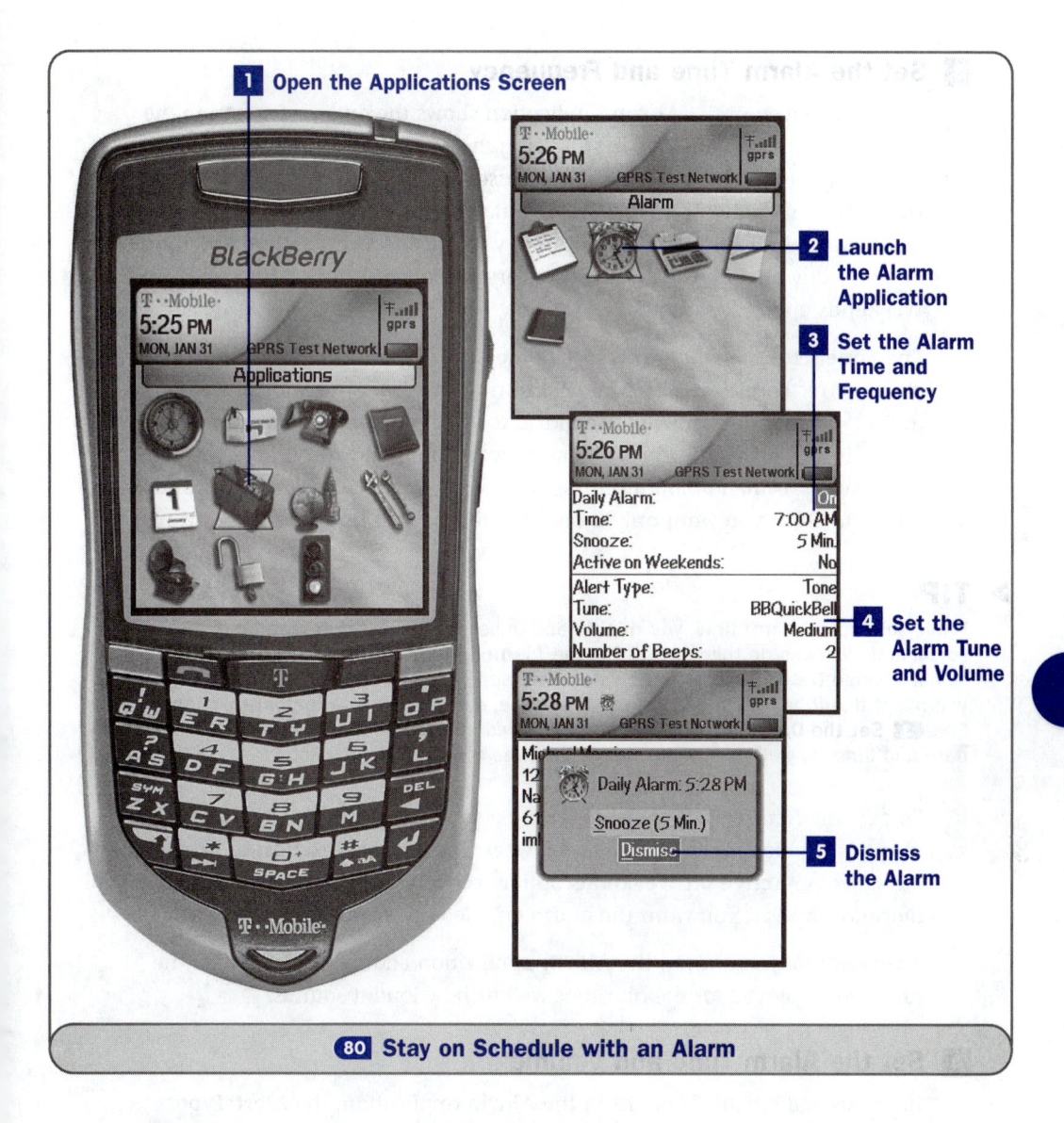

1 Open the Applications Screen

Scroll to the **Applications** icon on the **Home** screen and click the trackwheel. The **Applications** screen appears, showing a list of applications you can launch.

2 Launch the Alarm Application

Scroll to the **Alarm** icon and click the trackwheel. The **Alarm** application launches and appears.

3 Set the Alarm Time and Frequency

The main screen of the **Alarm** application shows the options for setting the alarm; you can set only one alarm using the **Alarm** application (although you can reset the alarm as often as necessary). The first option on the screen, **Daily Alarm**, enables and disables the alarm. The alarm is designed to be a daily alarm, so by enabling this option, you are effectively setting the alarm for every day of the week, or at least every weekday (if the **Active on Weekends** option is set to **Off**).

The **Time** setting is where you specify the time of the alarm—be very careful about correctly setting the **AM** or **PM** part of the time. The **Snooze** setting indicates how long you want the alarm to wait between snoozes. In other words, if the alarm goes off and you indicate that you want it to snooze, it will wait a specified amount of time and go off again. You can set the **Snooze** option to **Off** if you want only a one-shot alarm with no snooze feature.

▶ **TIP**

While setting the alarm time, you might need to set the current date and time. Fortunately, you can do this from within the **Alarm** application—just click the trackwheel, select **Change Date/Time** from the menu that appears, and click again. When traveling, you might find it helpful to change the time zone, even if it's just a temporary change. See **3 Set the Date and Time** for more detailed information about how to set the date and time, as well as how to change the time zone.

Finally, the **Active on Weekends** setting is where you specify whether the alarm is enabled for every day of the week (including weekends) or just weekdays. Set the **Active on Weekends** option to **No** if you only want a weekday alarm or to **Yes** if you want the alarm enabled all week long.

The remaining settings in the **Alarm** application enable you to specify the tune that is played for the alarm as well as how loud it sounds.

4 Set the Alarm Tune and Volume

In the second batch of options in the **Alarm** application, the **Alert Type** option determines the type of the alarm, which can be one of the following settings: **Tone**, **Vibrate**, or **Vibrate+Tone**. Although most people opt for the traditional **Tone** setting, in some circumstances you might want to be more subtle and use the **Vibrate** setting—just be sure you place your device on a surface where the vibration will get your attention (under your pillow maybe). To maximize the attention given out by the alarm, set the alert type to **Vibrate+Tone**.

Your BlackBerry device comes equipped with several ring tones, also known as *tunes*, which are also used to drive the alarm. The **Tune** option is where

80 Stay on Schedule with an Alarm

you select the tune that is played as the alarm sounds. Double-click the **Tune** option and scroll the list; listen to each sound until you find a good one for the alarm.

▶ **TIP**
Because the **Alarm** application relies on ring tones (tunes) as the basis for the alarm sound, you can download custom tunes to use for the alarm sound. I once set my traditional alarm clock to a radio station I liked…and I found that I sometimes slept through the music because it was music I liked. No problem—I simply changed the radio station to music I hated, and getting up got much easier! So, seek out an annoying tune that drives you crazy, and it will make a perfect alarm sound. See **52 Download New Ring Tones** to find out how to download new ring tones.

The alarm volume is just as important as the tune you select for the alarm. The **Volume** option is where you establish the volume of the alarm. This option can be set to one of the following values: **Low**, **Medium**, **High**, or **Escalating**. The **Escalating** setting results in an alarm that starts out low and gradually grows in volume to get louder. Use **Escalating** if you want an alarm that arouses you gently, or select **Medium** or **High** for a more direct approach; I can't imagine the **Low** setting being loud enough to wake anyone.

▶ **TIP**
Be sure to test the alarm volume in a setting similar to that in which you will be using it. You might need to set the volume a little louder than you initially thought to overcome other ambient noises.

The **Number of Beeps** setting determines how many times the tune is played for the alarm sound. This setting has a lot to do with the kind of tune you select. A short-and-sweet tune might require several beeps, while a full-length song will likely require only a single beep. Your options for this setting are limited to **1**, **2**, or **3**, so there isn't much flexibility with the number of beeps.

After configuring the alarm settings, click the trackwheel and select **Save** from the menu that appears. Click once more to save the settings. Now you can press the **Escape** button to exit the application and go about your business knowing that the alarm is now set and ready to go.

5 **Dismiss the Alarm**

When the alarm time rolls around, the alarm sounds and your device's screen turns on. If the **Snooze** option is enabled, you are given two options: snooze or dismiss the alarm. Snoozing causes the alarm to stop and reactivate soon thereafter based on the snooze time you set. Dismissing the alarm causes it to stop indefinitely—or at least until it is scheduled to go off again on the following day.

▶ **NOTE**
Your device must be powered off, locked, or in its holster for the alarm to sound. The idea is that you don't need the alarm to go off if the device is in use.

---

81 Make Notes with the MemoPad

→ **SEE ALSO**

🔲 **70** Apply Categories to Contacts
🔲 **78** Apply Categories to Tasks

Most people are familiar with the popular Post-It notes that are widely used in kitchens and on desks the world over. The concept of a Post-It note is simple but incredibly powerful: to provide a way of jotting down a quick piece of information that you don't want to forget. Just about any small piece of information can be written on such a note: a grocery list, a doctor's appointment reminder, a sketch for a process or product, and so on. I've personally used notes for all three of these types of information, and many more. So, what does this have to do with your BlackBerry?

BlackBerry devices include a built-in application called MemoPad that in many ways serves as an electronic Post-It note. MemoPad takes the Post-It idea to another level in that it allows you to assign each note a title and categorize it if you so desire. But the main idea behind the MemoPad application is to simply give you a convenient place on your BlackBerry to enter bite-size pieces of text information.

1 Open the Applications Screen

Scroll to the **Applications** icon on the **Home** screen and click the trackwheel. The **Applications** screen appears, showing a list of applications you can launch.

2 Launch the MemoPad Application

Scroll to the **MemoPad** icon and click the trackwheel. The **MemoPad** application launches and appears.

81 Make Notes with the MemoPad

1 Open the Applications Screen

2 Launch the MemoPad Application

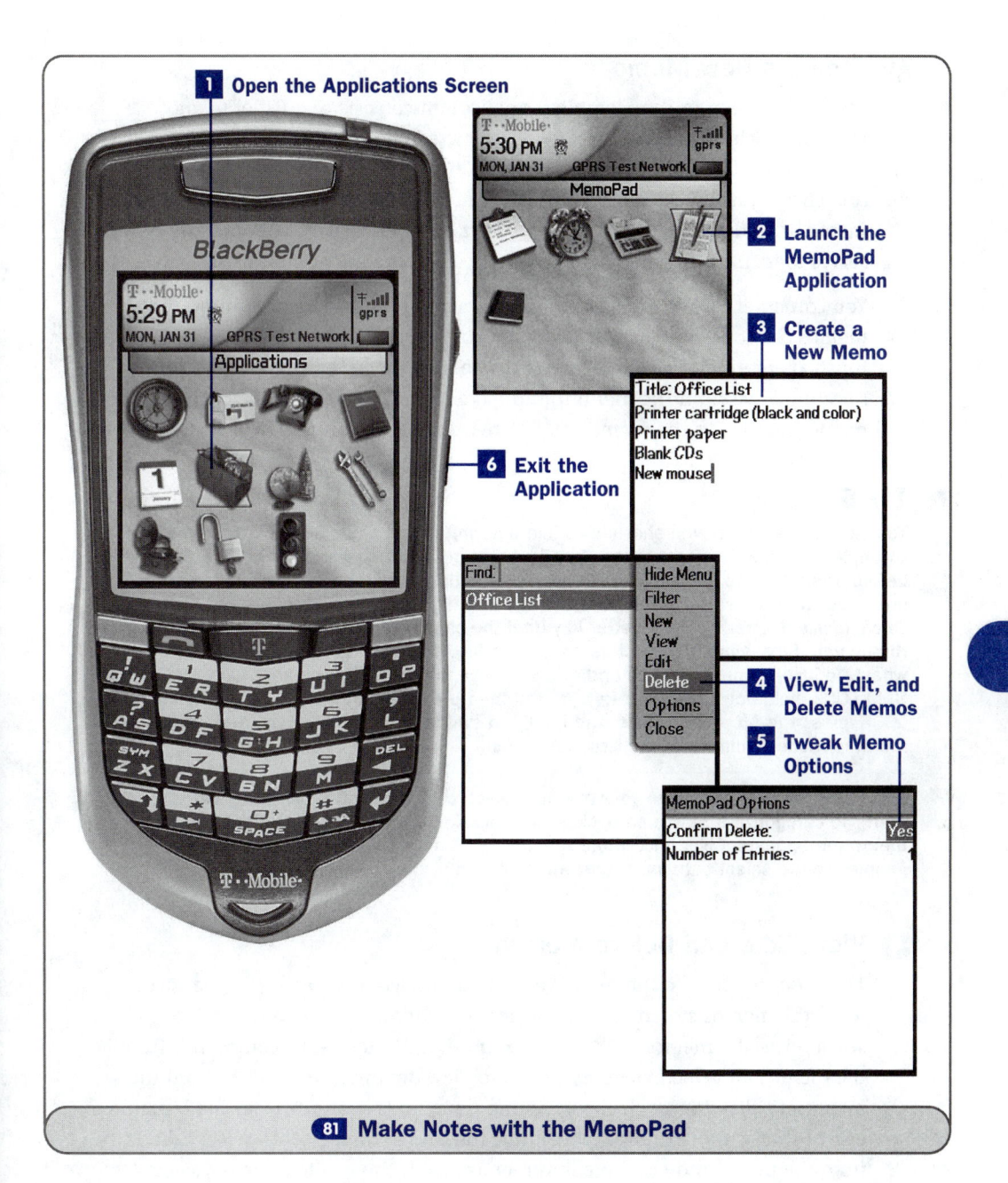

3 Create a New Memo

4 View, Edit, and Delete Memos

5 Tweak Memo Options

6 Exit the Application

81 Make Notes with the MemoPad

3 Create a New Memo

The main screen in the MemoPad application consists of a list of memos (notes), which is empty if you haven't yet created any memos. To create a new memo, click the trackwheel, select **New** from the menu that appears, and click again. A screen appears that enables you to enter details about the memo, including the title and memo text. After entering a suitable title that serves to identify the memo, you next focus on the memo text itself.

You can enter any text you want as the memo text. Just keep in mind that memos are composed as raw text with no special formatting. When you're finished entering the memo text, save the memo by clicking the trackwheel, selecting **Save** from the menu that appears, and then clicking once more. The memo is added to the memo list, where it is easily identified by its title.

▶ TIPS

You can use several typing shortcuts while entering text on your BlackBerry device. For example, to make the most of the *SureType* feature, enter an entire word letter by letter before attempting to select from the list of corrections. If you must make a correction, press the **Next** key (*) or scroll the trackwheel to highlight the correction, and then click. To capitalize a letter, hold the letter key until the capitalized letter appears. To scroll through all the available characters on a given key, hold the key and scroll the trackwheel. To insert a period at the end of a sentence, press the **Space** key twice. To turn on NUM LOCK, hold down the **Shift** key (#) and then press the **Alt** key; to turn off NUM LOCK, press the **Alt** key by itself. And finally, to switch between SureType and traditional multitap modes, hold down the **Next** key (*).

You might want to categorize your memos so you can filter and more easily sift through them. To categorize a new memo, click the trackwheel and select **Categories** from the menu that appears. Click once more to open the **Select Categories** screen, which enables you to select categories that are assigned to the memo.

4 View, Edit, and Delete Memos

The list of memos on the main **MemoPad** application screen provides access to all the memos stored on your device. To manage the memos, scroll to select a specific memo, click the trackwheel, and then select commands from the menu that appears. For example, to view a memo, select **View** from the menu and click the trackwheel. Editing a memo is similar to viewing a memo except that you are allowed to change the title or memo text—select **Edit** from the menu and click to edit a memo. Finally, to delete a memo, select **Delete** from the menu and click. You are prompted to confirm the deletion; click **Delete** to move forward with the deletion or click **Cancel** if you change your mind.

82 Crunch Numbers with the Calculator   323

▶ **TIP**
If you've taken the time to categories your memos, you can filter the memo list according to categories by clicking the trackwheel and selecting **Filter** from the menu that appears. Click once more to open the **Select Categories** screen, from which you can select the category of memos you want to show in the memo list; memos associated with a category you don't select aren't shown in the list. The exception to this rule is if you select a category to which no memos are assigned, which results in all the memos being shown. To restore the full unfiltered list of memos, just unselect the filter category.

5 Tweak Memo Options

The **MemoPad** application provides access to an options screen that allows you to set a single memo option and view your memo statistics. To open the **MemoPad Options** screen, start from the memo list, click the trackwheel, select **Options** from the menu that appears, and click again.

The **MemoPad Options** screen includes only one option, **Confirm Delete**, which is used to specify whether you want to confirm the deletion of memos. Setting this option to **No** speeds up the process of deleting memos, but it also removes the safeguard that prevents you from accidentally deleting a memo.

The **Number of Entries** field on the **MemoPad Options** screen isn't an option but instead provides you with the total number of memos on your device. This piece of information can help you quickly assess how many memos you have lying around.

6 Exit the Application

Press the **Escape** button to exit the application. Press the **Escape** button again to navigate back to the **Home** screen, or just press the **End** key once to exit the application and return directly to the **Home** screen.

82 Crunch Numbers with the Calculator

Whether it's calculating the tip at a restaurant or attempting to get a ballpark estimate on a mortgage payment, sometimes a pocket calculator is an invaluable tool. Because few of us have enough nerd pride to boldly carry a pocket calculator with us at all times, we have to settle for whatever else is handy. Fortunately, your BlackBerry device includes a calculator that works well for basic calculations, not to mention converting between English and metric units of measure. Hardcore number crunchers won't be abandoning their spreadsheets and financial calculators to embrace the BlackBerry's software calculator, but it does a great job of carrying out long division in a pinch!

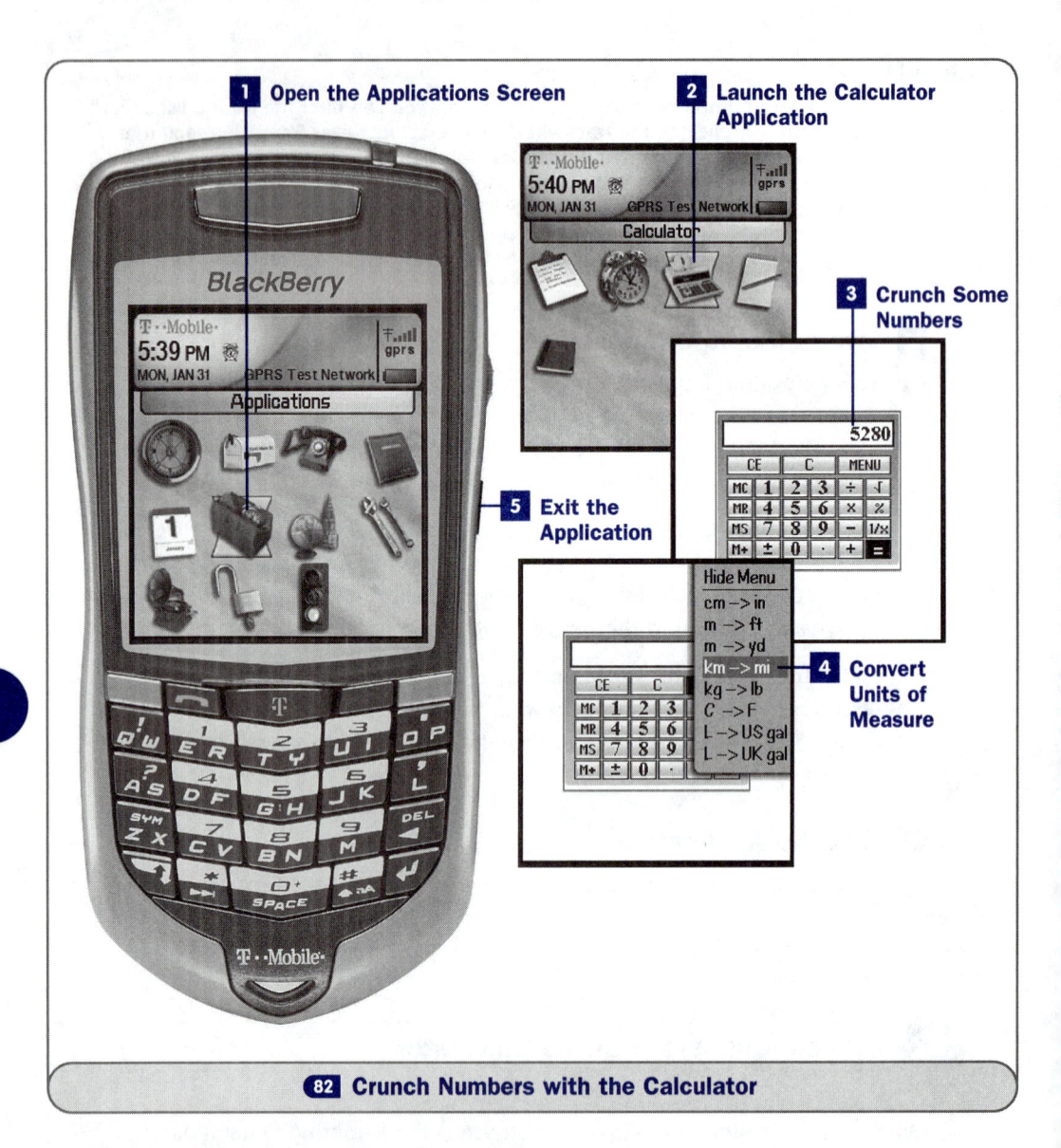

CHAPTER 14: Getting the Most Out of Helper Applications

1 Open the Applications Screen

2 Launch the Calculator Application

3 Crunch Some Numbers

5 Exit the Application

4 Convert Units of Measure

82 Crunch Numbers with the Calculator

1 Open the Applications Screen

Scroll to the **Applications** icon on the **Home** screen and click the trackwheel. The **Applications** screen appears, displaying a list of applications you can launch.

2 Launch the Calculator Application

Scroll to the **Calculator** icon and click the trackwheel. The **Calculator** application launches and appears.

3 Crunch Some Numbers

The **Calculator** application provides the basic functionality of a run-of-the-mill calculator with a few extra bells and whistles. To begin crunching numbers, just type the numbers on the keyboard and use the keys on the calculator's onscreen keyboard to carry out mathematical functions—use the trackwheel to scroll around and click to select the different functions. You can use the **Enter** key as a shortcut for the equals key on the calculator.

▶ **TIPS**

To scroll vertically down the calculator keys onscreen, hold the **Alt** key while scrolling the trackwheel.

The **L** key serves as a shortcut for the calculator's decimal-point key.

If you're like me and you always forget how to use the memory functions on a calculator, here's a brief refresher. The idea behind calculator memory is to allow you to store a single number for use in another calculation. To place a number in memory, type the number and click the **M+** key. To recall the number, click the **MR** key. To clear the number from memory, click the **MC** key. And finally, to replace the number with another number, type the new number and click the **MS** key. Also, if you click the **M+** key while a number is already stored in memory, the current number on the screen is *added to* the number in memory. If a number is stored in the calculator memory, it is displayed on the lower-left edge of the calculator.

4 Convert Units of Measure

Aside from allowing you to carry out basic calculations, the **Calculator** application enables you to convert between English and metric units of measure. To carry out such a conversion, type a number and click the **Menu** key on the calculator. Select **To Metric** or **From Metric** on the menu to determine which way you want to convert units. The menu changes to present a list of conversion options. Select the desired option, for example (**km -> mi**) to convert kilometers to miles, and click to carry out the conversion.

5 Exit the Application

Press the **Escape** button to exit the application. Press the **Escape** button again to navigate back to the **Home** screen, or just press the **End** key once to exit the application and return directly to the **Home** screen.

83 Manage Pictures with the Photo Album

→ **SEE ALSO**

   21 Change the Wallpaper
   51 Download New Wallpaper

Even though the BlackBerry 7100 series devices don't include such nifty gadgets as a built-in digital camera, photographs aren't entirely foreign to the BlackBerry experience. More specifically, the standard **Photo Album** application allows you to manage images on your device, including viewing them and setting them as wallpaper. What is somewhat unfortunate is that not every BlackBerry 7100 device is equipped to allow image attachments to email messages. If you use the BlackBerry Enterprise Server, you might have access to image attachments, but if not, it's up to your specific wireless provider to support image attachments. (Some do, some don't, and some support limited image file formats.) Even if your device doesn't allow you to send and receive images using email, you can still download images to your device from your desktop PC or from a website. The **Photo Album** application is how you work with images after they are stored on your device.

▶ **NOTE**
You aren't entirely out of luck if your device doesn't support image attachments in email messages. One option to consider is switching to a third-party email client application on your device. However, a less imposing option is to download an add-on that gives the standard BlackBerry email client image attachment functionality. One such add-on is BBImageViewer by Terratial Technologies. To find out more about BBImageViewer, visit the Terratial website at http://www.terratial.com/.

1 Open the Applications Screen

Scroll to the **Applications** icon on the **Home** screen and click the trackwheel. The **Applications** screen appears, displaying a list of applications you can launch.

2 Launch the Photo Album Application

Scroll to the **Photo Album** icon and click the trackwheel. The **Photo Album** application launches and appears.

3 View an Image

The main screen in the **Photo Album** application shows a list of all the images stored on your device, including a small thumbnail view of each image. To open and view an image, scroll the trackwheel to select the image, click, and then select **Open** from the menu that appears. Click once more, and the image is opened in full view on the screen.

83 Manage Pictures with the Photo Album

1 Open the Applications Screen

2 Launch the Photo Album Application

3 View an Image

4 Delete an Image

5 Exit the Application

83 Manage Pictures with the Photo Album

▶ TIPS

To cycle forward and backward through the images while viewing them, click the trackwheel, select **Previous** or **Next** from the menu, and click again.

You can set the **Home** screen image (wallpaper) from within the **Photo Album** application by selecting an image, clicking the trackwheel, and selecting **Set As Home Screen Image** from the menu. Click once more, and the selected image is set as the wallpaper. To reset the wallpaper to the default wallpaper, click, select **Reset Home Screen Image** from the menu, and click again. See 51 **Download New Wallpaper** for information on how to download new wallpaper images.

4 Delete an Image

You can delete an image from the image list or while viewing the image by clicking the trackwheel and selecting **Delete** from the menu that appears. Click once more to delete the image. You are prompted to confirm the deletion; click **Delete** to move forward with the deletion or click **Cancel** if you change your mind and decide to keep the image.

5 Exit the Application

Press the **Escape** button to exit the application. Press the **Escape** button once again to navigate back to the **Home** screen, or just press the **End** key once to exit the application and return directly to the **Home** screen.

---

84 Monitor Traffic and Surveillance Remotely

✔ **BEFORE YOU BEGIN**

50 Install a New Application Over-the-Air

To be brutally honest, very few wireless networks are currently operating at fast enough speeds to do much useful in the way of networked multimedia. *Networked multimedia* involves transferring video, music, and even large images over a wireless network. Still, even considering current wireless bandwidth limitations, some wireless multimedia applications can be useful now. For example, monitoring remote cameras using your mobile device can be incredibly empowering. Whether you're checking the flow of traffic to decide on a route home or monitoring your home security while away on a trip, wireless video monitoring is an enticing way to get the most out of your BlackBerry device.

You can go about monitoring a remote camera feed in a variety of ways. One application is particularly flexible in providing access to remote cameras: Terratial LIVE by Terratial Technologies. This application allows you to use your BlackBerry device to tap into both traffic cams (SkipTraffic LIVE) and security cams (Surveillance LIVE). All Terratial's online monitoring services require a subscription and fee, but you can try the service free by simply downloading the Terratial LIVE software.

84 Monitor Traffic and Surveillance Remotely

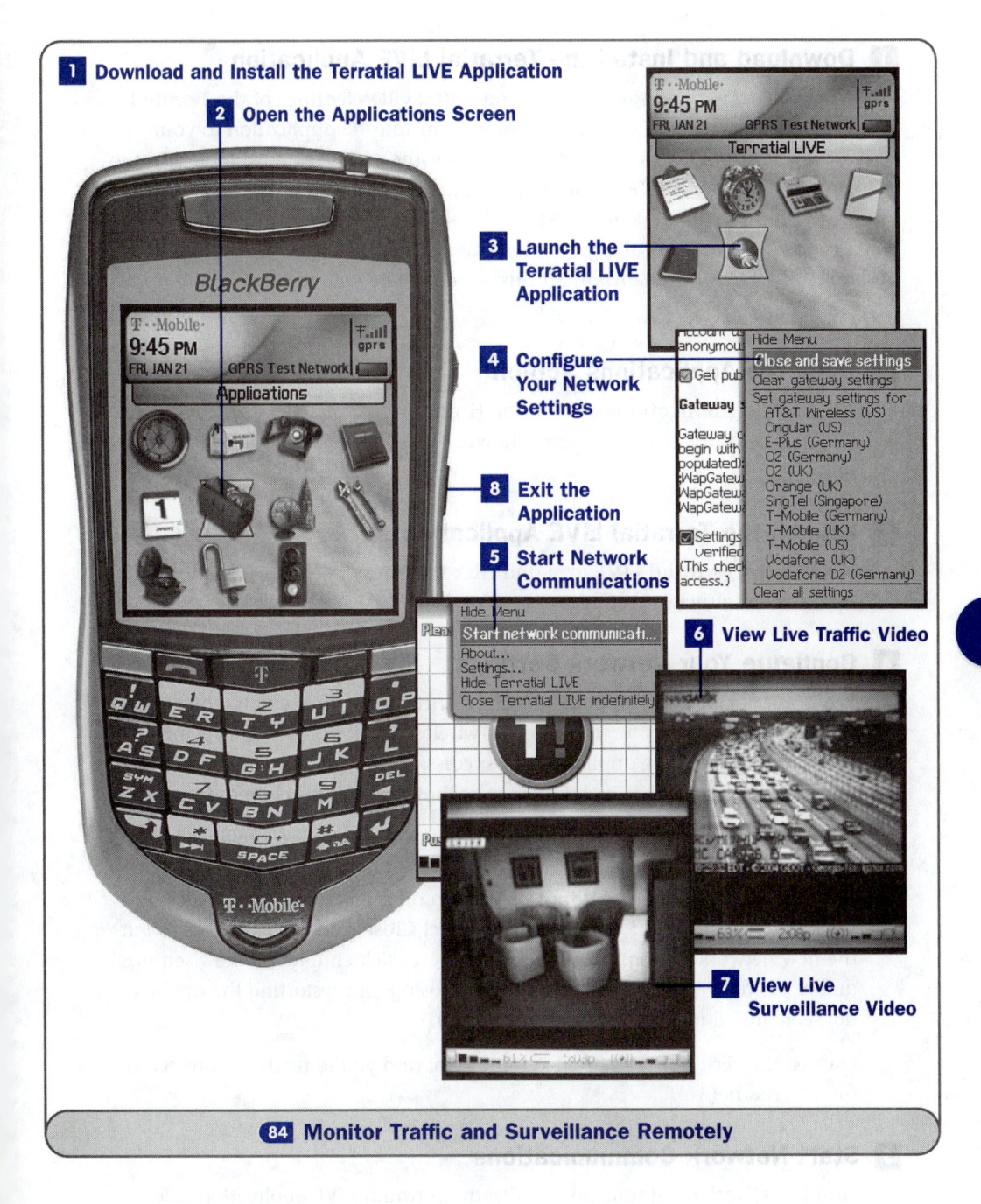

1 Download and Install the Terratial LIVE Application

2 Open the Applications Screen

3 Launch the Terratial LIVE Application

4 Configure Your Network Settings

8 Exit the Application

5 Start Network Communications

6 View Live Traffic Video

7 View Live Surveillance Video

84 Monitor Traffic and Surveillance Remotely

1. Download and Install the Terratial LIVE Application

To try the traffic and surveillance monitoring video features of the Terratial LIVE application, you must download and install the application to your device. Terratial LIVE is available as an over-the-air (OTA) download direct to your device from the Terratial website at http://www.terratial.com/downloads. Just visit this URL on your BlackBerry browser and follow the directions for downloading and installing the application. After you install Terratial LIVE, an icon is added to the **Applications** screen where you can launch the application.

2. Open the Applications Screen

Scroll to the **Applications** icon on the **Home** screen and click the trackwheel. The **Applications** screen appears, showing a list of applications you can launch.

3. Launch the Terratial LIVE Application

Scroll to the **Terratial LIVE** icon and click the trackwheel. The Terratial LIVE application launches and appears.

4. Configure Your Network Settings

When the Terratial LIVE application first starts, it prompts you to enter network gateway settings for your specific wireless service provider. This information is required for the application to successfully access the wireless network and communicate with Terratial's servers that provide live camera images.

To configure the network settings for your particular wireless provider, click the trackwheel and select your service from the menu that appears.
Click again, and the new settings are shown on the network settings screen. Click to open the menu once more and select **Close and save settings** to put the new network settings into effect. One more click enables the new settings and closes the Terratial LIVE application; closing and restarting the application is required for the settings to take effect.

Launch the Terratial LIVE application again, and you're ready to connect to the wireless network.

5. Start Network Communications

To start network communications with the Terratial LIVE application, click the trackwheel, select **Start network communications** from the menu that appears, and click again. You are then connected to the Terratial servers and given access to live channels. In this scenario, a *channel* is simply a group of

84 Monitor Traffic and Surveillance Remotely

camera feeds. Click the trackwheel to open a menu that shows the channels. If you're trying the demo version of Terratial LIVE, you'll find only a few channels, including a traffic channel and an office surveillance channel.

▶ **NOTE**

Some wireless service providers have limited their wireless Internet access for security purposes. You might have to enter configuration information on your device that is specific to your provider to have full Internet access, which is required for network-aware applications such as Terratial LIVE. The main piece of information you need is the access point name (APN) for your wireless provider, and possibly a username and password. Your provider should be able to provide you with this information, along with how to use it to enable full Internet access on your device.

6 View Live Traffic Video

To view live traffic video, select the traffic channel from the menu and click. In the trial version of Terratial LIVE, the traffic channel is called **AtlantaTrafficViews** and it shows images from traffic cams in Atlanta, Georgia. Your device spends a few moments downloading several camera images and then shows them in sequence by transitioning from one to the next.

▶ **NOTES**

If you're using the trial version of Terratial LIVE to try the application, you might not be shown actual live camera feeds. I noticed that most of the demo channels use archived images as opposed to live images for demonstration purposes.

Terratial's SkipTraffic LIVE service currently offers access to more than 1,500 traffic cams throughout the United States and many more in other countries. These traffic cams are organized according to your personal driving routes, so accessing them is made easy and intuitive.

7 View Live Surveillance Video

To view live surveillance video, select the office surveillance channel on the menu and click. In the trial version of Terratial LIVE, this channel is called **OfficeSurveillance** and it shows images from an unspecified office cam. Your device spends a few moments downloading several camera images and then shows them in sequence by transitioning from one to the next.

▶ **NOTE**

To view your own surveillance cams, you need to subscribe to Terratial's Surveillance LIVE subscription service. This service isn't cheap, at least not for a small office—a 1-year subscription costs about $1,000, over and above the cost of the surveillance cameras.

8 Exit the Application

Press the **Escape** button to exit the application. Press the **Escape** button again to navigate back to the **Home** screen, or just press the **End** key once to exit the application and return directly to the **Home** screen.

---

85 Use Your Device As a Flashlight and Mirror

✔ **BEFORE YOU BEGIN**

11 Install a New Application to Your Device

You probably never thought of your BlackBerry device as potentially serving as such a mundane tool as a flashlight or a mirror. However, an unbelievably simple add-on application enables your device to fill exactly these roles. I'm referring to MyFlashlight, an application developed by Stefan Adrian Burghelea that turns the screen on your device into a flashlight or mirror.

I have to admit to being a little let down that the MyFlashlight application didn't pull any crazy tricks with screen brightness or maybe an unusual refresh rate to generate incredibly increased luminescence. All MyFlashlight does is display a screen that is solid white (flashlight) or solid black (mirror). Even so, the solid white screen does indeed give off enough light to use it as a primitive flashlight, and there really is no other easy way to produce a solid white screen. The solid black screen is considerably less useful as a mirror when you consider that any electronic device with a shiny face can be used similarly. In fact, your BlackBerry screen turns into a "mirror" (solid black) by default any time you leave it alone and the screen shuts off. However, if you find yourself in a pinch and desperately need a flashlight, MyFlashlight could come in very handy.

1 Download and Install the MyFlashlight Application

The MyFlashlight application is available for purchase and download from the Handango mobile software store at http://www.handango.com/. Unfortunately, there isn't a demo version of MyFlashlight, but its purchase price as of this writing is 99¢. After purchasing MyFlashlight from Handango, you download a file to your desktop PC that allows you to install the application to your device. After installing MyFlashlight to your device, an icon is added to the **Applications** screen where you can launch the application.

85 Use Your Device As a Flashlight and Mirror   333

1 Download and Install the MyFlashlight Application

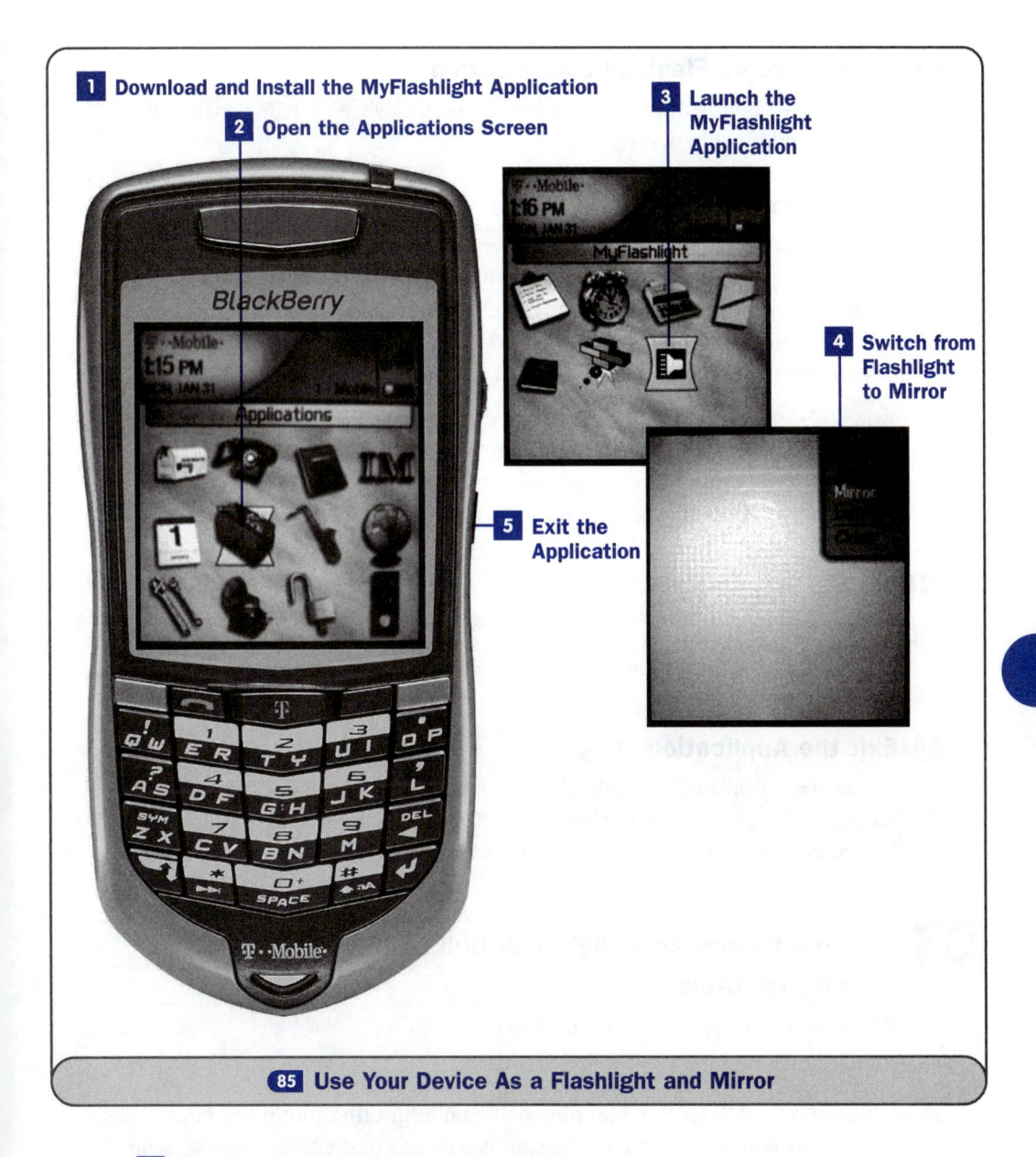

2 Open the Applications Screen

3 Launch the MyFlashlight Application

4 Switch from Flashlight to Mirror

5 Exit the Application

85 Use Your Device As a Flashlight and Mirror

2 Open the Applications Screen

Scroll to the **Applications** icon on the **Home** screen and click the trackwheel. The **Applications** screen appears, showing a list of applications you can launch.

3 Launch the MyFlashlight Application

Scroll to the **MyFlashlight** icon and click the trackwheel. The MyFlashlight application launches and appears.

4 Switch from Flashlight to Mirror

The initial screen for the MyFlashlight application is surprisingly simple. In fact, nothing is shown on it at all, and that's precisely the idea—maximize the number of white pixels on the screen to generate as much light as possible. There are no graphical tricks at work here, but the solid white screen does indeed provide some illumination in the dark.

Switching MyFlashlight to mirror mode simply turns the white screen black so you can see your reflection on the screen. To switch to mirror mode, click the trackwheel and select **Mirror** from the menu that appears. Click once more, and the screen turns black to provide mirror functionality.

▶ **NOTE**

I found the mirror feature of MyFlashlight to be significantly less useful than the flashlight feature. You might or might not decide that it's worth 99¢ for a simplistic flashlight on your device, but I found it to be a neat little application.

5 Exit the Application

To exit the MyFlashlight application, click the trackwheel, select **Exit** from the menu that appears, and click again. Then press the **Escape** button or the **End** button to navigate back to the **Home** screen.

86 Use Your Device As a High-tech Golf Scorecard

✔ **BEFORE YOU BEGIN**

11 Install a New Application to Your Device

Regardless of your skill level, if you play golf, you might find that using your BlackBerry device as an electronic scorecard is a simple and efficient way to keep up with your rounds. Technology has infiltrated the golf world in so many ways that it's a bit surprising more golfers don't already use their handheld devices and mobile phones as electronic scorecards. Now you can add your BlackBerry device alongside titanium club heads and GPS navigation systems on golf carts as a cutting-edge golf technology that can help improve your game.

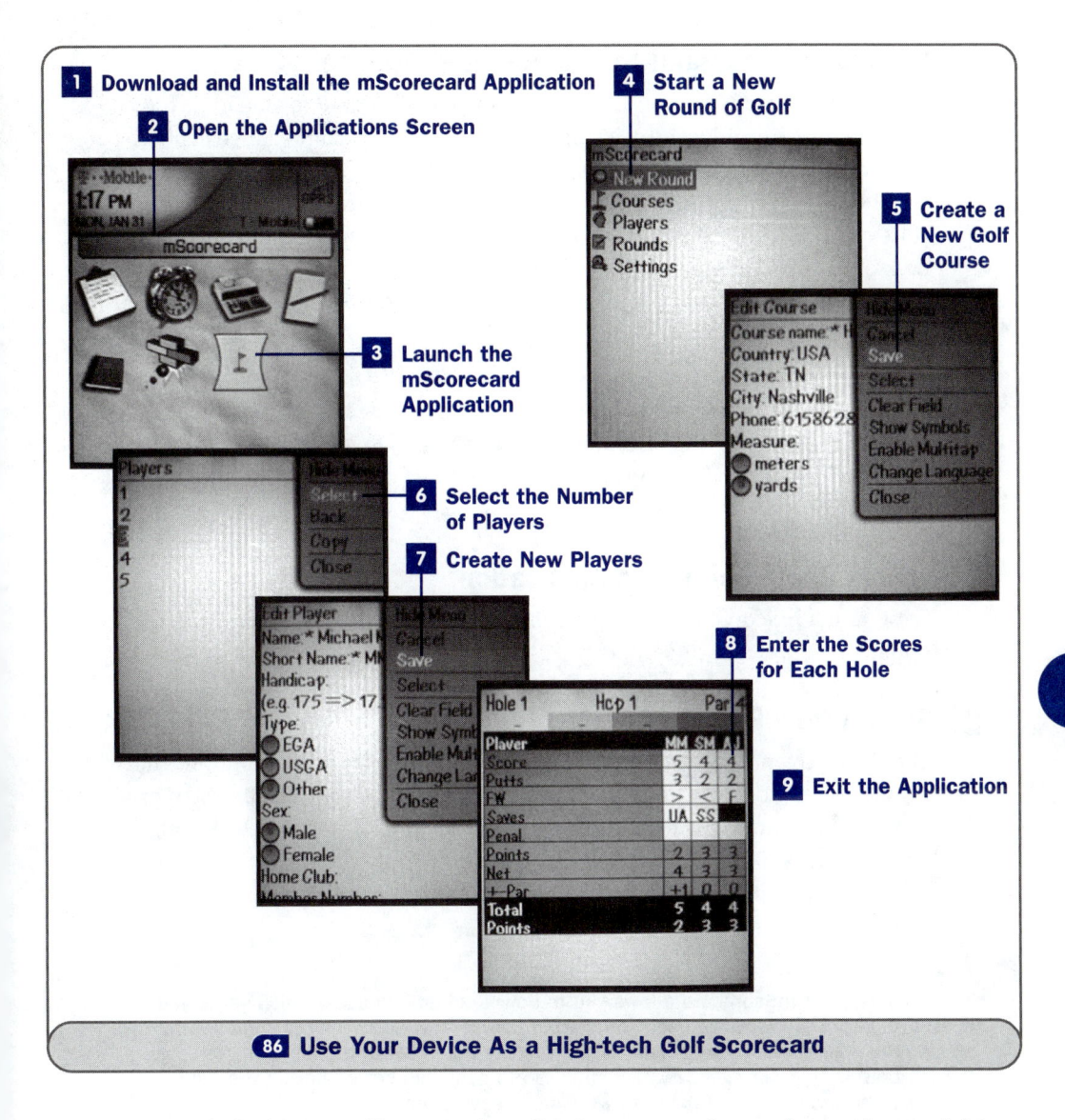

86 Use Your Device As a High-tech Golf Scorecard

1 Download and Install the mScorecard Application

2 Open the Applications Screen

3 Launch the mScorecard Application

4 Start a New Round of Golf

5 Create a New Golf Course

6 Select the Number of Players

7 Create New Players

8 Enter the Scores for Each Hole

9 Exit the Application

86 Use Your Device As a High-tech Golf Scorecard

Several BlackBerry golf scorecard applications are on the market, and you might want to spend some time analyzing each one to get an idea of which one suits your needs the best. Some of the applications I ran across are mScorecard, Wireless18, My Golf Card, and Golf Score Keeper. After tinkering with some of these applications, I decided to focus on mScorecard because it appears to be the most professional and full-featured of the BlackBerry golf applications.

1 Download and Install the mScorecard Application

The mScorecard application is available for purchase and download directly from the mScorecard website at http://www.mscorecard.com/. A free evaluation version of mScorecard allows you to run the application 10 times to see whether you like it; if you decide to purchase the application, its purchase price as of this writing is $19.99. To try mScorecard, download a file to your desktop PC and then install the application to your device. After installing mScorecard to your device, an icon is added to the **Applications** screen where you can launch the application.

2 Open the Applications Screen

Scroll to the **Applications** icon on the **Home** screen and click the trackwheel. The **Applications** screen appears, displaying a list of applications you can launch.

3 Launch the mScorecard Application

Scroll to the **mScorecard** icon and click the trackwheel. The mScorecard application launches and appears.

4 Start a New Round of Golf

The main screen in the mScorecard application includes a list of options that enable you to navigate to different parts of the application. The first step in using the application is to start a new round of golf. To start a new round, scroll the trackwheel to select **New Round** and double-click. The **Select Course** screen opens, which prompts you to select a golf course for the round.

▶ **TIP**

The full version of mScorecard allows you to download golf courses, which saves you the hassle of having to create courses yourself. Of course, this assumes the courses you play are available for download. You can check with the publisher of mScorecard (Velocor Corporation) to find out exactly which courses are available before buying the full version; visit the mScorecard website at www.mscorecard.com.

5 Create a New Golf Course

Unfortunately, because you're using mScorecard for the first time, there are no courses to select for the round. So, select **New Course** in the list and double-click to create a new course. The **Edit Course** screen appears, including several fields for entering details about the golf course. The only field you have to enter is **Course name**, which is simply the name of the golf course. After entering the details about the course, click the trackwheel and select

Save from the menu that appears. Click once more, and the course is saved; the screen changes to a hole-by-hole view of the course. Here you enter information about each hole, such as the par for each hole. An additional screen enables you to enter the slope for the course and other, more detailed, information. You can forego entering all this information for now if you're just trying to get a feel for using the application to keep score.

When you finish editing the new course and save it, you return to the **Select Course** screen where you can select the newly created course. Scroll to select the course and double-click the trackwheel.

6 Select the Number of Players

The next step in starting a new round is to specify the number of players. Just scroll the trackwheel to select the number of players, and then double-click.

7 Create New Players

Of course, mScorecard keeps up with players just as it keeps up with courses. You need to create players in the application that correspond to each of the players in the round. Select **New Player** on the **Player 1** screen and double-click to create a new player. The **Edit Player** screen appears, including several fields for entering details about the player. The only fields you have to enter are **Name** and **Short Name** (two characters), which are used to uniquely identify the player. You can enter as much additional player information here as you want, such as the player's handicap and golf association membership. After entering the details about the player, click the trackwheel and select **Save** from the menu that appears. Click once more, and the player is saved. You have to create a player or a course only once—from then on, you can just select the player when starting a new round or the course when playing on another day.

▶ **NOTE**
The short name of a player is displayed on the scorecard to identify the player, which helps conserve screen space.

You must repeat the player creation process for each player in the round; when you're done, you see each player listed on the **Player 1** screen. The screen is called **Player 1** because it is the screen used to select the first player in the round. So, select one of the newly created players and double-click. You are then asked to select the tee location for the player, after which you are asked to select the second player. Repeat the player selection process to select all the players for the round.

After creating and selecting the players, you are given a chance to enter the handicap for each player for the round. After setting the handicaps for the players, click the trackwheel, select **OK** from the menu that appears, and click again. The round starts and you can now begin entering scores for each hole.

8 Enter the Scores for Each Hole

You can be as detailed as you want when it comes to entering scores for the round of golf. The simplest approach is to just enter the score for each player on each hole, as you are accustomed to doing on a traditional paper golf scorecard. mScorecard takes things a bit further, though, by allowing you to get much more detailed; you can specify the number of putts, fairway hits, saves, and penalties for each hole, to name a few of the additional stats you can track.

▶ **TIP**

To scroll horizontally on the golf scorecard, hold down the **Alt** key while scrolling the trackwheel.

▶ **NOTE**

If you're a gambling golfer, you can use mScorecard to track side games while you're scoring the round. Click the trackwheel, select **Side Games** from the menu that appears, and click again to edit information related to gambling games played on the side.

When you finish entering the score for the first hole, click the trackwheel, select **Next Hole**, and click again. Continue scoring the rounds like this until you're finished playing. mScorecard automatically saves the round as you enter data, so you don't have to worry about saving.

9 Exit the Application

Press the **Escape** button to exit the application. Press the **Escape** button again to navigate back to the **Home** screen, or just press the **End** key once to exit the application and return directly to the **Home** screen.

15

Securing Your BlackBerry Device

IN THIS CHAPTER:

- **87** About BlackBerry Security
- **88** Secure the SIM Card
- **89** Turn On the Firewall
- **90** Protect Your Content
- **91** Safely Store IDs and Passwords on Your Device
- **92** Register Your Device with StuffBak

CHAPTER 15: Securing Your BlackBerry Device

It's difficult to get very far in any discussion about mobile computing without the topic of security coming up. And for good reason. When you start carrying around sensitive data on a mobile device that can communicate wirelessly, security concerns rise dramatically as compared with desktop PCs. There are several reasons for this, with the primary one being how easy it is to lose a mobile device and have it fall into the wrong hands. Another less-obvious but equally troublesome risk is the one associated with wireless networking—people tend to think of mobile devices in terms of mobile phones, but they really are mobile computers. More specifically, in the case of BlackBerry devices, they are mobile computers with a constant wireless network connection.

Fortunately, the BlackBerry 7100 series devices have security designed into virtually every level: Available mechanisms limit access to your device should it accidentally fall into the wrong hands, and a built-in encryption feature encrypts your data. There is also extensive support for advanced security standards to make browsing the wireless Web as safe as, if not safer than, browsing on a desktop PC. In addition to all the BlackBerry device's built-in security measures, you can employ several security strategies to help maximize the protection of your device.

87 About BlackBerry Security

→ **SEE ALSO**

- **5** Lock and Unlock Your Device
- **6** Password-Protect Your Device
- **67** About Bluetooth Security
- **88** Secure the SIM Card
- **89** Turn On the Firewall
- **90** Protect Your Content
- **91** Safely Store IDs and Passwords on Your Device
- **92** Register Your Device with StuffBak

Security on the BlackBerry 7100 series devices can be broken down into several types. Some security features largely work behind the scenes to encrypt data and network connections and generally ensure that no information is left exposed to anyone but you, the intended user. Other security is more visible but still operates more or less without much effort on your part. This latter type of security can be configured to some extent but still provides a basic level of protection without you having to do much. The final type of security is completely on your shoulders. This is perhaps the most important security of all in that it involves you being diligent about how you use your device and how you develop safe work practices to minimize security risks. It's worth examining each of these security types a bit

87 About BlackBerry Security

closer; then we'll focus on what you can do to use your device in a more secure manner.

The folks at Research In Motion (RIM) have gone to great lengths to make the BlackBerry 7100 series device one of the most secure mobile devices on the market. They know that the core user base of BlackBerry products is and has always been corporate users who often access highly sensitive data. For this reason, particular attention has been paid to security. Although it's expected that this security applies to users who have access to the BlackBerry Enterprise Server, you don't have to be a corporate user to benefit from the robust BlackBerry security architecture. As an example, one area where strict security standards are upheld is in the BlackBerry web browser, which supports secure connections through HTTPS, SSL/TLS, and WTLS. The goal behind these technologies is to provide authentication of data sent over a wireless web connection using *cryptography*. More specifically, these technologies prevent electronic eavesdropping, tampering, and forgery of data sent over a wireless connection by *encrypting* the data before it is sent.

▶ **KEY TERMS**

Cryptography—The field of knowledge associated with converting information from its normal, comprehensible format into an incomprehensible format, rendering it unreadable to anyone but the intended recipient.

Encryption—The process of converting information from its normal, comprehensible format into an incomprehensible format, rendering it unreadable to anyone but the intended recipient.

Encryption doesn't apply just to web browsing. If you use the BlackBerry Enterprise Server, encryption again enters the picture thanks to the S/MIME protocol, an email protocol that uses encryption to ensure that email messages can't be eavesdropped on while traveling between sender and recipient. With S/MIME, the sender and recipient each has a *digital signature* that uniquely and safely identifies them to each other. The digital signatures are used as part of the encryption and decryption process.

▶ **KEY TERM**

Digital signature—An electronic ID, logically akin to a handwritten signature, that is used to securely identify a person as well as encrypt and decrypt messages he sends and receives.

In addition to the built-in security features that operate behind the scenes on your device, some security features are a little more visible. As an example, content encryption allows you to encrypt all the data stored on your device so it can't be read or otherwise manipulated in a meaningful way. Although the encryption itself doesn't require any special effort on your part, enabling and disabling it is at your control. Taking a simple step back, the password-protection feature on your device is a security measure that operates seamlessly yet requires your assistance when it comes to enabling and disabling it. The SIM card on your device also offers a fair amount of security in that you can specify a password that allows only you to access the SIM card. If anyone else gets his hands on your phone, or even just the SIM card itself, he can't use it to make calls without the password. Again, this is an example of a security feature that is only as useful as you allow it to be.

The final type of security I alluded to earlier is more strategic than technological in nature. And because of this, it is the most important security of all. The worst mistake you can make as a BlackBerry user—or a user of any mobile device for that matter—is to rely on the built-in security of your device too much. It's not that I don't trust the built-in technological security features, it's just that I know people have a way of cleverly figuring out how to exploit human weakness. Therefore, the most important type of security is minimizing your human weaknesses when it comes to putting your device and its data at risk.

One of the best examples of what I'm talking about in regard to minimizing human mistakes has to do with upgrading to a new device. Numerous stories abound in which someone upgrades his device only to forget to clear the memory on his old device before getting rid of it. All the security in the world won't save you from handing your device over to someone with all its data intact. Granted, if it's password-protected and encrypted, you might not have much to worry about, but in many cases, people disable these features because they weren't planning on using the devices anymore. So, one example of using a bit of common sense to help protect yourself is to always clear the memory of your device if you ever plan on getting rid of it.

▶ **TIP**

To clear the memory of your BlackBerry device of all application data, navigate to the **Tools** screen and select **Settings**; then click **Security**. Click the trackwheel and scroll to select **Wipe Handheld** on the menu that appears. Click again, and then click **Continue** to wipe out all the application data on your device. Be forewarned that this is a dramatic step and should be done only if you are getting rid of your device or want a clean slate so you can set it up from scratch.

While we're on the subject of someone gaining access to your data, you can easily add insult to injury by not backing up your data regularly. If someone gets his hands on your device, even if it is fully protected, it won't do you much good if you haven't backed up the data. Sure, the thief might not be able to access your data, but if you don't have an extra copy of the data, you won't be able to access

87 About BlackBerry Security

it, either. It's therefore safe to add regular data backups to your list of common-sense security measures.

Instead of continuing on like this, it might be more useful to provide you with a concise list of common-sense security tips that can dramatically improve your odds of never losing data, never letting your device fall into the wrong hands, and ideally never permanently losing your device. That's right, I have a tip for dramatically increasing your odds of finding your device should you ever lose it. It just so happens that each security tip has an associated task with it, so refer to each task to find out more about how to put the tip in action:

- Enter your owner information so it appears prominently when your device is locked—**4 Make Yourself the Owner**.
- Lock your device so you don't accidentally press keys and inadvertently call someone by accident—**5 Lock and Unlock Your Device**.
- Password-protect your device so a password must be entered to gain access to the device after it is locked—**6 Password-Protect Your Device**.
- Back up your device regularly so you never put yourself at risk of losing significant data—**13 Back Up Your Device**.
- Clear all data from your device if you ever stop using or decide to get rid of the device—**15 Clear Personal Data from Your Device**.
- Set your device to automatically turn on and off so password-protection is automatically enabled when you leave the device idle—**16 Automatically Turn Your Device On and Off**.
- Understand security issues surrounding Bluetooth wireless connectivity and what you can do to protect yourself—**67 About Bluetooth Security**.
- Secure the SIM card using a password so no one can steal your device or SIM card and make phone calls on your dime—**88 Secure the SIM Card**.
- Turn on the firewall so you know exactly when a third-party application is attempting to access the wireless network—**89 Turn On the Firewall**.
- Enable content encryption so the data on your device is unreadable to anyone but you—**90 Protect Your Content**.
- Securely store IDs and passwords for websites and services on your device so you don't lose or forget them—**91 Safely Store IDs and Passwords on Your Device**.
- Register your device with StuffBak, the global lost-and-found service that boasts a 90% recovery rate on lost items—**92 Register Your Device with StuffBak**.

There you have it, a common-sense list of simple but effective security measures you can take to dramatically decrease the likelihood of experiencing a BlackBerry security breach!

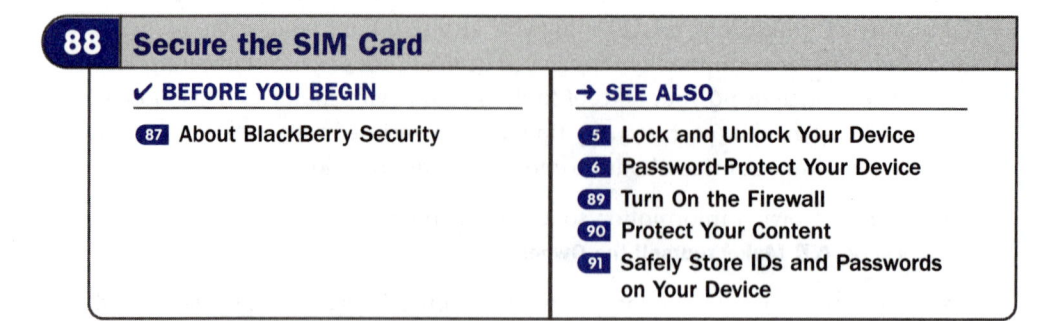

88 Secure the SIM Card

✔ BEFORE YOU BEGIN	→ SEE ALSO
87 About BlackBerry Security	5 Lock and Unlock Your Device 6 Password-Protect Your Device 89 Turn On the Firewall 90 Protect Your Content 91 Safely Store IDs and Passwords on Your Device

Like most mobile phones, your BlackBerry 7100 device includes a *subscriber identity module (SIM)* card whose primary purpose is to securely store the key that uniquely identifies you to your wireless service provider. Not only does the SIM card provide access to any contacts you might have stored on it (see 72 **Access the SIM Phone Book**), but it also serves as your device's access key to your wireless service provider. This means you can remove the SIM card from your BlackBerry device, place it in another device, and make calls on your wireless account. Of course, other people can do the same with your SIM card, which is a bad thing.

The way to prevent other people from stealing your SIM card and using it on their own devices is to enable SIM card security with a *PIN* code. A PIN code prevents your SIM card from being useful to someone else on her own device, and it prevents other people from being able to make calls using *your* device. In other words, SIM card security provides a way of locking out just the phone functionality of your BlackBerry device. This might or might not be a big deal to you, but it's an important feature of your device that you should know how to enable and disable.

1 Open the Tools Screen

Scroll to the **Tools** icon on the **Home** screen and click the trackwheel. The **Tools** screen appears, showing a list of tool options.

2 Open the Settings Screen

Scroll to the **Settings** icon and click the trackwheel. A list of options for which you can change the settings appears.

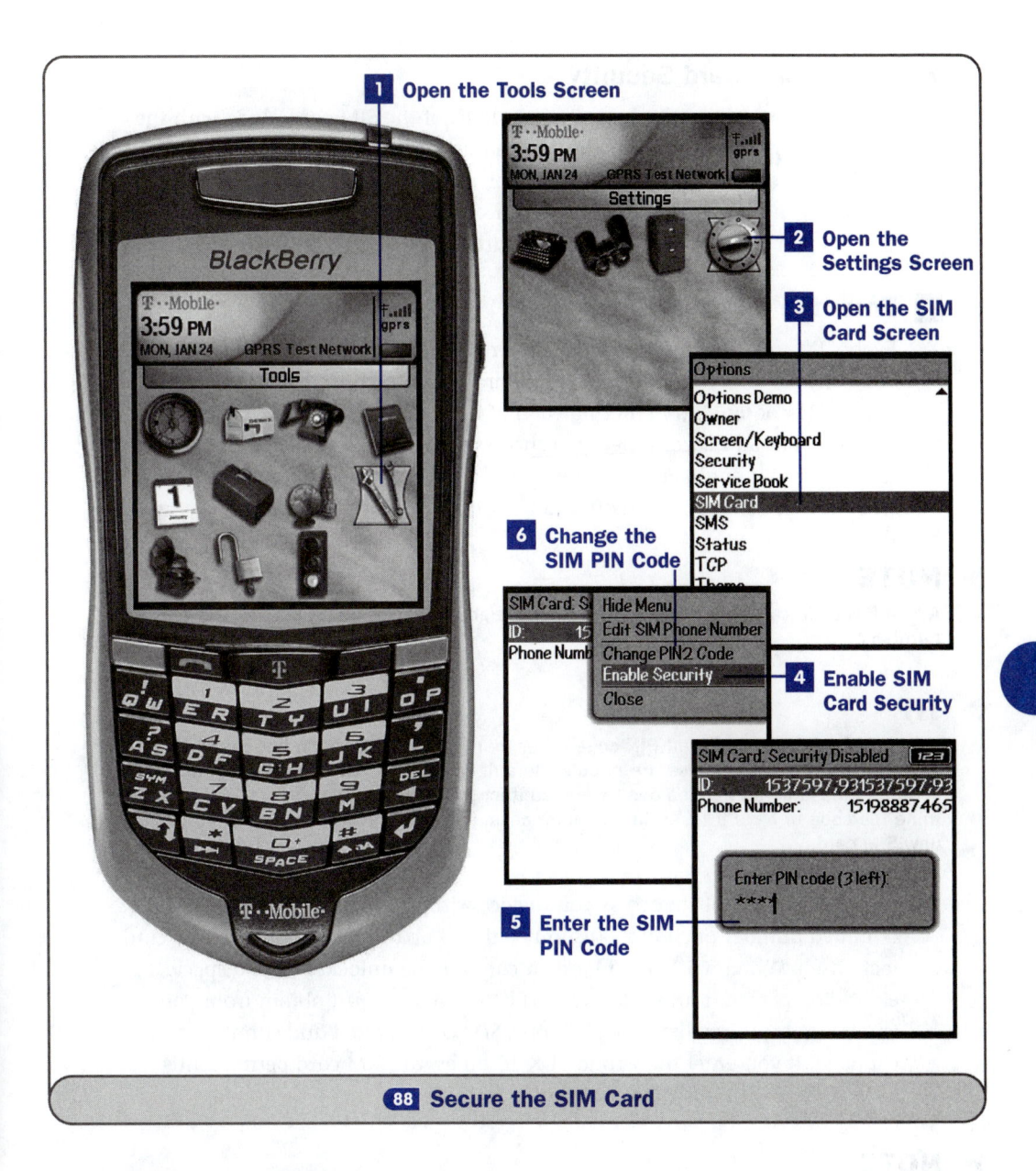

88 Secure the SIM Card

1 Open the Tools Screen

2 Open the Settings Screen

3 Open the SIM Card Screen

4 Enable SIM Card Security

5 Enter the SIM PIN Code

6 Change the SIM PIN Code

88 Secure the SIM Card

3 Open the SIM Card Screen

Scroll to the **SIM Card** option in the list of settings and click the trackwheel. The **SIM Card** screen opens.

4 Enable SIM Card Security

The **SIM Card** screen displays the unique ID of the SIM card along with the SIM phone number, which is the phone number of your BlackBerry device. To enable SIM security, click the trackwheel, scroll to select **Enable Security** from the menu that appears, and click again. A dialog box appears and prompts you to enter the PIN code for the SIM card.

5 Enter the SIM PIN Code

Every SIM card has a PIN code that restricts access to the card. If you've never explicitly set a PIN code for your SIM card, it likely has a default value of either **1234** or **0000**; try entering each of these values if you haven't set a PIN code for your SIM card. When you successfully enter the PIN code, security for the SIM card is enabled and the PIN code is required any time in the future when the device is powered off and back on.

▶ **NOTE**

A SIM PIN code can be anywhere from four to eight digits, including both letters and numbers.

▶ **TIP**

If your SIM card has a default PIN code other than **1234** or **0000**, do not change it to **1234** or **0000** because these are popular default settings. If you don't know your PIN code and these default codes don't work, contact your wireless service provider to determine the code or have it reset. In the worst case, your service provider will issue you a new SIM card.

> If someone attempts to access your device with an incorrect PIN code, she has a limited number of chances (usually either 3 or 10 tries) before the SIM card locks itself. When a SIM card locks, it can only be unlocked with a special eight-digit personal unblocking key (PUK) that you must obtain from your wireless service provider. The PUK for a SIM card is fixed and cannot be changed. If you enter the wrong PUK 10 times, the SIM card permanently locks itself, requiring you to obtain a new one.

▶ **NOTE**

Some SIM cards support an additional PIN2 code that can be used to provide security for additional SIM features. If your SIM card supports a PIN2 code, you can also set it using the **SIM Card** screen.

6 Change the SIM PIN Code

You should change the PIN code on your device if you've never explicitly changed it from the default setting. After you've enabled SIM card security, you can easily change the PIN code by clicking the trackwheel and selecting **Change PIN Code** from the menu that appears. Click again, and you are prompted to enter the existing PIN code followed by the new code. You actually have to enter the new code twice—once to initially specify it and again to verify it.

▶ **TIP**

If you've moved a SIM card from another mobile phone to your BlackBerry device and the SIM phone number wasn't updated, you can easily change it by clicking the trackwheel and selecting **Edit SIM Phone Number** from the menu that appears. Click again and enter the correct SIM phone number. Of course, there's a good chance that your mobile phone number didn't change, in which case changing the SIM phone number is unnecessary.

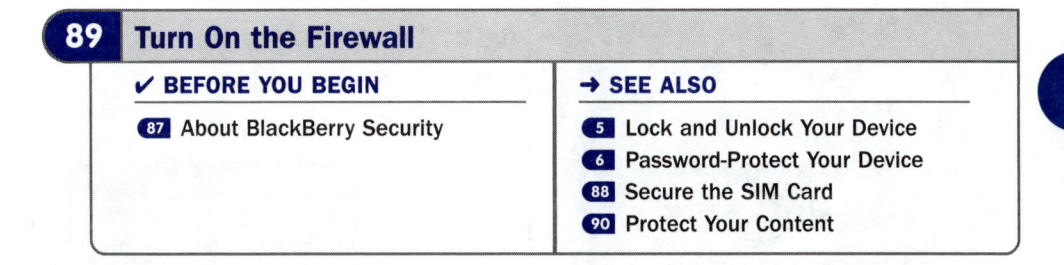

89 Turn On the Firewall

✔ **BEFORE YOU BEGIN**

87 About BlackBerry Security

→ **SEE ALSO**

5 Lock and Unlock Your Device
6 Password-Protect Your Device
88 Secure the SIM Card
90 Protect Your Content

You are probably already familiar with the concept of a *firewall*, which is a hardware and/or software layer that limits access to a network or computer. If you're using a desktop or notebook computer on a corporate intranet, you might already be accustomed to operating behind a firewall. The firewall feature built in to your BlackBerry serves a slightly different purpose than a traditional network firewall. The BlackBerry firewall serves to notify you when a third-party application makes an attempt to communicate over the wireless network.

The idea behind the BlackBerry firewall is that you are notified each time an application on your device attempts to access the wireless network, so in a way you serve as the manual gatekeeper for network access. You might view this as a hindrance, which is why the firewall feature is turned off by default. On the other hand, you might welcome such security if you don't regularly use third-party applications that access the network. The purpose of the BlackBerry firewall isn't to limit access to your device from outside, as you might expect from a traditional firewall.

CHAPTER 15: Securing Your BlackBerry Device

1 Open the Tools Screen

2 Open the Settings Screen

3 Open the Firewall Screen

4 Enable the Firewall

5 Exit and Save Changes

89 Turn On the Firewall

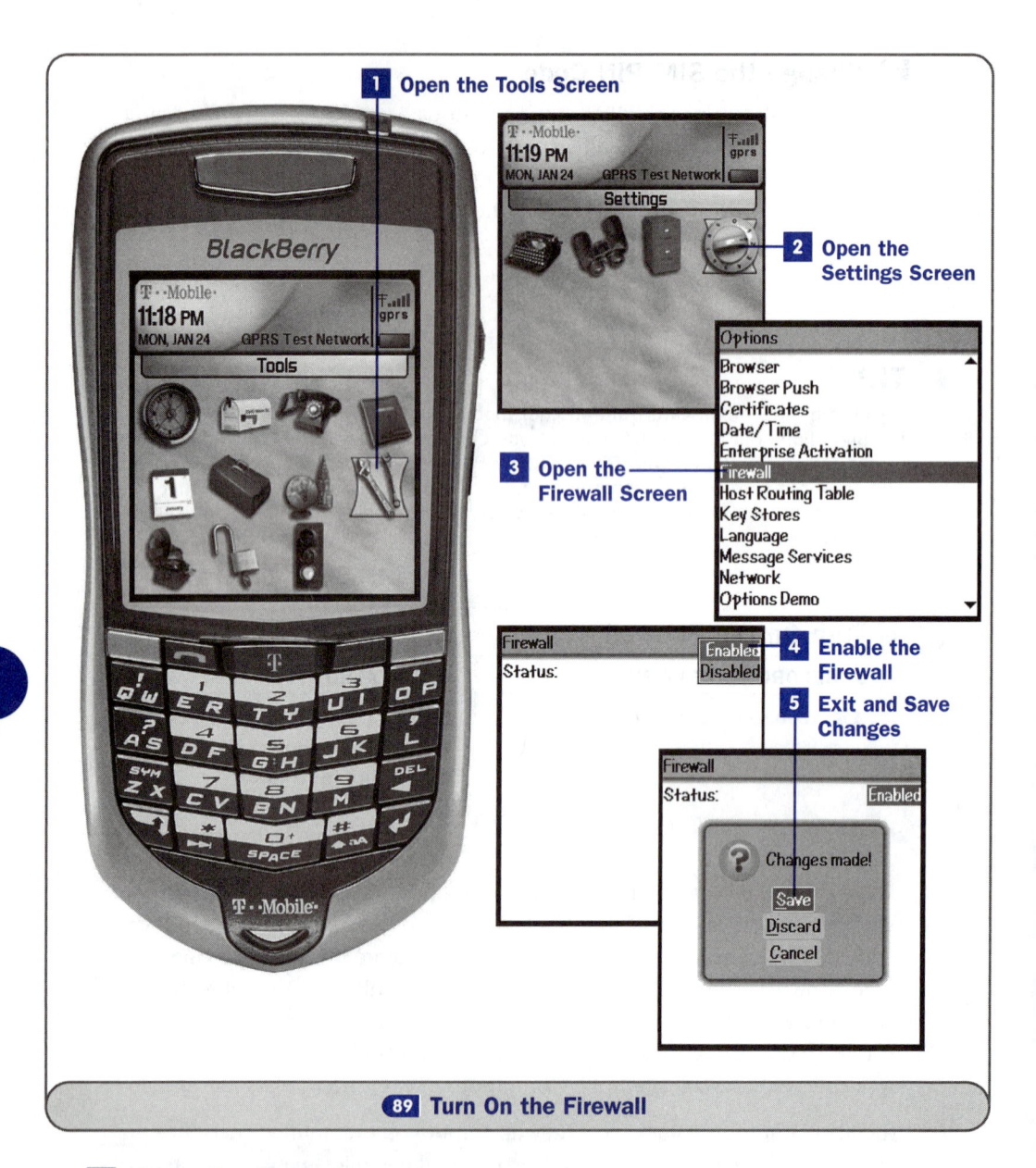

1 Open the Tools Screen

Scroll to the **Tools** icon on the **Home** screen and click the trackwheel. The **Tools** screen appears, displaying a list of tool options.

2 Open the Settings Screen

Scroll to the **Settings** icon and click the trackwheel. A list of options for which you can change the settings appears.

90 Protect Your Content 349

3 Open the Firewall Screen

Scroll to the **Firewall** option in the list of settings and click the trackwheel. The **Firewall** screen opens.

4 Enable the Firewall

The **Firewall** screen is surprisingly sparse, including only a single option for enabling and disabling the firewall feature. To enable the firewall feature, double-click the trackwheel and select **Enabled** from the pop-up menu that appears. Click to confirm the selection.

▶ **TIP**
To quickly change an option without having to go through the two trackwheel clicks required to open a menu and select **Change Option**, press the **Alt** key to view a list of options. Then scroll to the desired choice and click the trackwheel to select it. An even faster shortcut involves cycling to the next available choice by pressing the **Space** key.

5 Exit and Save Changes

Press the **Escape** button to exit the **Firewall** screen. If you changed the firewall setting, you are prompted to save or discard changes. When prompted, scroll the trackwheel to the **Save** option and click to save the changes. You then are returned to the **Settings** screen. Press the **Escape** button twice to navigate back to the **Home** screen, or just press the **End** key once.

---

90 Protect Your Content

✔ **BEFORE YOU BEGIN**
- **6** Password-Protect Your Device
- **87** About BlackBerry Security

→ **SEE ALSO**
- **5** Lock and Unlock Your Device
- **88** Secure the SIM Card
- **89** Turn On the Firewall
- **91** Safely Store IDs and Passwords on Your Device
- **92** Register Your Device with StuffBak

In addition to password-protection, which prevents someone from accessing your BlackBerry device after it has been locked, you should consider content protection to take things to another level. This involves encrypting all the data on your device so it isn't in a recognizable format until you actually access it. Content encryption doesn't usually put a noticeable strain on your device in terms of processing delays, so it's not a bad idea to enable it if you're concerned about data security.

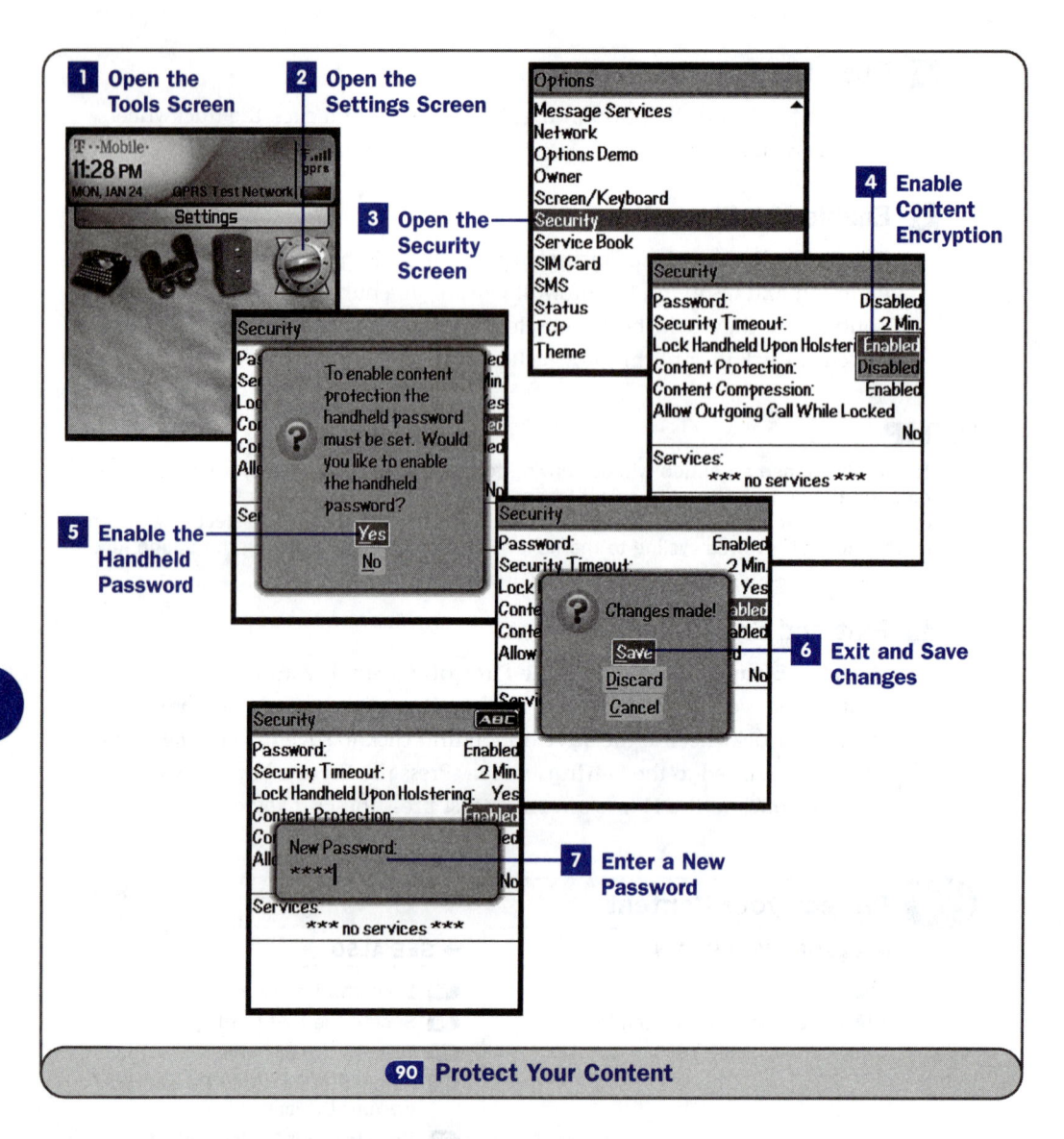

350 CHAPTER 15: Securing Your BlackBerry Device

90 Protect Your Content

Content compression goes hand in hand with content encryption and helps minimize the size of data. Content compression can be enabled with or without content encryption, and you should use it simply because it helps conserve memory. Unless you start noticing a significant delay in accessing data, I recommend using both content compression and content encryption for efficient and secure data storage.

90 Protect Your Content

1. Open the Tools Screen

Scroll to the **Tools** icon on the **Home** screen and click the trackwheel. The **Tools** screen appears, showing a list of tool options.

2. Open the Settings Screen

Scroll to the **Settings** icon and click the trackwheel. A list of options for which you can change the settings appears.

3. Open the Security Screen

Scroll to the **Security** option in the list of settings and click the trackwheel. The **Security** screen opens.

4. Enable Content Encryption

The **Security** screen includes several options, but the one we're focusing on is **Content Protection**. Enabling this option causes your device to encrypt all the data stored on it, improving data security. To enable content encryption, scroll to select the **Content Protection** setting (**Disabled** by default), double-click the trackwheel, and select **Enabled** from the pop-up menu that appears. Click to confirm the selection. After enabling content protection, you are immediately prompted to enable the handheld password.

▶ **TIP**
To quickly change an option without having to go through the two trackwheel clicks required to open a menu and select **Change Option**, press the **Alt** key to view a list of options. Then scroll to the desired choice and click the trackwheel to select it. An even faster shortcut involves cycling to the next available choice by pressing the **Space** key.

▶ **NOTE**
The **Content Compression** option is somewhat related to **Content Protection**, and it is enabled by default. Generally speaking, you should leave content compression enabled because it helps conserve precious device memory by compressing your data.

5. Enable the Handheld Password

To finish enabling content encryption (protection), you must agree to enable the handheld password (assuming that it isn't already enabled). This is the password used to protect your device after it is locked (see **6 Password-Protect Your Device**). To okay this setting change, scroll the trackwheel to select **Yes** in the dialog box that appears and click.

6 Exit and Save Changes

Press the **Escape** button to exit the **Security** screen. If you enabled content encryption, you are prompted to save or discard changes. When prompted, scroll the trackwheel to the **Save** option and click to save the changes. Because you've now enabled the handheld password, you are prompted to enter the new password.

7 Enter a New Password

Using the keyboard, enter the new password, making sure that it is at least four characters long. When you enter a password, each character is shown briefly as you type it before it is turned into an asterisk. This is helpful because your password will likely require different keystrokes depending on whether you use alphabetic or numeric input mode. Password entry is always carried out in multitap mode, but you can switch between alphabetic or numeric characters by briefly holding down the **Next** key (*). Alphabetic multitap mode is always selected by default when you enter a password, so I recommend sticking with an alphabetic password as opposed to a numeric one.

> **90** ▶ **TIPS**
>
> Keep in mind that you will be entering the password every time you unlock your device, which is likely quite frequently—especially if you have the security timeout set to a low value or are using the **Lock Handheld Upon Holstering** option (see **5 Lock Your Device**). For this reason, you should specify a password you can enter quickly. I prefer thinking of it as more of a PIN code, which means sticking with the minimum of four characters.
>
> Alphabetic multitap mode is the default mode for entering passwords, which means you'll have to constantly switch to numeric mode to enter a numeric password or press the **Shift** key for each number. I recommend using an alphabetic password instead of a numeric one so you don't have to change to numeric mode every time you enter the password. As an example, "CUTE" is a much better password option than its numeric equivalent, "7321".

Press the **Enter** key when you finish entering the password. Another screen appears, prompting you to verify the new password. Enter it again and press the **Enter** key.

Your BlackBerry device is now set to encrypt its data and require a password for access. The data isn't encrypted until the device is locked. When the device is locked, you see a small open lock near the top of the screen that indicates that data encryption is taking place. When all the data is successfully encrypted, the open lock turns into a closed lock.

91 Safely Store IDs and Passwords on Your Device

✔ BEFORE YOU BEGIN	→ SEE ALSO
87 About BlackBerry Security	5 Lock and Unlock Your Device
	6 Password-Protect Your Device
	88 Secure the SIM Card
	90 Protect Your Content
	92 Register Your Device with StuffBak

Anyone who uses the Internet regularly can attest to the frustration in having too many user IDs and passwords floating around. Many websites now require registration with an ID and password, which means you have to remember the ID and password if you want to access the website in the future. Although modern browsers do a good job of remembering this information to aid you in entering it, they don't necessarily help you if you're traveling or you delete your stored cookies. This is where a central repository of stored IDs and passwords comes in handy.

The **Password Keeper** application ships with most BlackBerry devices and allows you to enter user IDs and passwords for safe keeping. The idea is that you create a single password for **Password Keeper** and then use it to access your master list of IDs and passwords. This password list can extend beyond websites—you can enter PINs for bank accounts and just about any access code or password you want. Just be sure you are careful about setting the **Password Keeper** password because it holds the key to all the others.

1 Open the Tools Screen

Scroll to the **Tools** icon on the **Home** screen and click the trackwheel. The **Tools** screen appears, showing a list of tools options.

2 Launch the Password Keeper Application

To launch the **Password Keeper** application, scroll the trackwheel to select the **Password Storage** icon and click. The **Password Keeper** application begins by prompting you to enter a password for the application; this password is used to protect all the user IDs and passwords you'll enter into **Password Keeper**.

354   **CHAPTER 15:**   Securing Your BlackBerry Device

1 Open the Tools Screen

2 Launch the Password Keeper Application

3 Enter a Password for Password Keeper

7 Exit the Application

4 Create a New Password Entry

5 Enter the Password Details

6 Tweak Password Keeper Options

91

91 Safely Store IDs and Passwords on Your Device

> **NOTE**
> If you don't see the **Password Storage** icon on your device, the **Password Keeper** application might not have been installed by default on your device. This likely means you have an older version of the BlackBerry operating system; **Password Keeper** was added in version 4.0 of the BlackBerry OS. To find out how to upgrade the BlackBerry OS to the latest version, see "Upgrading Your Device to the Latest BlackBerry OS" in Chapter 1.

3 Enter a Password for Password Keeper

Using the keyboard, enter the password, making sure that it is at least four characters long. When you enter a password, each character is shown briefly as you type it before it is turned into an asterisk. This is helpful because your password will likely require different keystrokes depending on whether you use alphabetic or numeric input mode. Password entry is always carried out in multitap mode, but you can switch between alphabetic or numeric characters by briefly holding down the **Next** key (*). Alphabetic multitap mode is always selected by default when you enter a password, so I recommend sticking with an alphabetic password as opposed to a numeric one.

> **TIP**
> Alphabetic multitap mode is the default mode for entering passwords, which means you have to constantly switch to numeric mode to enter a numeric password or press the **Shift** key for each number. I recommend using an alphabetic password instead of a numeric one so that you don't have to change to numeric mode every time you enter the password. As an example, "CUTE" is a much better password option than its numeric equivalent, "7321".

You must enter the password twice to ensure that you entered it consistently. Scroll the trackwheel to select the **OK** button when you're finished entering the password and its confirmation, and then click. You are taken to the main **Password Keeper** screen, which contains a list of stored passwords and user IDs; initially this list is empty because you haven't created any password entries.

4 Create a New Password Entry

To create a new password entry, click the trackwheel and select **New** from the menu that appears. Click once more, and the **New Password** screen appears.

5 Enter the Password Details

The **New Password** screen is where you enter a new password to store in the **Password Keeper** application. A password entry consists of five pieces of information, which correspond to the following data fields: **Title**, **Username**, **Password**, **Website**, and **Notes**. The **Title** field simply stores the name of the password, which is typically the service to which it provides access, such as AOL, eBay, or Amazon. The **Username** and **Password** fields are fairly self-explanatory in that they represent the principle information being stored (username/ID and password). The website address of the service with which the password and username are associated is stored in the **Website** field. And finally, optional text notes regarding the password entry can be entered in the **Notes** field.

▶ **TIP**

If you struggle to create unique passwords that are difficult for potential hackers to figure out, consider allowing **Password Keeper** to create a random password for you. Just click the trackwheel, select **Random Password** from the menu that appears, and click once more. A random password is created and placed in the **Password** field for you. Keep in mind that you must log in to the actual website for the password entry and change your old password to the new random password.

After entering the specifics for the new password entry, click the trackwheel and select **Save** from the menu that appears. Click once more to save the entry and return to the main **Password Keeper** screen. There you see the new password entry in the list.

6 Tweak Password Keeper Options

The **Password Keeper** application includes some options you might want to change to customize the application so it better suits your needs. To access these options, click the trackwheel, scroll to select **Options**, and click again. Several of these options relate to the random passwords you can generate using **Password Keeper**. For example, you can set exactly how many characters are in the randomly generated passwords, along with whether the passwords contain alphabetic characters, letters, or symbols. I find that symbols are usually hard to remember and enter for passwords, so I recommend setting the **Random Includes Symbols** option to **False**.

The remaining options on the **Password Keeper Options** screen include **Confirm Delete**, which determines whether you have to confirm the deletion of password entries. The **Password Attempts** field determines how many attempts you are given to incorrectly enter the password for **Password Keeper** before the application clears out all the password entries and resets itself. This setting is designed to protect your passwords from someone trying to hack and figure out the **Password Keeper** password.

The last two options are related in that the **Allow Clipboard Copy** setting becomes important if you disable the **Show Password** setting. If you set the **Show Password** option to **False**, none of the passwords are shown within the **Password Keeper** application; they are instead displayed as a series of asterisks (*). This means you won't really have a way of looking at and determining what the password is. However, if you leave the **Allow Clipboard Copy** option set to **True**, you can select a password and copy it to the clipboard. You can then paste the password into a website in the BlackBerry browser and effectively look up and enter a password without ever seeing its actual value on the screen.

After changing any **Password Keeper** options, press the **Escape** button to exit the **Password Keeper Options** screen. If you changed any settings, you are prompted to save or discard changes. When prompted, scroll the trackwheel to the **Save** option and click to save the changes. You then return to the main **Password Keeper** screen.

7 Exit the Application

When you finish using **Password Keeper**, press the **Escape** button twice to exit the application and navigate back to the **Home** screen, or just press the **End** key once.

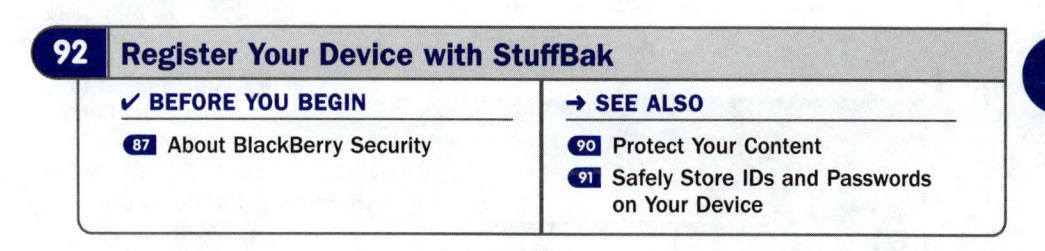

92 Register Your Device with StuffBak

✔ **BEFORE YOU BEGIN**

87 About BlackBerry Security

→ **SEE ALSO**

90 Protect Your Content
91 Safely Store IDs and Passwords on Your Device

You're probably familiar with the concept of a lost and found, where lost items are accumulated in one place so people can return later and retrieve the items. Lost and found is a popular service in restaurants, schools, offices, and other settings in the physical world. There is also a global lost and found in the virtual world that is in many ways more powerful than its real-world counterparts. A service called StuffBak enables you to register items and then hopefully get them back if you ever lose them.

The idea behind StuffBak is that you register an item with the StuffBak online service and then put a special decal on the item. If you lose the item and someone finds it, the decal contains detailed information about how to go online and report the item found, as well as how to get a reward. To make things even easier for the finder of an item, he doesn't have to pack the item or pay any shipping charges; there are numerous StuffBak drop-off locations (including all UPS Stores), as well as a StuffBak courier service that will pick up items.

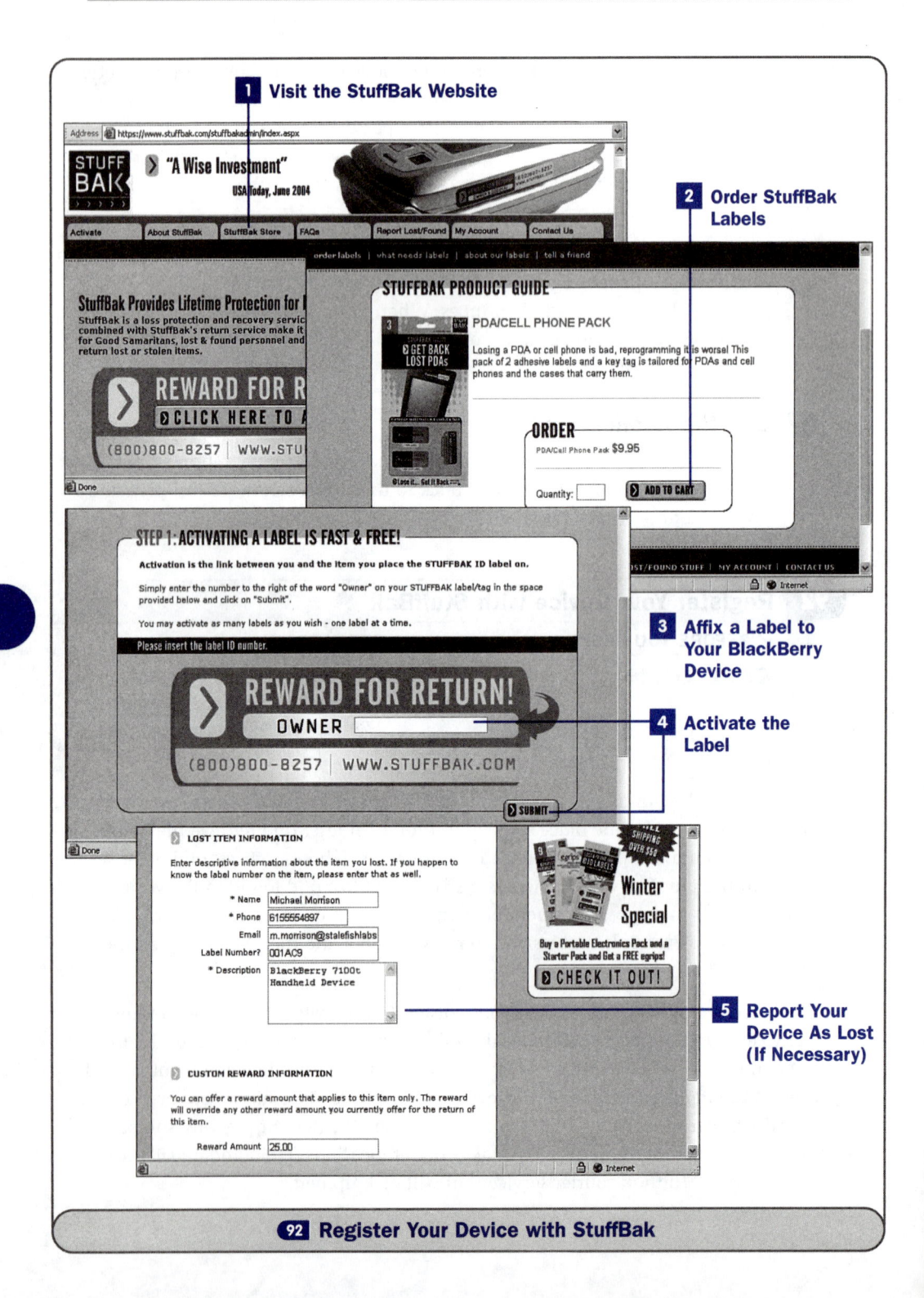

CHAPTER 15: Securing Your BlackBerry Device

1 Visit the StuffBak Website

2 Order StuffBak Labels

3 Affix a Label to Your BlackBerry Device

4 Activate the Label

5 Report Your Device As Lost (If Necessary)

92 Register Your Device with StuffBak

92 Register Your Device with StuffBak

On the other side of the equation, the person who loses an item pays a fixed $14.95 fee to StuffBak to claim the returned item, plus shipping and an optional reward to the finder. Think about it this way: Would you pay $14.95 or more (shipping plus reward) to get your BlackBerry device back if you lost it? I know I would! To get started with StuffBak, all you have to do is purchase a starter pack for as low as $9.95, which includes six labels in a variety of shapes and sizes. Thus, you can protect your BlackBerry device and five other items.

1 Visit the StuffBak Website

Registering your BlackBerry device with StuffBak begins with a visit to the StuffBak website, which is located at http://www.stuffbak.com/. Although you can navigate through the StuffBak website directly in the BlackBerry web browser on your device, I recommend using your desktop browser to make things easier. Either way, on the main StuffBak web page, navigate to the **StuffBak Store** and then navigate to **Variety Packs**.

2 Order StuffBak Labels

The **Variety Packs** area of the StuffBak store includes several variety packs of labels you can buy to get started with the StuffBak service. Unless you have some other ideas of things you might want to register with StuffBak, I recommend starting with the **PDA/Cell Phone Pack** for $9.95, which provides a couple labels for handheld devices and a key label you can use on your car/house keys. The cheapest option for getting started with StuffBak is $9.95, although you might want to order a larger pack of labels if you decide the service is worth it.

▶ **TIP**

Just in case you're suspicious about me recommending that you buy a product such as StuffBak labels, I have no affiliation with StuffBak whatsoever. It's a truly unique service that I've found particularly useful to users of mobile devices, myself included.

After deciding on a pack of StuffBak labels, you must go through the checkout process to purchase the labels and initiate the order. As part of this process, you create a StuffBak account, which means you'll have a username and password you can use to log in and keep track of your StuffBak "inventory" of registered devices.

▶ **TIP**

Consider storing your new Stuffbak username and password on your device using the **Password Keeper** application; see **91** Safely Store IDs and Passwords on Your Device.

3 Affix a Label to Your BlackBerry Device

When your StuffBak labels arrive in the mail, find a label suitable for your BlackBerry device and affix it to the side or back of the device. I found that the back of the device on the outside of the battery cover is a good spot because there is plenty of room. Now that the label is affixed to your device, all that's left to maximize the chances of recovering your device should it ever get lost is to activate the label on the StuffBak website.

4 Activate the Label

Navigate back to the StuffBak website at http://www.stuffbak.com/, and follow the **Activate** link from the main page. Enter the unique label number from the label of your BlackBerry device in the **Owner** field on the StuffBak activation page, and click **Submit**. Continue with the instructions to finish activating the StuffBak label and include your device in the StuffBak global lost and found repository. According to StuffBak statistics, you now have a 90% chance of recovering your device should it get lost.

5 Report Your Device As Lost (If Necessary)

In the unfortunate event that you actually lose your BlackBerry device, keep your fingers crossed that it will be found, reported to StuffBak, and returned to you. You can boost your chances that your device will be returned by reporting the device as lost on the StuffBak website. From the main StuffBak web page, follow the **Report Lost/Found** link, and then continue by navigating to **report my lost item**. You'll need to log in using your StuffBak username and password; then you can enter information about your lost item.

The key thing that reporting a lost item does is allow you to offer a reward for someone returning your item. You can enter any amount you want as a reward, just keep in mind that it will apply on top of the $14.95 StuffBak charge for returning the item, plus any shipping charges. Even so, the prospect of getting a device back that is worth several hundred dollars, plus your data—which could feasibly be priceless—is tough to put a hard value on. I recommend offering a $10 or $20 reward as a minimum to help improve the odds of getting a lost device back.

▶ **NOTE**

In addition to any reward you might offer, any person who returns an item to StuffBak is automatically given a reward from StuffBak in the form of $20 worth of StuffBak labels. It's a clever way to build the StuffBak community and promote the service.

Index

Numbers

1g networks, 6
2g networks, 6
2.5g networks, 7
2.75g networks, 7
3g networks, 7
411 phone directories, accessing, 242-245
802.11a/b/g protocols, 251

A

abbreviated dialing numbers (ADNs), 283
Access Number option (voice mail), 241
accounts
    BlackBerry Web Client accounts
        additional accounts, adding, 121-125
        creating, 100-104
        email filters, 125-128
Activate Handset command (Phone menu), 220
Activate Speakerphone command (Phone menu), 220
activating
    call waiting, 241
    headsets, 219
    speakerphones, 219
Active on Weekends setting (Alarm), 318
Add Bookmark command, 193
Add Bookmark dialog box, 193
Add Contact screen, 175
Add Filter page (Web Client), 127-128
Add Notes command (Call Log), 236
Add Subfolder command (bookmarks), 194
add-ins, 52

Additional Numbers option

Additional Numbers option (voice mail), 241
Address Book
- contacts
  - adding to mailing lists, 275
  - applying categories to, 277-279
  - calling, 273
  - creating, 270-273
  - removing from mailing lists, 276
  - saving, 273
  - sending messages to, 273
  - viewing, 273
- copying SIM contacts to, 283
- importing into BlackBerry Web Client, 107-110
- mailing lists, 274-276
- options, 279-281
- scrolling, 273

addresses (email), 116-119
ADNs (abbreviated dialing numbers), 283
Advanced Settings for Address Book window, 51
Advanced Settings for Calendar window, 51
Agenda format (Calendar), 287-290
Alarm application, 316-320
Alert Type setting (Alarm), 318
Allow Clipboard Copy option (Password Keeper), 356
Allow Duplicate Names option (Address Book), 281
Allow JavaScript pop-ups option (browser properties), 209
Alt key, 19
answering phone calls, 220
AOL Instant Messenger, 180
Application Loader Wizard
- installing applications, 53-56
- installing themes, 93-94
- removing applications, 56-59

applications
- add-ins, 52
- icons
  - hiding, 88
  - moving, 88
  - organizing, 86-89
  - showing, 88
- installing, 53-56, 196-199

PocketMac, 44
removing, 56-59
translator applications, 50
website resources, 53
applying categories to tasks, 308-311
appointments (Calendar)
- changing, 298
- creating, 294-298
- deleting, 299
- inviting attendees to, 298
- recurring appointments, 297
- responding to appointment invitations, 299
- saving, 298
- viewing, 298

attachments (email)
- sending, 113
- viewing, 138-141

Attachments screen, 140-141
attendees, inviting to meetings, 298
Auto Answer Calls option, 239
Auto End Calls option, 240
Auto On/Off option, 72-75
auto reply messages, 114-116
Auto Reply page (Web Client), 115-116
Auto signature setting (Web Client), 106
Auto Time Set feature, 27
automatic backups, 61
automatically turning on/off BlackBerry devices, 72-75
AutoText feature, 75-78
Available Offline option (bookmarks), 193

B

Back command (web browser), 186
backing up BlackBerry devices, 59-63, 342
Backspace key, 19
Backup and Restore Window
- backing up devices, 59-63
- clearing personal data from devices, 66-70
- restoring devices, 63-66

Berry 411, 242-245
BES (BlackBerry Enterprise Server), 8, 12, 99
BlackBerry 950, 8
BlackBerry 6200 series, 8
BlackBerry 6510, 8
BlackBerry 6750, 8
BlackBerry 7100g, 9
BlackBerry 7100r, 9
BlackBerry 7100t, 9-10
BlackBerry 7100v, 9-10
BlackBerry 7100x, 9
BlackBerry Bookmarks folder, 193
BlackBerry Desktop Manager
   Backup and Restore Window
      backing up devices, 59-63
      clearing personal data from devices, 66-70
      restoring devices, 63-66
   Connection Settings window, 45-48
   downloading, 42
   installing, 42-45
   Intellisync, 48-52
BlackBerry Desktop Software
   downloading, 42
   installing, 42-45
BlackBerry devices. *See also* security
   backing up, 59-63
   clearing, 66-70, 342
   connecting to desktop PCs, 45-48
   locking and unlocking, 30-32
   password protection, 32-36
   registering with StuffBak, 357-360
   restoring, 63-66
   turning on/off, 20, 72-75
   versions/series, 8-10
BlackBerry Enterprise Server (BES), 8, 12, 99
BlackBerry Redirector, 99, 160-165
"BlackBerry thumb," 5
BlackBerry Web Client, 98
   accounts
      additional accounts, adding, 121-125
      creating, 100-104
      email filters, 125-128
   Address Books, importing, 107-110

auto reply messages, 114-116
email messages
   attachments, 113
   composing, 111-114
   copying to another account, 119-121
   saving as drafts, 114
   sending, 114
options, 104-107
sent-from email address, changing, 116-119
Bluejacking, 263
Bluesnarfing, 263-264
Bluetooth
   capabilities, 249
   car kits, pairing BlackBerry devices with, 254-258
   classes of Bluetooth devices, 249
   compared to Wi-Fi, 251
   competitors to, 249
   definition of, 248
   deleting Bluetooth devices, 262
   headsets, pairing BlackBerry devices with, 254-258
   options, 258-262
   passkeys, 257
   portable Bluetooth keyboards, 251
   profiles, 250
   security, 262-265
      Bluejacking, 263
      Bluesnarfing, 263-264
      Bluetooth sniping, 264
      discoverable/invisible options, 264-265
      tips and guidelines, 265
   turning on and off, 252-254
   versions, 251
Bluetooth, Harald, 248
bookmarks, 191-195
   bookmark folders, 194-195
   copying, 194
   creating, 193-194
   deleting, 195-196
   editing, 195
   moving, 195
   navigating to, 188
   viewing, 194
Bookmarks screen, 193-194
Browser Configuration screen, 208

browser history

browser history, 190
browser options, 185, 206-210
    Browser Configuration, 208
    Cache Operations, 210
    General Properties, 208-210
browsing the web. See web browsing

C

Cache Operations (Browser Options), 210
Cache Operations screen, 210
Calculator, 323-325
Calendar, 286-290
    Agenda format, 287-290
    appointments
        changing, 298
        creating, 294-298
        deleting, 299
        inviting attendees to, 298
        recurring appointments, 297
        responding to appointment invitations, 299
        saving, 298
        viewing, 298
    Day format, 287-288
    Month format, 287-289
    navigating, 290-294
    options, 299-302
    synchronizing, 286
    Week format, 287-289
Calendar Options screen, 300-302
call forwarding, 224-227
Call Forwarding screen, 226-227
Call From Address Book command (Phone menu), 218
Call Log screen, 236-238
call logs, 234-238
    adding notes to, 236
    deleting, 237
    opening, 236
    options, 237-238
    viewing, 236
call timers, clearing, 215
Call Waiting, 241-242
calling contacts, 273

calls. See phone calls
car kits (Bluetooth), pairing BlackBerry devices with, 254-258
cards, SIM (subscriber identity module) cards
    PIN codes, 344-347
    security, 344-347
    SIM Phone Book, accessing, 281-284
categories
    applying
        to contacts, 277-279
        to memos, 323
        to tasks, 308-311
    creating, 277, 310
    deleting, 277, 310
Change Field Name dialog box, 273
changing. See editing
Choose Translator window, 50
Class 1 devices (Bluetooth), 249
Class 2 devices (Bluetooth), 249
Class 3 devices (Bluetooth), 249
Clear All Timers command (Status menu), 215
Clear Timer command (Status menu), 215
clearing
    BlackBerry devices, 342
    call timers, 215
    personal data, 66-70
clicking the trackwheel, 20
clients, PIM (personal information management), 109
ComFX, 201
Comma Separated Values (CSV), 109
Compose Email command (Messages menu), 134
Compose PIN command (Messages menu), 143
Compose SMS command (Messages menu), 147
composing email messages, 111-114, 134-137
conference calls, 220-224
Confirm Delete option
    Address Book, 281
    Calendar, 301
    MemoPad, 323
    Password Keeper, 356

phone, 240
tasks, 313
connecting BlackBerry devices to desktop PCs, 45-48
Connection Settings window, 47
contacts
   Address Book
      adding to mailing lists, 275
      applying categories to, 277-279
      calling, 273
      creating, 270-273
      removing from mailing lists, 276
      saving, 273
      sending messages to, 273
      viewing, 273
   instant messaging, 173-176
   SIM Phone Book, 283-284
Content Compression option, 36
Content Mode setting (browser configuration), 208
Content Protection feature, 349-352
Content Protection option, 36
controlling BlackBerry from desktop PCs
   applications
      installing, 53-56
      removing, 56-59
   backups, 59-63
   BlackBerry Desktop Software, installing, 42-45
   BlackBerry devices, connecting to desktop PCs, 45-48
   clearing personal data from devices, 66-70
   PIM data, synchronizing, 48-52
   restoring devices, 63-66
Convenience key, 20, 193, 197
conversations (instant messaging), 168
   carrying on, 176-179
   ending, 179
   saving, 169, 179
converting units of measure, 325
copying
   bookmarks, 194
   email messages to another account, 119-121
   SIM contacts to Address Book, 283
cryptography, 341

CSV (Comma Separated Values), 109
customizing BlackBerry
   application icons, 86-89
   Auto On/Off, 72-75
   AutoText, 75-78
   keyboard settings, 83-86
   profiles, 79-83
   screen settings, 83-86
   themes, 91-94
   wallpaper, 89-91

D

daily alarm, setting, 318-319
Date Selection dialog box (Calendar), 292
date/time, setting
   Date/Time screen, 24-27
   Web Client, 107
Day format (Calendar), 287-288
Default Call Volume option (phone), 241
Default Font Family option (browser properties), 209
Default Font Size option (browser properties), 209
default PIN codes, 346
Default Reminder option (Calendar), 301
Delete Bookmark command, 195
Delete command (Messages menu), 151
Delete Contact screen, 176
Delete Folder command (bookmarks), 195
deleting
   appointments, 299
   Bluetooth devices, 262
   bookmark folders, 195
   bookmarks, 195-196
   call logs, 237
   categories, 277, 310
   instant messaging contacts, 173-176
   mailing list members, 276
   memos, 322
   messages, 151-152
   pictures, 328
   SIM contacts, 284
   speed dial numbers, 231
   tasks, 308

How can we make this index more useful? Email us at indexes@samspublishing.com

Desktop Manager

Desktop Manager
   Backup and Restore Window
      backing up devices, 59-63
      clearing personal data from devices, 66-70
      restoring devices, 63-66
   Connection Settings window, 45-48
   downloading, 42
   installing, 42-45
   Intellisync, 48-52
desktop PCs, controlling BlackBerry from
   applications
      installing, 53-56
      removing, 56-59
   backups, 59-63
   BlackBerry Desktop Software, installing, 42-45
   BlackBerry devices, connecting to desktop PCs, 45-48
   clearing personal data from devices, 66-70
   PIM data, synchronizing, 48-52
   restoring devices, 63-66
Desktop Software
   downloading, 42
   installing, 42-45
Device Name option (Bluetooth), 261
Device Properties (Bluetooth), 261-262
devices. *See* BlackBerry devices
digital signatures, 341
Disabled command (Password menu), 34
disabling
   Bluetooth, 252-254
   Call Waiting, 241
Discoverable option (Bluetooth), 260, 264-265
dismissing alarms, 319
display language, selecting, 23
Do Not Forward (Call Forwarding), 227
downloading
   Berry 411, 243
   BlackBerry Desktop Software, 42
   mScorecard, 336
   MyFlashlight, 332
   ring tones, 203-206
   themes, 91
   wallpaper, 199-202

Drop Call command (Phone menu), 224
dropping callers from conference calls, 224

E

Edit Bookmark command, 195
Edit Forwarding Numbers screen, 226
Edit Notes command (Call Log), 236
editing
   appointments, 298
   bookmarks, 195
   Calendar view, 293
   call forwarding numbers, 226
   mailing lists, 276
   memos, 322
   PIN codes, 347
   sent-from email address, 116-119
   SIM contacts, 284
   SIM phone number, 347
   speed dial numbers, 230
   wallpaper, 89-91
email, 130-134
   attachments
      sending, 113
      viewing, 138-141
   auto reply messages, 114-116
   BlackBerry Enterprise Server, 99
   BlackBerry Redirector, 99, 160-165
   BlackBerry Web Client accounts, 98
      creating, 100-104, 121-125
      Address Books, 107-110
      options, 104-107
      sent-from email address, 116-119
   composing, 111-114, 134-137
   copying to another account, 119-121
   definition of, 131
   deleting, 151-152
   filters, 125-128
   forwarding, 99, 150
   marking as opened, 152
   marking as unopened, 152
   message folders, navigating, 152-153
   options, 104-107, 156-160
      Email Reconciliation, 159-160
      General Options, 158-159

organizing, 149-153
push email, 98
reconciliation, 157-160
redirecting, 160
replying to, 149
saving, 114, 153
searching, 154-156
sending, 114, 137
third-party applications, 99
viewing, 133-134
Emergency Call command (Phone menu), 215
emergency calls, 36, 215
Emulation Mode setting (browser configuration), 208
Enable Quick Entry option (Calendar), 301
Enabled command (Password menu), 34
enabling
    Bluetooth, 252-254
    firewalls, 347-349
enabling. *See* activating
encryption, 261, 341
End Call command (Phone menu), 220
End key, 19, 213, 220
End Of Day option (Calendar), 301
ending
    instant messaging conversations, 179
    phone calls, 220
Enter key, 19
Enterprise Server, 99
Escalating setting (Alarm volume), 319
Escape button, 20, 213
events (Calendar)
    changing, 298
    creating, 294-298
    definition of, 286
    deleting, 299
    inviting attendees to, 298
    recurring events, 297
    responding to meeting invitations, 299
    saving, 298
    viewing, 298
Extensible Messaging and Presence Protocol (XMPP), 180
extracting Zip file, 55

F

files
    attaching to email, 113
    Zip files, extracting, 55
filtering
    contacts, 277-279
    email, 125-128
    memos, 323
Filters page (Web Client), 127
fine-tuning BlackBerry
    application icons, 86-89
    Auto On/Off, 72-75
    AutoText, 75-78
    keyboard settings, 83-86
    profiles, 79-83
    screen settings, 83-86
    themes, 91-94
    wallpaper, 89-91
Firewall screen, 349
firewalls, 347-349
First Day Of Week option (Calendar), 301
flashlights, using BlackBerry devices as, 332-334
folders
    BlackBerry Bookmarks, 193
    bookmark folders, 194-195
    message folders, 152-153
    WAP Bookmarks, 193
Forward All Calls option (Call Forwarding), 226-227
Forward command (Messages menu), 151, 186
Forward Unanswered Calls option (Call Forwarding), 226-227
forwarding
    calls, 224-227
    email, 99
    messages, 150
frames, 186
Friendly Name setting (Web Client), 106

G

General Options
   email, 158-159
   phone, 239-241
General Properties screen, 208-210
Generating New Key window, 48
Get Link command, 188
Go To command (bookmarks), 189, 193
Go To dialog box, 189
golf scorecards, using BlackBerry devices as, 334-338
groups (Address Book)
   creating, 274-276
   editing, 276
   saving, 276
   sending messages to, 276
   viewing, 276

H

Handheld Application Selection window, 55, 58
Handheld Configuration window, 50
Handheld Data Preservation window, 70
hands-free car kits (Bluetooth), pairing BlackBerry devices with, 254-258
Hands-Free Profiles (Bluetooth), 250
headsets (Bluetooth), pairing BlackBerry devices with, 219, 250, 254-258
helper applications
   Alarm, 316-320
   Calculator, 323-325
   MemoPad, 320-323
   mScorecard, 334-338
   MyFlashlight, 332-334
   Photo Album, 326-328
   Terratial LIVE, 328-332
hiding application icons, 88
History command (web browser), 186
History screen, 190
Hold command (Phone menu), 219
holding phone calls, 218, 222
Home command (web browser), 186

Home Page Address option (browser configuration), 208
Home screen, 20-21
home screen images (wallpaper), 89-91
Human Interface Device Profiles (Bluetooth), 251

I

icons
   hiding, 88
   moving, 88
   organizing, 86-89
   showing, 88
IDs, storing safely, 353-357
ignoring phone calls, 220
IM+ Mobile Instant Messenger, 181
IM. *See* instant messaging
IMEI (International Mobile Equipment Identity), 103
Information field (Owner screen), 30
Infrared Data Association (IrDA), 249
Initial View option (Calendar), 301
installing
   applications, 53-56
   applications OTA (over-the-air), 196-199
   Berry 411, 243
   BlackBerry Desktop Software, 42-45
   mScorecard, 336
   MyFlashlight, 332
   themes, 91-94
instant messaging, 131-132
   contacts, adding/deleting, 173-176
   conversations, 168
      carrying on, 176-179
      ending, 179
      saving, 169, 179
   definition of, 131
   disadvantages, 169
   presence/availability, 170, 173
   services, 179-181
   setting up, 170-173
   unified instant messaging, 180-181
Instant Messaging screen, 172
Intellisync, 48-52

International Mobile Equipment Identity (IMEI), 103
invisible option (Bluetooth), 264-265
inviting attendees to meetings, 298
IrDA (Infrared Data Association), 249

J-K

Join command (Phone menu), 223
joining calls, 223

key terms
    add-ins, 52
    Bluejacking, 263
    Bluesnarfing, 264
    Bluetooth sniping, 264
    cryptography, 341
    CSV (Comma Separated Values), 109
    digital signatures, 341
    encryption, 341
    IMEI (International Mobile Equipment Identity), 103
    locales, 78
    macros, 77
    mailing lists, 274
    multitap input mode, 30
    over-the-air (OTA), 196
    passkeys, 257
    PIM clients, 109
    PIN (personal identification number), 48
    push email, 98
    reconciliation, 158
    service books, 185
    SureType, 18
    text messages, 131
    themes, 38
    translator applications, 50
    unified instant messaging, 181
    WAP (Wireless Application Protocol), 184
keyboards, 18-19, 213
    Keyboard Lock feature, 30-32
    settings, 83-86

L

labels (StuffBak), 357-360
Language screen, 23
language, selecting, 23
LANs (local area networks), 6
launching. *See* opening
links, navigating, 190
local area networks (LANs), 6
locales, 78
Lock Handheld Upon Holstering option, 35-36
locking BlackBerry devices, 30-32, 35-36
logs (call logs), 234-238
    adding notes to, 236
    deleting, 237
    opening, 236
    options, 237-238
    viewing, 236

M

macros, 77
mailing lists (Address Book)
    creating, 274-276
    definition of, 274
    editing, 276
    saving, 276
    sending messages to, 276
    viewing, 276
making phone calls, 216-220
    conference calls, 220-224
    emergency calls, 215
    headsets, 219
    smart dialing, 231-234
    speakerphones, 219
Mark as Private option (Calendar), 297
Mark Opened command (Messages menu), 152
Mark Unopened command (Messages menu), 152
MDS (Mobile Data Service), 185
measurements, converting with Calculator, 325

meetings

meetings
    changing, 298
    deleting, 299
    entering into Calendar, 294-298
    inviting attendees to, 298
    recurring meetings, 297
    responding to meeting invitations, 299
    saving, 298
    viewing, 298
MemoPad, 320-323
memos
    creating with MemoPad, 320-323
    deleting, 322
    editing, 322
    filtering by categories, 323
    options, 323
    viewing, 322
message folders, navigating, 152-153
Message handling settings (Web Client), 107
messages
    email, 130-134
        attachments, 113, 138-141
        auto reply messages, 114-116
        BlackBerry Redirector, 160-165
        composing, 134-137
        composing with Web Client, 111-114
        copying to another account, 119-121
        definition of, 131
        deleting, 151-152
        filtering, 125-128
        forwarding, 150
        marking as opened, 152
        marking as unopened, 152
        message folders, navigating, 152-153
        options, 156-160
        organizing, 149-153
        reconciliation, 157-160
        redirecting, 160-165
        replying to, 149
        saving, 114, 153
        searching, 154-156
        sending, 114, 137
        viewing, 133-134
    instant messaging, 168
        contacts, 173-176
        conversations, 168-169, 176-179
        disadvantages, 169

        presence/availability, 170, 173
        services, 179-181
        setting up, 170-173
        unified instant messaging, 180-181
    PIN (personal identification number) messages, 48, 132, 344-347
        definition of, 131
        deleting, 151-152
        forwarding, 150
        marking as opened, 152
        marking as unopened, 152
        message folders, navigating, 152-153
        organizing, 149-153
        replying to, 149
        saving, 153
        searching, 154-156
        sending, 142-145
    text messages, 130-134
        definition of, 130-131
        deleting, 151-152
        forwarding, 150
        marking as opened, 152
        marking as unopened, 152
        message folders, 152-153
        organizing, 149-153
        PIN messages, 131-132, 142-145
        replying to, 149
        saving, 153
        searching, 154-156
        SMS messages, 131-133, 145-149
        viewing, 133-134
Messages menu commands
    Compose Email, 134
    Compose PIN, 143
    Compose SMS, 147
    Delete, 151
    Forward, 151
    Mark Opened, 152
    Mark Unopened, 152
    Reply, 149
    Save, 153
    Search, 154
    View Folder, 153
Messages screen, 134
mirrors, using BlackBerry devices as, 332-334
Mobile Data Service (MDS), 185

mobile phone calls. *See* phone calls
mobile wireless networks (Bluetooth), 5-7
   capabilities, 249
   car kits, pairing BlackBerry devices with, 254-258
   classes of Bluetooth devices, 249
   compared to Wi-Fi, 251
   competitors to, 249
   definition of, 248
   deleting Bluetooth devices, 262
   headsets, pairing BlackBerry devices with, 254-258
   options, 258-262
   passkeys, 257
   portable Bluetooth keyboards, 251
   profiles, 250
   security, 262-265
   turning on and off, 252-254
   versions, 251
monitoring traffic and surveillance, 328-332
Month format (Calendar), 287-289
Move Bookmark command, 195
moving
   application icons, 88
   bookmarks, 195
   speed dial numbers, 230
mScorecard, 334-338
MSN Messenger, 180
multimedia, networked, 328
multitap input mode, 30
Mute command (Phone menu), 219
muting phone calls, 219
MyFlashlight, 332-334

N

navigating
   Calendar, 290-294
   message folders, 152-153
   web pages, 186-191
      bookmarks, 188
      browser history, 190
      links, 190
      URLs, 189

networked multimedia, 328
networks. *See* mobile wireless networks
New – Message page (Web Client), 111-113
New Address screen, 272
New Call command (Phone menu), 223
New Password screen, 355
New Speed Dial command (Phone menu), 230
Next key, 19
notes
   adding to call logs, 236
   creating with MemoPad, 320-323
   deleting, 322
   editing, 322
   filtering by categories, 323
   options, 323
   viewing, 322
Notes field (Address Book), 272
Notes screen, 236
Number of Entries field
   Address Book, 281
   Calendar, 302
   MemoPad, 323

O

opening
   call logs, 236
   Tasks application, 306
organizing
   application icons, 86-89
   text messages, 149-153
OS (operating system), 11-14
   advantages, 12-13
   limitations, 13
   push email, 12
   upgrading, 14-16
OTA (over-the-air) application installation, 196-199
owner information, entering, 27-30
Owner screen, 27-30

P

PANs (personal area networks). See Bluetooth
passkeys (Bluetooth), 257
Password Attempts option (Password Keeper), 356
Password Keeper, 353-357
Password menu commands, 34
passwords, 32-36
    passkeys, 257
    storing safely, 353-357
personal area networks (PANs). See Bluetooth
personal data, clearing, 66-70
personal identification numbers. See PIN messages
personal information management clients. See PIM clients
Phone Book (SIM), accessing, 281-284
phone calls, 212-215
    411 phone directories, accessing, 242-245
    answering, 220
    call logs, 234-238
        adding notes to, 236
        deleting, 237
        opening, 236
        options, 237-238
        viewing, 236
    call timers, clearing, 215
    conference calls, 220-224
    emergency calls, 36, 215
    ending, 220
    forwarding, 224-227
    headsets, 219
    holding/resuming, 218, 222-223
    ignoring, 220
    making, 216-220
    muting, 219
    phone options, 238-242
        Call Waiting, 241-242
        General Options, 239-241
        Voicemail Options, 241
    phone status, querying, 214-215
    receiving, 216-220
    smart dialing, 231-234
    speakerphones, 219
    speed dial list, 228-231
    voice mail, 215, 241
Phone Info screen, 214-215
Phone List View option (phone), 240
Phone menu commands
    Activate Handset, 220
    Activate Speakerphone, 220
    Call From Address Book, 218
    Drop Call, 224
    Emergency Call, 215
    End Call, 220
    Hold, 219
    Join, 223
    Mute, 219
    New Call, 223
    New Speed Dial, 230
    Resume, 219
    Split Call, 223
    Status, 215
    Swap, 223
    Turn Mute Off, 219
    View Speed Dial List, 228
Phone screen, 216
Photo Album, 326-328
pictures
    managing with Photo Album, 326-328
    wallpaper, 199-202
PIM (personal information management) clients, 109
    synchronizing with desktop PCs, 48-52
PIN (personal identification number) messages, 48, 132, 344-347
    definition of, 131
    deleting, 151-152
    forwarding, 150
    marking as opened, 152
    marking as unopened, 152
    message folders, navigating, 152-153
    organizing, 149-153
    replying to, 149
    saving, 153
    searching, 154-156
    sending, 142-145
platform, 11-14
    advantages, 12-13
    limitations, 13
    push email, 12
    upgrading, 14-16

players, adding to mScorecard, 337
PocketMac, 44
pop-up blockers, 102
portable Bluetooth keyboards, 251
Power button, 20
profiles
    Bluetooth, 250
    customizing, 79-83
    Web Client, 118
Prompt Before options (browser properties), 209
protecting BlackBerry devices. *See* security
protocols
    Bluetooth
        capabilities, 249
        car kits, pairing BlackBerry devices with, 254-258
        classes of Bluetooth devices, 249
        compared to Wi-Fi, 251
        competitors to, 249
        definition of, 248
        deleting Bluetooth devices, 262
        headsets, pairing BlackBerry devices with, 254-258
        options, 258-262
        passkeys, 257
        portable Bluetooth keyboards, 251
        profiles, 250
        security, 262-265
        turning on and off, 252-254
        versions, 251
    VoIP (Voiceover Internet Protocol), 4
    WAP (Wireless Application Protocol), 184-185
    WML (Wireless Markup Language), 184
    XMPP (Extensible Messaging and Presence Protocol), 180
push email, 12, 98

Q-R

Random Password feature (Password Keeper), 356
receiving
    instant messages, 178
    phone calls, 216-220
reconciliation (email), 157-160
Recurrence field (Calendar), 297
recurring appointments, entering in Calendar, 297
recurring tasks, 307
redirecting messages, 160-165
Redirector, 99, 160-165
Refresh command (web browser), 186
registering BlackBerry devices with StuffBak, 357-360
removing applications, 56-59
Rename Folder command (bookmarks), 195
renaming bookmark folders, 195
Repeat Animations option (browser properties), 209
Reply command (Messages menu), 149
replying to
    meeting invitations, 299
    messages, 149
restoring BlackBerry devices, 63-66
Restrict My Identity option (phone), 240
Resume command (Phone menu), 219
resuming phone calls, 218, 223
ring tones, downloading, 203-206
rounds of golf, starting in mScorecard, 336

S

Save command (Messages menu), 153
Save Image command, 202
Saved Messages folder, 153
saving
    appointments in Calendar, 298
    contacts, 273
    email messages as drafts, 114
    instant messaging conversations, 169, 179
    mailing lists, 276
    messages, 153
    tasks, 307
    web pages to message list, 190
scores (golf), entering in mScorecard, 338
screen settings, 83-86

scrolling Address Book, 273
SDNs (service dialing numbers), 283
Search command (Messages menu), 154
Search screen, 154
searching messages, 154-156
security, 340-341
    backups, 342
    Bluetooth, 262-265
        Bluejacking, 263
        Bluesnarfing, 263-264
        Bluetooth sniping, 264
        discoverable/invisible options, 264-265
        tips and guidelines, 265
    Content Protection feature, 349-352
    cryptography, 341
    digital signatures, 341
    encryption, 341
    firewalls, 347-349
    human errors, 342
    Password Keeper, 353-357
    passwords, 32-36
        passkeys, 257
        storing safely, 353-357
    SIM (subscriber identity module) cards, 344-347
    StuffBak, 357-360
    tips and guidelines, 343-344
    Wipe Handheld command, 342
Security menu commands, Wipe Handheld, 342
Security screen, 32-36
Select Address screen, 134-135, 143-144, 147, 276, 296-298
Select Categories screen, 273, 307
Select Category screen, 277-279, 310-311
selective backups, 62
Send key, 19, 213, 220
sending
    email, 114, 137
    instant messages, 177-178
    PIN messages, 142-145
    SMS messages, 145-149
sent-from email address, changing, 116-119
Serial Port Profiles (Bluetooth), 250
servers, BlackBerry Enterprise Server, 99

service books, 185
service dialing numbers (SDNs), 283
services, instant messaging services, 179-181
Shift key, 19
short-range wireless networks. *See* Bluetooth
showing. *See* viewing
side games, tracking in mScorecard, 338
signatures, digital, 341
SIM (subscriber identity module) cards
    PIN codes, 344-347
    security, 344-347
    SIM Card screen, 345
    SIM Phone Book, 281-284
SkipTraffic LIVE, 328-331
smart dialing, 231-234
SMS messages, 133
    definition of, 131
    deleting, 151-152
    forwarding, 150
    marking as opened, 152
    marking as unopened, 152
    message folders, navigating, 152-153
    organizing, 149-153
    replying to, 149
    saving, 153
    searching, 154-156
    sending, 145-149
sniping (Bluetooth), 264
Snooze setting (Alarm), 318
Sort By option
    Address Book, 281
    tasks, 313
sorting Address Book contacts, 281
Space key, 19
speakerphones, activating, 219
speed dial list, 228-231
Split Call command (Phone menu), 223
splitting calls, 223
Start Of Day option (Calendar), 301
status (phone), querying, 214-215
Status command (Phone menu), 215
Status menu commands
    Clear All Timers, 215
    Clear Timer, 215

StuffBak, 357-360
subscriber identity module cards. *See* SIM cards
Support Embedded Media option (browser properties), 209
Support Style Sheets option (browser properties), 209
SureType, 18, 137, 145, 148, 178, 322
Surveillance LIVE, 328-331
surveillance monitoring, 328-332
Swap command (Phone menu), 223
Symbol key, 19
synchronizing
    Calendar, 286
    PIM data with desktop PCs, 48-52
    tasks, 306

T

T-Mobile theme, 38
tasks
    applying categories to, 308-311
    creating, 304-308
    definition of, 304
    deleting, 308
    managing, 304-308
    marking as completed, 308
    options, 311-313
    recurring tasks, 307
    saving, 307
    sort order, 313
    synchronizing, 306
    viewing, 307
Tasks application
    applying categories to tasks, 308-311
    creating tasks, 304-308
    deleting tasks, 308
    managing tasks, 304-308
    marking tasks completed, 308
    opening, 306
    saving tasks, 307
    task options, 311-313
    viewing tasks, 307
Tasks Options screen, 313
telephone calls. *See* phone calls

Terratial LIVE, 328-332
Terratial website, 330
text messages, 130-134. *See also* email
    definition of, 130-131
    deleting, 151-152
    forwarding, 150
    instant messaging, 168
        contacts, 173-176
        conversations, 168-169, 176-179
        disadvantages, 169
        presence/availability, 170, 173
        services, 179-181
        setting up, 170-173
        unified instant messaging, 180-181
    marking as opened, 152
    marking as unopened, 152
    message folders, navigating, 152-153
    organizing, 149-153
    PIN (personal identification number) messages, 48, 132, 344-347
        definition of, 131
        deleting, 151-152
        forwarding, 150
        marking as opened, 152
        marking as unopened, 152
        message folders, navigating, 152-153
        organizing, 149-153
        replying to, 149
        saving, 153
        searching, 154-156
        sending, 142-145
    replying to, 149
    saving, 153
    searching, 154-156
    SMS messages, 133
        definition of, 131
        deleting, 151-152
        forwarding, 150
        marking as opened, 152
        marking as unopened, 152
        message folders, navigating, 152-153
        organizing, 149-153
        replying to, 149
        saving, 153
        searching, 154-156
        sending, 145-149
    viewing, 133-134
Theme screen, 37-39

How can we make this index more useful? Email us at indexes@samspublishing.com

themes

themes
  definition of, 38
  downloading, 91
  finding, 91
  installing, 91-94
  selecting, 37-39
  T-Mobile, 38
Time setting (Alarm), 318
time/date, setting
  Date/Time screen, 24-27
  Web Client, 107
timers, clearing, 215
Tone setting (Alarm), 318
trackwheel, 19
traffic, monitoring, 328-332
translator applications, 50
Trusted option (Bluetooth), 261
Tune setting (Alarm), 318
Turn Mute Off command (Phone menu), 219
turning on/off
  Auto On/Off, 72-75
  BlackBerry devices, 20
  Bluetooth, 252-254
  firewalls, 347-349

U

unified instant messaging, 180-181
uninstalling applications, 56-59
units of measure, converting with Calculator, 325
unlocking BlackBerry devices, 30-32
unzipping Zip files, 55
upgrading BlackBerry operating system, 14-16
URLs, navigating to, 189
USB, WUSB (Wireless USB), 250

V

Variety Packs (StuffBak), 359
Verichat, 181
version 1.0 (Bluetooth), 251
version 1.1 (Bluetooth), 251
version 2.0 (Bluetooth), 251
Vibrate setting (Alarm), 318
Vibrate+Tone setting (Alarm), 318
View Folder command (Messages menu), 153
View Speed Dial List command (Phone menu), 228
viewing
  appointments, 298
  bookmarks, 194
  call logs, 236
  contacts, 273
  email attachments, 138-141
  live surveillance video, 331
  live traffic video, 331
  mailing lists, 276
  memos, 322
  messages, 133-134
  pictures, 326
  tasks, 307
Viewing options settings (Web Client), 107
views (Calendar)
  Agenda, 287-290
  changing, 293
  Day, 287-288
  Month, 287-289
  Week, 287-289
voice mail, 215, 241
Voice Mail Options (phone), 241
Voicemail screen, 241
VoIP (Voiceover Internet Protocol), 4
Volume setting (Alarm), 319

W

wallpaper
  changing, 89-91
  downloading, 199-202
WANs (wide area networks), 5-7

WAP (Wireless Application Protocol), 184-185
WAP Bookmarks folder, 193
web browsing, 184-186
    bookmarks, 191-195
        bookmark folders, 194-195
        copying, 194
        creating, 193-194
        deleting, 195-196
        editing, 195
        moving, 195
        navigating to, 188
        viewing, 194
    browser configurations, 185
    browser options, 206-210
        Browser Configuration, 208
        Cache Operations, 210
        General Properties, 208-210
    MDS (Mobile Data Service), 185
    menu commands, 186
    OTA (over-the-air) application installation, 196-199
    ring tones, downloading, 203-206
    service books, 185
    title bar, 185-186
    wallpaper, downloading, 199-202
    WAP (Wireless Application Protocol), 184-185
    web pages
        frames, 186
        navigating to, 186-191
        saving to message list, 190
    WML (Wireless Markup Language), 184
Web Client, 98
    accounts
        additional accounts, adding, 121-125
        creating, 100-104
        email filters, creating, 125-128
    Address Books, importing, 107-110
    auto reply messages, 114-116
    email attachments, 113
    email messages
        composing, 111-114
        copying to another account, 119-121
        saving as drafts, 114
        sending, 114

options, 104-107
    Date/Time settings, 107
    Email identification settings, 106
    Message handling settings, 107
    Viewing options settings, 107
sent-from email address, changing, 116-119
Web Page field (Address Book), 272
web pages
    frames, 186
    navigating to, 186-191
    saving to message list, 190
Week format (Calendar), 287-289
Wi-Fi devices, 6, 251
wide area networks (WANs), 5-7
Wikipedia, 245
Windows Messenger, 180
Wipe Handheld command (Security menu), 342
Wireless Application Protocol (WAP), 184-185
wireless devices, 5
Wireless Markup Language (WML), 184
wireless personal area networks (PANs). See Bluetooth
wireless revolution, 3-5
Wireless USB (WUSB), 250
wireless web, 184
wizards, Application Loader Wizard
    installing applications, 53-56
    installing themes, 93-94
    removing applications, 56-59
WML (Wireless Markup Language), 184
WUSB (Wireless USB), 250

X-Y-Z

XMPP (Extensible Messaging and Presence Protocol), 180

Zip files, extracting, 55

Key Terms

Don't let unfamiliar terms discourage you from learning all you can about the BlackBerry 7100 series. If you don't completely understand what one of these words means, flip to the indicated page, read the full definition there, and find techniques related to that term.

Add-in A special helper application installed on your device to carry out a specific task, such as allowing you to view a file of an unsupported type. **Page 48**

AutoText A feature of the BlackBerry operating system that serves as a simplified spell checker and also carries out a more general text replacement. **75**

Bluejacking A minor Bluetooth security attack where another user sends you an unsolicited message using a Bluetooth connection. **262**

Bluesnarfing A serious Bluetooth security attack where another user gains access to the data on your device using a Bluetooth connection. **262**

Bluetooth sniping The process of using specially modified equipment to send and receive Bluetooth signals over a much longer range than intended. **262**

Cryptography The field of knowledge associated with converting information from its normal, comprehensible format into an incomprehensible format, rendering it unreadable to anyone but the intended recipient. **340**

CSV Stands for Comma Separated Values, a file format in which text data is listed in order and separated by commas. **107**

Digital signature An electronic ID, logically akin to a handwritten signature, used to securely identify a person as well as to encrypt and decrypt messages they send and receive. **340**

Encryption The process of converting information from its normal, comprehensible format into an incomprehensible format, rendering it unreadable to anyone but the intended recipient. **340**

IMEI Stands for International Mobile Equipment Identity, a unique number assigned to every mobile device. **100**

Locale A combination of a country/region and a language. **Page 75**

Macro A special symbol that references a piece of information stored on your device such as the date, time, owner name, or phone number. Using AutoText, macros make it possible to insert such information by simply typing a short word. **75**

Mailing list A group of contacts with whom you interact with as if they were a single entity; you can send an email message to an entire group of people by addressing the message to a single mailing list. **274**

Multi tap A popular handheld input mode in which you press a key multiple times to access the additional letters, numbers, and symbols printed on the face of the key. Switch from SureType mode to multi tap mode by holding down the Next key for about a second. **27**

Over-the-air Also shortened to OTA, the type of application installation that takes place over a wireless network connection to an application provider. The application is installed wirelessly "over the air," as opposed to using a direct connection with a desktop PC. **196**

Passkey A short password similar to a PIN code used to gain access to a Bluetooth device. **254**

PIM client Stands for personal information manager client, an application used to access and manage personal information, such as contacts, appointments, and tasks. **107**

PIN Stands for personal identification number, a number up to eight digits long that uniquely identifies your BlackBerry device. You use the device's PIN for configuration purposes as well as to send text messages directly to another BlackBerry device. **45**